# Under the Counter

**BCMCR New Directions in Media and Cultural Research**

Series editors: Oliver Carter, Kirsten Forkert, Nicholas Gebhardt and Dima Saber.

The Birmingham Centre for Media and Cultural Research's 'New Directions' book series aims to advance research and teaching in the broad range of media and cultural studies and to serve as the focal point for a community of scholars who are committed to critical inquiry and collaborative practice. Books in the series engage with developments in the field, showing how new theoretical approaches have impacted on research within both media and cultural studies and other related disciplines. Each volume will focus on a specific theme or issue, as well as exploring broader processes of social and cultural transformation. The series is committed to producing distinctive titles that challenge traditional disciplinary boundaries and question existing paradigms, including innovative scholarship in areas such as the creative industries; media history, heritage and archives; games studies; gender and sexuality; screen cultures; jazz and popular music studies; media and conflict; song-writing studies; and critical theory. The editors are also keen to encourage authors to experiment with non-standard approaches to academic writing.

# Under the Counter

Britain's Trade in Hardcore
Pornographic 8mm Films

*Oliver Carter*

Bristol, UK / Chicago, USA

First published in the UK in 2023 by
Intellect, The Mill, Parnall Road, Fishponds, Bristol, BS16 3JG, UK

First published in the USA in 2023 by
Intellect, The University of Chicago Press, 1427 E. 60th Street,
Chicago, IL 60637, USA

A catalogue record for this book is available from
the British Library.

Copy editor: MPS Limited
Cover designer: Aleksandra Szumlas
Cover image: Screenshot from *Chez Mrs Pirgeon* (1960–63).
Author's personal collection.
Production manager: Debora Nicosia
Typesetter: MPS Limited
Indexer: Paula Clarke Bain

Hardback ISBN 978-1-78938-658-5
Paperback ISBN 978-1-78938-664-6
ePDF ISBN 978-1-78938-659-2
ePUB ISBN 978-1-78938-660-8

Part of BCMCR New Directions in Media and Cultural Research
Print ISSN: 2752-4515 / Online ISSN: 2752-4523

To find out about all our publications, please visit our website.
There you can subscribe to our e-newsletter, browse or download our current
catalogue and buy any titles that are in print.

www.intellectbooks.com

This is a peer-reviewed publication.

*For Dad*

# Contents

List of Figures ix

Acknowledgements xv

List of Characters xix

Prologue: I Was a Teenage Porn Dealer xxv

Introduction: *Tonight at 8* 1

1. *Carnaby Kinks*: Obscenity, Permissiveness and the 17
   Dirty Square Mile

2. *Fisherman's Luck*: Making the Roller Market (1960–65) 51

3. *Up, Up and Away*: Entrepreneurship in Britain's 91
   Expanding Roller Trade (1966–69)

4. *House of Mirrors*: Regulating the Roller Trade (1970–73) 136

5. *Strip Poker*: Distributing Hardcore Films in Britain (1973–83) 173

Conclusion 217

Epilogue: *Truth or Dare* 224

Appendix 1: Labelography 238

Appendix 2: List of Rollers Seized from John Mason's Dean Street 314
   Office, 1 July 1969

Notes 318

Bibliography 333

Index 345

# Figures

Figure 0.1:   Screenshots from *Tonight at 8* (1966–67). Author's personal                    1
              collection.

Figure 1.1:   *Carnaby Kinks* (Evan Phillips 1968). Author's personal collection.             17

Figure 1.2:   (*top, left*) Peter Street, Soho, 2017 (photograph taken by author);           18
              (*top, right*) Walker's Court, 2021; (*below*) Brewer Street
              (both courtesy of Michael Venton).

Figure 1.3:   Walker's Court, looking towards Rupert Street in 1973. Tony                     41
              Sonenscher's The Court Bookshop at 10 Walker's Court, one
              of the largest bookshops in Soho, can be seen on the left.
              Courtesy of Robert Stallard/Mary Evans Picture Library.

Figure 1.4:   A selection of Soho postcards. Author's personal collection.                    44
              Faces obscured to protect the identity of performers.

Figure 1.5:   Examples of Soho Bibles. Courtesy of Lewis Parker and Rambooks.                 46

Figure 1.6:   A map of Soho's Bookstores in the late 1960s–early 1970s, drawn                 49
              from police records and constructed by the author using
              Snazzy Maps under Creative Commons Licence.

Figure 2.1:   Title card from *Fisherman's Luck* (1965–67). Author's personal                 51
              collection.

Figure 2.2:   Extract from Walton's glamour film catalogue (early 1960s).                     54
              Courtesy of 'Mal Mallister'.

Figure 2.3:   Advert for Paillard Bolex H16. Courtesy of 'Philip Black'.                      58

Figure 2.4:   Advertisement for a Todd Tank. Courtesy of 'Philip Black'.                      61

Figure 2.5:   Examples of early unbranded roller boxes: *Afternoon Lust*                      65
              (1964–67), *Turkish Delight* (1967–68) and *Black Magic* (1963–67).
              Author's personal collection. Faces obscured to protect the identity
              of performers.

Figure 2.6:   *100% Lust* (1966) released by Climax Films. Author's personal                  75
              collection. Faces obscured to protect the identity of performers.

Figure 2.7:   Advert for *Randy* (1966–67) from a Swedish mail-order company –   77
              Assman Productions – that refers to Christine Keeler. Author's personal
              collection. Faces obscured to protect the identity of performers.

Figure 2.8:   Unbranded 'Christine Keeler' 8mm film, likely to be of US origin   78
              and not Christine Keeler. Courtesy of 'Mal Mallister'.

Figure 2.9:   Business card for the Theanders' Bookshop. Author's personal   80
              collection.

Figure 2.10:  Blue Scene Films' release of *Fisherman's Luck* (1965–67).   82
              Author's personal collection. The female performer's face has been
              obscured to protect her identity.

Figure 2.11:  Screenshots from 16mm print of *Fisherman's Luck* (1965–67).   83
              Author's personal collection. The female performer's face has
              been obscured to protect her identity.

Figure 2.12:  Blue Scene Films mail-order catalogue. Courtesy of 'Phillip Black'.   85
              Faces obscured to protect the identity of performers.

Figure 2.13:  Blue Scene Films' release of *Lucky Girl* (1968).   86

Figure 2.14:  Scenes from rollers shot in the Victorian style flat: *Duet* (1968),   87
              *Turkish Delight* (1967–68) and *Lucky Girl* (1968). Author's
              personal collection. Faces obscured to protect the identity
              of performers.

Figure 2.15:  Screenshots from Blue Scene Films' *Manhunt* (1969). Author's personal   88
              collection. Faces obscured to protect the identity of performers.

Figure 3.1:   *Up, Up and Away* (1968). Image is taken from a Climax Films   91
              catalogue. Author's personal collection. Faces obscured to
              protect the identity of performers.

Figure 3.2:   Image of Michael Freeman from the early 1970s. Courtesy of   93
              Mike Freeman.

Figure 3.3:   Examples of Soho Postcards depicting hand-drawn pornography.   97
              These are similar to the goods Freeman produced and sold to
              Soho's bookshops. Courtesy of 'Tony M'.

Figure 3.4:   Evan 'Big Jeff' Phillips. Author's personal collection.   103

Figure 3.5:   Early first wave release of *Men* (1966–67) from Climax Films.   107
              Author's personal collection.

Figure 3.6:   Color Climax Corporation's referencing of roller titles – *Pussy*   108
              *Galore* (1966–67) and *Ring Up for Love* (1966–67) – in the
              names of magazines published in the early 1970s. Courtesy
              of *Vintage Erotica Forums*.

Figure 3.7:   Title cards demonstrating the three waves of Climax. From          109
              amateurish handwritten title cards to a more professionalized
              attempt at film production. Author's personal collection.

Figure 3.8:   *Gorgeous Blondes* Soho Bible, pictures likely taken during          112
              the filming of *Full Treatment* (1966–67). Soho Bible courtesy
              of Rambooks, roller box cover from author's personal collection.
              Faces obscured to protect the identity of performers.

Figure 3.9:   Advert for Uhler Reduction Printer. Author's personal collection.    115

Figure 3.10:  'Pornographer at the Pictures' title card. Author's personal         117
              collection.

Figure 3.11:  Box covers for *Degenerate's Orgy* (Mike Freeman 1968)               119
              and *Swap Orgy* (Mike Freeman 1968). Courtesy of Rambooks.
              Faces obscured to protect the identity of performers.

Figure 3.12:  Screenshots from *Degenerate's Orgy* (Mike Freeman 1968).            121
              Courtesy of Rambooks. Faces obscured to protect the identity
              of performers.

Figure 3.13:  Advert for Freeman's Nestville Photography Ltd mail-order            125
              operation from *Continental Film Review*. Courtesy of
              'Phillip Black' and the Erotic Film Society.

Figure 3.14:  Advertisement for Climax Original Films taken from issue 20          128
              of *Chick*, 1971. Author's personal collection.

Figure 3.15:  Extract from Climax catalogue. Author's personal collection.         129
              Faces obscured to protect the identity of performers.

Figure 3.16.  Screenshots from *Up, Up and Away* (1968). Author's personal         130
              collection. Faces obscured to protect the identity of performers.

Figure 3.17:  New labels, such as Private Films, Delilah Deluxe and Malmo          134
              Films, had appeared by the end of the 1960s. Author's personal
              collection. Faces obscured to protect the identity of performers.

Figure 4.1:   *House of Mirrors* (Anthony Collingbourne 1972). Author's            136
              personal collection. Faces obscured to protect the identity of
              performers.

Figure 4.2:   John Darby's garage, Rayner's Lane, Harrow. From the                 137
              National Archives, DPP 2/5303-1.

Figure 4.3:   List of 1970s roller labels.                                         142

Figure 4.4:   Links between Universal Films and Dolly Films, Svensk Films          143
              and Candy Films Author's personal collection. Faces obscured
              to protect the identity of performers.

Figure 4.5:    Screenshots from Universal Films' release of *Maidservant*        144
               (1970–72). Author's personal collection. Faces obscured to
               protect the identity of performers.

Figure 4.6:    An advertisement for hardcore 8mm films by Paramount             151
               Publications placed in *Film Making* magazine. The Durham
               post box address demonstrates the growth of the trade outside
               of Soho. Courtesy of 'Phillip Black'.

Figure 4.7:    Spar Sex Corporation's re-release of Climax's *The Bookworm*      154
               151 (1971–72) following the design of Colour Climax
               Corporation.

Figure 4.8:    Mail-shot  from one of Darby's mail-order operations.            157
               Author's personal collection.

Figure 4.9:    Promotional brochure for Donald Case's mini-movie                160
               machine business Fleetwood Films. Author's personal collection.

Figure 4.10:   Anthony Collingbourne, screenshot from *Timber* (1970–72).       161
               Courtesy of the Erotic Film Society.

Figure 4.11.   Other labels associated with Anthony Collingbourne:              163
               Academy, Double X, Fantasy and  Look. Author's personal
               collection. Faces obscured to protect the identity of performers.

Figure 4.12:   Screenshots from *House of Mirrors* (Anthony Collingbourne       164
               1972). Author's personal collection. Faces obscured to
               protect the identity of performers.

Figure 4.13:   *Traveller's Rest* (Anthony Collingbourne 1972). Author's        165
               personal collection. Faces obscured to protect the identity of
               performers.

Figure 5.1:    *Strip Poker* (1970–72) on International Films. Author's          173
               personal collection. Faces obscured to protect the identity
               of performers.

Figure 5.2.    David Waterfield, 1972. Courtesy of Patricia Clark.              178

Figure 5.3:    Flyer promoting the Compton Cinema Club and including            180
               membership application form. Author's personal collection.

Figure 5.4:    Advert for the Exxon Cinema Club. Author's personal              181
               collection.

Figure 5.5:    Releases from Color Climax Corporation and Lasse Braun.          183
               Author's personal collection.

Figure 5.6:    John Jesner Lindsay, image taken from his magazine               187
               *The Sexorcist*. Courtesy of Rambooks.

Figure 5.7:    *Nympho Artist* (John Lindsay, 1969–72) on Excelsior Film.    189
Author's personal collection. Faces obscured to protect the
identity of performers.

Figure 5.8:    *We Had to Do It* (1970–72) on Leidibird and *Joyride* (1970–72)    190
on Steinle Films. Both were re-released by Academy. Courtesy
of private collectors. Faces obscured to protect the identity
of performers.

Figure 5.9:    A selection of John Lindsay's European shot films:    192
*Tyrollean Love* (1970–72), *Artic Fuck* (1970–72),
*High Society* (1970–72) and *Alpine Lust* (1970–72).
Author's personal collection. Faces obscured to protect
the identity of performers.

Figure 5.10:   Produced for the German market, *Miss Bohrloch* (John    193
Lindsay 1972–73) starring Mary Millington on Walter
Bartkowski's Tabu De Luxe label. Author's personal collection.

Figure 5.11:   Advertisement for *The Pornbrokers* (Laurence Barnett and    195
John Lindsay 1973). The face of the female model has been
obscured.

Figure 5.12:   Mail-order advert for Lindsay's 8mm rollers, referring to the    199
Birmingham Trial. Author's personal collection.

Figure 5.13:   Screenshots from *Convent of Sin* (John Lindsay 1972–73).    200
Author's personal collection. Faces obscured to protect the
identity of performers.

Figure 5.14:   Lindsay's disclaimer used at the beginning of his rollers    202
referring to the Birmingham Trial. Author's personal collection.

Figure 5.15:   Advertisement for Lindsay's Taboo Cinema Club, 15–18    203
Great Newport Street, London. Author's personal collection.

Figure 5.16:   *Health Farm* (John Lindsay 1975–77) on Taboo Films.    207
Courtesy of 'Ken'. Faces obscured to protect the identity
of performers.

Figure E.1:    Title card from *Truth or Dare* (Mike Freeman 1981).    224
Courtesy of Mike Freeman.

Figure E.2:    *School-Girl träumt von King-Kong* (Gerd Wasmund/anon.    226
1977–79). Courtesy of Gerd Wasmund. Faces obscured to
protect the identity of the performer.

Figure E.3:    Adverts for the Holloway's hardcore video label Rippledale    228
and the Video Co. Exchange. Author's personal collection.

Figure E.4:    Holloways' VHS release of *Butterfly* (Joe Sarno 1972) on the            229
               Rippledale label. Courtesy of the Erotic Film Society.

Figure E.5:    Two adverts for Videx titles. Author's personal collection.              231
               Some faces are obscured to protect the identity of performers.

Figure E.6:    A selection of Videx releases on the VHS format. Courtesy               232
               of Dale Lloyd.

Figure E.7:    Advert for *Hard Dollar Hustler* (Alan Purnell 1977). Courtesy          233
               of Joe Rubin. Faces obscured to protect the identity of the
               performers.

Figure E.8:    Early adverts for David Waterfield and Patricia Clark's                 236
               Netherlands-based company Your Choice. Courtesy of
               Patricia Clark.

# Acknowledgements

British historian Raphael Samuel believed that history is the work of many hands and this book would not have been possible without the many people who supported, guided, helped and contributed to it. The inspiration for *Under the Counter* emerged out of a conversation with my dear friend John Mercer. When we first met in 2009, I asked him what he researched. 'Gay pornography', he responded and, back then, I had no idea that the field of Porn Studies existed. John supported this book from its inception and was kind enough to read over drafts and offer detailed notes. I cannot thank him enough for his mentorship and, most of all, friendship.

It was John who suggested that I attend the 2012 Gorizia Spring School and present a paper to their Porn Studies strand. Here, I was first introduced to the strand's convenors Enrico Biasin, Giovanna Maina and Federico Zecca, and a network of inspirational scholars who have all shaped my thinking. At this and subsequent occurrences of the Spring School, I met and discussed ideas with Clarissa Smith, Feona Atwood, Thomas Waugh, Susanna Paasonen, Eric Schaefer, Lynn Comella, Peter Alilunas, Kevin Heffernan, Sharif Mowlabocus and Linda Williams, amongst others. Thank you Enrico, Giovanna and Federico for building such a valuable and collegiate space. I look forward to my next visit.

Thank you to all my friends and colleagues at the Birmingham Centre for Media and Cultural Research, and especially to Tim Wall, recently retired associate dean for research, for creating the supportive environment that allowed this work to come to fruition. Centre director Nick Gebhardt has been a constant source of encouragement and it was he who suggested that I publish this book with Intellect as part of our newly introduced 'BCMCR New Directions in Media and Cultural Research' book series. A special mention to Simon Barber, Karen Patel, Annette Naudin, Gemma Commane, Iain Taylor, Nick Webber, Kirsten Forkert, Dima Saber, Pedro Cravinho and especially to Paul Long, who now enjoys the Melbourne sunshine. Thanks to all my wonderful Ph.D. students, who continue to enthuse me. Sulayman Bah introduced me to legal research methods, Kate Sivak made me think differently about my use of entrepreneurship, while

Christian Moerken and Sebastian F. K. Svegaard graciously helped with some of my primary research.

A British Academy small grant (SRG18R1\18023) enabled me to visit archives and interview people based in Denmark, the Netherlands and Sweden. Much gratitude goes to Mariah Larsson and her late husband Olof Fredrik Hedling who were so accommodating during my visit. This book is dedicated to Ole's memory; he was a kind and generous person with a great taste in music. Thanks also to Tommy Gustafsson, Taliah Pollock, Christian Isak Thorsen, Nicolas Barbano, Morten Thing, Jack Stevenson and Klara Arnberg.

Julian Marsh of the Erotic Film Society has been a pillar of support from the beginning of this project. His knowledge and expertise have been invaluable, always willing to offer ideas and, more importantly, challenge my thinking. We have enjoyed many long phone calls and countless text messages, sharing new discoveries and disappointments. Julian also assisted with the archival research, joining me at the National Archives and the British Library, or, when university work got in the way, he went by himself. Words cannot express how thankful I am for his time, expertise and his friendship.

Julian put me in contact with Simon Fletcher, who was producing a documentary about Mike Freeman. At that time, Freeman did not respond to my emails, but Simon had already visited him in Italy, filming an interview over the course of three days. Simon was kind enough to share his research and the unedited interview, leading to a successful partnership that resulted in the award-winning documentary series *Sexposed* and the documentary *Hardcore Guaranteed*. For these projects, we conducted many on-camera interviews with producers, distributors, performers and others involved in Britain's porn business. I draw on these interviews throughout this book; they would not have been feasible without Simon's involvement.

Which brings me to my interviewees. Thanking everyone who contributed to this research would require a separate book. I am especially grateful to those who wished to remain anonymous but were still prepared to share their experiences. Edward Goodman became a valued friend and advisor, whose years of expertise and personal archive of newspaper clippings were drawn on throughout the book. He also kindly took the time to read and offer notes on the first draft, as well as offering legal advice when things became a little murky. Similarly, David Hebditch read through various chapters and gave feedback. It may have taken four years to track him down, but it was worth the wait. Patricia Clark and Jayson Pannell offered me their time, particularly during a difficult period for them, for which I am most grateful. I have missed sharing coffees with Martin Tomkinson and listening to his stories of Soho's past. Willem van Batenburg and his partner were kind enough to invite me to their house and share Dutch waffles over coffee as we talked about his days making 8mm porn. Terry Stephens has always been great company and kindly put me in touch with his many contacts. Lindsay Honey took the time to meet and talk about his career, even though he was very unwell. Mike Freeman shared many phone calls, messages and archival documents over the years. He was undoubtedly a conflicting character with a difficult past, but I am sorry that he did not live to read *Under the Counter*. Freeman's story was the starting point for this research, and I am thankful for his involvement, even though many unanswered questions remain.

I am indebted to the collectors who graciously granted me access to their personal archives – 'Mal Mallister', 'Max', 'Ken', Julian Marsh, 'Ronnie X' and Julie M. 'Phillip Black' was especially generous, gifting old 8mm magazines and books. Huge thanks go to 'Dave' at Rambooks not only for sharing his family's stories, but also for inviting me to his warehouse and letting me go through his Aladdin's cave of material. Moreover, Dave read various chapters and corrected any factual errors. Thanks also to Tony Shrimplin of the Soho Museum, Brian Pritchard, Dale Lloyd, Lewis Parker, Laura Helen Marks, Joe Rubin from Vinegar Syndrome, Martin Brooks, Johnny Walker, Gregory, Michael Venton, Van Eck Video Services, Kip Darling and the inter-library loan team at BCU's library, Alexander Baron, Stephen Griffin, Bohemia Films, David McGillivray, James Morton, the posters at *Vintage Erotica*, Geoffrey Robertson, Tim Mitchell and Debora Nicosia at Intellect and the anonymous reviewers who offered detailed feedback on the first draft of this book. Apologies to anyone else I have missed.

As the forthcoming prologue shows, the idea for this book can be traced back to my adolescence and I thank my parents, Robert and Wendy, for telling me to not watch the poorly hidden pirated copy of *Breakfast Service*. Dad also unwittingly brought me home copies of *Video World* magazine, courtesy of his work colleague, which first made me aware of Britain's alternative economy of hardcore pornography. Sadly, my dad, Robert Carter, passed away on Sunday 7 August 2022. He always encouraged my work, and was constantly asking me when this book would be in print. I couldn't have asked for a better father. Dad, this one's for you. Finally, and by no means least, all my love goes to Katie and Evie. Thank you, Katie, for suffering this obsession over the past six years and for helping at the National Archives when you were heavily pregnant. On the day of my daughter's birth, I sat in a hospital room at St Thomas', using their Wi-Fi to access newspaper archives. Now this first volume is written, I look forward to us sharing more time together.

Parts of Chapters 1, 2 and 3 appeared in the journal article 'Original Climax Films: Historicizing the British hardcore pornography film business' (Carter 2018b). Elements of Chapter 4 can be found in 'The Watford Blue Movie Trial: Regulating "Rollers" in 1970s Britain' (Carter 2021), while parts of Chapter 5 can be found in the journal article 'Satisfaction guaranteed: Your choice and the transnational distribution of hardcore pornography between the Netherlands and Britain' (Carter 2022).

If anyone reading this book has further information to share, whether it be corrections, additions or any other details relating to Britain's under-the-counter pornography business, please contact me via www.under-the-counter.com.

# Characters

## The Producers

| | |
|---|---|
| 'Colin' | Part-time producer of glamour photographs, selling them to Soho's bookshops. Interviewed 27 June 2016. |
| 'Derek' | Claimed to have produced rollers in the early 1960s under the label Queen of Hearts. Interviewed 22 February 2020. |
| 'Sandra' | Mike Freeman's ex-wife who was involved in running Nestville Photography. |
| 'Skinny' Ken Taylor | Producer of postcards, typescripts and rollers from the early 1960s to early 1970s. |
| Alberto Ferro (aka Lasse Braun) | Braun was a successful transnational producer and distributor, beginning in 1961 and staying active until the 1990s. Died in 2015. |
| Anthony Collingbourne | Produced rollers from 1969 until 1972, working with distributor John Darby. Died in 2007. |
| Berth Milton | Publisher of the Swedish hardcore magazine *Private*. |
| Bob Byrne | Former employee of Mike Freeman. Started Climax Films with Evan Phillips in 1966. |
| Dave Wells | British performer and filmmaker from the early 1980s to 2000s. Worked with Ivor Cook. Interviewed 17 October 2018. |
| Donald 'Duke' Case | Real name Nick Valentine, Case fled to London after one of his New York massage parlours was bombed. Attempted to introduce mini-movie machines to Soho and filmed softcore content for them. Was arrested and expedited back to New York. |

| | |
|---|---|
| Evan 'Big Jeff' Phillips | Introduced to the business in 1965 by Mike Freeman. Initially employed as Freeman's distributor, but moved into roller production in 1966, starting the first branded label Climax Films. Phillips eventually moved his business to Denmark in 1969. Committed suicide in 1975. |
| Jens and Peter Theander | The Theander Brothers started the internationally successful Color Climax Corporation in late 1960s' Denmark. Prior to this, they sold British pornography in their Copenhagen bookshop. |
| George Harrison Marks | Glamour photographer and filmmaker. Shot hardcore for the European market. Died in 1997. |
| Gerd Wasmund | Known as Mike Hunter, Wasmund started out as a producer for Lasse Braun and then moved into film production. Interviewed 9 November 2020. |
| Ivor Cook | A professional photographer and early producer of hardcore pornography, including postcards, type-scripts and rollers. Worked for Berth Milton's Private as a senior photographer in the late 1970s/early 1980s. Died in 1985. |
| John Lindsay | Scottish pornographer who began filming rollers for John Darby in the late 1960s. Moved into distribution in the early 1970s, opening sex shops and cinema clubs. Also ran a modelling agency. Claimed to have been involved in eleven trials. Died in 2006. |
| Joop Wilhelmus | Dutch pornographer who published the magazine *Chick* and the child pornography magazine *Lolita*. Collaborated with John Lindsay. |
| Leonard Thorpe | Professional photographer who also made rollers in the late 1950s and early 1960s. Screened his films at blue movie shows. |
| Lindsay Honey | Better known as Ben Dover, Honey was introduced to hardcore film production by Mike Freeman, appearing in his early Videx titles. In the early 1990s, Honey's Ben Dover character became one of Britain's most successful pornographers. Interviewed 10 October 2017. |
| Martin Granby | Producer of postcards and rollers. Likely involved in the label Universal Films. Died in 2018. |

| Mike Freeman | Born Michael Muldoon, Freeman ran Nestville Photography, producing postcards, rollers and typescripts between 1964 and 1969, when he was jailed for murder. Freeman returned to the pornography business in 1979/80 following his release from prison, making hardcore films on video under the Videx label. He was jailed again in 1984 and moved to Amsterdam, the Netherlands, where he continued making films as Puff Video. He died in 2021. Interviewed between 3 and 6 April 2016. |
|---|---|
| Norman J. Warren | Made an early glamour film titled *Twist Contest* before moving into feature film production. Interviewed on 8 November 2019. Died in 2021. |
| Peter Walker | Started his filmmaking career by making glamour films on the Heritage label. Eventually moved into making feature-length horror and exploitation films. Interviewed 9 November 2018. |
| Russell Gay | Glamour photographer, filmmaker and publisher. Appears to have produced hardcore versions of his softcore films for the German market. |
| Terry Stephens | Producer of hardcore pornography from the late 1990s onwards. Former chair of the United Kingdom Adult Producers network. Interviewed 11 January 2017. |
| Willem van Batenburg | Dutch producer of hardcore pornographic films during the 1970s. Interviewed 13 October 2019. |

## The Distributors

| 'Dave' | Nephew of Tony Sonenscher who worked in Soho sex shops from the late 1970s onwards. Interviewed 1 December 2017 and 12 October 2018. |
|---|---|
| 'Ernie' | A casual supplier of hardcore pornography to South Wales. Interviewed 21 January 2021. Died 2022. |
| 'John' | Worked in one of Bernie Silver's Soho sex shops in the latter half of the 1970s. Interviewed 11 October 2018. |
| 'Mark' | Was casually employed to distribute imported pornography. Interviewed 1 November 2018. |
| 'Steve' | Runs a Soho sex shop and distribution company. Involved in the business since the mid 1970s. Interviewed 22 June 2020. |

| | |
|---|---|
| Ari Van Der Heul | Netherlands-based transnational pornography distributor. Collaborated with John Lindsay. |
| Bernie Silver | Gangster and pimp who was known as the 'Godfather of Soho'. Also ran Soho bookshops selling pornography. |
| David Waterfield | Ran two cinema clubs in North London that screened hardcore pornography. After serving a prison sentence for this, he started the Dutch company Your Choice with his then wife Patricia Clark, selling hardcore to British customers. |
| James Humphreys | Owner of Soho bookshops and magazine publisher. Died in 2003. |
| John Darby | Major mail-order distributor of pornography. Collaborated with John Lindsay and Anthony Collingbourne. |
| John Hawks-ford | Ran Soho bookshops from the 1950s to the 1960s. |
| Joseph 'Joey' Janes | Worked as a bookshop frontman from the 1960s until the 1970s, regularly employed by Tony Sonenscher. |
| Patricia Clark | Ex-wife of David Waterfield. Ran Your Choice when Waterfield moved to Thailand. Interviewed 16 July 2018. |
| Ronald 'The Dustman' Davey | Major producer of postcards and typescripts from the late 1950s until the early 1970s. Close friend of John Mason and Bill Moody. Died in 1990. |
| Ronald Eric 'John' Mason | Known as 'God' to those in Soho's pornography business, John Mason ran at least nine bookshops between the 1950s until the 1970s. Maintained close relationships with officers from the Obscene Publications Squad and a key figure in Soho's pornography trade. |
| Stuart Crispie | Employee of Evan Phillips who was involved in running Climax Films. |
| Tony Sonenscher | Ran one of Soho's largest bookshops – The Court Bookshop at 10 Walker's Court – among others. Died in 2012. |
| Walter Bartkowski | Also known as Charlie Brown, Bartkowski started by smuggling British pornography to Europe in the 1960s. In 1969, he formed Original Climax Films with Evan Phillips and introduced the Tabu brand to Germany around the same time. Regularly employed British roller producers to shoot content. |

## The Police

| | |
|---|---|
| 'Rob' | Retired London Metropolitan Police Officer. Interviewed 12 August 2016. |
| Commander Wallace 'Wally' Virgo | Senior CID officer who served in the Obscene Publications Squad from 1961 to 1962, promoted to Commander in 1970. Took payments from Soho pornographers. Found guilty of police corruption. |
| Detective Chief Superintendent Alfred William 'Bill' Moody | Former head of the Obscene Publications Squad. Had close relationships with John Mason and Ron Davey. Found guilty of police corruption. |
| Detective Inspector Leslie Alton | Took over leadership of the Obscene Publications Squad from Bill Moody between 1966 and 1968. Found guilty of police corruption. |

## The collectors

| | |
|---|---|
| 'Ken' | Interviewed 14 October 2019. |
| 'Mal Mallister' | Interviewed 12 September 2019. |
| 'Phillip Black' | Interviewed 3 September 2021. |
| 'RonnieX' | Interviewed 4 October 2021. |

## Others

| | |
|---|---|
| 'Soho George' | Soho resident and historian. Interviewed 5 September 2018. |
| Aidan McManus | Former employee of a Soho cinema club and now offers guided tours of Soho. Interviewed 8 June 2016. |
| Brian Pritchard | Retired film laboratory worker and co-author of *How Films Were Made and Shown* (2015). Interviewed 13 December 2019. |
| David Webb | Television and theatre actor who formed the National Campaign for the Reformation of the Obscene Publications Act. |

| | |
|---|---|
| Edward Goodman | Solicitor and chair of the Campaign Against Censorship. Was involved in the National Campaign for the Reformation of the Obscene Publications Act and acted as Mike Freeman's solicitor in the early 1980s. Interviewed 22 May 2020. |
| Lord Longford | Frank Packenham was a Labour politician who privately undertook an investigation into Britain's pornography business that became known as the Longford Report (anon. 1972). Died in 2001. |
| Martin Tomkinson | Journalist and author of *The Pornbrokers*. Interviewed 22 February 2017. |
| Mary Whitehouse | Moral crusader and leading figure of the British Christian movement the Festival of Light. Died in 2001. |
| Matthew Oliver | Private detective hired by Lord Longford's pornography inquiry to investigate Soho's bookshops. Uncovered the structure and organization of Soho's pornography economy and the police corruption that enabled it. |

# Prologue:
## I Was a Teenage Porn Dealer

### Breakfast Service *(1990)*

It sat there, in the top of a set of drawers in our living room. It was 1994, making me 14 years old. My dad explicitly warned me not to open the drawer and touch the videotape hidden in there. He purchased this from someone who visited his factory every week, offering a list of pirated films to buy. I recall us having copies of *The Crow* (Alex Proyas 1994) and *The Mask* (Chuck Russell 1994) that were evidently filmed with a camcorder in an American cinema and, through some underground, transnational network, somehow made their way to Birmingham in the United Kingdom to be copied by this bootlegger. Being a horror buff, the banned films on the list were of much more interest to me, purchasing copies of *The Exorcist* (William Friedkin 1973) and an uncut *Zombie Flesh Eaters* (Lucio Fulci 1979), amongst others. Not on the list but available on request was hardcore pornography.

Before the re-evaluation of the R18 certificate in 2000, the distribution of hardcore pornography in the United Kingdom was prohibited. However, it could be purchased through a thriving illicit economy, operating through mail-order and under-the-counter sales at sex shops. I also recall how pornography was traded amongst informal male networks. For instance, my dad's barber always used to offer him a copy of the 'latest Mike Tyson fight', despite Tyson not having fought for several months. Even at a young age, I realized that this was a codename for hardcore pornography in this masculine space.

One afternoon, my parents had gone out and left me to my own devices. The minute they departed, I went into the forbidden top drawer and took out the blank, black case that housed the pornographic film. It smelt of cheap plastic. The film had been intended for dad's sister, an elderly aunt who had asked my dad to obtain a porno movie for her so that she could 'finish her sexual education' – an unexpected request from my god-fearing 67-year-old aunt. Obliging as ever, my dad presented her with the film, which she did not enjoy as much as she thought she might. Now the film was in my hands, the smell of the plastic box filled my nostrils as I took out the cheap-looking cassette and, with nervous anticipation, I loaded it into our Sharp video player.

The television screen flickered as the film started. 'A Dolly Buster Production' read the on-screen text as a cheaply produced rock soundtrack played through the television speakers. The film's title was *Breakfast Service* (1990) and starred Dolly Buster, a German performer known for her blond hair, surgically enhanced breasts and numerous intimate body piercings. My nervous anticipation continued; after all, I was watching a forbidden film obtained through illicit means and was fearful of my parents returning home unannounced. Because of this, I regularly fast-forwarded through scenes. For my first hardcore porn viewing, it was quite a baptism. *Breakfast Service* was certainly hardcore, featuring scenes with anal sex and watersports. The dubbed German audio added a humorous element to the film; I could not say I found it particularly arousing, even as a teenage boy. At the end of the film, I rewound the tape, ejected it from the player, put it back in the plastic box, carefully placing it in the top of the drawer from where it came. I had finally viewed my first pornographic film.

## A porn pirate

Upon revealing my experience of watching *Breakfast Service* to a group of male friends at my secondary school, I realized that there was a demand for pornography. I already dabbled in selling on softcore, top-shelf porn magazines, such as *Mayfair* and *Razzle*. Having a relatively liberal uncle who was more than happy to buy porn magazines on my behalf, I resold them at double the cover price to friends at school. On one occasion, I was asked to obtain the recently released Pamela Anderson Playboy video, which retailed for £14.99. I charged £20, giving my uncle an extra £5 for the trouble of purchasing the video; I took no profit, as I also wanted to watch it, but recognized that I could make more money by duplicating the tape and selling copies.

Making a copy of a VHS tape was simple. I joined my parents' video recorder with my own cheap Hitachi video recorder through a SCART lead, placed the original tape in the master video recorder and recorded the output on a blank tape. I sold the tapes for £10 each, but reduced the price for certain friends. In 1995, I received my first cheque book and could now purchase goods via mail order. As an avid reader of video and film magazines from an early age, I noticed that the magazine *Video World* featured classified adverts for hardcore porn. Even adverts in the back pages of Sunday newspapers claimed to offer it for purchase. I was too naive to understand that such offers were too good to be true.

Now armed with a cheque book, I no longer required my uncle's services and ordered the films myself. For my first purchase, I responded to an advert in the *News of the World* that offered a porn compilation tape. A week later, I received the video. It turned out to be a compilation containing a series of possibly sexually explicit images edited together in a short clip. I was scammed and could not complain to the seller. What would I say? 'Excuse me, I was expecting hardcore pornography, which I know is not legally available in Britain, but you have ripped me off. Can I please have my money back?' I quickly learned my lesson and became more careful when purchasing from mail-order companies.

I noticed a full-page colour advert in the back pages of *Video World*: 'Guaranteed. Everything supplied by "Your Choice" is 100 per cent guaranteed to delight you. Should it fail to do so your payment will be refunded at your request with no quibble'. I sent for the free colour catalogue and, several days later, received an illustrated catalogue containing a list of films. The prices were high, £25 for one film. I risked placing an order for the film *An American Buttman in London* (John Stagliano 1992). I wrote the cheque and posted it to the address in Amsterdam. True to their promise, the film was received in a matter of days, oddly with a British postmark. It was undoubtedly hardcore pornography.

The VHS machines were connected, copies were made and sold to my school friends. With the profits generated, I purchased more films from Your Choice. To make more money, I needed to find a cheaper supplier, so I requested several catalogues from other mail-order companies. Strangely, I received more catalogues than I had asked for. One was from a porn swap shop. You sent the company your own hardcore tapes and could then choose new titles from their list, paying £25 for five films. My earlier experience of being ripped off was a warning that some adverts were too good to be true. On this occasion, I was wrong, receiving all five of the requested titles. However, the picture quality was not as good as that offered by Your Choice, indicating that these were copies of copies. Now I increased my profits and expanded the list of titles I was selling. To my parents' intrigue, I had to purchase a small VHS storage cabinet to hide the tapes. When more videos arrived, I would be asked what was inside. My reply: 'blank tapes [...] if you buy them through mail order, you get them cheaper than in shops'.

My small, illicit enterprise continued through to sixth form college, and even when I worked at my local supermarket, I found fellow male workers wanting to buy porn. With the advent of DVD, copying became even easier and more discreet. Getting access to the internet meant that I could easily order American porn DVDs from British-based companies. With hardcore pornography effectively legalized in 2000, importing was no longer problematic, and demand for my copies slowed. I still made the occasional copy when people asked, but my little side hustle was all but dead. With broadband internet and the distribution of pornography via torrents, I learned that I could download films, convert them to DVDs, and sell them for £5 each, half the price of the videotapes I sold. The advent of tube sites offering hardcore for free, such as PornHub and xHamster, made this all redundant, and my side hustle all but ended.

### *I Pornographer*

In 2012, I was writing up a chapter focusing on the fan-made *Fantom Kiler* films for my first book – *Making European Cult Cinema*. Following an interview with the director, Roman Nowiki (not his real name), I learned that these extreme reinterpretations of the Italian film cycle known as the *giallo* were produced in Stoke Newington, London – not Poland, as suggested by the promotion for the films. I was also interested in how the sexual content of the movies became increasingly harder, leading to Nowiki being employed by the Swedish company Private to make hardcore versions of *Fantom Kiler*. This made me wonder if there had been any academic work on the British pornography business. Despite some small mentions in books, I discovered that no detailed study of the trade existed. The most helpful studies were by non-academics.

A Google search pointed me towards a series of self-published autobiographies distributed via Amazon. The *I Pornographer* series of books, written by Mike Freeman, told the story of a British pornographer who began by making 8mm films and photographs in the latter half of the 1960s. He also claimed to be the first person in Britain to make and sell hardcore pornography on videotape in the early 1980s. Poorly edited and heavily focused on the sexual adventures of the author, the books contained nuggets of fascinating detail on the story of British pornography, from its origins in the bookstores of 1960s' London's Soho to the emergence of home video in the early 1980s. Freeman describes himself as a pioneer in the business. His stories seemed so sensational that I thought they were fictional, revealing criminal activities, such as murder and numerous instances of police corruption. I contacted Freeman by email to see if he would be interviewed. No response was received.

A few years later, a friend named Dale asked if I was interested in purchasing an archive of pornography. He told me how he was contacted via Twitter by the executor of an estate. Having built an online reputation for collecting VHS tapes, Dale was asked if he wanted to collect over 1000 pornographic VHS tapes from an address in London. Dale contacted a friend local to the area where this collection resided, hired a van and drove from Wolverhampton to Chelsea to collect it. Upon arriving, he immediately discovered that these were bootlegs containing hardcore gay pornography, not the rare commercial VHS tapes he had expected. Still, he and his friend collected as much as they could, including books and 8mm reels, put them into the van and stored them in the cellar of his friend's London pub.

'Do you know anything about a VHS label named Videx?', Dale asked in a phone call. I did. These were the films made by Mike Freeman in the early 1980s. Distributed by mail order only, Videx tapes have become sought after by British video collectors, rarely appearing for sale. Dale was looking to sell the collection. I spoke to fellow academic researchers John Mercer and Sharif Mowlabocus about the collection and the possibility of creating an archive. With their interest in gay pornography, we thought that the collection would be a valuable archive of sexual representation, but also offered an insight into how such material was clandestinely distributed in Britain. We purchased the archive and stored it in the photocopier room of a university, not knowing what to do with it.

We discovered that the collection's original owner was an anti-censorship campaigner and a television actor named David Webb. Webb was the chair of the National Campaign for the Reform of the Obscene Publications Act (NCROPA) and an avid collector of pornography. The papers of NCROPA had been donated to Warwick University's Modern Collections, digitized and hosted online. We had the majority of Webb's thoroughly catalogued VHS collection, 8mm film collection and personal 8mm recordings. Several years later, I met the executor of Webb's estate, a solicitor named Edward Goodman, who coincidentally was Freeman's solicitor for his 1983 obscenity arrest.

This book draws on these personal experiences and is the first of two volumes that construct a cultural and economic history of the British pornography business, focusing on the years 1960–2000, when it was a criminal offence to distribute hardcore pornography in the country. In this first volume, I discuss the emergence and development of a thriving alternative economy, producing and distributing 8mm hardcore films known as 'rollers' to the bookshops of London's Soho and outside of Britain via transnational agents. I identify some of the people who made these overlooked films and consider their practices as entrepreneurship. To do this, I draw on extensive ethnohistorical research, which includes primary interviews with those involved in the economy, and archival materials, such as legal documents, media reportage and the artefacts themselves. I show how these entrepreneurs manipulated Britain's complex framework for regulating pornography, initially operating in alliance with the corrupt members of the London Metropolitan Police until later working in opposition.

The first volume concludes by looking at how further regulations were introduced to control Britain's trade in hardcore pornography, following the shift from rollers to home video. A second volume will investigate how the economy moved towards legalization, looking at how companies used transnational links to distribute hardcore pornography into Britain, the introduction of hardcore satellite television broadcasts and the legal battles that resulted in the liberalization of hardcore in Britain. Although my teenage experiences of dealing porn pale in comparison with the pornography entrepreneurs I discuss in *Under the Counter*, they highlight the opportunism that existed in the economy, where money could be made from selling pornography before the onset of the internet and the shift from physical to digital commodities. This is the story of how physical hardcore pornography was manufactured and sold under the counter in Britain, from 1960 until 1984.

# Introduction:
## *Tonight at 8*

Trafalgar Square, London. One of Sir Edwin Lutyens' fountains expels water. Cut to an amusement arcade where two men and a woman play one of the many games. The shaky handheld camera pans to the right, showing the one-arm bandits and slot machines that line the wall. It pans back to the men and the woman, who leave the arcade arm-in-arm, revealing it to be a casino – likely in Leicester Square. This is confirmed when the threesome walks past the Café de Paris, which once sat beside Leicester Square on Coventry Street. They look in the window, pointing and smiling; the camera pans up to confirm the location, the bright lights of the sign flashing. It cuts to the marquee for the Prince of Wales Theatre, also on Coventry Street, where *Way Out in Piccadilly* is showing, starring the popular British entertainers Cilla Black and Frankie Howerd. This production opened on 3 November 1966, closing in July or August 1967, after Black was replaced. The camera pans down, showing the threesome strolling past the theatre. One of the men stops and points out a picture of Cilla Black, possibly suggesting the similarity between the short haircut of the anonymous woman and that of Black's. They laugh and walk on; the camera slowly moves right and focuses on a board reading '*Tonight at 8.00*'.

Another cut: now, the feet of the threesome are shown. They seem to be slow dancing together, moving around in a circle. The camera pans up, revealing that the men are groping the woman and removing her tights; the location appears to be a flat or a bedsit. While one of the men and the woman kiss, the other strips her. Now naked, the men playfully push each other away, competing for her attention. They climb on the bed and dance, shaking their penises up and down. The woman attempts to give oral sex but is unable to. A sudden cut – now they are all laying on the bed. One man is masturbated by the woman, while the other male masturbates the woman as he pleasures himself. Another cut – now a close-up – and, as the woman gives oral to one male, the other licks her nipple. A chair is brought into shot. The woman kneels as one man enters her from behind, and she gives the other oral sex. The camera zooms, showing a close-up of vaginal penetration. It zooms out to a medium long-shot, then

FIGURE 0.1: Screenshots from *Tonight at 8* (1966–67). Author's personal collection.

1

zooms again, but this time to a close-up of oral. Once again, it zooms out as they begin to kiss; it is possible that he may have ejaculated, but this is not clear. Suddenly they move to the bed, bodies intertwining, and the woman lays on one of the men while the other penetrates her. After the male withdraws, the camera zooms in again, seeming to indicate that he has climaxed inside her. The film ends abruptly, cutting to black.

In the British pornography trade, *Tonight at 8* (1966–67) would have been referred to as a roller because of how the reels rolled when played back on a projector. Rollers were black and white – sometimes colour – 200ft 8mm or Super 8 films produced in Britain. They are typically ten to twelve minutes in length and depict hardcore sex. Outside of Britain, such films were termed loops, stags or smokers (Di Lauro and Rabkin 1976). *Tonight at 8* (1966–67) stands out from all of the rollers I have viewed while researching this book. First, it evokes the moment when London was said to be 'swinging' (Mort 2010), and free love became part of the counter-culture movement (Albury 2018). Second, the opening narrative of *Tonight at 8* shares similarities with a police statement given by a female roller performer named 'Christine' while being interviewed for her involvement in the Watford Blue Movie Trial, a legal case I discuss at length in Chapter 4. A runaway from Northern England, Christine described how she met a man named Danny in the Playland amusement arcade, located in Piccadilly Circus. After spending the night with Danny, they met again the next evening in the same location, where he asked Christine to appear in a 'blue movie' for a payment of £10.[1] Christine agreed, and Danny made the arrangements. They both walked around the West End until their meeting with a man named Johnnie took place at the Pronto Bar, again in Piccadilly Circus. Shortly after meeting, Johnnie took Christine and Danny to a studio basement in Kings Cross, where she made an unnamed roller directed by a man named George.

Christine's statement highlights some of the methodological challenges when investigating this illicit trade, relying on sources with questionable reliability. Although her statement appears intentionally vague and elusive, Christine's account of making her first roller evokes the opening scenes of *Tonight at 8*, meeting in an amusement arcade and wandering around the West End until later having sex in a studio basement. Christine's statement is from 1973 and is obviously not describing the making of *Tonight at 8*. Nevertheless, it still highlights the role of the West End's association with vice (Mort 2010) and the roller trade, a relationship I explore in the next chapter. The performers in *Tonight at 8* are anonymous, and it is not clear who produced the film.[2] It is possible to narrow the date of production to between November 1966 and July 1967, as indicated by the theatrical run of the show *Way Out in Piccadilly*, showing how footage can often reveal clues about their clandestine origins.

According to the Adult Loop Database, a useful but often inaccurate online resource that catalogues small-gauge pornographic films, it is distributed by the label Climax. Between 1966 and 1972, Climax released around 200 individual titles and was the most dominant brand in the market. As rollers were under the counter, illicit goods circulating in the backrooms of Soho bookshops or sold via mail order, they were either printed using amateur or semi-professional technologies rather than in professional labs, resulting in limited prints. My inability to locate a copy of *Tonight at 8* possibly indicates that the film had a small print run, and few copies now survive. The source for the images used in Figure 0.1 is a poor analogue transfer that was likely duped from a videotape to DVD and encoded as a digital file. A copy exists in the Kinsey Institute's archive in Indiana, which houses a collection of approximately 361 rollers; to my knowledge, no other institutional archive holds rollers.

Despite the Obscene Publications Act 1959 outlawing the distribution of hardcore pornography in Britain, there existed a thriving economy, producing and distributing hardcore pornographic films, photographs and illustrated magazines (Hebditch and Anning 1988: 212). Like rollers, photographs were referred to as Soho Postcards and illustrated magazines were known as Soho Bibles or Soho Typescripts (Wickstead 2020), emphasizing the significant role Soho played in this economy. Although some have referred to this economy as nothing more than a 'cottage industry' (Sutherland 1982: 4), this book attempts to assess its scale and reach, focusing specifically on the roller market. Emerging when debates around permissiveness were prominent, at least 46 British labels made and released rollers between 1960 and 1979. As the labelography at the end of this book shows, I have traced over 1000 individual films produced in Britain during this period; there were likely more, but their small print runs mean that some will not have survived.

*Tonight at 8* also illustrates how the content of rollers contrasts with the typical British stereotype of prudish attitudes towards sex and sexuality (Marwick 2007: 171) and, as Schaefer (2005: 92) suggests, such early pornographic films can serve as 'documents of seduction and sex at the height of the sexual revolution'. Beyond their significance as an overlooked part of British film history, they matter because of their production context. For instance, rollers were often made with semi-professional filmmaking equipment by non-professionals, and the films were developed and printed in clandestine circumstances. Their legal context provides further understanding of the attempts to legislate and control hardcore pornography in Britain, while the entrepreneurial activities of those who made rollers serve as a window into the hidden enterprise cultures (Williams 2006) active in this period.

Over the past several years, there has been a renewed interest in the historical foundations of the pornography business. Before this, studies of the business were often 'insider accounts', such as autobiographies and biographies, 'journalistic snapshots' or 'anecdotal glosses' (Schaefer 2005: 86). Many works from the 1960s and 1970s were nothing more than an excuse to publish pornographic content. Such sources are not without value. For instance, Taylor (1970) provides a helpful insight into changes in pornography policy and serves as a fascinating time capsule of this period. However, it is easy to see that the book uses the text as an 'alibi' (Waugh 1996: 219-27) for the explicit images and illustrates the demand for hardcore pornography. According to Heffernan (2015: 38), earlier academic studies of hardcore pornography neglected to place 'economics at centre stage in the historical narrative'. Alilunas (2014: 63) points out that this work tended to focus on the textual features of the films, acknowledging that such an approach was necessary, particularly in the context of an anti-pornography discourse. For Alilunas, this has meant that 'industrial questions (and histories) have tended to receive the least amount of attention'.

Foundational studies on the history of the pornography business include the work of Slade (2000) and Schaefer (2002; 2005; 2007), whose writings have been particularly inspirational for my study. More recently, a number of studies have appeared that explore the history of adult film in America (Heffernan 2015; Alilunas 2016; Church 2016; Gorfinkel 2017; Strub 2011). Many of these observe the relationship pornography has with technology, economics and legalities, but focus on the American context. Outside of the United States, there has been comparatively little attention given to the histories of pornography in other countries, particularly in the post-war period. Sweden is an exception, with Larsson's (2016) study of 8mm Swedish pornography in the 1970s and Arnberg's (2010; 2012; 2017) work on Swedish pornographic magazines. There has also been interest in the German pornography business, particularly the mail-order entrepreneur Beate Uhse (Heineman 2011) and the beginnings of the Italian industry (Maina and Zecca 2021).

In regards to Britain, there exists a modest but significant corpus, mixing popular scholarship, biography and academic research. These tend to situate British hardcore pornography film making alongside the British softcore sex film (Sheridan 2005; McGillivray 2017) or wider British film history (Sweet 2006: 291). Others place British hardcore amongst the broader phenomenon of hardcore pornography. For example, Hebditch and Anning's (1988: 212) invaluable *Porn Gold* occasionally discusses the clandestine nature of British hardcore pornographic film production, conducting interviews with key producers from the period, such as Mike Freeman, Lasse Braun and Hans Moser as part of their investigation into national pornography industries. Flint (1999: 95–116) gives a historical chapter on the development of British pornography, and Thompson (2007) offers a chapter on 8mm British films, reviewing a small sample from the

1960s and 1970s, but shows little interest in their production or distribution. Journalistic work makes an important contribution, with Tomkinson's (1982) investigation into London's Soho pornography business mainly focusing on pornographic magazines, while Cox et al. (1977) discuss the relationship between the corrupt Obscene Publications Squad and Soho's pornographers. These sources have been valuable starting points for this research, though, as Alilunas (2016: 29) observes, they often 'lack citation or supporting evidence and can lead down twisting paths in the search of factual confirmation, or, worse can transmit inaccurate information'.[3]

In academic literature, one can find mentions of the post-war British pornography industry in Hunter (2013: 116–22), who draws on interviews with Mike Freeman and Lindsay Honey when briefly discussing the place of hardcore production within wider British 'trash' cinema. Similarly, Chibnall (2003: 45–47) contrasts elements of the film *Get Carter* (Mike Hodges 1971) with the British hardcore pornography business. Over the course of three pages, Chibnall identifies some of the leading players, such as Ivor Cook (who he incorrectly spells as 'Cooke'),[4] Evan 'Big Jeff' Phillips, John Lindsay and George Harrison Marks, and the police corruption in Soho that allowed them to operate but does not provide sources for his research. Both Hunt (1998) and Smith (2005) discuss the wider cultural context of the 1970s and the growth of the business, with the former briefly mentioning hardcore filmmaker John Lindsay. Inaccuracies are not exclusive to non-academic sources, with Thompson (1994) identifying John Lindsay as a softcore pornographer and, similarly, Upton (2016) also suggests that Mike Freeman was producing softcore pornography on home video. As this book will show, both claims are mistaken. Separately, these sources offer useful titbits of information about aspects of the British pornography business, but collectively they help to construct a timeline of how an economy came into existence and developed prior to the liberalization of pornography after the BBFC's re-evaluation of the Restricted 18 certificate in 2000 (Petley 2011; Perkins 2012; Hunter 2014).

Although this book focuses on the years 1960–84 and particularly 8mm film, it would be inappropriate not to acknowledge that Britain's economy of hardcore pornography existed prior to the 1960s. Stoops (2018) provides essential historical background for *Under the Counter*, piecing together Britain's pornography trade between 1900 and 1945. Using records from the courts and government combined with newspaper reports, Stoops uncovers a hidden trade that operated on a transnational scale, distributing pornographic commodities. This study gives a broad social history of the trade, providing the context for the post-war trade I discuss, which focuses more on the entrepreneurs who made and distributed hardcore pornographic films.

## *Pornography as an alternative economy*

An interest in the economics of pornography has been longstanding and has preoccupied scholarship too. Over the past ten years, several studies have emerged that seek to demystify and document the industrial context of pornography, such as Sullivan and McKee (2015) and Voss (2012), amongst others. These call for an engagement with ideas from political economy, highlighting how this approach can be productive for considering issues relating to cultural labour, policy/regulatory matters and other aspects of the 'nature of work under late capitalism' (Berg 2014: 75). However, the majority of these studies focus on the contemporary pornography industry. Some of the historical work discussed in the previous section has attempted to place a political and economic lens on the historical foundations of the contemporary pornography business, engaging with its technological (Alilunas 2016), legal or regulatory (Arnberg 2012; Strub 2011) and distribution contexts (Heffernan 2015; Larsson 2016). I have attempted to situate my own work amongst these debates, taking a cultural and economic approach to historicizing the British hardcore pornographic film business between 1960 and 2000, focusing specifically on the practices of entrepreneurs who actively produced and distributed such material in Britain when it was prohibited by law. Initially, I imagined this book to take the reader through the years 1960–2000, when it was a criminal offence to distribute hardcore pornography in Britain. Upon writing, I quickly realized that the weight of my research had generated enough material for multiple volumes.

Because of this, I concentrate on the years 1960–84, specifically exploring the production and distribution of rollers in an alternative economy, but also considering the emergence of home video in the late 1970s. In *Under the Counter*, I expand on previous work I have produced exploring alternative economies (Carter 2018a), where I studied the fan enterprise surrounding a particular cycle of European cult cinema known as the *giallo* – Italian post-war thrillers – arguing that 'fantrepreneurs' within an alternative economy used new technologies to produce artefacts that are distributed as commodities or gifts. To achieve this, they circumvented rules and regulations, such as laws and policies. These spaces are liminal, enabling experimentation and innovation until regulators find a way to control their activities, often resulting in an ongoing battle between the entrepreneurs and the regulators. Here, my use of the word 'alternative' is not intended to refer to radical or counter-cultural practices. I instead use it to indicate a different, or separate, economic space.

A focus on the radical dominates economic geography's approach to alternative economies, studying how alternative economies operate outside of the capitalist mainstream. Here, scholars explore varying forms of economic exchange and differing approaches to labour, organization and property (Gibson-Graham 2006).

Academics have been critical of this position, suggesting that alternative econo-mies are perceived as 'utopian experiments' (North 2007: xxii) that fill the gaps left by capitalism and therefore reinforce exploitative capitalist practices (Samers 2005). I find such ideas helpful in exploring the political and economic conditions that enable alternative economies to form. In the case of the pornography busi-ness, entrepreneurs have historically operated across 'both legal and financial grey zones' (Larsson 2015: 223). This is due to restrictive regulatory frameworks and the reputation pornography has for being a 'controversial economy' (Cannatelli et al. 2019). In this book, I use the concept of an alternative economy to indicate the existence of a distinct economic space between formal and informal media econo-mies (Lobato and Thomas 2015). It is often referred to as a grey economic space, which Roodhouse (2013: 16) defines as a market where practices are 'considered illegal but socially acceptable'. In criminology, the term 'twilight zone' has been used to describe 'the area where the legal and underground economies intersect or overlap' (McCarthy 2011: 26). I suggest that the British hardcore pornography business existed in an alternative economic space due to the activities of different entrepreneurs who manipulated the law to be able to produce and distribute their commodities. My focus, then, is on the practices of these entrepreneurs.

Central to this idea is how entrepreneurs spot inconsistencies in regulation and circumvent them, allowing for their commodities to be sold by lessening the threat of prosecution. Leeson and Coyne (2004: 4) define this process as 'evasive entre-preneurship', where entrepreneurs devote 'resources and efforts in evading the legal system' for their economic benefit. In Britain, the pornography business was tightly regulated under the Obscene Publications Act 1959. However, the vagueness of this highly criticized regulation (Robertson 1979; Woozley 1982) meant that it was open to interpretation. As Smith (2007: 54) argues, 'regulation and calls for censorship have not been simply repressive but have also been productive and an essential part of the material conditions in which pornography has developed in the UK'. To do business, entrepreneurs worked this messy regulatory framework to their advantage.

I show how entrepreneurship in an alternative economy is complex and multi-layered, with a range of economic actors performing different roles. For example, I draw on Schumpeter (2017), who sees the entrepreneur as a key player in economic development, mainly through their willingness to disrupt and innovate by creating new markets. Technology plays a vital role in this process. Coopersmith (1998: 95) suggests that accelerated technological change has always 'shaken the [pornography] industry [...] forcing companies to reinvent themselves to survive'. Occasionally, new technol-ogies catch regulators by surprise, falling outside of regulatory control and, until they catch up, entrepreneurs exploit such loopholes, as my discussion of home video in the conclusion to this book illustrates. Through their use of amateur and semi-professional filmmaking processes, these early innovators were – unbeknownst to them – creating a new market not only in Britain but one that also extended transnationally to parts of Western Europe and the United States.

Schumpeter's conceptualization of the entrepreneur has received criticism. For instance, Baumol (1990: 894) points out that entrepreneurs do not 'always follow the constructive and innovative script' Schumpeter proposes. Instead, Baumol sees entrepreneurs as opportunists who take different roles, engaging in productive, unproductive and disruptive practices. He recognizes that entrepreneurs do make productive contributions to society and the formal economy but also acknowledges that they are often involved in activities that offer 'questionable value to society' (Baumol 1990: 897), such as criminal or legally ambiguous enterprise. Later chapters explore how opportunistic entrepreneurs expanded the market, taking over from early innovators and motivated by the possible high profits offered through making and distributing pornography. Some are 'pariah capitalists' (Gertzman 1999), sharing similarities to the opportunistic black marketeers who profited from wartime rationing (Roodhouse 2013), while others adopt a moral discourse (Becker 1966), justifying their entrepreneurship as a way to bring change to a repressive system of censorship. Some exhibit the Thatcherite 'entrepreneurial spirit' well in advance of the enterprise culture agenda of the early 1980s (Gray 2002).

While the entrepreneurs I discuss share many similarities with the criminal entrepreneurs of which Hobbs (1988; 1995) writes, engaging in violence and other immoral acts, I also show how their participation in an alternative economy often blurs the boundary between criminal and lawful practices. Pornographers were not the only economic actors manipulating laws for their benefit. Rule enforcers, particularly the police, were equally entrepreneurial. Becker (1966) and Hobbs (1988) both identify the entrepreneurial qualities of police work, with the latter noting how detectives regularly skirt the boundaries of legality when making a case or to enhance their position in the force. I suggest that members of the Obscene Publications Squad, an arm of the Metropolitan Police who enforced the Obscene Publications Act 1959 in central London, were instrumental to creating an institutional framework (North 1990) for the alternative economy. In the 1950s, officers implemented a corrupt licensing system to control the distribution of hardcore pornography in Soho (Cox et al. 1977; Tomkinson 1982). This enabled pornography entrepreneurs to do business with the approval and protection of the police, inadvertently leading to the growth of Britain's pornography trade.

As North (1990: 3) writes, institutional frameworks are the 'rules of the game' that provide the incentive for trade. I argue that their interpretation of the Obscene Publications Act 1959 provided the framework for the alternative economy, using a combination of what North calls formal and informal constraints to guide entrepreneurs. As I show in the opening three chapters, this authorized hardcore pornography production and distribution, albeit under certain constraints, resulting in the growth of a transnational economy. Following the removal of the licensing system, Chapters 4 and 5 show how police and prosecutors shifted positions, using the law entrepreneurially to raid, arrest and prosecute pornographers. In response, pornographers attempted – unsuccessfully – to create a formal institutional framework for hardcore in Britain. *Under the Counter* explores this relationship between entrepreneurship and institutional change, highlighting, as North (1990) points out, how institutes continually evolve.

Given pornography's move from a physical commodity to an immaterial, digital commodity that is distributed, or streamed, for free via tube sites such as PornHub and xHamster, it may seem that this distinction has little purchase in the contemporary moment. However, as Alilunas (2016) observes, histories of the pornography business can further our understanding of new developments, such as how previous attempts to censor pornography relate to the control of 'online harms' or how new technologies enable entrepreneurial activity via income-generating content subscription platforms. *Under the Counter* highlights the ongoing challenges of regulating pornography and how entrepreneurs find ways to do business in the face of such uncertainties.

## *Investigating the illicit*

As McKee et al. (2020) find, defining pornography is notoriously difficult as the term has no singular meaning. Kendrick (1987: 31) sees pornography as a 'battlefield', naming an 'argument not a thing'. McKee et al. (2020: 1088) also note that Kendrick's definition calls into question debates around 'social and cultural relations of power'. Like Church (2016), I too use the term pornography rather than adopting recent suggestions to use 'adult film' (Church and Schaefer 2018: 142–43). While I see the adaptability and value of this, I adopt the broader term of pornography as it allows for the inclusion of other commodities produced and distributed by entrepreneurs alongside films, such as photographs and typescripts. To give further definition, I turn to Slade's (2000: 16) view of pornography as a 'market driven commodity' where artefacts are produced and distributed to meet market demand. As already identified, my focus is on the production and distribution of hardcore pornography, rather than the more licit form of softcore. Like the word pornography, hardcore is equally loaded. Simply put, hardcore pornography is the representation of 'non-simulated sex acts' (Schaefer 2005: 81) and, as Williams (1989) and Kendrick (1987) both point out, has been othered through numerous obscenity trials, raising questions about its social value and place in society. Therefore, an understanding of the law and its application is integral to any analysis of the pornography business. It can reveal past attempts to regulate and define pornography, and how these provide the structural conditions for trade. Moreover, such attempts to regulate often leave a trail of resources that researchers can draw on to document the business. I now briefly reflect on how I carried out the research for this book, considering the challenges faced when investigating illicit practices.

The methodology for this research draws on Kuhn's (2002) ethnohistorical study of 1930s' film audiences and their memories of cinema-going. She identifies the challenges of communicating with mature participants who have difficulties with recollection, a common issue I faced when conducting primary research for this project. According to Kuhn (2002: 6), ethnohistory can consist of 'ethnographic description and interpretation alongside oral historical inquiry and the historian's traditional source materials'. My adaptation of this approach included conducting semi-structured interviews with those involved in the industry from the 1960s to the present day, resulting in a total of 42. These consist of producers, distributors, performers, solicitors, collectors and casual workers. It proved impossible to interview officers involved in the Obscene Publications Squad, and only one retired Metropolitan Police officer agreed to share their broader experience of police work during the 1970s. Following Kuhn, I attempted to conduct a series of interviews with each participant, finding that this built trust and allowed time for memories to be rediscovered. Most of these have been with males, highlighting the gendering of the economy and the difficulty of locating females involved in making pornographic films. Some of these interviews were filmed and, with the permission of the interviewees, were used to make the six-part documentary series *Sexposed* (Simon Fletcher 2018).

Conducting the research for this book has been fascinating but frustrating. As the formative years of Britain's alternative economy of hardcore pornography can be traced back to the 1950s, its clandestine conditions have made it difficult to track down those involved. This may partly explain why there has been limited academic research on the subject. Many of those who participated in the economy operated under different names or have since changed their names through marriage or deed poll; others have passed away. Several interviewees repeatedly told me that I was 'five years too late', missing an opportunity to engage with many of the older Soho crowd who took delight in recounting their experiences. For those I was able to track down, and it often took years to locate some of the names I identified, many refused to take part, stating that they had moved on with their lives and did not wish to reconnect with their past. Others did not respond.

Although those involved in the making of rollers are nameless, there being no credits or attempt to document their production, it has been possible to identify people through media reportage, legal documents and other related ephemera. It regularly felt uncomfortable trying to discover these performers' contact details and I was conscious of intruding on their privacy. I found that many had left the business and moved on with their lives. For those I located and contacted by email or letter I found that few were willing to talk, making me realize that researching pornography's histories requires sensitivity and the building of trust. Because of this, I am very selective when choosing whose names to reveal in this research, especially with performers, even though they may be identifiable through public documents. Those I name either gave their permission, are already known for their involvement in pornography, have been identified in other academic research or have died. Some names have been changed at the interviewees' request to protect their identities and, on some occasions, I only give a first name or a surname.

At the heart of this book is an eight-hour semi-structured interview with Michael Freeman, who died in 2021. Freeman, formerly known as Michael Muldoon, was involved in the economy from 1964 to the early 2000s. He provided an invaluable first-hand account of the early years of the economy, through to the re-evaluation of the R18 certificate in 2000, when he produced his final films. My interest in the economy came from reading a series of self-published autobiographies titled *I Pornographer* by Freeman (2011). Freeman's claims seemed outlandish and exaggerated, telling stories about making rollers against a backdrop of police corruption and the London's underworld. Newspaper archives at the British Library corroborated many elements of Freeman's stories, and this method of triangulation became a crucial part of my methodology. Around this time, a documentary was being made about Freeman's life, titled *Hardcore Guaranteed* (Simon Fletcher 2019). Simon, the director, had also read *I Pornographer* and was equally fascinated by Freeman and wanted to document his life while he was still alive. Freeman agreed. Simon and I began a productive working relationship, collaborating on *Hardcore Guaranteed* and co-conducting numerous interviews, many of which are referred to throughout this book. Simon tracked Freeman down, discovering that he was living in exile in Southern Italy and, in April 2016, conducted a series of on-camera interviews. Following this, I undertook three phone interviews with Freeman and we conversed via Facebook Messenger, where he added first-hand detail to my ongoing discoveries.

The second part of my ethnohistorical approach involved archival research, locating various documents and artefacts that aid the historicization of the alternative economy. As highlighted by Williams (1989) and Dean et al. (2014), the ephemeral nature of pornography presents problems for researchers, as there are few specialist institutional archives to draw on, especially in Britain. Therefore, researching the historical foundations of the pornography business becomes a scavenger hunt, accumulating a 'critical mess' of material to make sense of (Schaefer 2012: 151). However, as Schaefer (2012: 151) points out, 'fortuitous convergences' often transpire from this. I began my archival research by attempting to collect a sample of the commodities produced and distributed by pornographers. Initially, this was poorly digitized captures of rollers and VHS films from the *Vintage Erotica* website, a community archive devoted to collecting, and preserving, pornography.[5] After building a physical sample of rollers, I quickly realized that their material properties – the packaging, the film stock – were as equally, if not more, revealing than the actual films (I elaborate on this in Appendix 1). No formal archive of rollers exists in Britain, with the most comprehensive collection being stored at the Kinsey Institute in Indiana, USA. Along with Di Lauro and Rabkin's (1976) film and title index, their database proved to be more exhaustive than the crowdsourced Adult Loop Database,[6] giving likely production dates for many rollers.[7] A lack of archives meant that I either needed to build my own or gain access to private collections, a challenge also acknowledged by Alilunas (2016: 39).

Gaining access to these personal archives relied on building trust with collectors, leading to them acting as 'sponsors' (Walsh 2004: 231), putting me in touch with others in their network and vouching for my integrity. I accessed seven substantial private collections of rollers and their owners kindly permitted me to scan images of boxes and view some of their titles. Once I established my own archive of rollers, I learned how to handle film after finding that titles in poor physical condition could easily be chewed up by a projector. This emphasized the precarity of these materials and led me to the purchase of a domestic 8mm scanner, allowing a sample of titles to be digitized in compressed high definition for closer analysis; 16mm films were professionally scanned. Many of the screenshots included throughout *Under the Counter* are taken from these scans. I reluctantly followed Kennedy and Davis' (2013) and Waugh's (1996) approach of distorting the faces of performers to protect their identities out of legal necessity.

Second, I turned my attention to media reportage, collecting magazines, articles from newspapers and relevant television broadcasts. Newspapers played a vital part in documenting the development of pornography in Britain, particularly with it being an ongoing subject of public interest. I sourced 829 newspaper articles, including articles from the Danish and Swedish press, highlighting the transnational nature of the economy.[8] These were located via microfiche at the British Library, but mainly through the British Newspaper Archive,[9] *UKPressOnline*,[10] the National Campaign for the Reformation of the Obscene Publications Act online archive[11] and the MediaStream service at the Royal Library, Copenhagen, Denmark. It is worth acknowledging the limitations of such sources. As Franzosi (1987: 6) identifies, 'the validity of newspaper information is questionable', but also points out that 'no data source is without error'. The editorial positions of tabloid newspapers often mean that pornography is portrayed negatively, presenting a skewed picture of events. While it is important to recognize the weakness of these sources, they still serve as valuable documents for pornography historians and starting points for further research. Magazines and periodicals such as *8mm Magazine*, *Forum*, *Experience*, *Continental Film and Video Review*, *Video World*, *Late Night Video*, *Personal Advertiser* and *Exchange and Mart* give further context, often containing interviews with some of the entrepreneurs, advertisements from enterprises and details of 8mm film-making practices.

It was newspapers and magazines that led me to undertake doctrinal research as they regularly made mention of legal cases. According to Hutchinson (2013: 9), doctrinal research is 'used to identify, analyze and synthesize the content of the law'. It involves 'locating cases and statutes, the use of indexes and citators, and the use of computer information retrieval systems such as Westlaw and LexisNexis' (McConville and Chui 2007: 3). This enabled me to understand the complex legal context for British pornography, as well as sourcing legal records that document the trade and the attempts made to regulate it. It also took me to the National Archives in London, discovering that they held many legal documents belonging to the Director of Public Prosecutions and the Metropolitan Police. Though not exhaustive, with only documents deemed culturally significant being kept, these document obscenity trials and investigations relating to police corruption and pornography. I scanned over 26,000 pages of legal documents. Three Freedom of Information (FOI) requests were made to open closed files, resulting in one being released, albeit heavily redacted, demonstrating not just the sensitivity of their contents but also the overprotectiveness of reviewers. I also learned that FOI requests can lead to files being closed or opening dates extended, doing more harm than good.

Collectively, these sources enabled me to shed light on this hidden enterprise, allowing me to understand how the alternative economy operated and learn how rollers were produced, distributed and regulated. Furthermore, the wide range and depth of sources have corroborated some of the apparent outlandish claims made by interviewees. As Hobbs (1988: 4) found in his research, 'criminals do lie', particularly in autobiographies and other insider accounts – another source I have sparingly drawn on to fill in any gaps. To address these limitations, I used multiple methods to help verify 'one set of data sources by collecting data from others' (Hammersley and Atkinson 2007: 183) and corroborate my findings. However, I realize that my historicization is based on my own interpretation of the material and the economy's lack of documentation. Like Bosworth (2001), I too draw on Farge (2013), who recognizes that there are always gaps in the archive when carrying out historical research, but it is possible to identify patterns that can be placed in context. Therefore, due to a lack of irrefutable evidence, I identify some of the likely candidates for making and distributing rollers in Britain. If I am wrong, I am happy to be corrected, welcoming future attempts to piece together the history of this forgotten trade. As Alilunas (2016: 30) highlights, researching pornography is a puzzle and relies on 'trace historiography' to make sense out of what has been left behind: 'the trace historiographer must often examine the smoke rather than the fire to determine how the fire started, what burned, and why'.

## Looking under the counter

The opening chapter explores some of the cultural and economic conditions for the emergence of the alternative economy of hardcore pornography, providing context for the chapters that follow. I begin by studying the Obscene Publications Act 1959, the primary legal instrument for regulating pornography in Britain. I suggest the limitations in this legislation presented an entrepreneurial opportunity for pornographers and police, leading to the introduction of an institutional framework for the alternative economy. I then consider the permissive society of the 1960s, showing how cultural shifts and changes in public policy made sex and sexuality a topic of public discussion. I situate Soho amongst this changing sexual landscape, identifying it as the economic centre for pornography distribution in Britain, discussing the key entrepreneurs who ran bookshops in this area, how they operated them and the corrupt licensing system that underwrote the economy. The chapter concludes by looking at how a culture of domestic hardcore production was established, with entrepreneurs selling their photographs and illustrated books to Soho's bookshops.

Chapter 2 considers the technological context for roller production, beginning with an exploration of how rollers fit into Britain's small-gauge film market and wider cultures of pornographic film production. I then move on to look at how small-gauge film technologies presented entrepreneurial opportunities, suggesting that movie-making magazines and handbooks served as instructional manuals for roller makers. Having discussed the conditions for production, I identify the early pioneers of roller production before focusing on the activities of Ivor Cook. I argue that these early entrepreneurs were innovators, creating a market for hardcore film in the alternative economy and, in the case of Cook, expanding its reach beyond Soho to Denmark.

Chapter 3 offers a broader understanding of entrepreneurship in the alternative economy by looking at the activities of Mike Freeman and Evan 'Big Jeff' Phillips. I study how these two pornographers took different approaches to their enterprise, with Freeman relying on his criminality and Phillips drawing on his experience as a small business owner to introduce the first branded label, Climax Films, in 1966. Both brought a commercial mindset to the economy, upscaling production and distributing pornography transnationally. I argue the Obscene Publications Squad's licensing system was an important factor in this growth, providing an institutional framework for the economy and setting the rules of the game, which Freeman disregarded, and Phillips followed.

Chapter 4 examines the expansion of the alternative economy in the early 1970s, as mail order became the dominant form of distribution, selling rollers and higher quality 8mm films imported from Denmark, which had fully legalized hardcore pornography in 1969. I argue that this expansion ultimately led to its regulation, with the popular press uncovering the Obscene Publications Squad's corrupt activities following an investigation into the pornography trade by politician and moral crusader Lord Longford. To illustrate this, I use the example of a forgotten obscenity trial referred to as the 'Watford Blue Movie Trial' by the popular press, which revealed the entrepreneurial activities of distributor John Darby and roller maker Anthony Collingbourne. Through a close reading of the Director of Public Prosecutions' documents relating to this trial, I show how police and prosecutors used a combination of laws to fill holes in the Obscene Publications Act 1959 and convict those involved. I argue that this case is indicative of a broader attempt to control the alternative economy, ultimately stunting Britain's roller trade.

The final chapter investigates a shift in the economy from production to distribution, as imported 8mm pornography replaced domestic production. Against the backdrop of a constantly shifting moral climate, I consider how John Jesner Lindsay and David Waterfield positioned themselves alongside politicians, anti-pornography activists and the police as moral entrepreneurs. Operating without a functioning institutional framework, I suggest that Lindsay and Waterfield acted as agents of change, seeking to legalize hardcore pornography in order to benefit from it. Central to this pursuit was claiming that their activities were moral and just. Throughout the chapter, I draw on their extensive legal battles to show how the Metropolitan Police responded to their increasingly publicized attempts entrepreneurially, seeking to close the loopholes that allowed Lindsay and Waterfield to do business. I close the chapter by reviewing how this battle of morality resulted in tighter regulation of Britain's pornography business, as the new Conservative government brought in tougher laws.

In the book's conclusion, I comment on the wider significance of the findings from my research into Britain's roller trade, discussing how entrepreneurship is a helpful framework for understanding the political, economic and cultural conditions pornographers operate in. I also consider some of the methodological limitations of the study. After the conclusion, I offer an epilogue that briefly considers the introduction of home video in Britain and the opportunities it created for pornography entrepreneurs. Here, the themes discussed throughout the book repeat themselves, with pornographers battling with the law and the eventual institution of another law – the Video Recordings Act 1984. But first, I return to the beginnings of the alternative economy, when the Obscene Publications Act 1959 was brought in to help separate artworks from pornography. As I show, the implementation of this controversial law created the material conditions for Britain's domestic trade in hardcore pornography.

# 1

## *Carnaby Kinks:* Obscenity, Permissiveness and the Dirty Square Mile

> *[A]s France has become more suppressive, her neighbour across the Channel has become increasingly permissive toward pornography, and it is Britain that currently supplies the majority – and the best – of the foreign stag material available in the American commercial market. Stag films (along with every description of photographic and literally pornography) are sold on a relatively open basis in London today [...] throughout the Soho area [...] they also suggest that there may be parts of London that are really as 'swinging' as its reputation.*
>
> (Knight and Halpert 1967: 186)

> *Our kind of porn really started in Soho, not in Sweden or Denmark as many believe. Denmark was just the only liberated country in Europe who would take it.*
>
> (Hans Moser, cited in Hebditch and Anning 1988: 212)

My first visit to Soho in 2009 was filled with nervousness and apprehension. Media reportage and popular representations in film and television had convinced me that the 'dirty square mile' was dangerous and unsafe. The Soho of today is very different to the Soho of the 1960s and 1970s. Like the other famous European red-light districts I visited as part of the research for this project – Vesterbro in Copenhagen, Denmark and De Wallen in Amsterdam, Netherlands – the traces of Soho's sexual economy are increasingly disappearing. According to Sanders-McDonagh and Peyrefitte (2016), this is being achieved through licensing laws, gentrification and corporatization. The many bookshops and sex shops that once existed throughout Soho are now replaced by eateries, clothes stores and other 'trendy' outlets. As Figure 1.2 shows, some remnants of Soho's sex trade still exist today. There is the vintage

FIGURE 1.1: *Carnaby Kinks* (Evan Phillips 1968). Author's personal collection.

FIGURE 1.2: *(top, left)*, Peter Street, Soho, 2017 (photograph taken by author); *(top, right)*, Walker's Court, 2021; *(below)*, Brewer Street (both courtesy of Michael Venton).

pornography DVD basement shop on Peter Street, and Walker's Court remains the primary location for sex shops. As you walk around, you might spot the 'Models' signs advertising the 'Soho Walk-ups', stairs that lead up to flats where sex workers operate, continuing Soho's long-held reputation for being the 'most famous red-light district in Britain' (Summers 1989: 208). In the 1960s, Soho was representative of swinging London, with events such as the Profumo Affair bringing international attention to its licentiousness (Mort 2010: 356). A highly sensationalized political sex scandal between 19-year-old model Christine Keeler and Secretary of State for War John Profumo, the Profumo Affair regularly featured in the popular news from 1961 to 1963, linking the political world of Westminster to the 'sexual world' of Soho (Mort 2010: 24). According to Mort (2010: 356), pornography and sex work 'were defining features of Soho's sexual economy, and this was underwritten by a fresh alliance between local entrepreneurs, the Metropolitan Police and Westminster Council'. Enabled by the ambiguity of the Obscene Publications Act 1959, the law used to control the pornography trade, a corrupt licensing system allowed the economy to function, minimizing the threat of arrest for those involved.

In this opening chapter, I consider the cultural and economic conditions for the emergence of an alternative economy that produced and distributed pornographic materials in the bookshops of Soho and beyond. Central to this was the regulatory framework for pornography in Britain. I begin by examining the Obscene Publications Act 1959 and how its ambiguities created a loophole that was exploited by pornography entrepreneurs and the Metropolitan Police. Second, I look at how other changes to regulation during the 1960s made sex a popular topic of public discussion. I suggest that the relaxed moral climate of this permissive society was a contributory factor in the emergence and development of this economy. Finally, I consider how Soho became representative of this changing sexual climate and the centre for pornography distribution in Britain, with corrupt members of a division of the Metropolitan Police named the Obscene Publications Squad forming an alliance with entrepreneurs running bookshops. This created a marketplace for selling commodities domestically produced by pornographers, such as photographs, typescripts and rollers. I argue that the entrepreneurial activities of the police established an institutional framework for the alternative economy that incentivized pornographers and allowed it to flourish.

## *Regulating pornography*

Entrepreneurs are typically framed as agents of change who rework existing institutional frameworks and, in turn, provide the incentives for 'political, social, or economic exchange' (North 1990: 8). For North (1990: 3–4), institutional frameworks are the 'rules of the game' and can consist of formal 'rules human beings devise' or informal 'conventions and codes of behaviour'. Using a sporting analogy, North suggests that players choose to either follow the rules of the game or break them to gain a competitive advantage. In the latter case, players exhibit an awareness of the benefits of breaking rules and the possible punishments for doing so. North names the law as a formal rule, noting that laws develop over time and therefore present different opportunities. Here, I am interested in how entrepreneurs interpret, play with and adapt laws for their own benefit. Increasing attention is being paid to entrepreneurs who evade formal structures and, through their enterprise, effect regulatory change. This process has been described as evasive entrepreneurship, which Elert and Henrekson (2016: 1) define as 'profit-driven business activity in the market aimed at circumventing the existing institutional framework by using innovations to exploit contradictions in that framework'.

Evasive entrepreneurship builds on Schumpeter's (2017) perception of entrepreneurs as rule breakers and innovators. Elert and Henrekson (2016) highlight how evasive entrepreneurs disrupt the legal system, often resulting in the review of current laws that either enable enterprise or criminalize it. Therefore, evasive entrepreneurs use legal loopholes to create new markets. Scholars tend to not equate evasive entrepreneurs with criminals, highlighting the blurring of the lines between what Baumol (1990) describes as productive entrepreneurship and unproductive or destructive entrepreneurship; entrepreneurial activity that does not make a productive or positive contribution to the economy. In this sense, the entrepreneur engages in what might be considered criminal acts but evades the law in order to generate profit and reduce the risk of arrest. I suggest that this creates an alternative economic space, where lines between formal and informal become unclear due to the disruptive activities of those who operate within it. For instance, in their study of the illicit art trade, Bichler et al. (2013) identify the diverse range of economic actors involved in the business, consisting of those who serve a criminal purpose, a smuggler, for instance, or another who takes a more formal role, such as the auction house selling a looted antique. They argue that this is an example of a 'market interlock', where the formal, grey and informal meet or, as I suggest, an alternative economic space with its own institutional framework and rules of trade. Here, formal and informal rules become intertwined and are geared towards preserving the economy.

As I show throughout this book, evasiveness regularly features in pornography entrepreneurship. Hence, to understand the economy's institutional framework, or the 'rules of the game' (North 1990), it is important to examine the primary legal instrument for controlling pornography in Britain – the Obscene Publications Act 1959. Like many of the permissive legislations introduced at the end of the 1950s and throughout the 1960s, its introduction was intended to be a 'liberalizing measure' (Manchester 1986: 33) and a response to 'authors and publishers who were concerned about the vagueness of the obscenity laws and anxious to differentiate between genuine works of art and pornography' (Tomkinson 1982: 29). Yet, as I will show, the inconsistency of the law allowed a range of entrepreneurial actors to interpret it in different ways, leading to the creation of an alternative economy of hardcore pornography; exactly the opposite of what the law set out to achieve.

Although its use has steadily declined over the years, the Obscene Publications Act 1959 was the 'primary statutory mechanism for regulating adult pornography' in the United Kingdom until the introduction of the Criminal Justice and Immigration Act 2008 (McGlynn and Ward 2009: 329). Yet, as Smith (2005: 149) notes, before the introduction of the Criminal Justice and Immigration Act 2008 there were four additional laws used to regulate pornography:

- The Customs Consolidation Act 1876 – covering the importation of indecent materials.
- The Post Office Act 1953 – prohibits the distribution of pornography by post.
- The Protection of Children Act 1978 – prohibiting the production and possession of child pornography.
- The Video Recordings Act 1984 – regulating the distribution of video recordings.[1]

As solicitor and chair of the Campaign Against Censorship, Edward Goodman explained, 'a mass of statutes and common law offences applicable to pornography' exist.[2] With this in mind, the following can also be added to the aforementioned:

- The Indecent Displays (Control) Act 1981 – preventing the public display of pornographic material.[3]
- The Public Order Act 1984 – preventing the display of insulting material.
- The Cinemas Act 1985 – consolidating the Cinematographic Acts (1909 and 1952) and the Cinematograph (Amendment) Act 1982, requiring cinemas to be licensed and show BBFC-certified films.
- The Criminal Justice and Public Order Act 1994 – outlawing indecent pseudo photographs of children.

Smith (2005: 149) acknowledges that the definitions of all of these laws are problematic and 'notoriously slippery'. Therefore, rather than providing a coherent legal framework for regulating pornography, they instead present a mess of overlapping laws that create confusion and make their application complex. Not only did this create legal loopholes for pornography entrepreneurs, but the ambiguities also meant that police and the courts could be entrepreneurial in their application of the law.

For example, the Customs Consolidation Act 1876 prevents the importation of 'indecent materials'; the Post Office Act 1953 prohibits the distribution of 'indecent or obscene' articles through the Royal Mail; and the Obscene Publications Act 1959 focuses on obscenity. According to *R* v. *Stanley* (1965), 'the words 'indecent or obscene' convey one idea, namely, offending against the recognised standards of propriety, indecent being at the lower end of the scale and obscene at the upper end of the scale'. Even so, the looseness of these terms can be used by the defence to lessen the sentence, arguing that an article is indecent rather than obscene, for example. This occurred in *R* v. *Waterfield* (1975), which I discuss in greater detail in Chapter 5. On appeal, the defence successfully argued that pornographic films imported from Denmark via the Netherlands by the defendant for screening and sale in his members-only cinema clubs were indecent rather than obscene. The judge finally determined that they were in 'touching distance of the border between indecency and obscenity'. Waterfield had his sentence reduced from three years to eighteen months.

Conversely, the ambiguities between indecency and obscenity could also be used by prosecutors to strengthen their chances of conviction, particularly in the mid 1970s when juries were increasingly finding hardcore pornography not to be obscene. Another strategy employed by the Director of Prosecutions was to draw on archaic common law charges, which Robertson (1979: 210) describes as 'judge-made law' as they come from court decisions rather than statutes. Charges such as conspiracy to corrupt public morals, outraging public decency and keeping a disorderly house were regularly used at the whim of prosecutors and judges seeking to control the activities of pornographers and deter others from entering the trade. A common law charge such as conspiracy carried 'a number of tactical advantages unavailable to the prosecution in proceedings brought under the Obscene Publications Act 1959', only having to prove to a jury that a conspiracy can involve at 'agreement', possibly even 'a nod or a wink' (Robertson 1979: 231–32). According to Cocks (2016: 267), conspiracy to corrupt public morals was used regularly throughout the 1960s and 1970s to circumvent 'not only the will of parliament, but also the intentions of legislators in the period after the Wolfenden Report of 1957'. He cites the case of *Shaw* v. *DPP* (1962) as an early example of the employment of common laws in an obscenity trial, which resulted in the defendant's prosecution.

I want to focus on how the Obscene Publications Act 1959 (including the amendments introduced in 1964) operates as a statute, identifying some of its vagaries and shortcomings as a piece of legislation, providing a legal context for the obscenity trials I discuss throughout this book and how it shaped the boundaries of the alternative economy. According to the opening text, its purpose is to 'provide for the protection of literature; and to strengthen the law concerning pornography'. The law was targeted at those who distribute obscene material rather than those who produce or possess it. It has always been legal to produce normative hardcore pornographic material in Britain, but not to sell it. A review of the British Board of Film Classification's R18 certificate in 2000 eventually allowed the sale of hardcore pornography in licensed sex shops, providing that the work does not contravene the Obscene Publications Act 1959 (Petley 2011; Perkins 2012). Possession is also permitted, on the basis that it is not for gain and does not contravene other laws, such as the Criminal Justice and Immigration Act 2018 or the Protection of

Children Act 1978. Under the Customs Consolidation Act 1876, the importation of 'indecent' material for personal use was a grey area. Until the early 1990s, customs seemed to be more concerned with intercepting large consignments of pornography, with smaller amounts sneaking through. However, as video tapes could easily be duplicated, customs began confiscating pornographic videos, fearing that one video cassette could result in innumerable copies once reaching Britain. O'Toole (1999: 146) mentions how this particularly affected gay men bringing gay pornography into the country.

In 1964, the Obscene Publications Act 1959 was amended to include gain, criminalizing those who stood to economically benefit from pornography. The 1959 Act was based on publication, making it an offence to publish an obscene article; this might consist of selling such an article to a customer in a shop and could even be through offering hire or gifting the article to another. As Robertson (1979: 71) explains, 'there must be some evidence connecting the defendant with the movement of the article into another's hands'. However, possession was not an offence. This came to light in *Mella* v. *Monahan* (1961), which argued that having a priced obscene article for sale in a bookshop did not constitute an offer of sale or could be defined as publication in accordance with the Obscene Publications Act 1959. To close this loophole, the 1964 Act criminalized the possession of obscene articles for commercial gain. Robertson (1979: 71) points out that this addition broadened the law, as only the intention of publishing for gain needed to be proven; evidence of its actual distribution was not required. Furthermore, gain is a broad term that could include other forms of economic exchange beyond money. The 1964 amendment also widened the control over pornography, responding to the rise in pornographic photographs and films. In *Straker* v. *DPP* (1963), the defence team for British art photographer Jean Straker argued that a photographic negative could not be considered an obscene article under section 1(2) of the Obscene Publications Act 1959; it could only be regarded as obscene if it was published (Pullen 2008).[4] The 1959 Act defined an article as 'containing or embodying matter to be read or looked at or both, any sound record, and any film or other record of a picture or pictures'. As a response to *Straker* v. *DPP* (1963), section 2(1) of the 1964 amendment now included

> anything which is intended to be used, either alone or as one of a set, for the reproduction or manufacture therefrom of articles containing or embodying matter to be read, looked at or listened to, as if it were an article containing or embodying that matter so far as that matter is to be derived from it or from the set.

Authorities now had increased legal powers to control the expanding British pornography trade. The 1959 act covered publication; the 1964 amendment criminalized possession for gain; and both could be used simultaneously alongside the common law charges I discussed earlier. Under section 2(1), those found guilty under the Obscene Publications Act 1959 were 'entitled to trial by jury' (Smith 2005: 155) and be liable for the following penalties:

a.  On summary conviction to a fine not exceeding £100 pounds or to imprisonment for a term not exceeding six months.
b.  On conviction on indictment to a fine or imprisonment for a term not exceeding three years or both.

The severity of the penalty would often be at the discretion of the judge. Steve, an owner of Soho sex shops since the 1970s, angrily recalled how he was sentenced by a judge with a reputation for harsh penalties for selling hardcore pornography.[5] If common law charges, such as conspiracy, were used, longer sentences and higher fines could be given at the judge's discretion.

## The problem with obscenity

For Robertson (1979: xviii), the Obscene Publications Act 1959 has not achieved its aims and has therefore 'suffered more criticism than any other contemporary piece of legislation'. Despite this, the 'test' for guilt, whether the offending article has the 'tendency to deprave or corrupt', has remained unchained since *R v. Hicklin* (1868). This is problematic for two primary reasons. First, the Obscene Publications Act 1959 comes from a particular period of history – the Victorian era – where there were regular attempts to 'legislate morals' (Roberts 1985: 611). At the heart of this law was a concern about whether obscene material might 'stimulate criminal appetites, undermine working-class incentives to lead a life of self-discipline and moral regularity and, not least, provide opportunities to deflate the moral pretensions of the upper ranks in society' (Roberts 1985: 613). Therefore, this outdated perception of obscenity still applies today, although attitudes towards sex and sexuality have changed considerably. It also raises questions about class and access to pornography, a matter I explore later in this chapter.

Second, the subjectivity of the term 'tendency to deprave or corrupt' is highly problematic. As Woozley (1982: 218) identifies, the language is unclear and is 'defined by reference to vague and elastic formulae' (Robertson 1979: 1). As a result, the test of obscenity relies on the case made by the prosecution to persuade the jury as to whether the offending articles meet these criteria and for the defence to persuade otherwise. As described in section 1 of the Obscene Publications Act 1959:

an article shall be deemed to be obscene if its effect or (where the article comprises two or more distinct items) the effect of any one of its items is, if taken as a whole, such as to tend to deprave and corrupt persons who are likely, having regard to all relevant circumstances, to read, see or hear the matter contained or embodied in it.

Therefore, it becomes the jury's duty to determine whether the intended audience for the material is likely to be depraved or corrupted by it. But, as *R* v. *Whyte* (1972) questioned, can pornographic articles sold in a bookshop deprave or corrupt their clientele when they might already be depraved and corrupted before purchasing the material?

Then there is also the question of whether the material can be deemed to have a 'public good'. As according to section 4, a person will not be convicted under section 2 or 3 if it can be justified that the article 'is in the interests of science, literature, art or learning, or of other objects of general concern'. The defence is permitted to draw on the 'opinion of experts' to support this claim.[6] The use of such experts is a common feature of many obscenity cases. In trials taking place in the mid 1970s, Robertson notes how

doctors, psychiatrists, psychologists and sociologists claimed that the publication of obscene material was justified, under section 4 [...] because it served 'an object of general concern' – namely the mental health and physical happiness of a community plagued by 'sexual dysfunction'.

(1979: 4)

This resulted in a number of high-profile pornography trials bringing unwanted media recognition, such as *R* v. *Lindsay* (1974), drawing further public attention to the material it was attempting to prohibit. As I show in Chapter 5, the defendant John Lindsay used the outcomes of his trial and the media attention it received as an alibi to legally sell the acquitted rollers in his sex shops. The opening titles of his films regularly stated that the films were cleared of obscenity charges and deemed to have a public good. In response, the law was tightened, with *DPP* v. *Jordan* (1976) 'limiting the public good defence to material with intrinsic merit as literature or learning' (Robertson 1979: 4). Therefore, whether an article can deprave or corrupt its likely audience is a complicated judgement to make and is heavily based on one's moral position. As Robertson (1979: 2) succinctly puts it, 'one person's obscenity is another person's bedtime reading'.

The subjectivity of obscenity has also affected how the law has been policed. For example, Robertson (1979: 5) notes how police forces across Britain had different perceptions on what would constitute an obscene publication, with Manchester confiscating relatively soft material, while police in Portsmouth 'tolerated the sale of anything short of child porn, bestiality or torture'. As I show later in the chapter, the greatest level of tolerance could be found in Soho, where the Obscene Publications Squad, more colloquially known as 'The Dirty Squad', entrepreneurially used the law to their advantage by operating an informal licensing system to permit the sale of hardcore pornography in Soho and economically benefit from it (Cox et al. 1977; Tomkinson 1982; Carter 2018). Unbeknownst to these corrupt police officers, their interpretation of the Obscene Publications Act 1959 created an institutional framework for the production and distribution of hardcore pornography in Britain. Producers and distributors became licensed and regularly paid fees to protect them from arrest.

This was enabled by section 3 of the Obscene Publications Act 1959, which gave police the power of seizure without needing to provide receipts for confiscated stock. Stock seized from unlicensed pornographers would often be sold on to others for profit. Tomkinson (1982) tells of how officers invited licensed Soho bookshop owners to visit Holborn Police Station. On arrival, they were given a tie to wear, signalling to others that they were members of the Criminal Investigation Department, and an Obscene Publications Squad officer accompanied the bookshop owner to the evidence store, where they could purchase stock. Tomkinson observes that they often purchased back stock that had been seized from their own premises.

As I have shown, the Obscene Publications Act 1959 was never fit for purpose. Its vague terminology allowed for interpretation and evasion by those producing and distributing materials, but also those who policed them. The police adapted the law to meet their own needs, instituting their own licensing system to control the pornography trade and profit from it. Later in this chapter I describe how this institutional framework for the economy was implemented and administered, and outline some of the other evasive techniques pornography distributors used to protect themselves from arrest. Before I do this, I turn my attention to how the Obscene Publications Act 1959 emerged alongside other laws in the 1960s, which drew attention to debates around permissiveness, with sex and sexuality becoming popular subjects of discussion. I situate the emergence of rollers and the growth of Britain's trade in hardcore pornography within this context, arguing that these political and cultural changes provided the ideal conditions for the alternative economy to develop.

## A permissive turn?

I have asked many of my interviewees who experienced the 1960s why they thought there was a sudden growth in the production and distribution of pornography in Britain at this time. All responded by talking to me about how the 1960s saw a relaxation in morals that affected people's attitudes towards sex and sexuality. The term 'permissiveness' or the 'permissive society' is often used to describe this moment in time, which Weeks describes as a

> legislative moment, producing a complex body of legislation passed in the decade after 1958, including reforms of the laws governing gambling, suicide, obscenity and censorship, Sunday entertainment, the abolition of capital punishment for murder, as well as liberalisation of various statutes governing sexual behaviour.
>
> (2012: 249)

For Hunt (1998: 34), this was a 'sociological shift, a consequence of the post-war economic boom which encouraged a kind of controlled hedonism'. The term has become one of much contention and is regularly critiqued by scholars. Weeks (2012: 249), for instance, suggests that advocates for permissiveness would have rarely used the term, while conservative moralists tended to use it in an almost 'scatological' manner. As demonstrated by my interviewees' responses, it is often perceived that there were major changes to society in this period. This is also expressed in the work of Marwick (1988: 19) who argues that a 'cultural revolution' occurred in Britain during the 1960s. He identifies this revolution as having six key features:

1. Affluence and consumerism.
2. Class, particularly the working classes having greater visibility.
3. Youth culture, evident in music and fashion.
4. Sexual attitudes and behaviour.
5. Fairness and freedom.
6. Frankness and openness.

Fisher (1993: 150–51) is critical of Marwick's view that 'Victorian Morality survived intact and unchallenged until the 1950s', believing that focusing too much on this moment in time is 'distorting', as it suggests there were no significant movements 'prior to this decade'.[7] For Mort (2010: 4), 'the permissive society was neither a revolution in English social life nor a radical break with the sexual cultures that preceded it', noting that restrictive policies and values introduced during the Victorian period remained in place. Weeks (2012), Fisher (1993) and Mort (2010) collectively recognize that permissiveness is a complex concept that cannot be simply reduced to a specific decade.

However, during this period, there were significant reformations to public policy that directly related to sexual culture, as well as numerous cultural events that made sex an oft discussed topic. For instance, the 1960s began with the *Lady Chatterley's Lover* obscenity trial in 1960, bringing public attention to erotic literature and the distribution of pornography in Britain. As mentioned in the introduction to this chapter, media reportage of the Profumo Affair sex scandal between the years of 1961 and 1963 ensured 'that sexual London was advertised across the world' (Mort 2010: 24). As I show in the coming chapter, the Profumo Affair became a key reference point for some of Soho's pornographers, particularly with the rollers *100% Lust* (1966–67) and *Randy* (1966–67) that were purported to feature Keeler.

Then there is the emergence of popular music, with the Beatles releasing their first album *Please, Please Me* in 1963. Weeks (2012: 328) notes that the term rock 'n' roll was a 'sexual synonym' with 'sexual outrage' playing a crucial part in its appeal to youth culture. The impact of this cultural form is evident in many rollers. Posters of popular music performers or albums are displayed on walls and record collections regularly appear in the background. Furthermore, 'nudist' films, such as *Naked as Nature Intended* (George Harrison Marks 1961), were passed for exhibition by the then British Board of Film Censors and shown in British cinemas (Trevelyan 1973: 101). Its director George Harrison Marks was also a pioneer of the British glamour film. As I discuss in the next chapter, glamour films were 'above-the-counter' goods openly sold in high street shops. Available on 8mm, Super 8 and, for a short period, 16mm film formats, glamour films usually had three- to four-minute running times and depicted softcore striptease, keeping strictly within the confines of the Obscene Publications Act 1959. These are only selected moments from the early 1960s, but collectively they highlight an increasing openness towards sex that challenges perceptions around the British being 'prudish' or 'sexually repressed' (Marwick 2007: 171).

Happening alongside these changing cultural conditions were significant reforms to public policy relating to sexual culture. I have already explored the Obscene Publications Act 1959, which was intended as a liberal measure, specifically protecting literary works, but also introduced to regulate the pornography trade (Manchester 1986: 33–35). The activities of the Wolfenden Committee in the late 1950s can also be seen as an important framing context for thinking about the 1960s, permissiveness and the sexual revolution. For Weeks (2012: 331), the committee's activities were 'both an expression of 1950s moral anxieties and a blueprint for the "permissive" legislation of the 1960s'. The committee assessed the law on homosexuality and prostitution, ultimately recommending 'the modification of criminal law as it affected certain areas of private morality, specifically prostitution by women and male homosexuality between consenting adults in private, while also suggesting harsher penalties for public indecency and soliciting' (Cocks 2016: 268).

The Wolfenden Report eventually resulted in the Street Offences Act 1959 and the Sexual Offences Act 1967. The Street Offences Act 1959 (Williams 1960) sought to decrease the 'public visibility' of sex workers while increasing penalties for soliciting (Mort 2010: 195). As Mort (2010: 195) observes, this created a 'national myth' that the Wolfenden Report led to a '90% reduction' in public soliciting. He points out that the report 'obsessively focused' on activities taking place in Soho and put the West End of London 'into the heart of governance' (Mort 2010: 23). It moved sex workers from the streets and into private spaces that were often owned by violent pimps, such as the Maltese Messina Brothers and Bernie Silver who dominated Soho's vice trade and economically benefited from this change in policy. I further discuss Silver's role in the alternative economy later in this chapter. Wolfenden's proposals to legalize sexual acts between men took longer, with the Sexual Offences Act 1967 introduced ten years after the report, permitting 'male homosexuality in certain circumstances (between two people over the age of twenty-one)' (Cocks 2016: 268). The committee's findings were published as a report in 1957. It immediately sold out, with 'unofficial, erotically packaged extracts marketed to an American readership', evidencing the significance of the report outside of the Britain, firmly placing attention on its attitudes towards 'sex and morality' (Mort 2010: 194).

Other notable statutes from the late 1960s relating to sexual freedom were the Family Planning Act 1967, the Abortion Act 1967, and the Divorce Reform Act 1969. Oral contraception in the form of the pill was made available in the United Kingdom in 1961 and could be prescribed by the National Health Service for 'therapeutic purposes' (Leathard 1980: 109). Upon its introduction, it received media attention, positive and negative. Institutions such as the Church of England believed its availability would 'encourage women's infidelity', therefore threatening patriarchal values (Leathard 1980: 1), while some journalists saw the pill as offering a revolution in 'sexual habits and attitudes' as well as offering 'emancipation' (Leathard 1980: 142). The introduction of the Family Planning Act 1967 formally made the distribution of contraceptives part of the NHS. It also permitted contraceptive advice to be given to all, including teenagers and the unmarried. As Leathard (1980: 142) acknowledges, there was 'a slow movement from confusion to order' due to a lack of hospital uptake and training of general practitioners.

The Abortion Act 1967 was a response to the practice of illegal abortions and those that were being carried out at the NHS or privately for 'therapeutic' reasons (Leathard 1980: 109). The Offences Against the Person Act 1861 criminalized abortion, and a life prison sentence could be given to the woman receiving the abortion and the person administering it. According to Lee et al., the Abortion Act 1967 did not repeal these prohibitions but, rather, carved out an exception which provided that the abortion will be lawful where two 'registered medical practitioners' agree 'in good faith' that an abortion should be provided under one of the grounds laid down in the Act.

(2018: 26)

Although this change in law was undoubtedly a step in the right direction, the law has remained controversial, particularly for medical professionals who have called for full decriminalization of abortion (Lee et al. 2018: 32). Prior to the Divorce Reform Act 1969, divorce was determined through 'blame', with one party placing blame on another. Brown (2000: 57) identifies that this 'difficult and unpleasant' law often resulted in the 'loss of maintenance' and 'loss of custody', but was used to dissuade people from divorce. The Divorce Reform Act 1969 replaced blame with irretrievable breakdown. Now either party could apply for divorce, with the case being based on facts rather than guilt.

An examination of these cultural shifts and amendments to regulation indicate that the 1960s was a period of societal change, particularly in relation to sexual culture. In the conclusion to his analysis of sex in Britain between 1900 and 1950, Humphries (1991: 217) acknowledges that the permissive moment of the 1960s was 'exaggerated', but did 'bring important changes in the sexual behaviour of young people' and suggested 'a new era of sexual freedom'. He also notes the significance of other contextual factors that contributed to this change, including the growth of the welfare state, the post-war economic boom and other aspects of social reform. Yet many of the reformations to legislation introduced during this period, as well intended as they may have been, were not without issue. Moral battles remained, such as the ten years taken to introduce the Sexual Offences Act 1967 following the findings of the Wolfenden Report, the difficulties implementing Family Planning Act 1967 or the on-going challenges with Abortion Act 1967, but also through the use of antiquated common laws as a legal instrument to control such changes to sexual culture and society. For Cocks (2016: 268) this is evidence of prosecutors testing the new moral boundaries rather than a contrived 'backlash against permissiveness'. Journalist Martin Tomkinson described the permissive moment as a 'loosening of the belt' of morality and perhaps this is a useful way of understanding the limited impact of these changes.[8]

It is in this decade when a domestic trade in the production of hardcore pornography began to grow. I do not see this as mere coincidence. As Drucker (2015: 16–17) points out, opportunities for entrepreneurship are not just relative to 'economic events', but can also be explained by changes to 'values, perception, and attitude'. For him, the introduction of an entrepreneurial economy is a 'cultural [...] economic and technological event'. Hence, the societal changes I have described, including amendments to laws, can be seen as contributory factors to the emergence of hardcore pornography in Britain. Future chapters demonstrate how entrepreneurs sought to exploit these new cultural and regulatory conditions that were perceived as permissive, situating themselves amongst this new backdrop of increased, yet limited, sexual freedom. It is not my intention to demonstrate that this alternative economy is further evidence of a permissive society, especially when Denmark's permissive experiment resulted in the decriminalization of all pornography by 1969. Instead, I see it as further evidence of a cultural and economic response to the changes I have explored in this section. London's Soho came to represent many of these changing attitudes. Moreover, it was the epicentre of the alternative economy and a space where pornography entrepreneurship flourished, due to an exploitation of the Obscene Publications Act 1959.

## The Dirty Square Mile

According to Collins (2004), sexual enterprise in Soho can be dated back to the early eighteenth century with the Hoopers Hotel brothel that existed on Soho Square. Soho's reputation for vice has been longstanding. I have already discussed how the Street Offences Act 1959 drove sex workers off the street and into premises, mostly above shop flats, that were owned by members of London's underworld. In Victorian London, the trade in pornographic materials was originally based on Holywell Street, before shifting to Soho in the early 1900s (Nead 1997). Nead (1997) outlines how the original incarnation of the Obscene Publications Act 1857 sought to control the trade in 'dirty books' that circulated in this urban space, but managed to survive until the end of the Victorian period. The trade soon relocated to Soho, embedding itself amongst its established sexual economy, and by the 1960s there was a growth in sex-related enterprises (Collins 2004: 1796). Amongst the many clip joints, strip clubs and brothels were bookshops selling hardcore pornography. I now consider Soho's role in the alternative economy and how it functioned as the main distribution centre for British pornography. I focus on the entrepreneurs who ran bookshops, initially the main outlet for distributing pornography in Britain, and how this enterprise was underwritten through a corrupt licensing system introduced by the Obscene Publications Squad. This, I argue, formed an alternative economy of hardcore production and distribution, which had its own governance, practices and economic rules.

Tony Sonenscher – also known as Tony Boffa or Italian Tony – was the son of Italian immigrants. According to a description found in police files, he was a short man with a slim build, short dark hair, and a 'swarthy' complexion. In the late 1950s, he and his brother ran a florist stall at Birmingham's Rag

Market, a democratic and social trading space that attracted entrepreneurs and diverse consumers. As McRobbie (1989: 31) recognizes, rag markets have traditionally offered employment opportunities for immigrants and others who might struggle to secure typical jobs. She also discusses the social aspect of this type of work and acknowledges that illicit goods were often circulated in this economic space. At the beginning of the 1960s, Sonenscher relocated to Soho, leasing a record shop at 10 Walker's Court in partnership with the popular entertainer Kenny Lynch, seeking to profit from the demand for popular music. Like Birmingham's rag market, Soho had a similar spirit. It was known for its bohemian and cosmopolitan culture, traditionally being home to people from a range of nationalities. Aidan McManus, an interviewee who used to work in Soho's adult cinemas and now gives guided tours of Soho, believes that 'no one comes from Soho [...] it doesn't discriminate', therefore making it a place of tolerance.[9] Historically, it has attracted immigrants from many different countries, such as France, Greece, Italy and Malta, bringing different cuisines to the area and a range of craft practices. The name Soho itself is said to originate from a hunting cry, as back in the 1500s it was a hunting ground (Summers 1989). The thrill of the hunt seems to have lived on. Whether it be residents hunting out a business opportunity by opening a shop or running a stall at the local street market, consumers hunting for a bargain or food at the many cafés and restaurants, or the 'punters' hunting for sex or pornographic goods.

The Kenny Lynch Record Centre was not a successful venture, partly because Lynch and Sonenscher were unable to maintain the rent for the shop and pay back the credit owed to the record companies. According to Joey Janes, one of Sonenscher's employees, he suggested that they reopen the store as a bookshop.[10] Bookshops emerged in Soho during the 1940s (Tomkinson 1982: 16). The innocuous term 'bookshop' was a convenient cover; these shops specialized in selling pornography. The early shops from the 1940s usually had a front room, where inoffensive material would be openly sold, and a back room where the more explicit material was kept. Douglas offers a useful description of these spaces operated:

> the counter was topped by a false wall with a hatchway cutting in it via which one made one's purchases. A door let in this wall, which was covered with scores of personal contact magazines, gave onto the inner room. This counter, however, also contained two closely-packed boxes full of carefully sealed packets of photographs [...] The customers entered the shop openly and were strictly divided into the casual browsers who spent a considerable time working through the openly displayed merchandise and those who went straight to the counter and asked for specific requirements. One customer, who asked for some 'special books', was invited into

the back room from which he emerged a few minutes later with a bulging brief-case. Requests for 'men and women' or 'sex photos' also met with an invitation to the back room as did the request of a young man in dark glasses who tremulously asked if they had 'any of men?' 'Homo stuff?' queried the assistant, before issuing the standard invitation.

(1969: 63)

The gatekeeper of this backroom was the 'chair'; a forbidding male figure sat behind the counter of the shop who decided whether to grant a customer access. If permitted entry, the customer likely found a suitcase containing the illicit stock that could readily be removed from the shop should members of the police decide to inspect the premises. Casual browsing was not allowed, and the chair kept a watch on the time spent in this backroom. During the 1940s, this stock typically consisted of 'highly literary works of art' and commanded high prices: 'books would regu-larly fetch £20–£50 and on occasion as much as £250 or £500' (Tomkinson 1982: 17). Tomkinson notes how much of this material originated from France, suggest-ing the existence of informal transnational trade networks across Soho's French community, smuggling material in from the continent.

By the 1950s, approximately six bookshops operated in Soho in 1956, mainly located in the courts connecting Wardour Street with Brewer Street. In 1959, a journalist named Gerald Byrne published two articles on 30 August and 13 September in the *Empire News and Sunday Chronicle*, a newspaper that eventu-ally merged with the popular *News of the World* tabloid. Byrne's stories claimed that police corruption was rife in Soho, with bookshop owners bribing police offers for permission to trade. Byrne's accusations led to a police investigation by the Criminal Investigation Department (CID) of the Metropolitan Police. A 27-page report on the investigation from 30 December 1959 details its findings. Byrne met with the investigating officer, who notes that Byrne had a reputation for 'sensational' writing and was known for making 'unfounded' allegations. In the meeting Byrne agreed to assist the investigation but not be formally part of any enquiry. Conveniently, his research notes had been destroyed in a fire. The complaint related to:

the alleged control of bookshops selling pornographic literature which is said to bring in an annual income of three million pounds and of police receiving bribes from the 'controllers' for protection and information of intended searches [...] the bribes [...] amount to £2000 weekly. He further alleges that in order to avoid the heavier penalties provided by the [Obscene Publications Act 1959] 'stooges' act as a 'stand in' for proprietors and are thus able to be treated as first offenders.

The report found that none of the six men named in Byrne's article were currently involved in the bookshop business, yet it acknowledges that they collectively owned the leases of around eight bookshops in Soho, with a pattern of the businesses changing hands after the proprietor, or chair, had been convicted. It concludes that all allegations made against the officers named by Byrne were either 'unfounded or unsubstantiated' and that Byrne himself was unreliable, signalling the end of the investigation.

Byrne's investigation uncovered the system of ownership that allowed bookshop proprietors to distance themselves from the business should they be raided by the police. Hence, the chair was the leaseholder, made responsible for the running of the shop and therefore liable for arrest. As the protection offered by corrupt police officers was limited, the chair system served as another instance of evasive entrepreneurship. Ten years later, Byrne's allegations were proven right when a private investigator uncovered the inner workings of the economy and the police corruption that supported it (see Chapter 4). It also transpired that one of the bookshop owners named by Byrne was one of the largest porn entrepreneurs in the 1950s.

## The bookshop owners

'FILTH IS HIS TRADE', reads the headline of an article by Duncan Webb in *The People* (29 April 1956). Webb calls for the Dirty Squad, or the Dirt Squad as he has termed them, to arrest one of the 'pornography princes of London'. John Hawksford had already been convicted twice in the 1950s for publishing obscene photographs, the last being on 24 November 1953. He kept a relatively 'low profile' but had a 'near legendary status for meanness' (Tomkinson 1982: 18). Webb names Modern Books on 48 Dean Street as one of Hawksford's bookshops, selling 'the vilest books, photographs and postcards ever put on sale'. Webb shares his experience of visiting Modern Books, describing how the front of the shop offered 'reputable books', but the backroom stocked 'pornographic books and pictures'. Despite Webb's unhelpful moralistic tone, he still outlines one of Hawksford's successful models of enterprise and one that would be a standard method of economic exchange across Soho bookshops. 'The library side is more profitable', states Webb, summarizing how Hawksford hired out books at £10 a time, with £5 being paid back to the customer on return. He speculates that each book is loaned out at least 50 times a year, offering higher profits. Webb also discloses that Hawksford visits other Soho bookshops, selling pornography wholesale to smaller traders. Hawksford's exchange model became commonplace in Soho's economy. Not only did this guarantee future access to stock, it also made pornographic materials more affordable for customers, being able to claim back money. One of Hawksford's main pornography suppliers was a former council dustman named Ron Davey, whose specialty was obscene photographs and, later on, typescripts. Davey's enterprise is discussed later in this chapter.

The Soho bookshop I find most fascinating is the Long Shop. 'Colin', a semi-professional photographer and one of the economy's casual producers, remembers it being no more than five feet in width, sitting in-between a public house and a shop at 51A Old Compton Street.[11] This demonstrates the demand for space in Soho to open a bookshop on one of its main thoroughfares. Tom Fletcher – a 'Bohemian character […] with shoulder length hair and a Gauloise cigarette permanently drooping from the left corner of his mouth' – was the owner, becoming wealthy through selling 'French books' (Tomkinson 1982: 17). Fletcher unwittingly brought one of those most dominant entrepreneurs into the bookshop business. Known as John Mason, or simply as 'God' for reasons that will become apparent later, Ronald Eric Mason's entry into the trade was accidental.

In a police statement from the Obscene Publications Squad criminal investigation, Mason recounts his involvement in the economy.[12] With Fletcher needing a carpenter to fit shelves in the Long Shop, Mason's wife recommended that he employ her husband as a handyman. Mason, a former scene shifter at the Globe theatre, began working for Fletcher in 1952 and quickly progressed from carpenter to salesman, learning the rules of the alternative economy. Part of this involved regular meetings with a detective constable from the Metropolitan Police in a public house. Both Tomkinson (1982: 17) and Hobbs (1988) acknowledge the role of the public house in illicit business and how it provides an informal networking space for entrepreneurs. For Hobbs (1988: 142), 'it is in the pub that deals are struck, and information regarding cheap goods, stolen commodities, and exchanges of skills are relayed'. Furthermore, it is a space where police might socialize with criminals, particularly in the East End of London. As Hobbs (1988: 142) points out, the backgrounds of police and criminals were not too far apart. This may explain why corruption was so commonplace in the Metropolitan Police and how those in the pornography trade were able to maintain close relationships with officers.

Mason's story also acts as a window into the Obscene Publications Squad's licensing system and the institutional framework of the alternative economy. The officer named by Byrne in his 1959 exposé, Swain, is also identified by Mason, receiving a weekly retainer from Fletcher in exchange for providing information on officers in the Obscene Publications Squad and whether there were 'any pressures on the police on the sale of pornographic literature'. After learning the trade, Mason opened his own shop on Old Compton Street, paying Swain's replacement, Sergeant MacLeod, a deposit. Mason was denied, as his proposed shop happened to be too close to the Long Shop. By 1955, Mason received permission to open a shop at 5 Walker's Court, paying MacLeod £15 a week for a licence. Shortly after, West End Central carried out a raid on Soho's bookshops as a murder had taken place in one of them.[13] Mason had his stock seized and was convicted at the Central Criminal Court, receiving a twelve-month prison sentence. Mason expressed frustration at this arrest, believing that his licence should have provided protection. MacLeod informed him that the arrest was part of a murder investigation and therefore outside the Obscene Publications Squad's jurisdiction.

Mason quickly became aware that the licence only offered limited police protection, primarily the opportunity to do business with minimal police interference. Raids remained an occupational hazard, but licensed bookshops received forewarning, usually via a phone call relaying the codeword 'WH Smith' or 'Menzies', the names of British high-street newsagents. This gave time to either remove hardcore material or leave out damaged or unwanted stock (Manchester 1986: 38). Having lost the lease on 5 Walker's Court, Mason opened a shop at 4 Gerrard Street. Again, Byrne's allegations prove to be accurate. Mason's business model heavily relied on the use of chairs to run his shops. These front men leased one of his shops from his company, SJD Properties Limited. The ideal chair had a clean criminal record and signed a release to ensure there was a legally binding contract in place. Therefore, if the police raided the shop, Mason would be immune from prosecution, with blame falling on the chair and others who worked there. More often than not, chairs were fully aware of this relationship, risking risk of arrest, a fine – usually paid by the owner – or a prison sentence in exchange for a wage. As I mentioned earlier, the chair system was another legal loophole used by bookshop owners to protect themselves from arrest and prosecution.

Mason's statement exposes officers who took regular bribes. As Rose-Ackerman (1996: n.pag.) recognizes, 'Businesses selling outlawed goods and services are especially prone to extortion'. However, the licensing system was mutually beneficial, enabling both parties to make money. In exchange, pornography entrepreneurs operated with little interruption and police maintained a control over the trade. Payments were slipped inside newspapers and usually exchanged in public houses. In 1958, as part of a crackdown on bookshops by the new head of the Obscene Publications Squad, Inspector Gerrard, Mason was put out of business for twelve months. Police contacts later informed him that he could continue in the bookshop trade on the basis that nothing pornographic was on show. In response to this guidance, Mason opened a driving school in the front of 4 Gerrard Street, selling pornography from the back, and eventually another at 4 Green's Court. Around this time, his current police contact, Detective Webb, introduced Mason to Detective Sergeant Bill Moody.

Moody became Mason's new contact and was paid £175 a month for a licence to run both shops. Moody briefly left the Obscene Publications Squad and was replaced by DS Wally Virgo, who commanded £200 a month. In 1965, Moody returned to the Obscene Publications Squad as a detective inspector, demanding that Mason pay £350 to open a third shop at 10–11 Moor Street. As Mason's empire of bookshops grew, so did the payments. When police arrested one of his chairs for selling an illustrated typescript, or Soho Bible, to a Roman Catholic youth club leader, Mason had to pay an extra £1000 to Moody, who arranged for another officer – Leslie Alton – to conduct the interview. Mason, already paying his monthly licence, was frustrated by this additional fee, but passed it off as an additional business expense. In 1969, he claims to have given a further £14,000 to Moody after another chair was arrested when police uncovered obscene films during a raid on his Dean Street office.

In addition to making payments, Mason maintained a close, personal relationship with the Obscene Publications Squad, particularly Moody. Mason invited officers to his annual birthday party; Moody even attended his daughter's wedding. This friendship with the police brought many benefits. The Obscene Publications Squad stored seized materials in the lower basement of Holborn Police Station. Moody offered to sell Mason these materials, resulting in Mason being given a CID tie to wear so that officers would not question his presence. Mason selected the items he wanted, and Moody arranged for the stock to be delivered to his Dean Street office. Mason paid between £300 and £500 in cash to Moody, who counted it out in front of him in a 'business like manner'. Mason remarked that these prices were 'less than half' of what he usually paid elsewhere for stock and that others in the trade purchased materials from the Obscene Publications Squad. Journalist Martin Tomkinson told me that Mason was often buying back his stock that had been seized. By the early 1970s, Mason ran at least six Soho bookshops, paying a monthly licence of £1000. He spent half of the year overseas and had associates run his businesses. Mason's strong association with the police and status in the trade led to others awarding him the nickname 'God' due to the power he was afforded. He also acted as a sort of moral gatekeeper for the trade, informing police of those producing child pornography or bestiality to the police, as will become apparent in Chapter 3.

Mason's story might seem repetitive, with him paying greater amounts of money to corrupt police officers. However, it indicates how the licensing system functioned and highlights the extent of the growing corruption taking place in the Obscene Publications Squad. According to Manchester (1986: 37), the Obscene Publications Squad enjoyed 'total control in its field', growing from five officers in 1957 to fourteen in the early 1970s, demonstrating the expansion of the economy. By the late 1960s and early 1970s, there was more money to be made, as imports from Denmark, where pornography had been decriminal-ized, were being smuggled into Britain. The smaller number of officers taking 'drinks' from bookshop owners also grew, being indoctrinated into a culture of corruption that had been taking place since the 1950s. As pornographer Mike Freeman explained, 'the corruption was something so deep and extensive that you couldn't get in the [Scotland] Yard unless you took a drink [...] everyone was bent, the whole fucking Yard!'[14] The police were not the only ones who enabled the economy to function. London's underworld also had a stake and worked in alliance with members of the Obscene Publications Squad to offer their own form of regulation and control.

## The underworld

'Let me tell you what Fat Bill said [...] if you're not paying the Dirty Squad, you're paying the gangsters', Mike Freeman remarked. Fat Bill was most likely Billy Hicks, a bookshop worker and relative of Tony Sonenscher. Freeman recounted how members of the underworld visited Hicks' shop, attempting to exort money in exchange for protection. Hicks calmly put his hand below the counter and, instead of taking pound notes out of the cash box, presented a hand grenade; the message to the gangsters was clear. Hicks was already paying the police and had no intentions of paying the underworld. The Obscene Publications Squad and powerful entrepreneurs like Mason were not the only ones who policed the alternative economy. From the 1940s onwards, London's underworld had more control over the activities in Soho than the Metropolitan police, starting with criminal entrepreneurs such as the Maltese Messina Brothers – brutal pimps who consolidated vice in Soho (Summers 1989: 211). Despite being a square mile, Soho's narrow streets made it an ideal contained space for criminal activity and difficult to police (see Figure 1.6). This was partly due to its many courts, offering a possible escape route towards Oxford Street, Regent Street, Shaftesbury Avenue and Charing Cross Road. Furthermore, the sheer scale of vice in Soho presented challenges for the police, hence why corrupt relationships also extended to gang-sters like Bernie Silver.

I asked journalist Martin Tomkinson, who regularly visited the Coach and Horses public house in Soho during his time working for the magazine *Private Eye* and shared drinks with police officers, gangsters and pornographers, why these relationships existed. He described it as 'effective policing', with the police work-ing with gangsters such as Silver or bookshop owners like Mason to help them control vice in Soho. Tomkinson believed that this allowed the police to 'find out about crimes before they happened' and make an early intervention. In his study of criminal entrepreneurship in London's East End, Hobbs (1988: 194) recognizes that police also demonstrate entrepreneurial flair, making 'cases in the same way that business entrepreneurs make money'. Therefore, relationships with criminals become a key part of their entrepreneurial practice, helping to solve cases, but can also present opportunities for corruption. It is worth mentioning that police wages around this time were low. A former London police officer from the early 1970s named 'Rob' told me that he could understand why officers took bribes at this time 'because the pay was crap'.[15]

The most powerful underworld figure in the 1960s and 1970s Soho was Bernie Silver. Mason might have been named God by those in the pornography trade, but Silver was more ominously known as the 'godfather of Soho' (Summers 1989: 212). When the Messina Brothers faded from the scene, following a detailed exposé on their activities by journalist Duncan Webb and the resulting police crackdown, Silver took their place. Formerly from the East End, Silver, alongside his enforcer, a former Maltese police officer named 'Big' Frank Mifsud, moved into Soho. They started by running a strip club in Brewer Street, eventually growing their empire. Tomkinson described Silver as a 'glorified pimp' who was involved in flat-farming – a highly exploitative practice that involved landlords letting flats to sex workers at high rents – due to his ownership of flats in Soho. Coincidentally, the criminal investigation into the earlier discussed allegations made by journalist Gerald Byrne names Silver as police informant and is evidence of his close relationship with members of the Metropolitan Police. Such was Silver's power in Soho that he commanded respect. Tomkinson recounted two anecdotes that emphasized Silver's authority. First, whenever Silver visited the Coach and Horses public house, he always ordered a vodka and orange from the bar. As a sign of respect, anyone meeting with Silver ordered the same drink. Second, Tomkinson recalled a disgruntled member of Soho's underworld approaching him in the street, unhappy about an article Tomkinson had written for *Private Eye*. Silver, who happened to be walking along the street, noticed the loud verbal abuse given to Tomkinson and shouted 'c'mere you cunt' to the unhappy man. Silver gave him a strong warning, nodded to Tomkinson and walked on; Tomkinson said that he never had any further problems in Soho after this incident.

While this may seem typical of many colourful tales about powerful gangsters (Hobbs 1995), Tomkinson saw it as significant. It showed that Silver had the power to stop incidents before they happened, revealing why he was such a valuable resource for the police. As Linnane (2016: 250) notes, Silver and Mifsud 'imposed a kind of peace in [Soho] for two decades', managing Soho on behalf of the police, while also being able to carry on their illicit practices – Silver too was paying the police for a licence to operate his bookshops. However, peace might be too strong a word, as Silver and Mifsud regularly used violence and intimidation to control Soho. Two people linked to Silver, a sex worker and a 'gofer', both died after falling out of the windows of Soho flats. 'John', who worked in one of Silver's bookshops, nervously told me about a shoplifter who stole from one of Silver's shops.[16] The thief was grabbed by one of Silver's employees, taken up to the room upstairs, hanged from the ceiling by a hook which was attached to his tied hands, stripped and cut down his back with a bayonet. As John stressed: 'no one stole from Bernie'. Powerful messages such as these spread across Soho, strengthening Silver's reputation.

Silver's entry into the bookshop business was inevitable, expanding his criminal empire across Soho. Given the profits that could be generated from selling pornography, it is easy to understand why Tony Sonenscher opened the Court Bookshop at 10 Walker's Court between 1964 and 1965 (see Figure 1.3). Like many of those selling pornography, Sonenscher took no interest in it; it was nothing more than an in-demand, highly profitable commodity. It was suggested to him by his associate Joseph Janes, whose involvement in Soho's economy dated back to 1935. In keeping with the usual system of using front men, Sonenscher registered the business under Janes' name to protect himself. At first, the shop operated without a licence from the Obscene Publications Squad. Because of this, they only sold small amounts of pornography, as the suppliers to bookshops, such as the pornographers or wholesalers like Ben Holloway and Gerald Citron, were nervous about stock being seized and not receiving payment. This shows how the licence also provided status in the economy, demonstrating that they were serious operators and vetted by the police.

Janes obtained small amounts of stock through his Soho network to keep the shop in business. After seven weeks of opening, Chief Inspector Leslie Alton visited the shop. Armed with a warrant, Alton found the small stock of hardcore pornography in the back room. He returned a month later, again discovering their inventory, and reported Janes. This summoned a visit from Bill Moody, who warned Janes that they could not stay in business. Janes states that he questioned Moody on why other shops remained open. Moody informed him that several public complaints had been made and that there were already too many shops in Soho selling pornography. At the time, Janes was not aware that members of the Obscene Publications Squad had already approached Sonenscher, advising him to become licensed. Feeling cheated, Janes left the shop just before his court date. He shortly discovered that Sonenscher partnered with Brian Young, a close acquaintance of Alton's. Now the shop was doing 'big business in pornography', becoming one of the largest bookshops in Soho. Eventually, Janes returned to the Court Bookshop as a salesman, earning £75 per week. Given the average weekly wage for an adult male in the late 1960s was around £20, Janes' stated earnings illustrate how much money those working in bookshops earned.

FIGURE 1.3: Walker's Court, looking towards Rupert Street in 1973. Tony Sonenscher's The Court Bookshop at 10 Walker's Court, one of the largest bookshops in Soho, can be seen on the left. Courtesy of Robert Stallard/Mary Evans Picture Library.

The licence made Sonenscher a wealthy man. At the beginning of each month, he met with Obscene Publications Squad officers at a pub in Victoria to pay his fee. Like Mason, Sonenscher understood the value of maintaining a good relationship with the police. Alongside the bookshops, he also had a tiling business with his brother-in-law Frank and Kenny Lynch. All of the Obscene Publications Squad officers had their houses tiled free of charge, demonstrating how gifts and favours were exchanged to build relationships. For Sonenscher, this was a family busi-ness, employing his brother-in-law, cousins and other close relations. Janes notes how Sonenscher only trusted family members with handling the large amounts of money the Court Bookshop generated. He opened two other bookstores, one at 45 Old Compton Street, which Janes alleges was in partnership with Silver, and another at 54 Charing Cross Road. Sonenscher's legacy lives on through his nephew 'Dave', who runs the bookshop Rambooks in North London, specializing in the sale of vintage pornography.

Mason and Sonenscher's stories offer an understanding of the alternative economy's institutional framework. Within this economy were the entrepreneurs running bookshops selling pornography, the entrepreneurial activities of the Obscene Publications Squad and the rules of trade established through their informal licensing system and the criminal entrepreneurs who assisted the police in controlling the trade. Simply put, Soho was the primary distribution network for hardcore pornography in Britain. Later chapters show how the trade expanded beyond Soho, but also demonstrate how it continued to play a crucial part in the organization of the economy. I now consider the types of goods sold in Soho's bookshops prior to the rise in roller production. I suggest that photographs and illustrated books were precursors to 8mm British hardcore films and also describe how producers of such goods found a place in the economy, selling pornographic materials to bookshops for distribution.

### Soho Postcards and Bibles

For Manchester (1986: 32), the sudden growth in Britain's pornography trade can be explained by the economic situation of the 1960s and the post-war recovery. Increased employment opportunities and a rise in wages resulted in an expanding middle class. Therefore, 'people were prepared, it seems, to spend at least some of their new found wealth on pornography'. Manchester also recognizes that pornography typically commanded high prices. As mentioned in the previous section, Soho's post-war trade in pornography was initially dominated by material imported from the continent, with French books and photographs the most prominent commodity available for purchase.[17] Such books commanded anywhere between £5 and £40 for those that were of a higher production quality. With the average working male earning a week wage of £14 in 1960, purchasing a French book would have been roughly the equivalent to a month's salary for most of the population.[18] As Kendrick (1987: 77) observes, debates around class and access to pornography are inextricable. Referring to an erotic book titled *The Mysteries of Verbena House* (1882), Kendrick notes how only 150 copies were published at the cost of four guineas – the equivalent of two weeks wages for a member of a lower-middle-class English family. Purchasing pornography was reserved for the wealthy; this remained so by the early 1960s and, to some extent, 2000, when the sale of hardcore pornography was legally permitted in Britain. The high costs represented its status as an illicit commodity, but as Kendrick argues, it also placed it in the preserve of the upper classes, 'shielded away from common view by barriers of class and gender' (Kendrick 1987: 49).

However, around the early 1960s, domestically produced hardcore pornography became increasingly commonplace in the backrooms of Soho bookshops. Prior to rollers, sets of photographs in packs of five, known as Soho Postcards in the trade, were sold to the bookshops by their makers. According to 'Colin', a producer of such materials in the late 1960s, Soho Postcards retailed for either £1 for a pack of five black and white postcards or £2 for a colour set, indicating the higher demand for colour. 'Colin' sold his photographs to the bookshops for seven shillings and six pence per set (roughly 38p) giving the bookshop a profit of around 62p per set and evidencing the high profit margins for distributors such as Tony Sonenscher and John Mason. 'Colin', like other pornographers selling to bookshops, collected his money on return once the items had been sold, which often involved long delays for small-time players in the economy. Such a model of economic exchange is known as sale or return and was predominately used across Soho's bookshops. The informality of the economy meant that no formal contracts were drawn up, therefore pornographers could easily be exploited. 'Colin' claimed to have not been motivated by profit. For him, Soho Postcards and glamour photography were a side-hustle to his employment as a printer, allowing him to meet models and make a little money out of his hobby. It was not just opportunistic amateurs or semi-professionals who were attracted to the business of making pornography. Those willing to risk making pornography production a full-time pursuit could make significant profits, with some having exclusive deals with bookshops. According to Tomkinson (1982: 19), one of the most prominent producers of Soho Postcards was a man known as the 'The Dustman'.

Tomkinson (1982: 19) describes Ronald Ivor Davey as 'an engaging, sociable, giant of a man'. He was also a dustman, working for Hammersmith Borough Council for around eight years until an injury led to him making his photography hobby a full-time pursuit. Davey's other pastime happened to be nudism. It was John Hawksford who advised Davey to combine his two hobbies, taking explicit photographs of his fellow nudist club members to sell to Soho's bookshops. Davey reveals more in a police interview from 1975:

> I first became involved in pornography in the early fifties as a supplier to bookshops in the West End. I actually took the photographs and from the negatives reproduced large numbers of those photographs for distribution. At that stage I would take them into individual bookshops and sell them to the persons behind the counter.[19]

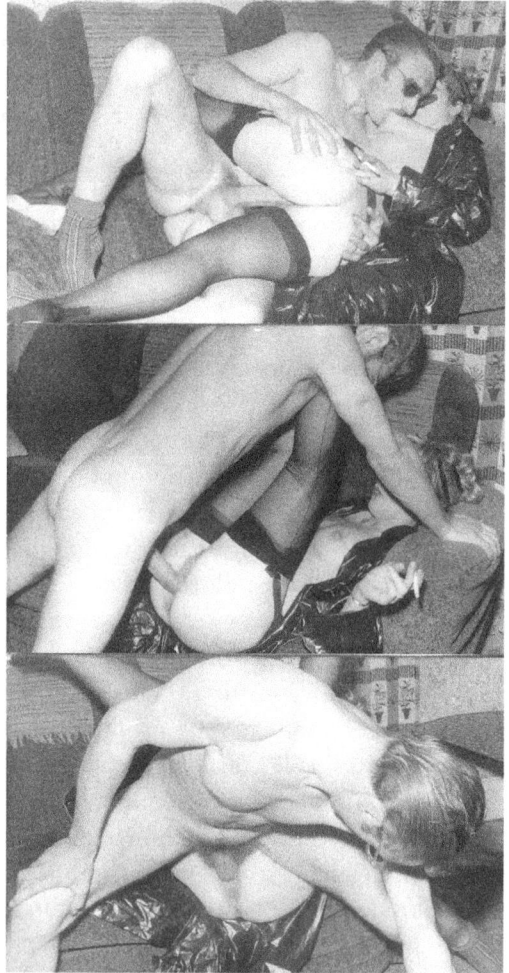

FIGURE 1.4: A selection of Soho Postcards. Author's personal collection. Faces obscured to protect the identity of performers.

Waugh (1996: 286) indicates that by 'the end of the nineteenth century, worldwide underground networks existed for the distribution of illicit photos explicitly depicting sexual activities'. Davey was certainly not the first to utilize the medium of photography for this purpose, with amateurs gaining access to cameras and film in the 1890s when Kodak introduced 'roll film and mass-market handheld cameras' (Waugh 1996: 28). Davey likely taught himself how to develop and print images through handbooks and popular magazines such as *Amateur Photographer* and other guides, which detailed the necessary workflow. All the required equipment, including the chemicals needed for developing images, could be purchased from high street shops like Ilford's or Jessops, or via mail-order companies.

Like distributors, producers of pornography also required a licence from the Obscene Publications Squad to permit them to trade. By the late 1950s, Davey's business in Soho Postcards became known to the police. He was stopped in Soho by an officer named Inspector Murray, who pursued Davey for some time. Davey met Murray every week, usually on a Friday night in a West End pub or restaurant, to buy him a meal or a drink. These regular meetings ensured that Davey could continue to operate. He even offered Murray the use of his caravan, eventually gifting it to him. Murray was replaced by another officer named Monahan. Instead of food and alcohol, Monahan asked for a monthly payment between £30 and £40, meeting in a West End pub to exchange the money. Davey now became licensed, permitted by the police to produce pornographic photographs. However, in early 1960, he was raided by the police. Davey suspected that this raid was related to his relationship with Murray and the gifting of the caravan. Following the investigation of four premises linked to Davey, he was found to be in possession of around 16,000 'improper' negatives and over 18,000 photographs. The court estimated that Davey was making £40 a week, around three times the average weekly wage. He was sentenced to six months imprisonment for publishing 744 'improper' photographs of men and 105 similar photographs of women, indicating that Davey was producing for both heterosexual and gay audiences. An article in the *News of the World* (10 April 1960) states that the magistrate had never before seen 'such a vast volume of absolute filth'.

After serving four months in prison, Davey restarted his pornography business. He formed a friendship and lucrative partnership with John Mason due to his hold over the porn business in Soho and strong connections with the Obscene Publications Squad. Tomkinson (1982: 28), who regularly drank at the same pub as Davey, identifies him as 'the biggest single producer of porn' in the early 1960s. With photographs and erotic books being the two most popular selling products in the bookshops, Davey combined the two goods into one, publishing illustrated books that were known as Soho Bibles, but also referred to as Soho typescripts or just typescripts (Wickstead 2020). Very much forgotten in British pornography history, a Soho Bible is an amateur produced book that serves as a precursor to the 8mm roller. As Figure 1.5 shows, Soho Bibles usually featured a pornographic image on the front cover, either hand-drawn art or a photograph. The titling was done with either a stencil or a Letraset text transfer system. Inside, the book contains an erotic story, hastily written by one of the many willing authors paid to fill the pages, illustrated with several photographs, often glued to a blank paper page. All the papers are then stapled together, producing a crude-looking hybrid between a book and a magazine.

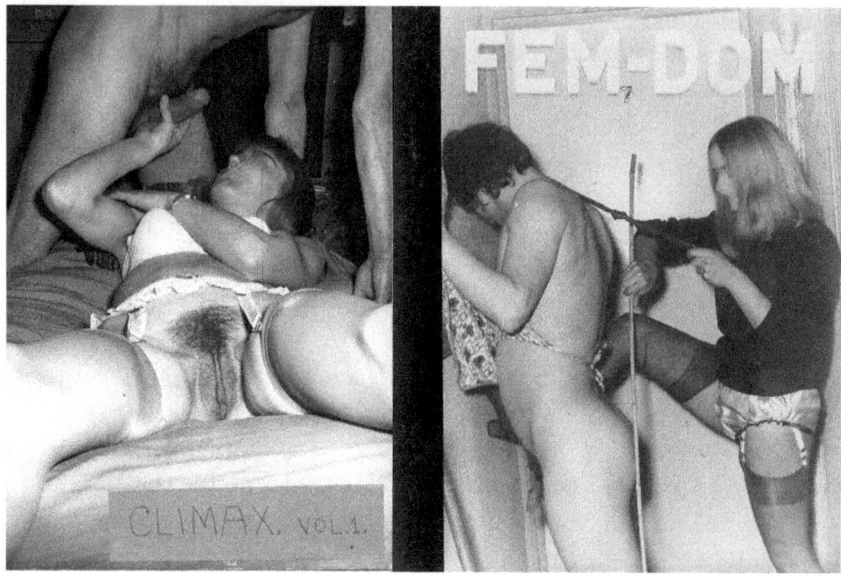

FIGURE 1.5: Examples of Soho Bibles. Courtesy of Lewis Parker and Rambooks.

For obvious reasons, credits are not given, signifying their illicit origins. References to a publisher are sometimes provided, such as Bon Homme Press or Rendez-vous Press (possibly a play on the name 'Ron Davey'?). Soho Bibles were duplicated using a Gestetner, an early instance of a photocopier. Around 500 copies could be made at a time by turning the wheel of the machine by hand. Davey required three Gestetners to keep up with the demand for his 'Millionaire Dustman' typescripts, as they became known in the trade, referencing the money they generated. Mason had exclusive distribution, selling them in his Soho bookshops. Davey wholesaled Soho Bibles to Mason for £3–£4, and Mason sold them to customers for £25, again showing the high retail prices bookshops charged (Tomkinson 1982: 35). In one weekend, 300 copies could be sold, potentially generating over £1000 for Davey and £6000 profit for Mason (Tomkinson 1982: 35).

Davey and Mason were close friends with Detective Chief Superintendent Bill Moody. Not only did they drink together in pubs, but they also visited each other's houses, went on holidays together, played rounds of golf and Davey regularly invited them to his freemasonry functions.[20] Davey was even known to be Moody's driver when he was not chauffeuring Mason around London, taking him to attend crime scenes (Tomkinson 1982). In police files, Davey states that he now paid the Obscene Publications Squad between £60 and £80 a month for his licence to produce pornography and was back to buying his contact officer,

Culver, food and drink at West End establishments. In the latter half of the 1960s, Davey approached Culver about opening his own bookstore in the West End. Following a negotiation, Davey paid £100 a month for the licence to run a shop located on Monmouth Street, but this was short-lived. He moved on to have an involvement in two bookstores in Charing Cross and Paddington, both outside Soho. Interestingly, Davey did not have to pay the Obscene Publications Squad to licence these premises, showing how the corruption was strongly centred around Soho.

Denmark's legalization of hardcore pornography in 1969 meant that magazines with higher production values were imported into Britain, replacing Soho Bibles. The growth of rollers in the mid 1960s also affected Davey's business. In his police statement, Davey maintained that he was a minor player, unlike the other pornographers active in Soho, yet Tomkinson (1982: 19) names Davey as the 'biggest single producer' in the late 1950s and early 1960s. 'Colin' recalled an encounter with Davey that is also indicative of his status in Soho:

> I encountered Davey in a bookshop in Walker's Court when I was collecting money from them. The Chair was giving me the usual excuses for not being able to pay me, then in came Davey. Suddenly, the Chair produced a roll of banknotes big enough to choke a horse! When Davey left I said to the Chair 'If you can pay him, you can pay me'.

It is not known what happened to the former Dustman who pioneered Soho Postcards and Soho Bibles. His 1975 police statement gives the occupation 'Maintenance Engineer', implying that he moved away from the trade. He passed away in 1990.

## Conclusion

Police documents indicate that by the end of the 1960s there were around 52 bookshops in London's West End (see Figure 1.6), a ten-fold increase from five shops in 1955 (Manchester 1986: 31), signifying the growth of the economy in a fifteen-year period. A further 35 shops stretched across wider London, usually near train stations where there was heavy footfall. The grouping together of enterprises has been termed clustering (Porter 1998). According to Porter (1998: 78), 'clusters are geographic concentrations of interconnected companies and institutions in a particular field'. He also notes that clusters include 'linked industries' and are crucial to creating economic competition. From these come innovation, new enterprises and high levels of productivity. The clustering of bookshops alongside other sex-related enterprises in and around Soho was central to the functioning of the alternative economy, providing retail outlets for pornographers to sell their goods. In turn, bookshop owners retailed the items at increased costs.

Due to the clandestine nature of the trade, it is difficult to accurately determine the financial scale of this economy. As I have shown in this chapter, considerable amounts of money were exchanged between bookshop owners and pornographers, but just how lucrative was it? According to Robertson,

> the weekly gross of a police-protected Soho shop was estimated at £10,000 and one bookseller who was actually prosecuted in 1971 had been netting a weekly profit of £2000 during his two years of operation, beside which his £2000 fine appeared derisory.
>
> (1979: 9)

Another source is the report generated by the Longford Committee (Anon. 1972). Independently financed by Labour MP Frank Packham, more widely known as Lord Longford, the committee was tasked with investigating Britain's pornography trade. Although perceived as a moral crusade, the Longford Report employed a private investigator named Matthew Oliver who uncovered the inner workings of the alternative economy and the police corruption involved. In Chapter 4, I discuss how this ultimately resulted in the fall of the Obscene Publications Squad's licensing system and an investigation into police corruption. The Longford Report (Anon. 1972: 34) estimates that, in 1972, 'the "hard pornography" trade represents at least a ten million pounds a year turn-over, and "soft pornography" many times that amount'. The report also highlights the low-investment, high-profit nature of the economy, suggesting that it is not uncommon for retailers to make '80 per cent profit on cost'. The use of a sale or return model also reduced economic risk, with unsold goods being returned.

This chapter has considered the cultural and economic conditions for the emergence of an alternative economy that produced and distributed hardcore pornography in Britain. I have shown how a cumbersome legal framework for regulating pornography presented an economic opportunity for corrupt police officers and pornographers to exploit. I have described their practices as evasive entrepreneurship and suggested that the licensing system introduced by the police provided an institutional framework for the alternative economy. By becoming licensed, pornography entrepreneurs legitimized their criminality, receiving protection from the police. I also suggested that the so-called permissive society of the 1960s brought sex and sexuality to the forefront of public discussion. Here changes to public policy and cultural shifts were central to the emergence of the

1. 11 Archer Street
2. 12 Archer Street
3. 16 Archer Street (Newsagent)
4. 25 Berwick Street
5. 37 Berwick Street
6. 69 Berwick Street
7. 79 Berwick Street
8. 36 Berwick Street
9. 85 Brewer Street
10. 46 Broadwick Street
11. 95 Charing Cross Road
12. 96a Charing Cross Road
13. 54 Charing Cross Road
14. 23a Cranbourne Street
15. 16 D'Arblay Street
16. 48 Dean Street
17. 88 Dean Street (Newsagent)
18. 93 Dean Street
19. 4 Earlham Street (Circus Bookshop)
20. 32 Frith Street
21. 38 Frith Street
22. 62 Frith Street
23. 31 Gerrard Street
24. 33 Great Windmill Street
25. 53 Greek Street (Greek Bookshop)

26. 4 Green's Court
27. 10 Irving Street
28. 16 Lisle Street
29. 20 Lisle Street
30. 12 Little Newport Street
31. 13 Monmouth Street
32. 10-11 Moor Street
33. 5 Newport Place
34. 8 Newport Place
35. 22 Noel Street (Aphrodisia Aid Sex Boutique)
36. 40 Old Compton Street
37. 11 Old Compton Street (Casino Bookshop)
38. 51a Old Compton Street (The Long Shop)
39. 3 Peter Street
40. 31 Peter Street (Love Easy Boutique)
41. 5 Rupert Court
42. 55 Rupert Street
43. 57 Rupert Street
44. 200 Shaftesbury Avenue
45. 3 Soho Street
46. 617 Soho Street
47. 26 St Anne's Court
48. 10 Walker's Court (Court Bookshop)
49. 5 Walker's Court
50. 32 Wardour Street
51. 26 Wardour Street

FIGURE 1.6: A map of Soho's Bookstores in the late 1960s–early 1970s, drawn from police records and constructed by the author using Snazzy Maps under Creative Commons Licence.

alternative economy. Finally, I explored Soho's place in this economy, identifying it as the primary marketplace for pornographic goods and, through the stories of John Mason and Tony Sonenscher, detailed how the licensing system functioned.

Having established the conditions for hardcore pornography enterprise in Britain, I now move on to focus on the entrepreneurs who manufactured the 8mm films known as rollers. The next chapter concentrates on Ivor Cook, one of the forerunners of pornographic film production in Britain. It considers the role of film-making technologies that enabled this enterprise and how the trade began to expand beyond Soho.

# 2

## *Fisherman's Luck*: Making the Roller Market (1960–65)

### *Introduction*

*[O]ne of the few things that we produce better than anybody else, I would say, is now pornography. The standard is very, very high. In fact, we export it. Which I find fascinating. Because prior to that, most of the pornography came from the Middle East, Far East, France, Germany, Sweden. And the standard wasn't nearly as good as we produce now.*
(Stuart McCabe 1968)[1]

On the morning of 5 October 1962, Detective Sergeant Marshall of the London Metropolitan Police was granted a warrant to search the house of Ivor Cook. Cook's name had been passed on to the police alongside other individuals 'engaged together in printing obscene books, filming and reproducing obscene pictures and subsequently selling their wares to the proprietors of low-class book shops in London and Aldershot'. At 10:45 a.m., Marshall and two of his colleagues entered Cook's house in South East London, immediately discovering four 8mm 'obscene films' in the hallway. When questioned about their origin, Cook claimed to have purchased them from a shop in Soho for £17 each, intending to keep two and sell the others on. As the search progressed, Marshall and his team found and seized a 'quantity of photographic equipment'. Amongst the equipment were cards for printing photographs, suggesting that Cook was producing Soho Postcards and selling them via bookshops. 'They are old cards', Cook told Marshall, 'I forget what they are about now, they could refer to photographs, as I told you before I used to take portraits'.

In his report of the search, Marshall seems mystified by the lack of any photographic negatives on the property, aside from the ones already present in the seized equipment; when developed, these were found not to be obscene.[2] Marshall

FIGURE 2.1: Title card from *Fisherman's Luck* (1965–67). Author's personal collection.

describes Cook as a 'cute individual [...] actively engaged in the processing and selling of obscene films and photographs'. He notes that Cook was spending far more than his income as a rent collector and denied knowing others named in the conspiracy to produce obscene publications for gain. On 16 November 1962, Marshall learned through an anonymous tip that Cook stored 'obscene material' at a photographic studio in Latymer Road, Hammersmith. After searching the studio, Marshall and his colleagues found evidence of photographic practice, but nothing suggestive of an obscene publication. Marshall learned that an 'Ivor Collins' had rented the space for two years. When collecting his seized photography equipment, Marshall asked Cook about the studio. Cook admitted to hiring the space, but declared that his photography enterprise had ended due to a lack of business.

Marshall's report indicates that he was highly suspicious of Cook. As this chapter shows, Marshall's suspicions were well-founded, as Cook was one of the early producers of rollers: black and white – sometimes colour – 8mm films around ten to twelve minutes in length depicting hardcore sex. This report is significant as it is the earliest institutional document I discovered that implicates someone producing and distributing hardcore pornographic films in Britain. In this chapter, I explore the emergence of unbranded rollers between the years 1960 and 1965. In the previous chapter, I considered the cultural and economic conditions for the alternative economy producing and distributing hardcore pornography. Now, I look at the technological context, exploring how early entrepreneurs like Cook used amateur and semi-professional film technologies to create a new market for rollers and were involved in establishing transnational links that expanded the reach of the economy beyond the confines of Soho.

### Before rollers

The appearance of rollers occurs at time when a commercial market for 8mm films was already well established. Due to a lack of research, it is difficult to ascertain the scale of this market in Britain. Arguably, its halcyon days were between the mid 1950s and late 1970s before being superseded by the video cassette recorder. The market grew in the mid 1950s as 8mm projectors became more affordable and accessible to the expanding middle class. Introduced by Kodak in 1932, the 8mm format was a cheaper option for amateur filmmakers and offered people the opportunity to watch films in the privacy of their own home (McKee 1978: 105). The Second World War and the rise of television stunted the growth of 8mm as a domestic technology until British distributors like Walton released short edits of classic silent comedies starring Charlie Chaplin and Laurel and Hardy. McKee (1978: 106) believes that this appealed to a new generation of 'film buffs' with increasingly disposable incomes who were eager to see classic Hollywood films not shown on television. Coincidentally, Walton was one of the first distributors to release glamour films, an 'above-the-counter' precursor to the roller.

Chibnall (2003: 46) defines the glamour film as 'three-minute softcore reels featuring [...] models in states of undress'. Initially released on the domestic 8mm format, but also available on 9.5mm, Super 8 and 16mm, these short films were popular in the late 1950s and the 1960s. They depicted short stripteases, much like those taking place in Soho's strip clubs, such as Paul Raymond's Revue Bar on Walker's Court or the five clubs owned by Murray Goldstein.[3] Many glamour films play on Soho's reputation for vice, with titles such as *Soho Striptease* (Pete Walker 1960), the Carnaby Kinks label and the film *Down Town* (Pete Walker no date) opens with footage of a woman walking through Soho to audition at what is seemingly a strip club. At this time, screen nudity was still problematic, and 8mm film was not subject to approval by the then British Board of Film Censors. Therefore, glamour films could show moving naked flesh, providing that they did not contravene the Obscene Publications Act 1959. Glamour films commanded higher prices than other films on the format because of their content and were openly sold in high street shops or through mail order. A Walton catalogue from the early 1960s offered 50ft 8mm black and white prints for £1 4s or colour for £3 6s. 100ft 9.5mm and 16mm were costlier – £2 5s for black and white, colour £6 10s (see Figure 2.2).

The economic opportunities offered by this new format attracted many producers, including George Harrison Marks, Russell Gay, Stanley Long[4] and Pete Walker. A former vaudeville comedian, Walker, started producing glamour films in 1958 and distributed them via the label Heritage Films. They were filmed on a 16mm camera in under an hour and distributed on both 8mm and Super 8 in cardboard boxes with a glamour style image of the starring model on the front. According to Schaefer (2002: 7), '16mm came to be considered a semi-professional – but still a nontheatrical-gauge', whereas 8mm, as an affordable production format, was considered amateur, and 35mm was the dominant, professional mode of production. Walker's films were openly sold in high-street photography shops, Soho's bookshops and through mail order. According to Chibnall (1998: 35), Walker found this to be a highly profitable enterprise, issuing 'one hundred a year' and 'nearly four hundred by the time he sold the business' in the late 1960s. In a filmed interview from 2016, Walker reflects on his glamour film past, stating that the films could command twice the cost price of non-adult 8mm movies and would 'sell ten times as many'.[5] He also acknowledges that the films were 'taboo' at the time, but perfectly legal to make and distribute.

Chibnall (1998: 35) believes that Walker's interest in the glamour market was financially driven; he 'could not resist the opportunity to exploit it'. When I interviewed Walker in 2018, he expressed the same motivations, stating that he only made glamour films for the money, using the profit to produce 35mm

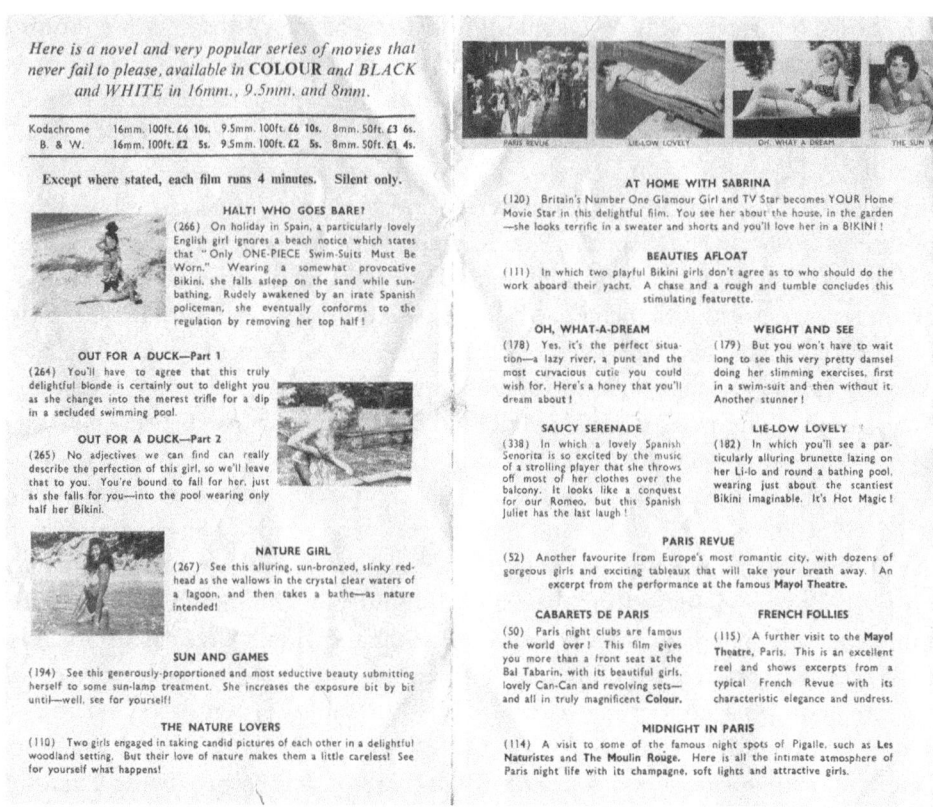

*Here is a novel and very popular series of movies that never fail to please, available in COLOUR and BLACK and WHITE in 16mm., 9.5mm. and 8mm.*

| Kodachrome | 16mm. 100ft. £6 10s. | 9.5mm. 100ft. £6 10s. | 8mm. 50ft. £3 6s. |
| B. & W. | 16mm. 100ft. £2 5s. | 9.5mm. 100ft. £2 5s. | 8mm. 50ft. £1 4s. |

**Except where stated, each film runs 4 minutes. Silent only.**

**HALT! WHO GOES BARE?**

(266) On holiday in Spain, a particularly lovely English girl ignores a beach notice which states that "Only ONE-PIECE Swim-Suits Must Be Worn." Wearing a somewhat provocative Bikini, she falls asleep on the sand while sunbathing. Rudely awakened by an irate Spanish policeman, she eventually conforms to the regulation by removing her top half!

**OUT FOR A DUCK—Part 1**

(264) You'll have to agree that this truly delightful blonde is certainly out to delight you as she changes into the merest trifle for a dip in a secluded swimming pool.

**OUT FOR A DUCK—Part 2**

(265) No adjectives we can find can really describe the perfection of this girl, so we'll leave that to you. You're bound to fall for her, just as she falls for you—into the pool wearing only half her Bikini.

**NATURE GIRL**

(267) See this alluring, sun-bronzed, slinky red-head as she wallows in the crystal clear waters of a lagoon, and then takes a bathe—as nature intended!

**SUN AND GAMES**

(194) See this generously-proportioned and most seductive beauty submitting herself to some sun-lamp treatment. She increases the exposure bit by bit until—well, see for yourself!

**THE NATURE LOVERS**

(110) Two girls engaged in taking candid pictures of each other in a delightful woodland setting. But their love of nature makes them a little careless! See for yourself what happens!

**AT HOME WITH SABRINA**

(120) Britain's Number One Glamour Girl and TV Star becomes YOUR Home Movie Star in this delightful film. You see her about the house, in the garden —she looks terrific in a sweater and shorts and you'll love her in a BIKINI!

**BEAUTIES AFLOAT**

(111) In which two playful Bikini girls don't agree as to who should do the work aboard their yacht. A chase and a rough and tumble concludes this stimulating featurette.

**OH, WHAT-A-DREAM**

(178) Yes, it's the perfect situation—a lazy river, a punt and the most curvacious cutie you could wish for. Here's a honey that you'll dream about!

**WEIGHT AND SEE**

(179) But you won't have to wait long to see this very pretty damsel doing her slimming exercises, first in a swim-suit and then without it. Another stunner!

**SAUCY SERENADE**

(338) In which a lovely Spanish Senorita is so excited by the music of a strolling player that she throws off most of her clothes over the balcony. It looks like a conquest for our Romeo, but this Spanish Juliet has the last laugh!

**LIE-LOW LOVELY**

(182) In which you'll see a particularly alluring brunette lazing on her Li-lo and round a bathing pool, wearing just about the scantiest Bikini imaginable. It's Hot Magic!

**PARIS REVUE**

(52) Another favourite from Europe's most romantic city, with dozens of gorgeous girls and exciting tableaux that will take your breath away. An excerpt from the performance at the famous Mayol Theatre.

**CABARETS DE PARIS**

(50) Paris night clubs are famous the world over! This film gives you more than a front seat at the Bal Tabarin, with its beautiful girls, lovely Can-Can and revolving sets— and all in truly magnificent Colour.

**FRENCH FOLLIES**

(115) A further visit to the Mayol Theatre, Paris. This is an excellent reel and shows excerpts from a typical French Revue with its characteristic elegance and undress.

**MIDNIGHT IN PARIS**

(114) A visit to some of the famous night spots of Pigalle, such as Les Naturistes and The Moulin Rouge. Here is all the intimate atmosphere of Paris night life with its champagne, soft lights and attractive girls.

FIGURE 2.2: Extract from Walton's glamour film catalogue (early 1960s). Courtesy of 'Mal Mallister'.

films for theatrical distribution.[6] Similarly, cult horror film director Norman J. Warren also made an early glamour film named *Twist Contest* (Warren n.d.). According to Warren, a distributor required a glamour film and offered the job to him. As someone with the ambition to enter the British film business, Warren saw it as an opportunity to be involved in film production.[7] For Chibnall (2003: 46), the glamour film business demonstrated that there was a market for adult films. As competition amongst British glamour filmmakers grew, others began to differentiate by making hardcore pornography for distribution on 8mm.

Early hardcore pornographic films date back to the early 1900s (Knight and Alpert 1967; Di Lauro and Rabkin 1976), with Buenos Aires an early 'principal center of production' (Di Lauro and Rabkin 1976: 46). However, the clandestine origins of pornographic film make its history difficult to trace. There are a variety of synonyms for hardcore pornographic films, such as loops, blue movies and pornos, which often refer to different viewing contexts. The most commonly used term is 'stag film', which Waugh (1996: 309) defines 'an explicit sexual narrative, produced and distributed, usually commercially, to clandestine, non-theatrical male audiences, between 1908 and 1970, principally in Europe and the Americas'. Di Lauro and Rabkin (1976) believe that stags were pioneered by France between the 1920s and the 1950s, though markets also existed in Latin America, Germany and the US. Slade (2000: 105) notes that early stags first appeared as 'single reels of 12 minutes' on 35mm film until the 1930s, when 'amateurs switched to 16mm formats', leading to an increase in production. According to Schaefer (2002: 7), 16mm was marketed as an amateur format accessible to 'middle and upper-class families'. As he points out, the Second World War changed the status of 16mm, as it was used in 'combat and newsreel photography, as well as the burgeoning educational market', before being adopted by US-based adult filmmakers in the late 1960s to make hardcore features.

Slade (1984) sees the 8mm format as central to reviving the American stag film in the 1950s until they were 'outpaced by the English' at the start of the 1960s (Slade 2000: 105). This claim is supported by Knight and Halpert (1967: 186) who note that Britain supplied 'the majority – and the best – of the foreign stag material available in the American commercial market'. In Britain, pornographic movies were often referred to as 'blue movies' by the popular press. However, in the Soho trade, British-produced hardcore films distributed on 8mm were known as rollers, because of how the film reel would roll when played through a projector. Rollers first appear in the early 1960s. Before this, many of the pornographic films sold in Soho's bookshops were imported from France, supplied via transnational networks. An article from the *Western Mail* (3 June 1959) tells how the British government plan to 'fight the obscene film trade'. A quote from Lord Denning, the then 'Law Lord', comments on the smuggling of 'grossly obscene' films into Britain. Another article in the *Daily Mirror* (24 March 1948) describes Scotland Yard's efforts to track down 'a gang of men and women making indecent films'. The films are said to originate from France and the article mentions how Scotland Yard are working with the French Sûreté to 'help stop the smuggling of such films into this country'.

Evidence indicates that hardcore films were produced in Britain before 8mm rollers, but distributed on a very limited scale and usually on 16mm. Two 16mm films housed in the Kinsey Institute's archive are said to be of English origin – *Easiest Way* (1930–35) and *English Joys* (1940–43). I have not been able to confirm whether these were hardcore productions, or indeed British. Two collectors I interviewed claimed to have seen hardcore films pre-dating the 1960s. 'Philip Black' owns several 16mm films he believes were produced by moonlighting members of the General Post Office Film Unit (GPO):[8] 'They were quite professional [...] I made the connection because the star of one of the stags turns up in a GPO short film from 1936'.[9] Another collector, 'RonnieX', recalled visiting the home of a major film collector and dealer: 'he told me his father used to shoot 16mm colour films of his girlfriends engaged in sexual acts during the early 1940s [...] I was shown a great example and the quality was outstanding'.[10] RonnieX's anecdote is significant as it implies that amateurs were documenting their own sexual exploits on 16mm film. It is not clear if these were intended for commercial distribution. In her study of early British pornography, Stoops (2018: 72) found that 'few pornographic films' were produced in the early twentieth-century, citing an investigation into a film company who collaborated with a shipping firm to export pornographic films to Karachi. Stoops believes that pornographic films existed in 'significant enough quantities' but were mainly exported through transnational networks rather than sold in Britain.

Further indication of hardcore films being domestically produced in Britain prior to the 1960s can be found in an article from the Swedish newspaper *Aftonbladet* (8 August 1937), which speaks of 'illegal movie clubs' showing 'smuggled uncensored film'. It tells of how smugglers evade customs, and how audiences of such screenings are made up of the 'curious' or 'perverts' who 'enjoy the disgusting entertainment'. The article comments on the profitability of these showings and alludes to the existence of 'secret studios' making pornographic films in Britain. Collectively, these primary and secondary sources suggest that the production of hardcore pornography in Britain before 1960 was disorganized, secretive and a small-scale activity. Furthermore, the use of 16mm made them accessible to a limited audience who had the means to view such films. The introduction of the lower cost 8mm format was significant for the emergence of rollers. There existed an already established small-gauge film market for roller makers to exploit and, more importantly, the technology to produce films was accessible to amateurs and semi-professionals.

## Making rollers

According to Doyle (2013), technology is integral to the 'economic success' of any media industry. In previous work, I have explored how new technologies create opportunities for enterprise (Carter 2018). For Schumpeter (1939: 84–85, 2017), entrepreneurs are innovators who disrupt markets by introducing new products and ultimately create a new market within an economy. Schumpeter's model of entrepreneurship has been criticized for placing innovation within the context of large-scale organizations and for being too limiting, particularly for understanding marginal economic activity (Hagedoorn 1996: 887–88). Despite these shortcomings, I want to take Schumpeter's general notion of entrepreneurs as innovators and creators of new markets and apply it to the disruptive activities of early roller makers. In the previous chapter, I discussed how the Obscene Publications Squad's informal licensing system provided an institutional framework for an alternative economy of hardcore pornography, permitting entrepreneurs to produce commodities to sell via Soho's bookshops. Photographs and typescripts appear to have dominated the market and were manufactured outside the formal economy by amateurs, semi-professionals and professionals. These items could be produced in-house using commercially available materials. I now explore how entrepreneurs used 16mm and 8mm filmmaking technologies to disrupt the economy and create a new market in the alternative economy for hardcore films. I explain how they devised their own means of production to bring these products to market and likely drew on amateur filmmaking networks to aid their practice.

Like the glamour filmmakers discussed earlier, most roller makers shot on 16mm and distributed on 8mm. An article from the magazine *Amateur Cine World* (29 September 1966) identifies how 16mm offered filmmakers many advantages over 8mm. First, picture resolution was better; second, it was easier to edit due to the larger frame size; third, as there was less demand for equipment, it was a buyer's market; fourth, 16mm sound projectors were cheaper than 8mm ones, and, finally, 16mm gave access to a broader range of film duplication, printing and processing. For example, filmmakers could shoot on negative film and have a work-print produced to edit; duplicates could also be made without the original film suffering.

According to roller maker Mike Freeman, the most popular camera in the 1960s was the Swiss-made Paillard Bolex H16 (see figure 2.3). Occasionally, a Bolex H16 can be seen drifting into the frame of rollers, as is evident in *Chez M. Pirgeon* (1960–64), evidencing that it was commonly used. Cleveland and Pritchard (2015: 293) remark on how the Bolex H16 appealed to the 'serious amateur' or 'semi-professionals making 16mm films'. For Turquier (2016: 156), 'non-mainstream' filmmakers preferred the camera for 'its robustness, reliability, relative inexpensiveness, and [...] for the array of aesthetic possibilities it allowed'. These possibilities were linked to its features – light, well made and reliable, usable in a range of filming conditions and a turret lens system that offered three easily selectable options. They were also attractive to avant-garde filmmakers because of in-camera special effects, such as different filming speeds, time-lapse arrangements, and filter slides, amongst others. A drawback with the Bolex H16 was that its spring drive motor only provided 30 seconds of continuous filming before needing to be rewound by hand. Bolex eventually introduced an external electric drive motor to eradicate this. Moreover, the camera held only 50ft or 100ft of film, giving four minutes of film at sixteen frames per second. As most rollers used at least 400ft of 16mm film, several reel changes were necessary.

An article in *Amateur Cine World* (29 September 1966) article prices a used early Bolex H16 model at around £60, with later versions costing between £100 and £150. In comparison, a new 8mm Bolex camera cost £45. A seller of such

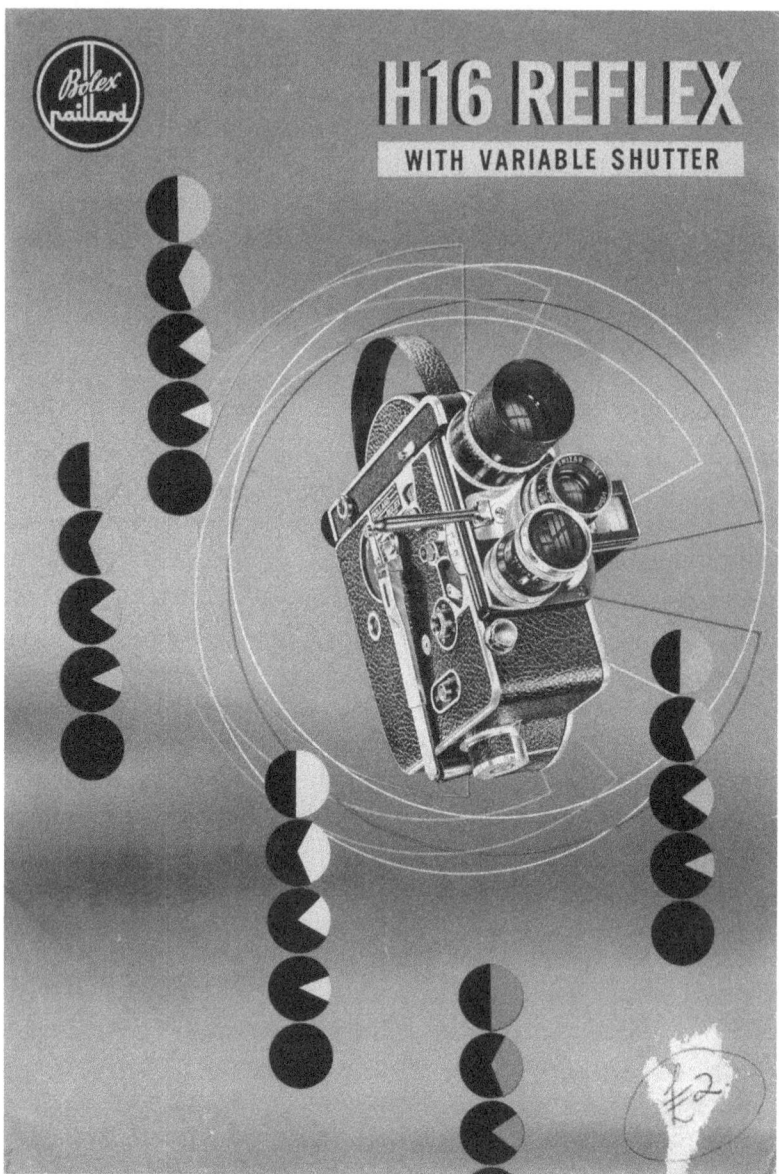

FIGURE 2.3: Advert for Paillard Bolex H16. Courtesy of 'Philip Black'.

cameras advertising in *Amateur Cine World* (17 March 1966) includes the text 'URGENTLY REQUIRED BOLEX 16mm. EQUIPMENT', hinting at their demand. Other adverts show that 16mm film came in either 50ft or 100ft spools, colour film costing around £2 to £3 for 50ft, while 100ft cost between £3 and

£5, depending on the brand. Therefore, stock for a 400ft roller shot on 16mm would cost at least £15 in 1966, adding at least an extra 100ft for edited footage. Alongside the growing affordability of camera equipment was a 'national culture of amateur cine-clubs' across Britain (Reekie 2007: 104). Central to this culture were handbooks and cine magazines such as *8mm Magazine* and *Amateur Cine World,* assisting those who were interested in learning how to use the technology, giving them access to the equipment and a like-minded community. When I interviewed the Danish pornographer Willem van Batenburg, he proudly showed me his copy of a Bolex H16 guidebook from the 1960s.[11] Van Batenburg told me that this was his 'bible' on how to use the Bolex H16, not having received any formal training in filmmaking. This highlights how cine-clubs, magazines and production handbooks were educational resources and informative for those wanting to learn the craft of small-gauge film production. For roller makers, they were particularly helpful as guides on how to process and print films.

As the distribution of hardcore pornography in Britain was criminalized under the Obscene Publications Act 1959, it was tricky to process and print rollers. Therefore, creative solutions were necessary. Films could be sent to a commercial laboratory for processing, but an attentive worker might notice the potentially obscene material and report it to the police. Italian pornographer Lasse Braun sent his first 8mm production *Golden Butterfly* (Lasse Braun 1967) to a Kodak laboratory for processing, assuming that it would be one of many going through the automated machinery, evading the attention of laboratory workers. Although his gamble paid off, Braun realized this approach was unsustainable and decided to seek out alternative options.[12] Interviewees also described adding innocuous footage at the beginning and the end of a film to evade the attention of laboratory staff and minimize the risk of it being discovered. A second option was to find a willing laboratory employee who, for a fee, would process the film 'out of hours'. Former film laboratory worker Brian Pritchard told me that many laboratories ran 24 hours a day for seven days a week, making it possible for such side hustles to take place at night when there was a skeleton staff.[13] Roller maker Evan Phillips is said to have preferred this route prior to moving to Denmark in 1969 and establishing his own laboratory (*Sunday People,* 6 February 1972: 11).

The negative could also be smuggled or shipped abroad to an overseas film laboratory. According to Hebditch and Anning (1988: 79), some of 'the gentlemen of Soho' sent their films to Sven Nielsen in Lyngby, Denmark, to be processed and even duplicated. Nielsen owned his own film laboratory and advertised its services in his adult magazine *Vue*. This option carried risks, including customs seizure, potential piracy and a delay in receiving the developed negative. It also involved additional costs, especially if a courier was needed to smuggle the film in and out of Britain. In the early 1970s, roller maker John Lindsay often filmed in European countries where pornography was legalized as it meant he could easily have the film processed by a professional laboratory and smuggle it back into Britain for printing.[14] Another option was to avoid commercial and use do-it-yourself (DIY) techniques. I spoke to Brian Pritchard, a former film laboratory worker and expert on film processing, about whether it would be possible to process a 16mm film outside of a laboratory:

> Unlikely [...] the processes [for colour film] were very complicated, and you weren't able to buy processing solutions; they had to be made up from raw chemicals, and the chemicals had to be mixed correctly in the correct proportions. Obviously, if you wanted to do black and white, that's a lot easier.

Developing machines were prohibitively costly, therefore Pritchard believes that roller producers likely relied of the services offered by 'garage labs'.

A garage lab was a semi-professional setup, the word 'garage' indicating their informality. According to Pritchard, 'there were quite a few [...] during the 60s and 70s and they concentrated on producing 8mm only'. Garage labs were run by people who had the means and skill to develop film, often using semi-professional, commercially available equipment advertised in *Amateur Cine World* or *8mm Magazine*. One such processing device was known as a Todd Tank. As an advert for the device in Figure 2.4 shows, the Todd Tank had a Ferris wheel-like frame which held the negative. Working in a darkroom with safe lighting, the operator wound the film onto a spiral drum sitting in a chemical bath. Rotating the drum, either by hand via the attached handle or an electric motor, the film dipped into the developing chemicals for a designated amount of time. Afterwards, the chemicals were replaced with water to rinse the film. If reversal film was being used, a hardening solution was required, followed by a water rinse. Then, a bleaching solution, a further rinse and another exposure to white light. An additional run through developing fluid was necessary, followed by a rinse, fixing solution and final six water rinses. While on the drum, the film needed to time to dry before being wound on to a reel and made ready for printing. Bomback (1958) states that this precise and lengthy process took at least 60 minutes, depending on the film's length. This emphasizes the precision, skill and patience required to achieve decent results. It also may explain why early unbranded rollers were produced in low quantities as it was a labour-intensive activity.

In addition to Todd Tanks or other semi-professional developing devices, it was possible to build homemade solutions. In his work on British underground film making, Reekie (2007: 111) discusses how 'experimental practice' underpinned the amateur film movement. He notes how cine magazines like *Amateur*

AT HOME; IN INDUSTRY; IN HOSPITALS, INSTITUTIONS, RESEARCH LABS., GOVT. DEPTS., AND IN SCHOOLS, Cine Films are processed with the

# TODD TANK

Models with capacities from 33ft. to 210ft. Send PC. for TODD TANK Brochure and/or Memo 12, giving details of OUR PRO-CESSING SERVICE for all PNI 9·5mm: d/8mm. & 16mm. (whether supplied by us or bought elsewhere) including Kodak Plus X and Tri X and ex-Govt. films

## MICROFILMS LTD.
### ST. ANDREWS STREET, DUNDEE

FIGURE 2.4: Advertisement for a Todd Tank. Courtesy of 'Philip Black'.

*Cine World* provided a communal space for amateurs and semi-professionals to share DIY approaches to film production, including step-by-step guides on how to process and print films using homemade equipment. Such publications could have served as 'how to' manuals for early roller makers, particularly for those wanting to find ways to bypass commercial laboratories and keep production in-house. In one of a series of articles on 16mm production, *Amateur Cine World* (15 September 1966), Francis Williams offers a diagram of his wooden motor-driven processing drum and outlines how it can be used to develop a 16mm negative. His instructions illustrate the precision needed to get decent results. However, amateur and semi-professional approaches were not without fault and involved trial and error, with the developer having to learn from their mistakes to avoid repeating them. According to Bomback (1958: 151–52), the following faults were common:

- Picture too light or too dark (development too long or too short).
- Yellow stain (bleaching not fully completed).
- Blisters or recirculation (solutions not at the right temperature).
- Bleaching too slow (incorrect solution).
- Streaky picture (drum rotation too slow).
- Drying spots (film not dried properly).
- Buckling of film (film stretched during processing or too much heat used to dry the film).
- Negative density wrong (film underexposed).

Such imperfections are often present in the prints of some rollers, being transferred from the developed negative, revealing the types of practices used to process the film. For instance, a print with few flaws suggests that the roller was likely professionally developed in a commercial laboratory, while a print showing fading, blemishes or blotches can be indicative of a garage lab or home processing. The early roller *Chez M. Pirgeon* (1960–65) shows instances of chemical damage, with a yellow stain possibly being indicative of incorrect bleaching or not drying the film properly. Therefore, it is possible to identify the likely origins of certain rollers by closely examining the film itself.

After developing the negative, a contact printer was required to duplicate the films. Printing a 16mm shot film on to the 8mm format was especially difficult for roller makers who were unable to use commercial laboratories. Brian Pritchard told me that one of the first challenges would be reducing a 16mm negative to 8mm. According to Pritchard, an optical device could be used to print from the 16mm negative to 8mm film or produce a double 8mm negative from the 16mm positive. The double 8mm negative could then be contact printed and then separated into single 8mm film using a splitter device. Roller maker Mike Freeman confirmed that he preferred the latter process as it made duplication faster, allowing for two 8mm copies at a time. Pritchard pointed out that either of these reduction printing techniques required specialist equipment, making it plausible that professional labs might have been engaged to produce double 8mm negatives for roller makers to duplicate using their own contact printers. Semi-professional devices, such as the American company Uhler's range of contact printers, were available with optical reduction fittings but costly to import. Mike Freeman purchased two of these machines to print his rollers, and I describe how these worked in the next chapter.

Homemade contact printers were also possible. In an article from *Amateur Cine World* (22 September 1966), Francis Williams presents his model for a DIY printing device, stressing that the process is

> really very simple [...] all that is necessary is a device to hold the negative in firm contact with the positive stock while it is being exposed to the printing light, and some method for advancing the two films together, either continuously by means of a sprocket or step-by-step with a claw.
>
> (404)

Williams' design is based on an ordinary 16mm projector with some modifications, running at twelve frames per second to produce one print. He makes a credible case for the benefits of a homemade printing machine over a professional one, suggesting that it can make a more exact contact print than that offered by fast-moving professional machines, but underlines that the film needs to be handled cleanly to attain good results. A reader inspired by Williams' device wrote a letter to *Amateur Cine World*, describing a printing device designed by members of his amateur film club. The author claims his machine prints 100ft of film in five minutes and has given eighteen months of successful use. Once a run of films had been contacted printed, they were packed and ready to be wholesaled to Soho's bookshops.

Through a combination of formal and informal means, entrepreneurs were able to manufacture hardcore films, finding ways around using film laboratories. The availability of small-gauge filmmaking technologies allowed roller makers to shoot on 16mm and print on 8mm film for wider distribution. Magazines, handbooks books and the expertise of cine clubs, instructed roller makers on how to use filmmaking equipment and conceive their own post-production practices, keeping it in house in order to avoid drawing attention to their illicit activities. This empowered them to bring a new product into the alternative economy for hardcore films, disrupting a market that was dominated by photographs and typescripts. I now want to consider some of the early innovators of British hardcore 8mm films and discuss their practices. This unveils more details about roller production and distribution.

### The early pioneers

I have been able to identify four roller entrepreneurs active between the years 1960 and 1965 – Leonard Thorpe, Ivor Cook, Ken Taylor and 'Derek'. In the early stage of this alternative economy, rollers appear to have been distributed with no branding. Instead, they were simply packaged in blank cardboard boxes or boxes with an explicit photograph, often taken during filming, glued to front. Such packaging may either have the film title handwritten on the box. However, the common practice was to Letraset[15] the title on the photograph (see Figure 2.5). The lack of any identifying features suggests an attempt by their producers to distance themselves, making it difficult to identify the makers of unbranded rollers. The films open with either a handwritten title card or use a more professional looking titling kit. Handwritten titles can help to identify films made by the same producer. For example, the opening titles of *Chez M Pirgeon* (1960–65), *Hotel Sexi* (1960–65), *Lavabora* (1960–65) and *La Dolce Vita* (1960–65) use the same distinctive handwriting. The choice of titling for these rollers is also interesting, using either French, Italian or Spanish language to perhaps create the illusion that they were not made in Britain. An examination of the film stock reveals the name 'Ilfords', a British brand regularly used by roller makers, as confirmed by Mike Freeman and Evan Phillips. The foreign sounding titles may also be a reference to racy reputation of European arthouse films that were shown in private members only cinema clubs to escape the British Board of Film Censors (Trevelyan 1973: 122–23; Spicer and McKenna 2013).

The earliest known roller maker was an entrepreneur named Leonard Thorpe. On 10 January 1960, *The People* wrote about the 'ghoul who makes money from evil films', including a picture of the 47-year-old Thorpe loading an 8mm film onto a projector. A professional freelance photographer from Finchley, London, Thorpe is revealed to be involved in running illicit blue movie shows. These were held in private spaces where a projector could be mounted, such as flats, factories and the function rooms of public houses or working men's clubs. In today's parlance, they might even be described as pop-up porn cinemas or 'secret cinemas' (Gustafsson 2016). The small footprint of an 8mm projector meant that it could easily be concealed in a suitcase next to some films and smuggled into a suitable location, attracting little attention. As Gustafsson (2016) identifies in his study of Swedish informal blue movie shows during the 1920s and 1940s, such events made pornographic films more accessible, especially for those who might not have had the financial means to purchase and screen such material, let alone know how to access to it. Therefore, these pop-ups offered a space outside of the home to view pornographic films.

Yet not all blue movie shows were money making enterprises. A collector named 'Mal Mallister' recalled viewing his first rollers:

> It was the early 1970s, and I was working at this factory. One day, the manager told me to go this shop over the road and to collect some films; they were *Traveller's Rest* on Anglo Continental, *Tour de Love* on Look and *Equal to Mummy* on Climax. So, I did. They were from under the counter of the shop. I took them back, and the

FIGURE 2.5: Examples of early unbranded roller boxes: *Afternoon Lust* (1964–67), *Turkish Delight* (1967–68) and *Black Magic* (1963–67). Author's personal collection. Faces obscured to protect the identity of performers.

manager got the projector out and screened them to the lads. I eventually bought those films from that shop and still have them today.

Mal mentioned that the screening was to male workers. Waugh (2001: 280) notes that such exhibitions regularly took place in 'homosocial' spaces, while Williams (1989: 73) suggests that male bonding was a central pleasure for those who watched stags in communal settings. Factories are regularly identified as locations for blue movie shows. For instance, in 1966, the screening of rollers at a Castle Bromwich car factory made the front pages of many national newspapers, telling of how they were attended by 80–100 male night-shift workers (*Daily Mirror*, 25 April 1966).

Other newspaper articles show that blue movie shows were a regular occurrence in London. In an on-going investigation into these enterprises, a journalist named Peter Forbes reveals the activities of a car-hire service specializing in picking up tourists from Soho and taking them to view 'obscene films' in Marylebone (*The People*, 12 July 1964: 15). Forbes recounts how one of his team was approached by a young man offering to 'show you around' for a cost of £5. When quizzed what that meant, the young man responded, 'you'll see – and if you don't like it you can get your money back'. The investigator agreed and noticed the young man call out to another standing in a shop door across the road. This was the driver who took the investigator to a house in Marylebone to see a blue movie show. On arrival, the investigator queried the price and was told: 'some of these films cost £35 each – what are you complaining about?'. The 30-minute show was held in the basement of the house and members of the male audience are said to be tourists. The investigator noticed a woman operating the projector located at the back of a room.

Later, a tout approached another reporter on Soho's Old Compton Street and, after agreeing, was taken to a flat in Newport Court. Here, they found a projector sat on a table and a screen above a chest of drawers. Again, £5 was the fee, indicating a standard tariff for these illicit screenings. According to one of the organisers, the films had been purchased in Soho that very day at the cost of £20 each; the titles of the films are not offered. Three further males attended the show and, at the end, were offered the 'services of a woman' who stood in front of the flat's doorway; I explore the relationship between blue movie shows and sex work shortly. Following further digging, Forbes discovered that two young men in their mid twenties ran the film shows. Forbes watched one of their cars for five hours, observing that sixteen men were picked up on Old Compton Street and taken to Charlotte Street, Marylebone. In keeping with his usual approach, Forbes approached both men, who told him that they each generated £100 per from the six-month long operation.

Stories like these appear regularly throughout the 1960s, demonstrating the popular press' fascination with pornography and an on-going concern about the impact of permissiveness. Leonard Thorpe's case differs from these examples in that he is said to screen his own films, making him the earliest documented producer of rollers (*The People*, 10 January 1960: 4). The article indicates that Thorpe used 'call girls as actresses' and also persuaded 'men and women friends to take part in them for free'. Those attending his film shows paid an extremely high £50 entry fee; over three times the average male weekly wage. Many were 'directors of companies' and clients of Thorpe's professional photography business: 'they are the kind of people who can afford fifty quid a time – on expenses'. This again highlights the relationship between class and access to pornography, as discussed in the previous chapter. While Thorpe screened his silent rollers, which are said to be colour prints, he gave the audience a sort of director's commentary about how he made them and the performers who took part in them.

Thorpe also arranged for sex workers to attend the screenings, who made themselves 'friendly' with the male audience for £2; 'further services' cost £3. Newspaper articles and police documents show that sex workers were often present at blue movie shows. As Koch (1990: 18) observes, the relationship between pornographic films and sex work is longstanding: 'pornographic films were above all bought and screened by brothels, which hoped to entice their customers with filmic offerings while earning money from services rendered through selling tickets for the screening'. British blue movie shows appear to subvert the economic model Koch (1990) describes, with people attending the shows for the purpose of viewing a pornographic film and 'personal services' being offered at an additional cost. Some blue movie shows also incorporated live sex shows. *Regina* v. *Murray and Others* (1965) tells of blue movie shows taking place above a flat on Berners Street in Soho. In addition to viewing rollers, customers could watch a husband and wife give a live show for £15 or pay £10 to just watch their performance.[16]

Thorpe provided the unnamed journalist with a summary of his business. To arrange a film show with two sex workers cost £25. His projector cost £90, while a second one with sound cost £300, perhaps an indication of how he invested into this enterprise and the kind of profits he generated. Thorpe says that he also purchased films for £50 each, swapping them with others, ominously remarking 'buying them on the open market is too dangerous'. This may explain why he moved on to making his own films, admitting that he has produced 'quite a few' and that it took him 'years to build up my lists of models and men for them'. Thorpe is said to be making colour rollers, a rare commodity in the early 1960s. As retired film laboratory work Brian Pritchard pointed out earlier in this chapter, colour film was costly and difficult to process. Thorpe's identification as a professional photographer might be an explanation for him having the ability to produce colour rollers and shows how photographers adapted to making films.

To evade the law, Thorpe is said to have only put on blue movie shows when invited to a client's house. This, he believed, meant he could not be accused of depraving or corrupting his clientele under the Obscene Publications Act 1959 as they were consenting to attend the showing. Additionally, Thorpe never used the same location more than once. These efforts were unsuccessful, as Thorpe was later found guilty of 'running obscene film shows', resulting in a four-month prison sentence and a fine of £22 (*The People*, 3 July 1960: 9). Considering the profits Thorpe claimed to be generating through his blue movie shows, £22 is a small amount. Thorpe's activities demonstrate the different types of entrepreneurial activity that related to rollers. Rather than distributing via Soho Bookshops or mail order, Thorpe is said to be offering private screenings to wealthy clients. Because of this, Thorpe appears to have operated outside of the safety of the alternative economy, not having the police protection that could have allowed him to operate unhindered. This is typical of others who ran blue movie shows, eventually falling foul of the law and prosecuted using the antiquated common law charges Keeping a Disorderly House or Conspiracy to Corrupt Public Morals (Cocks 2016). Blue movie shows later evolved into cinema clubs, which used loopholes in the Obscene Publications Act 1959 and cinema laws to show hardcore pornography. I discuss these in greater detail in Chapters 4 and 5.

Another producer active in the first half of the 1960s was 'Derek'. As explained in the introduction to this book, many of the people involved in the alternative economy have either died, are impossible to trace or do not want to talk about their past. When finding someone who is alive, there is always some trepidation about whether they will talk about their involvement. I met 'Derek' through an associate who arranged for me to speak to him at his market stall. Unfortunately, 'Derek' would only speak in this setting, being a little hesitant and secretive about his enterprise.[17] He did not give much away, but provided a valuable first-hand account of roller production. 'Derek' started making rollers in the early 1960s. He blamed his age, which seemed to be mid 70s, for not remembering the exact date. He claimed to have released a total of 100 8mm films, of which six were made by himself. 'Derek' said that the boxes containing his movies always had a queen of hearts playing card stuck to them, indicating a very early attempt at branding, and that one of his rollers was titled *Peeping Tom* (*n.d.*). Unlike other roller producers, 'Derek' shot on 8mm film rather than 16mm and described himself as an opportunistic amateur who made hardcore pornography purely for profit. Using 8mm instead of 16mm would have been cheaper and made duplication slightly easier. He sourced performers in and around Soho, approaching women at bars and clubs, asking if they would participate in his films, again signifying Soho's role in the alternative economy.

'Derek' recalled the motivations of one female performer: 'she was a hostess, doing it all for her young daughter. She eventually earned enough [money] to retire and put her little girl in private school'. He regularly used a well-endowed male performer who worked as a representative for a shoe company and did not ask for payment. Once the films were shot, 'Derek' tasked an associate named Dennis with processing and printing them as he lacked the technical know-how. Dennis ran a shoe shop in Peckham, south London, that had a garage lab in a small room at the back. According to 'Derek', Dennis also sold pornography under-the-counter: 'a priest was a regular customer. He laid the money on the counter, and then picked up a brown paper bag containing postcards and walked off […] he never said a word'. As well as selling to Soho's bookshops, 'Derek' claimed that people in Soho's pubs could be tempted to buy his rollers for an extraordinary £100 each. This would have been a huge amount of money in the early 1960s, and contrasts with the prices described by other interviewees and those reported in police documents. Although 'Derek''s pricing seems unlikely, if true, it might point to the scarcity of rollers in this early period of their existence.

'Derek' left the trade, as making them had 'become too much trouble', mentioning a tabloid investigation into his enterprise; something I have been unable to verify. Instead of making rollers, 'Derek' moved to distributing imported pornography. Later in life, he released films on the newly introduced home video formats and unintentionally became embroiled in the video nasties moral panic of the early 1980s (Kerekes and Slater 2000; McKenna 2020). After learning film editing at night school, he made a series of documentaries about the Second World War, releasing them on the Video Home System format (VHS). He was also an early entrepreneur in the British video games business, issuing around ten titles for devices such as the Sinclair and Commodore home computer systems.

'Derek' was a fascinating yet frustrating interviewee. In our brief conversation, he provided further context on early roller production and valuable detail on the use of garage labs. However, he refused to elaborate on certain points, especially those relating to criminality. For instance, he refused to comment on the corruption in the Obscene Publications Squad. 'Derek''s career trajectory exhibits a willingness to embrace the economic opportunities offered by new technologies, transitioning from 8mm production to video tape and computer games. His career illustrates how entrepreneurs move between illicit and licit spaces and apply the skills they acquired to different media forms.

Unlike Thorpe and 'Derek' little is known about Ken 'Skinny' Taylor. His name is mentioned as part of the police investigation that resulted in Watford Blue Movie Trial, an obscenity case that features heavily in Chapter 4. In a police interview, roller producer Anthony Collingbourne recounts how he encountered Taylor:

> Sometime in the early 1960s I met a man whom I subsequently knew to be Ken Taylor. On reflection I think this was shortly after my release from prison in about 1962. [He] had a studio called Columbia Studios in a little side turning opposite the Edgeware Hospital [sic.]. The first time I went into the studio [...] I went there to buy some pornographic films from Taylor. I remember visiting Taylor on one occasion at his home which is a flat above a firm called Premiere Motors in Colindale on the main Edgware Road. Shortly after meeting him, I started appearing in the films he was making as an actor. Taylor paid me for this service.[18]

Collingbourne later resumed his acquaintance with Taylor in 1969 when he opened a photography studio in Watford. He speaks of how Taylor used the studio to make rollers on the basis that Taylor showed Collingbourne and an associate how to make them. Collingbourne describes Taylor as living beyond his means and that this led to him selling an American processing machine to Collingbourne, suggesting that Taylor invested in equipment to simplify developing rollers. Tantalizingly, a newspaper article on the Watford Blue Movie Trial 'allegedly' links Taylor to the Profumo Affair, but goes no further (*Evening Echo*, 8 June 1974: 5).

From Collingbourne's account, Taylor appears to have participated in the alternative economy for over ten years and was licensed by the Obscene Publications Squad – a document from the Watford Blue Movie Trial names him as a police informant. Despite this, it is difficult to link Taylor to any rollers or labels, aside from those he is said to have assisted Collingbourne in making in the files relating to the Watford Blue Movie Trial. Collingbourne reveals that Taylor was a former partner of Ivor Cook, the roller producer I introduced in the opening of this chapter. For the remainder of the chapter, I consider Cook's place in the alternative economy and how he was involved in developing transnational links to Denmark and Sweden, expanding the trade beyond Soho.

### The professional – Ivor Cook

In much of the literature on British hardcore 8mm films, Cook is regularly identified as an important figure. For instance, Thompson (2007: 224) states that Cook was the 'brilliant eye whose "Climax Films Present" trademark precedes some of the most exquisitely realised British stags ever made', a claim repeated by Hebditch and Anning (1988) and Chibnall (2003). Aside from one newspaper article,

I found no other evidence connecting Cook to Britain's most prolific roller label, which I discuss at length in the next chapter. Cook appears to have been a fixer for Climax Films, helping Evan 'Big Jeff' Phillips and his associates start their business. Cook kept a low profile and operated within his means, rather than attempting to upscale his enterprise. Therefore, he left little trace of his practice. Interviewees who either worked with Cook or knew of him told me that Cook was initially a respected professional photographer who produced Soho Postcards and sold them to Soho's bookshops. 'Colin', a producer of glamour photographs, remembered him as a highly proficient photographer. Dave Wells[19], a performer, producer and director who was active in the early 1980s fondly recalled working with Cook, referring to him as a 'sweet man', while German pornographer Hans Moser (cited in Hebditch and Anning 1988: 213) saw Cook as 'a real gentleman in all the other shit', referring to the corruption and criminality taking place in Soho at the time when Cook was active.

Cook is a useful entrepreneur to focus on as he appears to have a played a significant part in the development of rollers, drawing on his background as a professional photographer to make films and distribute them via the alternative economy. Additionally, Cook's role as a fixer appears to have contributed to the emergence of labels like Climax, as well as utilizing transnational partnerships to extend distribution beyond Soho and into Denmark. As outlined in the introduction to this chapter, the Obscene Publications Squad were aware of Cook's involvement in making Soho Postcards and rollers as early as 1962, suggesting that he sold his goods to Soho's bookshops for some time. The investigation also indicates that he was part of a firm, which included Robert Shaw and Martin Granby. Shaw moved on to publishing softcore pornography magazines in the late 1960s and early 1970s and Granby, who I discuss in chapter four, went on to make his own rollers. Cook appears to have had many partners in the early 1960s, hinting at some sort of organization to his enterprise and taking more of a professional approach to his work.

Interviewees regularly remarked on Cook's professionalism. 'Colin' informed me that 'Ivor was in it in a big way – the first with colour prints and rollers'. Fellow photographer and roller producer, Mike Freeman also remembers Cook:

> He lived out in Molesey, Surrey. He was a professional. He had a big colour machine with four rolls of colour coming over [...] his pictures were always impressive to me [...] he used to use uniforms a lot [in his pictures and films] [...] I found this intensely erotic, so I started doing things like that. I had the greatest respect for him.[20]

Cook seems to share much in common with Leonard Thorpe. Both are said to have had a background in professional photography, giving them knowledge and understanding of framing, lighting, composition and image processing. They also had access to professional equipment, as Freeman indicates with his mention of Cook's colour processing machine; an expensive technology in the early 1960s that required technical skill to operate. By the mid 1970s, Cook was clearly an established professional photographer with his own studio, as an advert printed in an issue of *British Journal of Photography* (1974: vol. 121) demonstrates:

> six Colorama backgrounds nine-foot wide. Front Projection Studio for hire. Transflex system used with either Robel 66 [sic] or Linhof Technicha 4 in × 5 in. Small library of transparencies available. Lighting systems are Broncolor and Bowens Multilec with full range of accessories. Usual facilities, dressing rooms, etc., no parking restrictions. Five minutes from Hampton Court. For full details of hire of studio and/or front projection contact Ivor Cook, Hurst Park Studios, The Precinct, Hurst Road, West Molesey, Surrey [phone numbers removed].

Cook regularly advertised in the *British Journal of Photography*, a publication intended for professionals rather than mass-market magazine *Amateur Photographer*. The advert shows a significant financial investment in high-end photography equipment, likely funded by his profits from Soho Postcards and rollers. I have shared this advert with a number of professional photographers who informed me that the facilities would have been high-end for their time, indicating a successful photographer.

### A licensed pornographer

When interviewed by the Metropolitan Police on the 26 November 1975 as part of Obscene Publications Squad corruption investigation, Ivor Cook summarized his participation in the alternative economy.[21] Identifying himself as a 'professional photographer by trade', Cook states that he started producing and distributing pornography in the early 1960s, initially manufacturing Soho Postcards before expanding to rollers. He tells of how he sold these goods to the chairs of Soho bookshops, suspecting that this activity brought him to the attention of Obscene Publications Squad and resulted in the investigation described in the opening to this chapter. Cook recalls how officers found 'six obscene films', resulting in him being summoned to Scotland Yard where Obscene Publications Squad officers asked him to sign a disclaimer. Here, Cook was told by an officer named Webb to contact a man named Frankie Hulpert if he wanted to continue his pornography business. Cook arranged to meet with Hulpert in a public house, who advised Cook to become licensed and that this would cost £15–£20 per week. Hulpert acted as an intermediary between pornographers and the police, helping them to maintain a distance between the two parties and collecting payments on behalf of the Obscene Publications Squad. At first, Cook paid Hulpert weekly, then monthly, meeting at public houses in the West End of London to exchange money. Cook notes how Hulpert was 'uncouth', having to repeatedly buy him and his associates – who Cook assumes were police officers – drinks. Cook believed this to be an 'imposition', but understood the benefit of the license, as it allowed him to carry on unhindered.

Later, Hulpert asked Cook to meet with Detective Inspector Bill Moody, then Head of the Obscene Publications Squad. This led to repeated meetings where Cook purchased alcohol and meals for Moody, as well as 'handing him a drink' – a £25 cash payment. He soon found that the protection offered by this licence was limited when he was arrested on 9 July 1966 as part of a raid on a blue film show taking place at Cornwall Gardens, South Kensington. The front page of the *Kensington Post* from 26 November 1966 reveals more. Cook was one of four men and one woman later sent for trial because of their involvement in 'an obscene film show where girls invited customers to avail themselves of their services'. A man named King, his wife and a male associate were

> charged with conspiring together and with other persons unknown to corrupt the morals of and to debauch such persons as might be induced, or permitted, to resort to the address in Cornwall Gardens for the purpose of viewing an obscene film, or obscene films.

They were also accused of unlawfully opening, keeping and maintaining a disorderly house, again illustrating how common laws were utilized to regulate blue movie shows.

Cook, identified as a 'photo-finisher', and his German associate, were charged with 'conspiring together and with other persons unknown to contravene the provision of the Obscene Publications [Act]'. The raid resulted from yet another investigation by *The People* newspaper. A journalist named William Gardner made contact with King's wife, who offered him 'entertainment'. Mrs King made mention of 'blueys' – another British synonym for pornographic films – and invited the journalist to a basement flat at Cornwall Gardens on 6 July where 'she and plenty of other girls would be present'. On arrival, the doorman introduced Gardner and his photographer to Mr. King. The films shown all featured 'couples having intercourse' and they were propositioned by 'a girl who offered her services'. The entry fee was £5, though Peters said they usually charged 'between £15 and £20', but also ran 'country house parties' – orgies, as according to Gardner – that cost £30. Gardner paid £10 to watch a 'lesbian act' and three separate women offered sex for £5.

Gardner reported the show to the police and revisited the flat with an officer on Saturday 9 July. They were turned away, as the Kings 'had some film business to discuss and plan with others', asking them to visit later. On Gardner's return, the doorman refused entry, mentioning 'something about the police'. Giving evidence at the trial, Chief Inspector Moody told how the flat was under surveillance that very night and that Mr King reported Gardner and his associate to a passing police officer for attempting to 'gate-crash' their party. The officer asked what type of party it was, and Mr King invited him inside, triggering the raid. Moody recalled Cook's German associate carrying a 'hold-all and a wooden box which contained photographic equipment and photographs'. When questioned what the equipment was for, Cook's associate quipped, 'it is part of the gear we use. We are kinky, man. This is a kinky household'. At trial, Cook was asked: 'some of the photographs are of this flat and they are all obscene. Some have Mrs. King on them. You are obviously here to take photographs. Did you take these?'. Cook replied, 'look, I am a first-class photographer. The quality of these speak for themselves. Of course I did not take them, but I like that sort of thing'. When asked why he was there, Cook replied, 'For the party, of course. We are all a bit kinky'. All the defendants pleaded not guilty.

In the police interview, Cook recalls how he destroyed negatives when the police raided Cornwall Gardens, as he had been 'taking obscene photographs of the occupants'. He was unaware that police were watching the flat. Cook mentions how Moody acted as if they had not met before, questioning him in a 'normal manner'. After the raid, Hulpert channelled messages to Cook, informing him that Moody was not happy with Cook being at the address, but there was little chance of him going to prison. While awaiting committal, Cook continued business though claimed to have 'decreased' his production after being told to stop. Cook met with Moody before the trial, paying him £200 in cash to look after his 'interests at the Old Bailey' court. Moody agreed. At the end of 1967, Cook attended the trial with the other defendants at London's Central Criminal Court, now pleading guilty to conspiring with his German associate and other persons unknown to contravene the provision of the Obscene Publications Act 1959. He was fined £200, or the alternative of 6 months imprisonment; Cook paid the fine off in stages. With Moody no longer in charge of the Obscene Publications Squad, having moved to another department, Detective Inspector Leslie Alton took over and asked to meet with Cook. He told Cook that he was 'dissatisfied' with the money he was paying, wanting him to increase it to £50 per week, much like what he said to bookshop owner John Mason, as identified in chapter one. Cook told

Alton that 'business wasn't that good' and negotiated a payment of £30 per week to be handed to Hulpert.

Like the other roller makers discussed in this chapter, Cook's output is difficult to identify. According to pornographer Mike Freeman, Cook 'was brilliant, but infrequent'. Cook seems to corroborate this, telling the police he produced 'on average about 50 films a month as well as photographs'. This would not have been 50 individual titles per month, but 50 copies of a roller, possibly indicating the challenges Cook faced when duplicating his films. Freeman remembers Cook's early rollers being presented in a generic cardboard box with a photograph on the front with no other identifying features, similar to ones pictured in Figure 2.5. Hebditch and Anning (1988: 213) suggest that Cook, who they incorrectly name Ivor Cooke, made '*Pussy Galore, First Audition, End of Term* and *100% Lust*', but frustratingly provide no further evidence to indicate how they linked Cook to these films. It seems that this linkage of Cook to these films has led to authors associating Cook with Britain's most successful roller brand Climax Films, making the identification of his films even more challenging. Hebditch and Anning's (1988: 213) connection of Cook to the film *100% Lust* is significant (see Figure 2.6). They state that the film is rumoured

FIGURE 2.6: *100% Lust* (1966) released by Climax Films. Author's personal collection. Faces obscured to protect the identity of performers.

to star Christine Keeler of the Profumo Affair in a hardcore scene, an allegation repeated by Flint (1999), Thompson (2007) and McGillivray (2017).[22]

Another Climax Films title – *Randy* (1965–66) – was also marketed as starring Keeler. This is evidenced in a listing found in a 1967 German mail-order catalogue selling rollers, postcards and typescripts (see Figure 2.7). A collector shared an 8mm film that features a topless photograph of Keeler on the front as well as her name; it is not clear what the content of this film is (see Figure 2.8).[23] As Di Lauro and Rabkin (1976) recognize, many early stags purport to star Hollywood actresses or other celebrities, but these are usually an exploitation marketing technique to incite rumour and sell the film. For instance, the stag *The Personal Touch* (n.d.) is rumored to star Hollywood actress and singer Barbra Streisand (Thompson 2007: 176). In actuality, this was a British woman who regularly performed in Climax Films' rollers, such as *Auto Sex* (1968). Evidently, this ploy worked with *100% Lust*, as Mike Freeman recalled it being one of the most popular rollers sold in Soho's bookshops. Whoever made *100% Lust* attempted to obscure the performer's face as much as possible, trying to capitalize on a very slight likeness to Keeler. The performer may not be Keeler, but her linkage to this film further strengthens Mort's (2010: 24) claim that Keeler and the Profumo affair brought global attention to 'sexual London'. As I show in the coming section, it was also an important reference point for British pornographers like Cook.

## From Soho to Copenhagen

Although I cannot validate Hebditch and Anning's (1988: 213) assertation that Cook made *100% Lust*, I found that he did export postcards claiming to feature Keeler to Denmark. This is well documented by the Danish press. When exploring the travels of Italian pornography entrepreneur Lasse Braun, Larsson discusses how 'opportunistic transnationalism' was a dominant feature of his enterprise. Larsson (2018: 158) identifies how Braun regularly moved geographic locations and based his operation in countries that offered certain economic advantages, such as a more permissive legal framework towards pornography, or the means to professionally process and print. This might also be understood as yet another instance of 'evasive entrepreneurship', with Braun seeking to find ways circumvent laws in order to operate with little interference and maximize profits. In contrast, Cook's use of transnational networks was not to improve his means of production, but to develop his business and generate greater profits. Examining Cook's transnational enterprise demonstrates how British pornography entrepreneurs played a key part in expanding the alternative economy beyond Soho and building relationships with international pornographers.

On 22 December 1966, the *Berlingske Tidende* reported that a 39-year-old Englishman named Baron had been arrested in Copenhagen after threatening an

# SUPER PORNO FILM

**1026 UNEXPECTED GUESTS, 60 m, black/white, 8 mm.**
Preis DM 250.—. Price $ 70.—. Sv. Kr. trehundra.
Personen: 2 Mädchen + 2 Männer. Number of persons: 2 girls + 2 men.

Ein Ehepaar besucht ein anderes Ehepaar und sieht, dass die Wirtsleute im Schlafzimmer Beischlaf haben. Hierüber werden sie so aufgeregt, dass sie auch selbst anfangen. Später wechseln sie Partner und verschiedene Kombinationen werden versucht, bis sie alle vier gleichzeitig Auslösung bekommen.
A married couple pays a visit to another couple and discovers that their hosts are busy having intercourse in their bedroom. The visitors become so excited that they themselves start straight away. Later on they change partners and various combinations are tried out until all of them at the same time reach sexual orgasm.

**1037 THE WHORE, 40 m, black/white, 8 mm.**
Preis DM 250.—. Price $ 70.—. Sv. Kr. trehundra.
Personen: 1 Mädchen + 1 Mann. Number of persons: 1 girl + 1 man.

Eine Dirne versucht, ein wenig Geld für sich zu behalten. Der Zuhälter wird rasend, legt sie über das Knie und zieht ihre Hosen herunter. Danach prügelt er das Mädchen mit der Hand und mit einem Rohr durch. Schliesslich öffnet er in seiner Erregung seine Hosen und lässt seinem Samen über ihr Gesicht und Busen spritzen.
A whore tries, to keep some of the money herself. The pimp becomes furious, puts her over his knees and pulls down her pants. Thereafter he beats her up with the hand as well as with rattan. At last he opens up his trousers, and in excitement over the punishment he lets his sperm squirt over her face and breasts.

**1029 PHANTOM FUCKERS, 60 m, black/white, 8 mm.**
Preis DM 250.—. Price $ 70.—. Sv. Kr. trehundra.
Personen: 3 Mädchen + 2 Männer. Number of persons: 3 girls + 2 men.

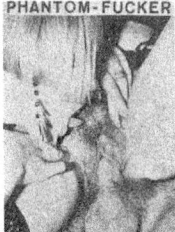

Drei Mädchen sitzen auf einem Sofa, als zwei maskierte Männer auftauchen und sie dazu zwingen, sich zu entkleiden und vor dem Sofa niederzuknien. Danach werden sie gepeitscht und dazu gezwungen, den einen Mann zu lecken und mit ihm Beischlaf zu haben. Sie müssen seinen Samen auflecken und von einem Glas mit Urin trinken. Ein Film, der Erotik unter Zwang zeigt.
Tree girls are sitting on a sofa, when two masked men force their way to the girls, force them to undress and kneel on the sofa. After the girls have obeyed them, the men begin to beat up the girls and force them to suck the one man and have intercourse with him. They are then forced to lick up his sperm and to drink a glass of his urine. A film, which really shows sexual sadism.

**1030 RANDY, 60 m, black/white, 8 mm.**
Preis DM 250.—. Price $ 70.—. Sv. Kr. trehundra.
Personen: 1 Mädchen + 1 Mann. Number of persons: 1 girl + 1 man.

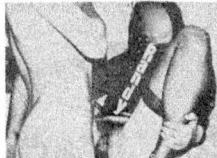

Ein junges Paar (das Mädchen ist das vielbesprochene englische Fotomodell,' Christine Keeler) zeigt einen sehr avancierten Beischlaf unter neuen und spannenden Winkeln. Der junge Mann leckt sorgfältig die Geschlechtsteile des Mädchens und steckt gleichzeitig seinen Finger in Anus des Mädchens.
A young couple, of which the girl is the very famous English model, Christine Keeler, shows a very advanced intercourse in new and exciting angles. The young man carefully sucks the girl's sex and inserts at the same time his finger in her anus.

FIGURE 2.7: Advert for *Randy* (1966–67) from a Swedish mail-order company – Assman Productions – that refers to Christine Keeler. Author's personal collection.

FIGURE 2.8: Unbranded 'Christine Keeler' 8mm film, likely to be of US origin and not Christine Keeler. Courtesy of 'Mal Mallister'.

Antiquarian bookshop owner named Jensen with violence.[24] The Danish police were investigating whether a 'criminal syndicate in London' had sent Baron to demand money from the bookshop, though Baron denied these claims. Jensen met an 'English photographer' in 1965 offering 'lewd films and photos' with some featuring Christine Keeler for 36,000 Danish Kroner (DKK). Again, the mention of Keeler identifies her as an internationally renowned figure whose reputation was exploited by British pornographers such as Cook. It is plausible that Cook mentioned Keeler's name to increase the price of his products, with Jensen paying the photographer DKK20,000.[25] Acting on behalf of the photographer, Baron visited Jensen to collect £1300, telling Jensen that he was part of 'a criminal syndicate in London'. When Jensen told Baron that he did not have the money, Baron threatened to cut his face with a razor blade and bomb the shop and his ex-wife's apartment with dynamite. Baron warned him that three other men from the syndicate would carry out these threats. When in court, Baron denied acting on behalf of a criminal organization and claimed to be collecting the money on behalf of 'a good friend'. He admitted that his threats were a lie and an attempt to scare Jensen into paying his debts.

On the same day, the story made the front page of the *Demokraten* and named Baron's 'good friend'. It tells of Baron crying in the dock, wanting to be released so that he can go back to his family in Birmingham in time for Christmas after pleading guilty to a charge relating to 'threats of violence of a particularly dangerous nature'. In court, Baron admitted to collecting the DKK20,000 for 'an English photographer named Ivor Cook'. During the hearing, the prosecutor gave additional background information relating to the case. In 1965, Jensen became acquainted with a man from England named 'Walter' who sold pornography on behalf of British pornographers. 'Walter' was later arrested by the police, imprisoned for twenty days and then deported. Further details on this matter can be found in a 19 May 1966 article from *Berlingske Tidende*, which reported that a 44-year-old German was arrested at his hotel, following an 'anonymous report'.

After the police found '180 pornographic images and movies in his luggage', the man admitted to regularly distributing the materials in Denmark and Sweden, but denied any wrongdoing. Another purpose of his travels was to build relationships between the producers of magazines in Scandinavia and bookshops in Britain. The article states that materials found were produced in Britain and the police believed he was conducting 'extensive international trade'. In court, Walter denied that his trade was illegal. Going back to the article in *Demokraten*, it identifies that Walter put Jensen in contact with Ivor Cook, who was known for producing 'porn films and pictures of high quality'. Cook visited Copenhagen in the spring with content for Jensen to purchase, but Jensen struggled to obtain the large amount of money Cook requested, owing DKK16,000. Jensen struggled to sell Cook's pictures, as 'another English company' sold pornography to other bookshops at lower prices.

Instead of payment, Cook asked Jensen if he could arrange an abortion for his fourteen-year-old daughter, who had 'become pregnant during a party'. This is intriguing as I have found no evidence that Cook had a daughter, only a son – might this have been arranged on behalf of a friend, or perhaps an underage performer in one of his films? Jensen hosted the girl, who disobeyed him and purchased items on credit that he later paid for. Jensen believed this reduced his debt from DKK16,000 to DKK 11,000. However, Cook demanded DKK20,000 as he was 'in need' of the money, hence why Baron was sent to collect the debt. Given the timeline, it is likely that Cook required money when he was arrested during the Cornwall Gardens raid. Cook had paid Moody £200 to help with his trial, but was asked to decrease production. This might suggest why Baron was sent to Denmark to extort the money.

More significant is the involvement of the mysterious German named 'Walter', exporting Cook's films and photographs to Denmark.[26] His full name was Walter Bartkowski, also known by his pseudonym – Charlie Brown. A German-Polish prisoner-of-war during the Second World War, Bartkowski remained in Britain, working as a steward on cross channel ferries operating between Dover and Calais.

He became Soho's 'top porn smuggler', distributing 'slides [transparency photographs], picture sets and 8mm black and white films' on their behalf, giving access to a larger market (Hebditch and Anning 1988: 212–13). It is alleged that six of Cook's rollers were purchased by two Danish brothers Jens and Peter Theander via Bartkowski and sold in their bookstore 'Rådhusantikvariatet', located on Studiestræde 17, in Copenhagen, Denmark (see Figure 2.9).[27] This shop opened in 1966, when section 234 of the Danish Criminal Code criminalized the distribution

FIGURE 2.9: Business card for the Theanders' Bookshop. Author's personal collection.

of pornography in Denmark (see chapter four). Like the bookshops in Soho, shop windows displayed innocuous material, with harder products available under-the-counter (Hebditch and Anning 1988: 54). I speak more about the activities of the Theander brothers and the Danish context for British pornography later in this book, as well as Bartkowski's involvement in the trade.[28]

## Blue Scene Films

Identifying Cook's rollers is difficult as they had small print runs and no branding. The Danish case does show that Cook was using Christine Keeler's notoriety to sell his films and photographs, making it possible that he was involved in the production of *100% Lust* and *Randy*, which were both promoted as films starring Keeler. I suspect that Cook eventually branded his films in 1969 under the label Blue Scene Films, re-releasing his older rollers as well as new films that he made in Scandinavia, where he could legally process them. Blue Scene Films differs to other roller labels. Its catalogue of rollers, of which I have been able to identify 42 different titles (see the labelography is Appendix A for further detail) re-releases films made in London between 1964 and 1969 alongside new content filmed in Sweden from 1969 to 1972. To further confuse matters, the packaging for Blue Scene Films includes the text 'produced in Denmark'. Therefore, the person, or persons, behind Blue Scene Films was involved in the British pornography trade from 1964 onwards, making Cook a plausible candidate. The Adult Loop Database tenuously associates the label with pornographer John Lindsay due to the film *Fisherman's Luck* (1965–67) being filmed outdoors, like many of his other films. However, *Fisherman's Luck* pre-dates Lindsay's involvement in the trade, which I discuss in Chapter 5.

*Fisherman's Luck* was likely produced between 1965 and 1967, with the Kinsey Institute specifically dating it to 1966. I located a copy of the film on 16mm, as well its later 8mm re-release on Blue Scene (see Figure 2.10). Like stags, some early rollers were printed on 16mm as well as 8mm, catering towards the smaller 16mm market and perhaps for showing at blue movie shows. These had very small print runs and now rarely surface. According to Brian Pritchard, 16mm films were easier to pirate than 8mm, which might explain why so few were printed on this gauge. An *Amateur Cine World* article from 18 November 1965 echoes this. It tells of how prolific glamour film producer, and occasional maker of hardcore pornography, George Harrison Marks stopped printing his glamour films on 16mm after discovering that 'hundreds of pirated 8mm reduction prints were being made from them and sold in various parts of the world' without his knowledge. Yet 16mm prints are immensely valuable as they have a higher resolution than 8mm, especially when digitally scanned at 4k resolution, revealing greater detail in the frame and offering potential clues to their origins.

FIGURE 2.10: Blue Scene Films' release of *Fisherman's Luck* (1965–67). Author's personal collection. The female performer's face has been obscured to protect her identity.

*Fisherman's Luck's* title card, as shown in Figure 2.11, is distinctive and differs from others I have viewed. The film is set in a rural area close to a lake or a river. It starts with a young woman wearing a pinafore dress strolling through the woods. She walks past a man wearing a garish paisley shirt, possibly dating the film to 1966 or even 1967. He is fishing. As he casts off, the hook catches her dress. He unhooks her, and she sits to next him, sharing a cigarette while he continues to fish. After some close-up eye contact to signify their intimate connection, they both kiss, the camera focusing on the man's lips as he moves towards the woman. They stand up and the camera follows them as they walk towards a tree – they kiss as she leans back on the tree, his hands attempting to go further than she wants, gently pushing him away. It cuts again to the couple walking hand-in-hand to a secluded area in the bushes. The woman lays down, and the man repeatedly attempts to seduce her until she gives in to his advances. Keeping their clothes on, he takes out his penis through his fly, lifts her dress, removes her underwear and enters her, cutting to a close-up of the penetration. Now it cuts to the woman on top, the camera showing close-ups from the front and the back. It now seems to present a close-up of doggy style before cutting to a close-up of the woman's face, looking bored and uninterested. They then move back to the tree before going

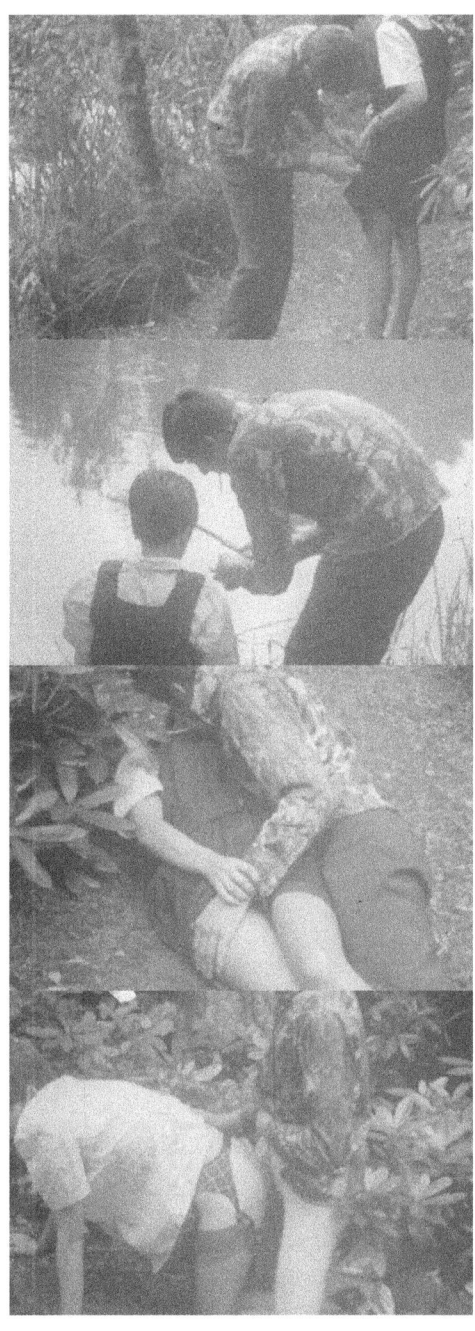

FIGURE 2.11: Screenshots from 16mm print of *Fisherman's Luck* (1965–67). Author's personal collection. The female performer's face has been obscured to protect her identity.

through a similar routine of sexual positions, finishing again with doggy style and the man ejaculating away from the body. The roller cuts to a long shot as the couple kiss and walk out into the open, again hand-in-hand. The film ends.

*Fisherman's Luck* is a slightly disjointed film, possibly due to its outdoor location and the threat of a passerby discovering its production. Shooting sex in these conditions also looks to have been a challenge. The producer relies on the use of close-ups to show penetration, which is often obscured by the performers' clothing. Still, the film shows skill, using careful editing to construct a narrative.[29] The Kinsey Institute link the film to another early roller titled *Part-Time Job* (1962–63), as it may also feature the female performer wearing the same pinafore dress. Like *Fisherman's Luck*, *The Part-Time Job* shows ambition. The exposition of *The Part-Time Job* is similar to that found in glamour films and takes its lead from mainstream, narrative filmmaking. It involves a woman, later named as Valerie, looking in the window of a shop for a part-time job. The name Valerie is a possible reference to Valerie Singleton, a presenter on the popular BBC children's television show *Blue Peter* from 1962 to 1972 who sported a similar haircut. Unlike other rollers, *The Part-Time Job* uses fade-ins and outs, showing proficiency with editing. Frustratingly, there is plenty of exterior footage and a shot of the male performer reading a copy of the *Evening Standard*, but the poor quality of the digital file makes it impossible to decipher these significant clues that might help to identify when it was made. *The Part-Time Job* also uses inter-titles, like those used in silent films, to carry the narrative; these are handwritten on a chalkboard.

Listed in a mail-order catalogue offering other Blue Scene Films titles (see Figure 2.12),[30] *The Part-Time Job* is distinctive for its professionalism, particularly in its attempt to tell a story. Going back to *Fisherman's Luck*, the male can be identified as 'Big' John English. The well-endowed English, as the nickname 'Big' implies, appears in numerous rollers from different labels, spanning the branded and unbranded periods. In the late 1970s to the early 1980s, he became a reliable 'stud' for German and Scandinavian producers such as Mike Hunter (aka Gerd Wasmund) and Color Climax.[31] English also appears in a magazine titled *Seduction Susan*, published in 1970 by the Theander Brothers' company Color Climax, alongside a thin male who regularly performed in many Blue Scene Films titles. The photographs in this issue were shot in a flat that has a Victorian appearance, featuring a piano, mahogany furniture, wooden panels and a chaise longue, which the performers have sex on. This significant location is also used in several rollers originating from the mid to late 1960s that Blue Scene Films later re-released, suggesting a potential link between Blue Scene Films and the Theander Brothers.

Like *Fisherman's Luck*, *Lucky Girl* (1968) is filmed around the same period (see Figure 2.13). It is located in the same Victorian flat as *Seduction Susan* and features 'Big' John English and the thin male. Rabkin and Di Lauro (1976: 86)

FIGURE 2.12: Blue Scene Films mail-order catalogue. Courtesy of 'Phillip Black'. Faces obscured to protect the identity of performers.

FIGURE 2.13: Blue Scene Films' release of *Lucky Girl* (1968). The film was likely made and released as an unbranded roller in 1968 and re-released by Blue Scene Films between 1969 and 1972. Author's personal collection. Faces obscured to protect the identity of performers.

believe this location to be either a stately home or an expensively furnished flat. It is more likely that this location was someone's home that doubled as a studio for hire. The photographs from *Seduction Susan* imply that the flat is close to Earl's Court underground station, and therefore may be located around Chelsea/Kensington. Curiously, underneath Cook's advert for his studio in the *British Journal of Photography* is another offering the services of a 'well equipped Kensington Studio for hire, £11 a day, £6 half-day, Victorian room setting also for hire'. As magazines tended to list adverts by the same advertiser directly underneath each other, could it be that this is Cook offering the same studio used to film his rollers? As indicated by Figure 2.14, other rollers re-released by Blue Scene Films that also use this location are *Fanny* (1967), *Incestral Home* (1967), *More Suds and Sex* (1967),[32] *Invitation Sex* (1969), *What the Butler Saw and Did* (1965–67), *Turkish Delight* (1967–68) and *Duet* (1968).[33] The unbranded rollers *Music Masters I* (1965–67) and *Music Masters II* (1965–67) do not appear to have been re-released by Blue Scene Films, but make use of the same flat and male performer.[34]

By 1969, Blue Scene Films becomes a label and releases films shot in Sweden. *Manhunt* (1969–72) is a colour roller filmed in Sweden, as identified by Swedish road signs (see Figure 2.15). A man, the thin performer from the rollers shot in

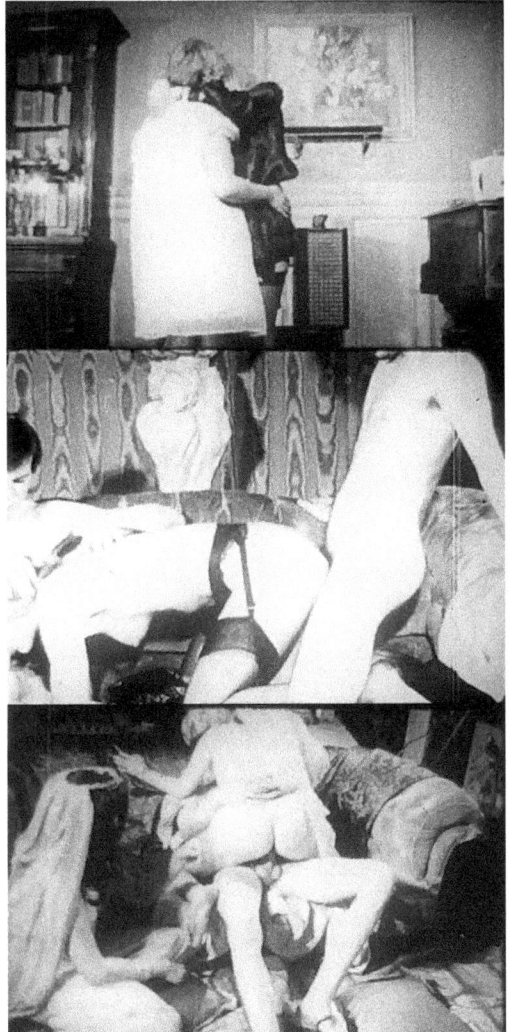

FIGURE 2.14: Scenes from rollers shot in the Victorian style flat: *Duet* (1968), *Turkish Delight* (1967–68) and *Lucky Girl* (1968). Author's personal collection. Faces obscured to protect the identity of performers.

the Victorian flat, stops his car to help two stranded female motorists. He looks at the car's engine, is knocked unconscious by one of the women, pushed into the backseat of their car, drugged and taken to their flat. To wake him up, one of the women urinates on him, and they end up having group sex. At the end, the man is put back in the car at gunpoint and dropped off, dazed and confused. Outdoor settings used in other Blue Scene Films rollers, including *The Hunter* (1969), *Free*

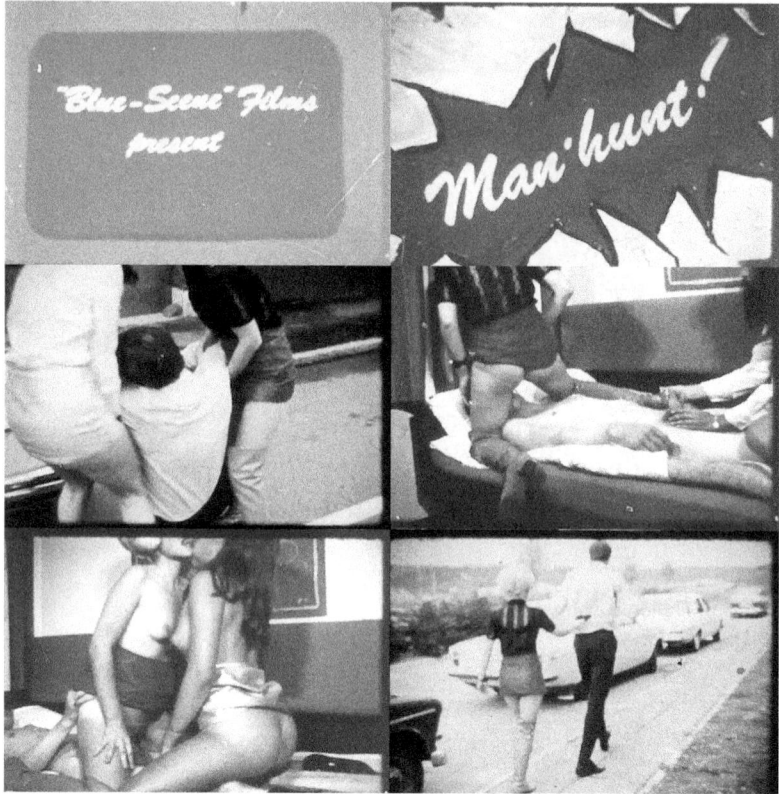

FIGURE 2.15: Screenshots from Blue Scene Films' *Manhunt* (1969). Author's personal collection. Faces obscured to protect the identity of performers.

*Sample* (1969) and *After Sales Service* (1969) also reference Sweden, or possibly Denmark, hinting at a transnational filmmaker crossing borders to shoot films and potentially process them before returning to Britain.

It cannot conclusively be determined that Ivor Cook was the person behind Blue Scene Films, but the evidence I have found points towards his involvement for four reasons. First, the label released older British rollers and new productions, suggesting someone involved in the business for an extended period. As I have shown, Cook began shooting rollers at the turn of the 1960s and in 1962, the Metropolitan Police found six films in his possession, leading them to declare that Cook was 'actively involved in the processing and selling of obscene films'. Second, there is the Victorian flat, which appears in a series of rollers re-released as Blue Scene Films titles and links, albeit weakly, to Cook through an advert placed in the *British Journal of Photography*. Third, I discovered a wealth of colour Soho

Postcards, many of which were taken at the Victorian flat and during the making of rollers re-released by Blue Scene Films, such as *Turkish Delight*. With Cook known for being a pioneer of colour Soho Postcards, it is likely that he produced these photographs.

Finally, the relationship with Sweden and Denmark is significant. I have discussed how Cook visited Denmark to sell his rollers and postcards, as well as having them distributed via Walter Bartkowski. Given these links, Cook could have been travelling to make films in Sweden and Denmark, following Denmark's legalization of pornography. Here he would have been able to process the films after making them. Additionally, there is a link to the Theander brothers and Color Climax, with Cook allegedly selling rollers and Soho Postcards to them in 1967. Did Cook supply the photographs used in the magazine *Seduction Susan*, which were also circulated as Soho Postcards?[35] The magazine credits Jens Theander, but the brothers regularly re-published old Soho Postcards in issues of *Color Climax*, perhaps as an acknowledgement to the British pornography they once sold in their Copenhagen bookstore before their Color Climax Corporation became a successful 'international commodity' (Heffernan 2016: 130).

## Conclusion

According to newspaper reports, there were 61 convictions for 'offences relating to obscene film in London' in 1965 (*Belfast Telegraph*, 19 November 1965). The *Daily Telegraph* (11 November 1965) clarifies that this figure related to blue movie shows rather than arrests for the selling of rollers, suggesting that the production and distribution of hardcore films was still very much a marginal economic activity at this time. As this chapter has shown, the challenges of printing and developing rollers using amateur or semi-professional means limited their output. Therefore, between 1960 and 1965, rollers appear to have been in short supply. In the following chapter, I show how other entrepreneurs built on the work of the early innovators discussed here, finding ways to increase their productivity and generate higher profits. The purpose of this chapter has been to consider the technological context for roller making, exploring how entrepreneurs exploited an increasing public demand for pornography by using the popular 8mm format to distribute films. I have shown how amateur and semi-professional filmmaking technologies were used to shoot, process and duplicate rollers. I suggested that entrepreneurs drew on amateur film cultures, particularly filmmaking handbooks and magazines, to guide their practice and avoid using professional film laboratories.

The early roller entrepreneurs discussed in this chapter disrupted the alternative economy, creating a new market for hardcore films alongside other commodities such as photographs and typescripts. In this case of Cook and Taylor, both had backgrounds in professional photography, easing their transition to filmmaking. As later chapters show, Cook's reputation for professionalism led to him becoming a fixer or mentor for other roller producers, facilitating their practice. Furthermore, Cook's background reveals how entrepreneurs within the alternative economy developed transnational networks in order to bring their products to international markets. Cook was evidently attempting to use swinging London's international reputation to sell his products, referencing the Profumo Affair and Christine Keeler. This suggests that British pornography during the 1960s was becoming an internationally saleable commodity, prior to the growth of Denmark's own business in the late 1960s. The following chapters explore how the alternative economy of hardcore pornography in Britain expanded. Through the support of the Obscene Publication Squad's licensing system, rollers moved from being a limited commodity to becoming a dominant product in the alternative economy.

But what of Ivor Cook? After his obscenity arrest in 1966, Cook seems to have evaded the attention of the police, benefiting from the licensing system. He worked within his means, maintaining a small-scale enterprise. Because of this, Cook left little trace of his business. Like many other British producers, Cook appears to have ceased making rollers around 1972 following the *Sunday People's* exposé of the alternative economy and the resulting crackdown on police corruption. In a police interview, he claimed that cheaper imports from Denmark put him out of business, though he is clearly an untrustworthy interviewee, changing his story over the course of three statements. Producer and performer Dave Wells, who Cook photographed in the early 1980s, informed me that he became the senior photographer for Berth Milton's *Private* who were responsible for publishing the first colour hardcore pornography magazine in Sweden, 1965 (Arnberg 2012). Cook's transnational networks and reputation as a professional photographer may have led to this appointment, further illustrating the international recognition his postcards and rollers received from other pornographers. Cook unexpectedly died of a heart attack on 5 September 1985, aged 58, leaving more questions than answers about his role in Britain's alternative economy of hardcore pornography.

# 3

## *Up, Up and Away*: Entrepreneurship in Britain's Expanding Roller Trade (1966–69)

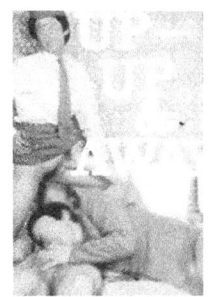

### *Introduction*

'Star's killing reveals blue film racket', reads the headline of an article in the 21 December 1969 edition of the *News of the World*. Pictured left is Michael Muldoon, who later changed his name to Michael Freeman, centre is his wife Sandra, and far right is Gerry Hawley. The article tells of how the athletically built Hawley regularly performed in Freeman's rollers and tried to take over Freeman's business. Freeman murdered Hawley in May 1969, dumping his heavily tattooed body in Epping Forest, Essex, which also happened to be the location used for some of his films. An associate of the notorious East End gangsters the Kray Twins, Hawley had '14 convictions for violence' and had met Freeman in Brixton prison, who was serving an 18-month prison sentence for conspiring to publish an obscene article, under section 2 of the Obscene Publications Act 1959. At the time of Hawley's murder, the *News of the World* article claims that Freeman was earning an average of more than £2000 a week from his pornography business, making 'sometimes 500 per cent profit' from his rollers. When Freeman's premises on Great Windmill Street, Soho, were searched, famed London Metropolitan Police officer Bert Wickstead discovered 120 canisters of film. On arrest, Freeman alleged that a man named Tony and his female associate were responsible for Hawley's murder. At the trial, Freeman admitted that he alone murdered Hawley, who was under the influence of the psychedelic drug lysergic acid diethylamide (LSD). Freeman was found guilty and given a life sentence. His wife Sandra and brother-in-law Kenneth

FIGURE 3.1: *Up, Up and Away* (1968). Image is taken from a Climax Films catalogue. Author's personal collection. Faces obscured to protect the identity of performers.

Eighteen, a partner in the business, were both found innocent of murder, but guilty of impeding the course of justice. The court placed Sandra on probation, and jailed Eighteen for three years.

'I stabbed him in self-defence, 89 times', said Mike Freeman, sitting in front of a camera in the garden of his house in an undisclosed location in Southern Italy while being filmed for the documentary I produced – *Hardcore Guaranteed* (Simon Fletcher 2019). 'What I've done basically with my life', he added, 'is made people experience pleasure. I've not killed millions of people [...] I've killed one person who was trying to kill me and my family'. Freeman claims to have been the 'porn king of Soho', selling postcards, typescripts and rollers to bookshops and exporting to Denmark, Sweden, Germany and the Netherlands. Whereas Ivor Cook kept a low profile, allowing him to stay working in the pornography business for around 25 years, Freeman's inability to work within the alternative economy's institutional framework resulted in his downfall. As this chapter shows, Freeman's ambitions and disregard for authority eventually led to a life sentence for murder, serving ten years in prison. Until his death, Freeman maintained that Hawley had been sent to assassinate him on behalf of the Obscene Publications Squad and that he murdered him out of self-defence. Admittedly, this sounds far-fetched but, as I show, Freeman's unwillingness to conform to the conditions of the licence offered by the Obscene Publications Squad ultimately made him a liability, his actions threatening to expose the alternative economy and specifically the police corruption that enabled it to operate.

In the 1960s, Freeman's participation in the economy was limited to four years, as he was in and out of prison. Yet, in this brief period, he had a considerable impact on the trade, not only in his production of rollers, but also through his bringing of Evan 'Big Jeff' Phillips into the business. With Freeman in prison for most of 1966, Phillips became the first person to brand rollers, introducing the label Climax Films. This led to a surge of competing brands, as the roller trade grew in the latter half of the 1960s. In this chapter, I show how the activities of Freeman and Phillips offer a more detailed understanding of entrepreneurship with Britain's alternative economy of hardcore pornography. I consider how Freeman's and Phillips' opportunistic approach to enterprise contrasted, with Freeman regularly drawing on his criminality and Phillips utilizing his experience as a small business owner. I argue that both brought a commercial mindset to the production and distribution of hardcore pornographic films, but this was driven by the Obscene Publications Squad's licensing system.

### 'A born entrepreneur'

Michael Freeman, pictured in Figure 3.2, was born Michael John Muldoon – colloquially known as Mick or Micky – in Vauxhall, London, on 10 February

FIGURE 3.2: Image of Michael Freeman from the early 1970s. Courtesy of Mike Freeman.

1939 and died in June 2021. Prior to his death, Freeman released a series of self-published autobiographies titled *I Pornographer* and appeared in the documentary *Hardcore Guaranteed* (Simon Fletcher 2019). Between 3 and 6 April 2016, Freeman gave a detailed interview, discussing his career in and out of the pornography business. However, significant gaps remain, particularly during the early years when he was making rollers. His ex-wife Sandra's self-published book *Knock Down Ginger* (Joyce 2011) gives more detail on Freeman's early activities,[1] while newspaper articles concerning Freeman's arrests and Central Criminal Court records relating to Hawley's murder also help to fill in some of the gaps.[2]

In the 60 files that document the Director of Public Prosecution's investigation into the Obscene Publications Squad's corrupt activities there are numerous police statements provided by those involved in Britain's pornography business. Often presented alongside these are their criminal records, which highlight that many engaged in unlawful activities prior to joining the alterative economy. The Obscene Publications Squad's licensing system legitimized criminal activity, permitting licensees to engage in illicit practices with minimal threat of arrest. Because of this, the alternative economy was a sort of 'safe space' for criminals, blurring the boundaries between criminality and legitimacy. Freeman's enterprise demonstrates how criminals found a home in Britain's pornography business, but also shows how they were controlled by the police to ensure that the economy was protected and sustained. Therefore, pornographers were required to operate within the institutional framework I described in Chapter 1, or face removal from it, as Freeman's story reveals.

Freeman's criminality manifested at a young age. At school, he led a gang and became associated with the Teddy Boy subculture. According to Jefferson (1993: 67), Teddy Boys were a 'response to the post-war upheaval and destruction of the socially cohesive force of the extended kinship network. Thus the group life and intense loyalty of the Teds can be seen as a reaffirmation of traditional slum working-class values'. Class is significant to Freeman. In the interview, he often referred to his working-class origins as an essential part of his make-up, but also his motivation for success and money. Freeman was brought up in Brixton's Guinness Trust Buildings, a philanthropic housing project providing accommodation to the working class at low interest rates (Malpass 1999). The Teddy Boys were also known for defending their territory, engaging in acts of violence, and Freeman was no stranger to confrontation. He recalled stealing items, such as food from a local bakery or boxes from unattended trucks, to sell at school. As Hobbs (1988: 136–38) notes in his research on East End criminal entrepreneurship, petty criminality amongst London youths appeared at an early age, allowing for the acquisition of a 'business acumen' that served them in later life. Freeman describes himself as a 'born entrepreneur', believing that his experiences as a youth in Brixton, London, prepared him for the pornography business: 'another thing I used to do was go down Brixton market and drag the fruit barrows back to the sheds [...] and get sixpence each [...] I always had money [...] as well as sneaking into shops and stealing'. After leaving school, he briefly worked as an apprentice with a ladies' hairdresser and then became a copy editor for a London newspaper, which introduced him to publishing.

Freeman quickly fell afoul of the law, leading to an ongoing mistrust of the police and authority that jeopardized his involvement in Britain's pornography business. He first clashed with the police when he was 14 or 15 years old, being charged with possessing a firearm and then placed in a remand home. He also spent time in a French prison, though it is not clear why. Freeman's criminal record details numerous petty crimes. Further insight into his criminality is offered by his wife Sandra in her autobiography. Her 'mad ride' with Freeman, as she describes it, started in 1960, when they first met in Brixton. Spending a lot of time on her own, she was quickly drawn to the attention Freeman offered, becoming her 'saviour' and 'protector'. By 1961, Sandra tells how they made money 'illegally', specializing in stealing cars and swapping licence plates:

> Mick knew an expert who made dodgy plates. He knew the right combination of letters and numbers for the year of the car – so that it didn't look suspicious – if old numbers and letters were stuck on it the police would spot it for a ringer straightaway.

They also stole car radios, selling them for £7 to £15. Police arrested Freeman for this in November 1960 and disqualified him from driving for five years; not that this stopped him from stealing and driving cars. Sandra also talks about how Freeman would 'blag', creating distractions and robbing people of their money. He was also 'violent', stabbing a lorry driver in the thigh, removing him from the cab and beating him with a crowbar. As Gottschalk (2009: 22–23) suggests, participation in gangs and trouble are two early formative stages of the criminal entrepreneur. Freeman's early criminality informed his later entrepreneurship. Here he developed attributes that enabled him to succeed in Britain's pornography business, as well as building a vendetta against the police that impeded his ability to sustain a career.

Sandra also makes mention of Freeman's entrepreneurial spirit, reminiscing about when Freeman attempted to 'go straight'. One of his business ideas was to buy cheap yellow dusters from a warehouse specializing in soiled goods and dip each one in wax polish to produce 'impregnated dusters'. Freeman believed people would buy a two-in-one product that simply required heating the sheet to activate the wax. He packed them in a labelled bag that read 'This Product has been Made and Packed by the Blind and Disabled', pretending that he sold them on their behalf, pitching to customers that they were 'all the rage' in America. As it was December 1962, they also sold calendars. Sandra alleges to making around '£400' from the sale of the impregnated dusters and calendars. Freeman setting his mother's kitchen on fire while making the dusters put an end to this venture and they returned to stealing car radios. In many ways, Sandra's description of Freeman's enterprise mirrors that of the 'spivs' who operated against the backdrop of austerity in Britain's post-war black market. Roodhouse (2013: 243) defines the spiv as 'a penny capitalist flogging goods of unknown origin to a public hungry for controlled goods', who first came to widespread attention in autumn 1945 and was represented in popular media as the 'working-class anti-hero' (194). Freeman's experience of hawking goods later proved useful when selling his pornography to Soho's bookstores.

After learning that Sandra was pregnant, he attempted to become a member of the Royal Fusiliers, a regiment of the British Army. Sandra believes Freeman joined the army to lay low, after carrying out a job for members of London's criminal underworld; she does not elaborate on what crime he committed. Freeman acquired the birth certificate of an associate and joined the Royal Fusiliers under a false name, seeking to distance himself from his criminal record. Stationed in Germany and concerned about his true identity being discovered, Freeman went AWOL, returning to Clapham, London, in 1964. Sandra was 17 years old when she gave birth to their first child. Around this time, Freeman entered the pornography business. One of Freeman's hobbies was drawing. He claimed to have attended evening classes at St Martin's Art School in Charing Cross. Being sexually curious from a young age, Freeman sketched erotic drawings, usually pictures of naked women, and sold to schoolmates. While at St Martin's, Freeman was approached by an anonymous man who:

> said 'I like your drawings'. I said 'it's pornography', and he said, 'I don't care, I'm not a prude'. To cut a long story short, we ended up going to a guy named Tommy in Frith Street; he had a little book shop. He looked through them [...] 'okay, I'll give you a pound each for them', I think it was. There was about ten drawings there. To me, £10 was a lot of money in the sixties [...] I said, 'do you want anymore' and he said 'yes', so I went back and did another 50 or so [laughing] [...] took them back, and he brought them.

This again highlights the demand for domestically produced pornography in the early 1960s, with drawings being an attractive commodity for the bookshops of Soho to sell. £10 in 1964 was just over half the average wage for an adult male. While in the bookshops, Freeman noticed the Soho Postcards:

> I saw them hanging up in a little packet [...] he [the bookshop chair] was taking photographs and shrink wrapping them or putting them in a plastic bag and sellotaping them. He was selling them at five for a pound. From there, I decided to go into photographs and started doing them myself.

Unlike the entrepreneurs discussed in the previous chapter, who I suggested were innovators and disrupters, creating a new market in the alternative economy for pornographic films, Freeman is more of an opportunist. As Kirzner (1973) suggests, entrepreneurship is not always about innovating. For him, an entrepreneur is an 'opportunistic trader' who spots an opportunity to exploit (Smith 2009: 259). Contrasting with professional photographer Ivor Cook, Freeman had nothing more than a passing interest in photography until realizing that it was a skill he could exploit.

According to Sandra, the bookshop owner advised Freeman to photograph his erotic sketches and sell the reproductions. To learn the craft, Sandra remembers Freeman going to the library and hiring books about photography. He stole two cameras from a shop and acquired the necessary equipment for developing and printing photographs. A darkroom was built in the cupboard of their flat where Freeman produced prints of his erotic artwork, taking 50 prints of each set to sell to the Soho bookshops. Figure 3.3 shows the type of materials Freeman manufactured. One bookshop chair told Freeman that erotic drawings were a specialist market and did not sell quickly. Freeman responded by moving to manufacture Soho Postcards, believing the competition to be 'complete rubbish' and lacking

FIGURE 3.3: Examples of Soho Postcards depicting hand-drawn pornography. These are similar to the goods Freeman produced and sold to Soho's bookshops. Courtesy of 'Tony M'.

quality. To generate profits and pay for models, Mike convinced Sandra to appear in his first pictures, taking solo shots of her and them having sex.

For the first shoot, Freeman purchased items from a department store for Sandra to wear. She was 17. At that time, a nude image of a 17-year-old was legally acceptable, providing that it was not obscene, contrary to the Obscene Publications Act 1959. According to the Sexual Offences Act 1956, the age of consent was 16.[3] After developing the photographs, they 'selected thirty for six sample packets of five pictures in each packet'. Freeman remembers taking them to the Soho bookshops:

> The first day I went over to the West End [...] [I] had a bag full of these little photos. I didn't know whether they'd have them or not because I hadn't tried to sell anything. I even went into his shop [the Frith Street shop where he had sold his erotic artwork]. He brought them. 'Oh, you're doing them yourself now, are you?' he said. 'Okay, I'll have three sets', which was fifteen shillings. I went round all the shops and got this from everyone. So, when I went home, I had this big wad of money. To me, it was a fortune.

Whereas Freeman's other hustles failed, he quickly realized that he could make quick cash from producing pornography. As journalist and author Martin Tomkinson explained to me, the alternative economy of pornography was 'cash-rich, people will pay lots and lots of money [...] or you can make lots and lots of money, but it was an easy come, easy go type atmosphere'. Sandra tells of Freeman returning home from Soho, where '26 bookshops' ordered 36 packets. To meet these orders, Freeman calculated that he had to print 4680 postcards, realizing that an automated process was necessary to expand his enterprise.

Additionally, bookshops required fresh content to attract new purchases from customers. A friendship with a man named Tony developed, who expressed an interest in appearing alongside his wife for Freeman's postcards. He also asked Sandra to perform with Tony's wife. Although reluctant, Sandra 'knew that [she] would have to do what Mick wanted'. Freeman again assured her that this was a short-term solution until he could find and pay other models. In the November of 1964, Freeman went into business with Tony, renting the front room of his house and turning it into a makeshift laboratory. Freeman now needed to access materials. Taking the £100 earned from his drawings, Freeman cut a deal with the photography shop Ilford's. Presenting himself as a professional photographer, he paid the salesman an extra £25 for preferential treatment, setting up an account so he could get what he required. With the darkroom set up, Sandra describes a hectic scene of the two couples taking turns to work 24 hours a day to meet the orders placed. Freeman constructed a basic drying machine to help accelerate the process, again showing how do-it-yourself equipment was utilized. After fulfilling the orders, Freeman obtained a £600 developing and printing machine from the photography retailer Ilford's. Sandra recalls:

Mick had said to the bloke he knew there, pulling out a wad of cash. Stick that in your pocket. I am going downstairs to buy all my paper and chemicals. It will take me a couple of trips to the car, which is outside on the pavement. Make yourself scarce 'cos on one load I'm going to walk out with that machine. Make sure all the instructions and any bits I need are in the box. Don't say it's gone until later in the day when anyone could have taken it. You okay with that?' The bloke had agreed – why not?

Freeman had 'slipped him a oner [£100]', his persuasiveness saving £500. Henry (1978: 4) describes such informal economic exchange as 'fiddling'. These are 'perks, legitimate fringe benefits or entitlements that are 'allowed' to workers as a result of their being employed'. With this machine, the process became smoother and more manageable. Freeman had also taken sample copies of new postcards, featuring Sandra and Tony's wife 'Paula' performing together,[4] to show to the bookshop chairs, leading to more orders.

Sandra learned how to use the machine and became further involved in the production, taking a brief break from appearing in front of the camera. According to Sandra, Tony found another performer – a 14-year-old girl who allegedly 'became Mick's best model and worked for him for years'. Freeman's disregard for the age of consent shows how he regularly flouted the law in the blind pursuit for profit, selling the postcards across Soho. As I show later in this chapter, this eventually resulted in his arrest. They moved the laboratory to a rented house in Purley, South London, where Freeman installed a new dryer, further professionalizing the process. In the interview, Freeman described how he intended to produce a higher quality commodity than his competitors, making his work unique and, therefore, sought after. He also aspired to be a legitimate businessman, eventually registering a company named Nestville Photography with Companies House – intentionally choosing a bland, generic name to front his pornography enterprise. Sandra quickly discovered that Freeman performed with other female models, placing a strain on their relationship, particularly when she found she was pregnant with their second child. She also claims that Freeman became increasingly abusive, referring to 1965 as his 'anything goes' period, where profit became his sole motivation.

Freeman's early entrepreneurship offers a window into the types of characters that were drawn to the alternative economy. He shares similarities with 'Derek', who I discussed in Chapter 2, being attracted to the economic opportunities afforded by producing pornography and learning skills along the way. As I have shown, Freeman had no formal training in photography or filmmaking, only a hobby as an artist that he turned into an opportunity by selling drawings to Soho's bookshops. Although he was not a professional, Freeman repeatedly remarked on having professional aspirations, believing that the use of expensive equipment would make his enterprise more efficient as well as improving the physical quality of his products. It was in mid 1965 that Freeman began to think about reinvesting his profits into producing rollers. He discussed this prospect with his contact at Ilford's, but ended up recruiting Evan Phillips to assist him in making them.

## Big Jeff

On 19 November 1965, *The News* included an article with the headline 'THREE MEN IN COURT: *Schoolgirls' adventures in West End*'. The use of the word 'adventures' is somewhat misleading, given the nature of the case. In 1964, Scotland Yard had introduced Operation Innocents out of concern for young people being attracted to the bright lights of the West End and becoming involved in vice. This was a response to the unfortunately named Jack the Stripper case, also known as the Hammersmith Nude Murders – a series of six unsolved murders in London between 1964 and 1965 (Jarossi 2018). A number of the victims were reported as being sex workers, with one, Irene Lockwood, having an association with blue films (*Daily Express*, 11 April 1964). As some of the victims were said to have frequented Soho and the wider West End of London, the Metropolitan Police sent 'special squads into Soho to round up teenage schoolchildren wandering the streets and hanging around the dimly lit coffee bars and basement jazz clubs'. Operation Innocents was intended to stop children from being 'tempted into vice by the shady characters who infest Soho at night'. A Soho historian who goes by the name of 'Soho George' told me about what attracted him to Soho as a teenager in the early 1960s:

> It had a life of its own, you know. It had this smell because of all the different foods you could get there, and then there was a crackle of the neon lights. You couldn't help but be drawn to it.[5]

It is not clear whether Operation Innocents was impactful. However, the experience of the three 14-year-old schoolgirls who came to the West End from the West Country on 23 September 1965 suggests otherwise.

*The News* and the *Post Mercury Gazette* (3 December 1965) document the case. On 24 September, Freeman and Tony picked up the three schoolgirls from the Eros Statue at Piccadilly Circus, not far from Soho. They were asked if they would like to be paid to model for photographs, and offered £5 an hour. Having only £2 left between them, they agreed. The girls were taken to a photography studio where 'sexual offences took place and photographs were taken'. Freeman paid them another £15 to stay in a hotel. One of the girls claims that they were warned: 'if they went to the police he would see that the photographs were passed around their home town'. Two days later, Tony and another associate named Mick arranged to collect the girls from the same location to take more photographs. Again, they were paid £5. This time a 'private house' was used, but 'similar offences' took place: 'we ended up naked [...] and this time Tony had intercourse with me'. Another girl confirmed the story and told how she had intercourse with Mick while Freeman took photographs. The following morning, the police picked up the girls for undisclosed reasons.

On 6 October 1965, a raid on a bookshop in South London resulted in the seizure of 'thousands of obscene photographs'; some of these featured the three girls. On 8 October, police saw Freeman 'abandoning a large quantity of obscene photographs', resulting in a car chase. Freeman managed to escape capture, but abandoned his car, leaving 'many hundreds more photographs' in the boot. Again, some of these included the three girls. Detective Inspector Moody took control of the case, eventually leading to the arrests of Freeman, Tony, Mick and the owner of the private flat, who was charged with 'permitting the three girls to be in his apartment for the purpose of intercourse'. The others were charged with conspiracy to contravene the Obscene Publications Act 1959 and indecent assault. Tony and Mick were charged with unlawful intercourse with the 14-year-old girls under the Sexual Offences Act 1956.

Freeman appears to have excluded this event from his autobiography, but did recount it during the on-camera interview.

> I had a phone call from Fat Bill [a Soho bookshop owner] who told me that there were three girls on the game, and they wanted to do porn. They looked young, but not really young. The age [required by models] was 16. Actually, they were 14–15. I wanted to take the photos 'cause I knew how much money I could make from them. I got these girls, and I smudged them up [took their photos]. I didn't have sex with them [...] I took photographs of them. I didn't touch any of them. Tony, my friend did, he was banging away like a rabbit. I brought out these photos, and I was rich. The orders were enormous.

Freeman claims that the girls were in London as they had run away from the West Country, where they were in a 'home for being sexually aware at a young age'. Although problematic, this case is significant for several reasons. First, as Hobbs (1988) argues, it shows how criminal entrepreneurs justify their activities as enterprise. Freeman did not show any remorse for taking the pictures, repeatedly emphasizing the profits they generated for him. Second, it demonstrates how entrepreneurship is a morally ambiguous pursuit (Buckley and Casson 2001), and often wholly immoral. Finally, as I will now discuss, the incident gives an insight into the regulation of the alternative economy, and how the licensing system introduced by Obscene Publications Squad was intended to exclude those who might threaten its existence.

At this point in his career, Freeman operated without a licence from the Obscene Publications Squad. Freeman told how Stanley Lowe, the chair at Monty Rosen's Long Shop at 51a Old Compton Street, repeatedly warned him that he needed a licence to trade:

> Stanley said, 'look, Mike, you're earning now, you've got to pay Old Bill'. I said, 'fuck them bastards'. I hated the police, had hated them my whole life. I thought I'm earning money; what do I want to pay them for? I believed it [pornography] was going to be legalised [...] I was very political about the whole thing. I certainly wasn't going to pay the police, so they tried to get me after that.

Following the discovery of the photographs of the underaged girls, Freeman soon found that the majority of Soho's bookshops had blacklisted him. Shops were instructed by the Obscene Publications Squad to not purchase Freeman's goods, indicating how the licensing system was intended to remove undesirables from the trade to conserve the economy. In the Director of Public Prosecution files relating to the investigation of the Obscene Publications Squad, I found mention of the powerful bookshop owner John Mason reporting Freeman to his police contacts for taking and selling these pictures. It transpires that Mason acted as a moral guardian for the economy, refusing to sell child pornography or excessively violent pornography in his shops, perhaps further evidence of why he was referred to as 'God'. With Mason owning many shops and exerting such power, this greatly affected Freeman's ability to earn.[6] The 8 October 1965 car chase was the first of many instances where Freeman attempted to outwit the police, 'a merry dance', he gleefully called it. To get around his blacklisting, he employed a frontman named 'Big Jeff' to supply the bookshops.

Freeman said he met the notorious London gangster Reggie Kray during a previous stay in prison and was on friendly terms with him. In the early 1960s, the Krays were looking to move their operations from the East End of London to the West End, opening the El Morocco Club on Gerrard Street, next to Soho, in 1965. The club attracted celebrity attendees as well as being a meeting place for gangsters. Freeman says that he received an invite from Reggie Kray and, not wanting to disrespect him, visited the El Morocco with Sandra. The Krays were aware of Freeman's pornography business, and while at the club, Reggie introduced him to a man named Evan Phillips: 'Reggie said this guy is rich [...] runs the accommodation bureau in Shaftesbury Avenue; he gets houses and all that'.

Freeman and Phillips quickly struck up a friendship, coincidentally both having wives named Sandra, and then regularly saw each other socially. Evan John Phillips was born on 12 January 1942 in Hammersmith, London (see Figure 3.4). His parents were Welsh and, unlike Freeman, was from a middle-class background: 'He was a rich, young boy [...] he started working for me. We had a partnership'. Phillips was later arrested as part of the crackdown on the alternative economy. While in prison, he gave a detailed interview to police investigating corruption in the Obscene Publications Squad.[7] This 34-page interview summarizes Phillips' career as Britain's 'first blue film millionaire' (*Sunday People*, 6 February 1972). In this interview, he makes no mention of the Krays, but states that Freeman approached him around May 1965 when he was looking to rent a house. Phillips assumes that Freeman 'must have been impressed by my attitude to business', asking if he would be 'interested in reproducing films for him'. It seems odd to think that such an offer would be made so quickly without Freeman knowing Phillips. Therefore, it is plausible that Reggie Kray introduced them, but Phillips chose not to name the Krays in his statement.

Phillips knew nothing about photography or pornography at this time but sensed a business opportunity. Freeman told him that he was involved in the sale of Soho Postcards and now wanted to 'extend his range to include films'. He offered Phillips £100 per week to come into business with him and help source the equipment required to make rollers. While making his enquiries, Phillips met two other men, Byrne and Ward, who also reproduced postcards for Freeman.

FIGURE 3.4: Evan 'Big Jeff' Phillips. Author's personal collection.

Together, they located a company that imported film developing and printing machines into Britain, finding that it would cost £700 to purchase the necessary machinery. To raise the capital, Phillips sold his house. With his accommodation business not offering him decent financial rewards, he worked for Freeman selling postcards to Soho's bookshops on his behalf, under the name 'Big Jeff'. The film equipment was scheduled to arrive in January 1966, but by February 1966, the police finally arrested Freeman for the schoolgirl postcards. While on remand at Brixton prison, Moody visited Freeman and told him there was

> more to life than stepping on the accelerator. Go into court, plead guilty, and I can get you off the dangerous driving charges [from the car chase]. If not, you'll get four years [...] I've spoken to the judge, and he's agreed to give you 18 months imprisonment [...] you'll be out in the year [...] when you get out, give me a tinkle.

Freeman pleaded guilty and, as Moody promised, received an 18-month prison sentence. While jailed, Phillips and his associates started their own business, leaving Sandra to fend for herself. In *Knock Down Ginger*, she recounts the challenges of running the postcard operation and how the Obscene Publications Squad pressured her.

In a police interview taken from the Obscene Publications Squad investigation, a photographer and porn distributor named Babington tells how he ended up working for Sandra while Freeman was in prison.[8] Babington was attending a course in photography at an art college when he met Sandra, who employed him to 'print obscene photographs from negatives' that she would supply. Babington had trouble getting paid for his work, so he visited the Soho to understand how the economy worked. Babington decided to bypass Sandra, directly supplying the bookshops: 'this was a simple matter of going into the bookshops, showing the person in the chair the pictures and taking orders'. After a short while, Babington got to know those in the economy and was warned that he needed to pay the police for a licence. He found a partner named Mitchell, who already had strong ties to Soho's bookshops, leading to them being licensed by the Obscene Publications Squad. Their early operation involved reprinting Freeman's photographs – without his or Sandra's knowledge – as well as those taken by Mitchell. Eventually, Babington diversified, specializing in importing films and magazines from Denmark. He was arrested in 1972 after attempting to import 10,849 magazines, 22,838 catalogues, 183 films and 109 sets of playing cards via Dover and London Heathrow. His sentencing made the front page of the *Daily Mirror* (29 September 1972). The article outlines his 12-month suspended prison sentence and £12,000 fine, becoming embroiled in the crackdown of the economy following the discovery of corruption in the Obscene Publications Squad, which I discuss in the next chapter. Babington's brief role in the economy shows how profitable it could be for those wanting to earn large amounts of money in a short space of time.

## Climax Films

While Sandra tried to keep Freeman's business running, Phillips quickly learned about the powerful myth of Big Jeff. One day, while delivering postcards to Soho, he was approached by a bookshop chair known as 'Chicko', who ran John Mason's shop at 4 Green's Court, Soho. He told Phillips, who he knew as Jeff, that the Obscene Publications Squad were looking to arrest a man named Phillips. It transpired that the Obscene Publications Squad thought Phillips was the 'Mr Big' working with Freeman, suspecting that he was involved in the sexual offences committed against the 14-year-olds. Phillips revealed his true identity to Chicko, denying being party to the crime. Chicko agreed to set up a meeting with Mason, who Phillips named the 'biggest man in the pornography business' in his police statement. During their meeting, Mason introduced Phillips to two officers in the Obscene Publications Squad. Phillips distanced himself from Freeman's offence and told how he wanted to sell postcards and, eventually, rollers. Again, this shows the power Mason held within the economy through his close relationship with corrupt police officers, acting as a sort of gatekeeper. Phillips asked for permission to carry on trading. An officer named Culver permitted him to continue, but a further meeting would be necessary to discuss the matter. Two weeks later, 'Old Bill' – Soho slang for 'the police' – visited Phillip's house in Kew, Surrey, presenting him with a search warrant. Phillips recalls what happened after a search of his premises was completed: 'Culver said "we don't mind you working. We can't guarantee it will be 100% but it's 99% cover and it will cost you a oner [£100] per month" […] I said, "well that will be very satisfactory with me"'. To make a good impression, Phillips paid the money in advance. Culver told him that they would meet every month at a public house to make the payment. Mason later told Phillips that this fee was 'very fair', and he paid 'something in the region of £1000 a month' for his licence, revealing how the licence fee had a sliding scale – the greater the earnings, the higher the fee.

Unlike Freeman, whose loathing of the police meant he avoided a licence, Phillips understood the benefits of being in league with the Obscene Publication Squad. Freeman's criminal background also contrasts with Phillips' experience as a business owner, taking a more conventional approach to producing and distributing pornography. This acumen allowed Phillips to grow a successful transnational enterprise, changing how rollers in the alternative economy were packaged. At this point, rollers were unbranded, and their distribution was small-scale, as discussed in the previous chapter. Phillips' innovation was to brand them, much like the popular 8mm glamour films, which had recognizable labels, such as Pete Walker's Heritage Films, Russell Gay's Venus and George Harrison Marks' Kamera. Phillips' label, Climax Films, appears to have been launched in mid 1966. This is significant, as it is the first use of the brand name Climax, and is several months before the Danish pornographers Jens and Peter Theander introduced their iconic brand, first in 1967 with the magazine *Klimaks* ('Climax' in Danish), which eventually became Color Climax in August 1968 (Madsen 2013).[9] The early years of Climax's operation are briefly detailed in Phillips' police interview, but are also mentioned in a magazine interview with roller performer 'Big' John English (*Whitehouse*, No. 32) and *The People/Sunday People* newspapers (8 November 1970; 6 February 1972).

According to English, Phillips and Byrne started Climax Films with a 'working capital of £350'. The *Sunday People* states that they began by using 'secondhand 8mm equipment, poorly processed and printed at film laboratories by technicians working at night without the knowledge of their employers'. Byrne rented a bedsitter at 2A, 23 Nevern Place, Earl's Court, London, which was regularly used for making the films; Phillips paid Byrne's rent in lieu of using the flat as a makeshift studio. Phillips states that he shot the early films with Byrne assisting; neither had experience of film production. Performers were found via 'various contacts in the West End', and English, who performed in several early Climax rollers, states that they put adverts in 'papers'. According to Crispie, a former bookshop chair who Phillips later employed to assist in running Climax Films, female performers were paid £20 to £30 per film, while men earned £10. When interviewed by *The People*, Crispie alleges that 'the boy in the first film had been a drug addict [...] and the girls were young [...] 15 years old at the time of filming'. It is difficult to ascertain whether this claim is true, nor is it possible to identify this early title as no accurate list of Climax Films rollers exists with a list of their production dates. In her work on Britain's early porn trade, Stoops (2018: 228) believes that the use of underage performers 'received no attention whatsoever' from authorities. Freeman's arrest for making and selling underage photographs suggests that this position had changed, although it is likely that underaged models were still exploited by unscrupulous producers.[10]

*The People* acknowledges Ivor Cook's early involvement in Climax Films, helping Phillips to get the business started. Given Cook's experience and reputation as technician and a producer of rollers, it is plausible that he assisted Phillips in Byrne in some of the earlier titles, showing them how to use the equipment and establishing a workflow. This may explain why Hebditch and Anning (1988) associate Cook with certain Climax Films titles. Climax Films rollers were packaged in distinctive orange boxes, with the brand Climax Films – later Climax Original – on the top, with the text 'black and white' printed on the bottom alongside the length of the films (see Figure 3.5).[11] They were sold to Soho's bookstores, retailing for £15 each. Like Cook, Phillips initially struggled to generate enough copies of the films to satisfy the demand for product. Whereas Cook operated within his means, Phillips had the ambition to grow Climax Films, scaling up production and producing a higher material standard of product.

Following Cook, Phillips also exported his films to Scandinavia via porn smuggler Walter Bartkowski, where they were sold in bookshops. Earlier, I suggested that the Theander Brothers' brand Color Climax was inspired by Phillips' label, as they sold his rollers at their antique bookstore Rådhusantikvariatet in Copenhagen (Carter 2018). Interestingly, the Theanders also named three magazines after the early Climax rollers *Pussy Galore* (1966–67), *Ring Up for Love* (1966–67) and *Carnaby Kinks* (1968), further supporting this claim (see Figure 3.6).[12] Phillips' relationship with Bartkowski eventually turned into a partnership when they sensed an opportunity to grow the business by moving Climax Films to Denmark in 1969, where pornography was now legalized. I discuss this later in the chapter.

FIGURE 3.5: Early first wave release of *Men* (1966–67) from Climax Films. Author's personal collection.

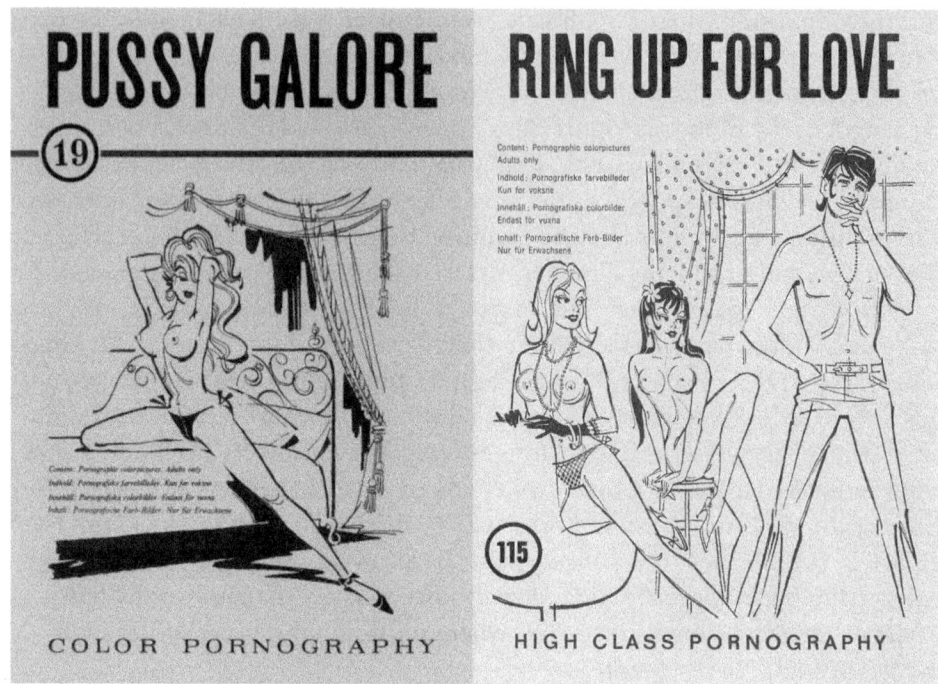

FIGURE 3.6: Color Climax Corporation's referencing of roller titles – *Pussy Galore* (1966–67) and *Ring Up for Love* (1966–67) – in the names of magazines published in the early 1970s. Courtesy of *Vintage Erotica Forums*.

I refer to the years 1966–67 as the first wave of Climax Films' releases. These are often identifiable by handwritten titles that precede the film (see Figure 3.7), indicating their amateurish origins, as well as the use of Ilford's film stock. During this period, they released at least 51 titles, many of which were shot in the Earl's Court bedsit. The films tend to feature group sex between men and women, a common trope of British rollers. One-on-one sex scenes are rarer, with *Escort Agency* (1966) and *Bondage* (1966–67) being exceptions. However, even in the early years of Climax, Phillips understood the need to diversify output and cater to different audiences. For example, they produced one gay roller (*Men*, 1966–67) and another featuring a trans performer having sex with another male (*In Drag*, 1967). I have already discussed two early Climax rollers in this book: the apocryphal Christine Keeler film *100% Lust* (1966), supposedly shot by Ivor Cook, and *Tonight at 8* (1966–67), a title associated with Climax Films, that I argue represents swinging London in the mid 1960s. *Ring Up for Love* (1966–67) is a typical film from this first wave of Climax rollers. It begins with a handwritten title card, rather than the more professional titling system that

FIGURE 3.7: Title cards demonstrating the three waves of Climax. From amateurish handwritten title cards to a more professionalized attempt at film production. Author's personal collection.

would later be adopted in Climax's second wave, when they increasingly professionalized production.

The film features two young blonde women in a flat, likely Byrne's Earl's Court bedsit. This setting is regularly used in many of the early Climax rollers and is easily identified by the floral curtains shown in the background and the location of the bed. *Ring Up for Love* opens with a close-up of the faces of each woman. They are talking and smiling. The camera zooms out to reveal that they are dressed in their underwear and discussing a vinyl record. There might be no sound, but it is evident that the doorbell has been rung, and the camera follows one of the women as she goes to the door, using the intercom system to find out who is visiting. Her shadow on the door shows that the filmmaker is using lighting. The film cuts, and we see a medium close-up of the women. One looks towards the camera and appears to be instructed by the filmmaker to remove their underwear. After doing so, the women walk toward the sink in the corner of the room, where a long shot reveals that they are washing their vaginas, accentuated by a close-up, and suggesting they are preparing for their visitor.

A long shot shows them drying each other, but one of the women leaves and walks towards the door to answer it. A male appears in the shot. The camera is behind the sofa that they all fall on, kissing and groping each other. Now the camera moves to the front of the sofa and zooms in to capture the women giving the man oral sex. The man points to his left, and the film cuts to a long shot of the women on the bed, zooming in on them kissing and masturbating together. They move into a 69 position, and the male comes back into shot, joining in and having intercourse with one of the women; the other uses a dildo. They engage in a range of sexual positions until the man ejaculates after receiving oral sex. The film does not end with the cum shot but reveals that the male has maintained an erection and continues to have sex with the women. He seemingly ejaculates again over the vagina of one of the women, and the film cuts a piece of paper with 'FIN' handwritten.

While many of the unbranded rollers discussed in the previous chapter, such as *Fisherman's Luck* (1965–67) and *The Part Time Job* (1962–66), show some understanding of narrative filmmaking and seek to emulate professional production practices, *Ring Up for Love* is a much rawer film. The primary purpose, it would seem, is to capture the immediacy of the sexual act. Slade (2006: 38–39) argues that the majority of pre-1960s stags were 'inept', referring to their clandestine origins and nonprofessional makers. He also suggests the exhibition context for stags demanded that the films signified illicitness through 'their deliberate clumsiness and vulgarity'. Although Slade refers to early stags, some rollers are also demonstrative of ineptness and this, I argue, is often due to the inexperience of those who produced them, as well as the limitations of the equipment they used. Home processing techniques, for instance, often resulted in errors or blemishes that connote illicitness. However, there is no evidence to suggest that rollers were intentionally made to look illicit. Retired film laboratory worker Brian Pritchard repeatedly commented on how roller makers would have been motivated by economics, producing as cheap a product as possible to maximize return.

This, Pritchard believes, is why production quality was not a primary concern, or necessarily a possibility, in the early years of roller production.

Early Climax Films' rollers like *Ring Up for Love* are evidently not made by a skilled filmmaker, but a nonprofessional whose primary intention is to document what is happening in front of the camera with few edits to simplify post-production. Many of Phillips' productions were shot back-to-around or within a short span of each other. *The Teen Scene* (1966–67) and *Love for Sale* (1967–68) feature the same two blonde female performers as *Ring Up for Love*. An interview with Climax performers in the Danish magazine *Chick* (issue 20, 1970) uncovers more detail about Phillips' approach to making rollers. When asked how much they earn, one performer claims that they were usually paid for three hours of work, but if filming ran over, they would be paid for each extra hour. In addition to making films, this time was also used to shoot photographs for distribution as Soho Postcards or to illustrate Soho Bibles. For example, photographs likely taken during the filming of the Climax rollers *The Good Life* (1966–67) and *Full Treatment* (1966–67) feature in a Soho Bible titled *Gorgeous Blondes* (see Figure 3.8), showing how Phillips generated a range of commodities from just one shooting session. While performers received a one-off payment, entrepreneurs exploited their labour by reproducing materials and benefiting from their sale.

After eighteen months, Phillips was 'in full swing of producing new films and photographs regularly and distributing them in Soho', but he became 'fed up' with making the films himself and wanted to remove himself from that side of the business, focusing more on running the company. Moody had now left the Obscene Publications Squad, ironically leading an investigation into police corruption (Cox et al. 1977) and Detective Inspector Leslie Alton replaced him. Phillips runs through how Alton immediately made changes to the licence fee, evidencing how the police were aware of the economic potential offered by the expansion of the alternative economy:

> It was then decided by Alton that everybody with cover [the licence] should pay double what they were before […] he indicated that the […] pornography business in general was growing rapidly, and there were more people who had to be paid out of the kitty.

Phillips attended weekday evening meetings, taking place at a public house named The George and the Dragon, with Mason, Ron Davey, Soho bookshop chair George Vinn and a former Obscene Publications Squad officer called Andrews, who was now working for Mason. The purpose of these gatherings was to 'discuss all the various happenings in the porn business. I would get news of people who were being nicked or information which may have been of interest to anybody in company at the time'. Phillips' statement corroborates claims made by John

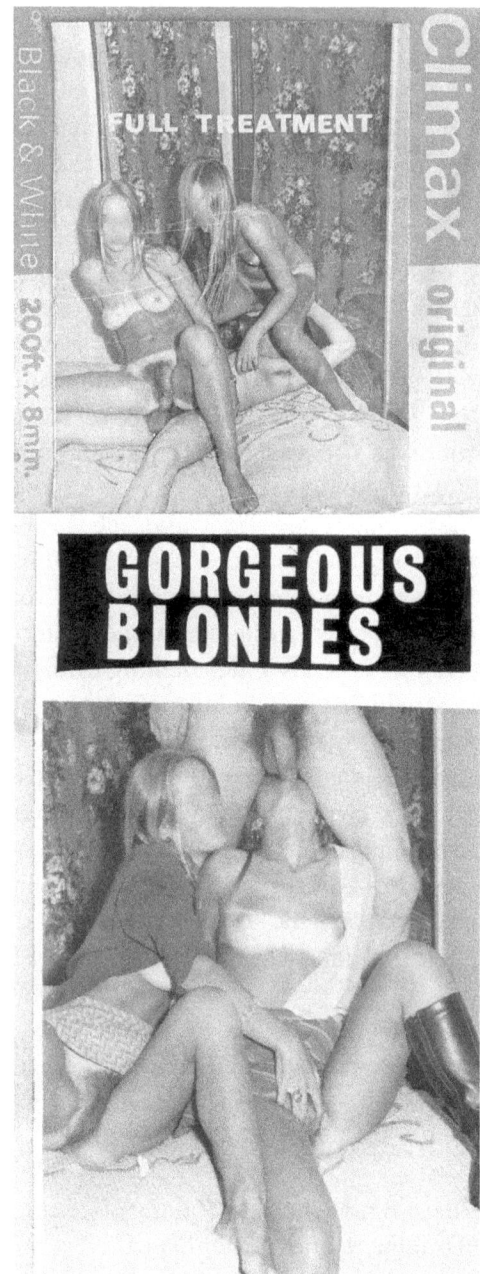

FIGURE 3.8: *Gorgeous Blondes* Soho Bible, pictures likely taken during the filming of *Full Treatment* (1966–67). Soho Bible courtesy of Rambooks, roller box cover from author's personal collection. Faces obscured to protect the identity of performers.

Mason, which I presented in Chapter 1. He shares how officers announced searches of bookshops in advance so that those with licences knew to remove stock from the shops or put out old, unwanted stock for seizure. Phillips also alleges that Bill Moody still took payments from pornographers and kept in touch with developments in the economy, despite being in a different department. Phillips met Moody for meals and paid him £100 'not that there was any actual threat by Moody to prosecute me', it was a way 'to be friendly and keep in touch'. Evidently, Phillips understood the advantage of maintaining a good relationship with police. By 1968, Phillips claims that Climax Films was a financial success, and he was making vast sums of money from his enterprise. Although he offers no indication of these profits, his increased licence fee – now doubled to £200 – implies that he was becoming a significant player in the economy.

Kirzner (1973: 14) believes that entrepreneurs 'notice profit opportunities that exist because of the initial ignorance of the original market participants'. As a business owner who was drawn to alternative economy because of its low investment and potential high-profit margins, Phillips brought with him commercial mindset. While others avoided branding, Phillips appears to have seen it as a way to disrupt the marketplace and was able to do so because of his police cover. The impact of this approach is described in a police interview with roller maker Martin Granby:

> At first it was sufficient for me to just have the spool with the film on it, but very shortly after Jeff Phillips came on the scene, he was a very big time operator and he marketed his films in boxes with proper titles. I of necessity had to compete with him and box and title my films.[13]

Therefore, this act of branding shifted how rollers were packaged, with other competitors like Granby, who I discuss in the next chapter, following Phillips' lead and expanding the market.

## Pornographer at the Pictures

By spring 1967, Freeman was due for release from Pentonville Prison, having served a year of his 18-month sentence just as Bill Moody promised. In *Knock Down Ginger*, Sandra notes how he immediately expressed his intention to resume his photography business and make rollers. According to *I Pornographer*, Freeman quickly rented two hotel rooms, one to use as a studio and another to house his equipment. He photographed Sandra and another unnamed model, developed them and took the postcards to Soho's bookshops. Fat Bill, who worked at Sonenscher's The Court Bookshop at 10 Walker's Court, advised Freeman to start paying for a licence. Recalling the unpleasant conditions of Pentonville Prison and how Moody had kept his promise, Freeman understood that it was good business to have the support of the police, providing him with the protection to operate. He appears to have felt betrayed by Phillips, who abandoned Sandra and created Climax Films, using the equipment Freeman asked Phillips to source. In the interview, Freeman spoke of how he paid the now wealthy Phillips an unexpected visit at his house in Kew, Surrey, and pressured him into giving money to restart Nestville Photography. Not wanting trouble, Phillips agreed and advised Freeman to get a licence from the Obscene Publications Squad. Freeman used Phillips' money along with finance from what Sandra refers to as 'unnamed sources' to purchase filmmaking equipment and establish his own discreetly located laboratory in Bermondsey, South East London. At first, he employed Sandra and his brother-in-law Kenny Eighteen as assistants, feeling he could trust them more than outsiders like Phillips and Byrne.

Fat Bill arranged for Freeman to meet his police contact, Detective Cheval. They met at a small coffee bar next door to the Court Bookshop in Walker's Court. Freeman recalled how Cheval was apprehensive about offering him a licence, believing him to be a 'gangster'. Freeman assured Cheval that he was the director of Nestville Photography, a formally registered business. Eventually, Cheval agreed to recommend Freeman for a licence. A few weeks later, Cheval arranged a meeting with the then Head of the Obscene Publications Squad, Leslie Alton. Cheval proposed Freeman's licence to Alton, who expressed concerns about Freeman's criminal associations, but agreed to offer the licence on a trial basis. As Alton went to the toilet, Cheval beckoned Freeman to follow and exchange the £10 he had in a brown envelope – the initial monthly cost of his licence. Freeman says that a further meeting took place at New Scotland Yard to set the conditions of his licence. Freeman's recollections offer a unique insight into how the licensing system operated. His licence came with four conditions: no mail order, no exporting outside of Britain; no underage models; and to provide a copy of every film and set of postcards he produced. It is likely that the 'no underage models' condition related to his previous charge and was an attempt to dissuade him from doing it again. The cost of the licence would be 25 per cent of his monthly earnings, again showing that licences differed for each entrepreneur within the economy and was likely based on the amount of money they were earning.

Now licensed, Freeman began to shoot films using a 16mm wind-up Bolex H16 camera. Contrasting with Phillips, who is said by the *Sunday People* to have used film laboratories out-of-hours to process and print his films, Freeman planned to do it himself in his own laboratory, having purchased two 16mm Uhler-branded optical printers from Michigan, USA. As mentioned in Chapter 2, the Uhler was a semi-professional device that allowed for a contact print to be made from either the negative, positive or interpositive. These were expensive machines, as the catalogue in Figure 3.9 shows, costing USD 950 each. Yet, they could reduce 16mm

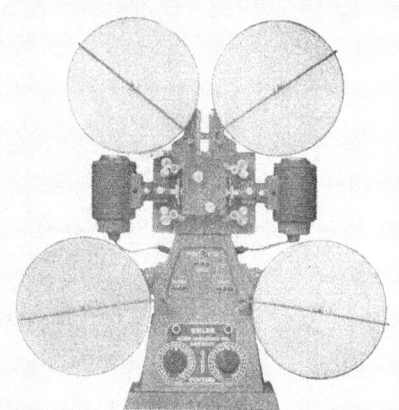
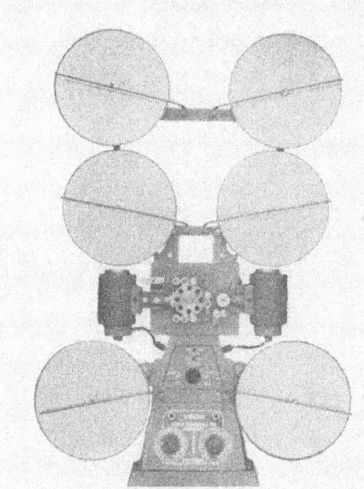

FIGURE 3.9: Advert for Uhler Reduction Printer. Author's personal collection.

to 8mm, and vice versa, making them an ideal machine for those needing to have control of the printing process. However, the Uhler was far from perfect. Retired film laboratory worker Brian Pritchard described how such devices worked and their limitations:

> if you just want to copy one film onto another of the same size then it was normally done by contact printing, so you'd have a sandwich of the negative and the print stock, and it runs through a printer past a light source. This sounds like a semi-pro solution to me. Contact printing [...] was fast, it didn't give you the finest quality, but it was very fast to print.

Sandra recalls using the Uhler in *Knock Down Ginger*:

> The machine was dark grey metal and stood about three feet high on the bench. There was one huge spool on the left for the continuous negative. Mick explained that the same film was repeated five times with four foot of leader in between each film. The leader was a blank piece of film and this is where it was spliced, once it had been developed in the tanks. I picked up the process easily and had no problems working the machine. The enlarger for the stills had a foot switch so you could use both hands for speed.

As Pritchard recognizes, the Uhler was a flawed solution to the challenge of printing rollers, often resulting in inconsistent prints. However, it was fast and allowed Freeman to upscale his production. Using an Uhler had another benefit. 16mm film could be purchased and used for both filming and printing. Freeman talked about how he would buy 16mm from Ilford's, then split it himself to make it 8mm gauge, saving money and speeding up the duplication process.

Freeman aimed to be Phillips' main competitor. From 1967 to 1968, he set himself the target of making a new film every two weeks and 60 new photographs per week. Freeman never saw Ivor Cook as a threat, as he was only intermittently producing, but Phillips consistently issued new titles for distribution across Soho. Freeman named his first label Eros Films, through which he issued the 'Pornographer at the Pictures' series. These early films are now difficult to locate and rarely appear for sale. The largest collection exists at the Kinsey Institute in Indiana, enabling me to identify 53 individual titles, suggesting that Freeman kept to his production schedule. The films begin with the text 'Pornographer at the Pictures presents' on what appears to be a magnetic board, followed by the film's title (see Figure 3.10). Early films are identifiable by a series number. Kinsey lists the film *Homework* (1967–68) as

116

FIGURE 3.10: 'Pornographer at the Pictures' title card. Author's personal collection.

number 2 in the Pornographer at the Pictures series; the first film is not apparent (see Appendix 1 for further information). Sandra suggests that the first film they made was *Wrens at Play* (1967–68), though the Kinsey Institute identifies this as number 22 in the series.

Sandra implies that these films featured 'young girls', and Freeman shows a predilection for this type of content with at least eleven titles mentioning the words 'teenage', 'school' or 'young'. When questioned about this, Freeman responded that he catered to the demand for schoolgirl-themed pornography and it was nothing more than a business decision. The titles of the films show that he produced two bestiality films (*Dog Fun*, 1967–68 and *Dog Orgy*, 1967–68), representations of incest (*Incest*, 1967–68; *Family Fun*, 1967–68), but the majority depict the standard roller trope of group sex. Freeman claims to have sold them to bookshops for £5, where they retailed for £15–16, making at least £400 a week from his films alone. He extended to making Soho Bibles, writing the stories and employing someone else to manufacture them. Another new employee worked in the laboratory and assisted Freeman in making the films.[14]

When making a film at a flat in Herne Hill, London, which belonged to one of his regular employers named Susan, Freeman discovered the benefits of the licence. Susan was a hairdresser who Freeman met through his contacts in Soho bookshops. It seems that many performers were found via connections in the West End, with some being in relationships with people associated with the bookshops. Sandra indicates that Susan was one of Freeman's favourite models who resembled the famous fashion model Twiggy, a look that Freeman was eager to exploit. During the filming of a threesome taking place in Susan's flat, a neighbour across the street noticed the powerful lights and discovered the film being made. After informing the police, Freeman was raided:

> I was in the room filming, and there was a knock on the door. Susan said, 'it's the police'. I said, 'fuck off'. 'We know what you're doing in there, Michael; it's the police'. I took the film, hid the camera and put the lights on the floor. 'Come and open the door or we will knock it down. We know what you're doing', said the copper from the porn squad with another copper in plain clothes. I knew he was bent.

One of the Obscene Publications Squad officers advised Freeman not to film at the location again, as it was outside of their jurisdiction. The officer knew Freeman was licensed. Still, Freeman 'took out some money, gave them £40 each, giving them a drink', wanting to make sure they were happy before they left. He now realized that 'the licence was a good thing; I could do what I wanted without being hassled'. While Phillips saw the advantage of being in good favour with the police, Freeman's rebellious nature and blind ambition to be 'the porn king of Soho' began to cause problems for the Obscene Publications Squad.

## Blackballed

As well as recruiting performers through contacts Freeman also advertised in contact magazines. He struck up a relationship with *Personal Advertiser*, a small publication sold in Soho bookshops containing classified adverts. The owners required photographs for the magazine, which Freeman supplied, and, in return, he placed adverts asking for models, showing the reciprocity in the economy. Few copies of this magazine survive, aside from some issues from the early 1960s, held by the British Library. Early copies show that it was a very basic publication containing advertisements for pen pals, people looking for accommodation and mail-order operations selling glamour photographs and films. In 1968, he received a response from a couple who were interested in appearing in a film. A fortnight later, Freeman visited them, discovering that they lived on a Royal Air Force (RAF) base in Norfolk. On the first visit, the camera malfunctioned, necessitating another visit to make the film. The 22-year-old female and her 32-year-old husband – an RAF officer – agreed to perform, resulting in *Swap Orgy* (1968). By this time, Freeman introduced a second label named Venus Films,[15] issuing new content and re-releasing earlier Eros Films' titles. It appears that having a range of brands was a common tactic used by roller entrepreneurs to create the impression of new content and therefore maximize profits. *Swap Orgy* was issued on Eros Films, later reissued as *Degenerate's Orgy* (1968) on Venus Films (see Figure 3.11) and his third label Action Films. *Degenerate's Orgy* uses a more professional looking title card, likely

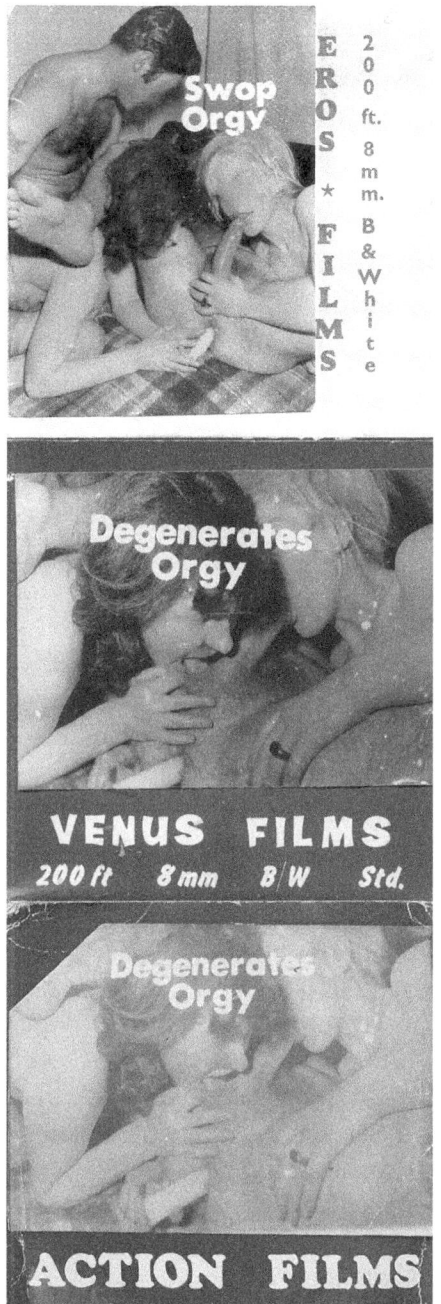

FIGURE 3.11: Box covers for *Degenerate's Orgy* (Mike Freeman 1968) and *Swap Orgy* (Mike Freeman 1968). Courtesy of Rambooks. Faces obscured to protect the identity of performers.

made using titling equipment (see Figure 3.12). The film illustrates how Freeman's style was similar to Phillips, documenting sex rather than trying to construct a narrative.

*Degenerate's Orgy* features four performers: the RAF couple, Susan and Gordon, one of Freeman's reliable male performers. Freeman must have been giving direction, as the film's opening shows a long shot of performers looking at the camera, talking to the director. Rather than being edited out, such exchanges regularly occur in rollers, offering some insight into the role of the director. Slade (2006) questions why these exchanges were not edited out, suggesting that it was a feature of the stag film. I see inclusions as evidence of hasty postproduction and quality not being a primary concern for roller makers. A crude cut takes the viewer to a wider long shot, revealing the male of the RAF couple masturbating his wife while they watch the other performers have sex; Susan is on top of Gordon. The female from the RAF couple inserts what looks to be a candle in Susan's anus; it seems that her husband is struggling to maintain an erection during filming, a challenge many male performers face. Now Freeman shows both couples having sex, one in missionary position, another having the woman on top. Freeman cuts to a close-up of Gordon's penis inside Susan, then cuts to a close-up of Susan's face. Back to a wide long shot of both couples, quickly returning to Gordon and Susan; it is obvious which couple is getting Freeman's attention. The female of the couple smiles at the camera and pleasures herself with a bottle, kissing Susan, eventually taking another candle from the fireplace – unlit, of course – and slides it inside of Gordon's anus as Susan gives him oral sex. He cuts to Gordon having sex with the RAF officer's wife from behind as she gives oral sex to Susan. He then cuts to a close-up of Gordon ejaculating on her rear before ending the film with a close-up of the officer's wife still giving oral sex to Susan. A title card reads: The End.

On 14 September 1969, the *News of the World* reported: BORED RAF WIFE STARRED IN BLUE FILMS. Another article featured in the same newspaper two weeks later (*News of the World*, 28 September 1969). Both give background to the production of *Swap Orgy/Degenerate's Orgy* and the impact the release had on its performers, but also show how Freeman's enterprise was drawing attention from the tabloid press, threatening to expose the alternative economy. In Brixton, South London, police stopped two men carrying a sack 'full of blue films and pornographic photographs'. This led to the on-base arrest of the RAF officer who appeared in *Swap Orgy/Degenerate's Orgy* and an investigation into whether 'disgraceful conduct' had occurred. For the 28 September article, his wife gave her account:

> I wrote off to a box number and about a fortnight later a man turned up in a car. He said he operated the camera, insisted that I entertain him. My husband used to sit downstairs while this went on. He never liked the idea. I honestly didn't know that

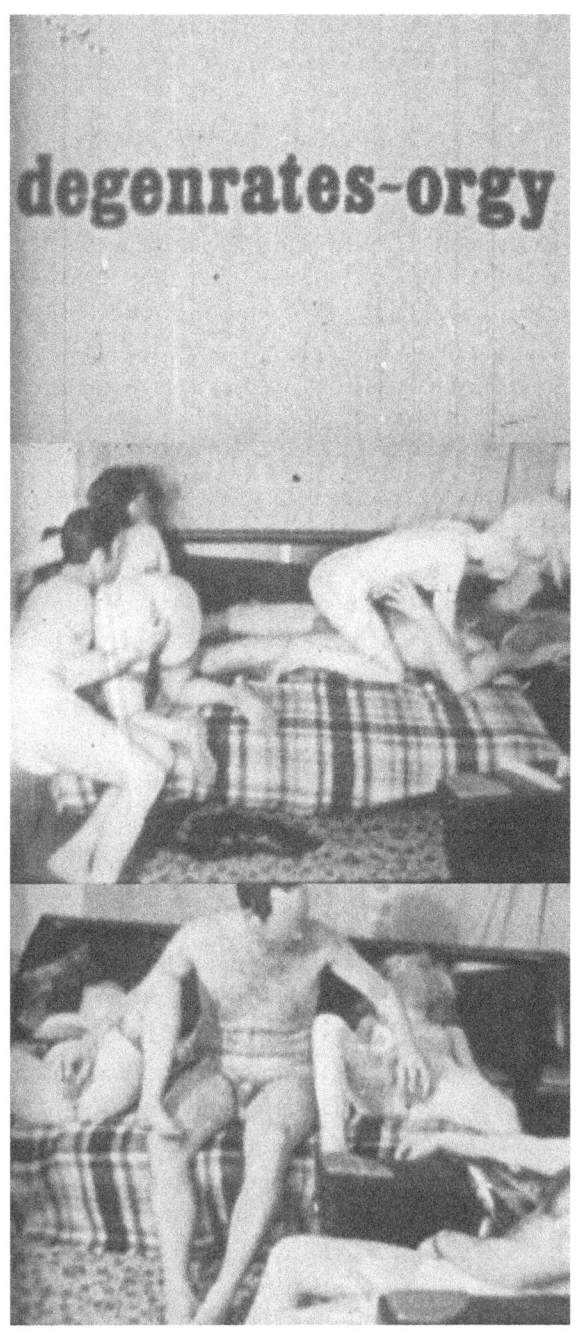

FIGURE 3.12: Screenshots from *Degenerate's Orgy* (Mike Freeman 1968). Courtesy of Rambooks. Faces obscured to protect the identity of performers.

some of the things we did were against the law [...] I always thought that what went
on in the privacy of one's own home was nobody's business.

The Wing Commander, who acted as the RAF investigator for the case, further
described what took place, drawing on a statement given by the RAF sergeant.
After his wife had placed an advertisement in *Personal Advertiser*, offering her
services as a model, a man named 'Jones' replied, asking if she would like to make
a strip film. 'Jones' was Freeman's pseudonym, revealing how false names were
often used in case of any recrimination. The wife agreed to participate and several
weeks later Freeman turned up with 'another man and girl'. The sergeant, who is
quoted in the article, returned home to discover his wife naked and with the other
man: 'I didn't feel too good about it, but didn't have the nerve to do anything'. He
states that she was paid £10 for her performance; far less than the usual amount.

No film was made that night 'because the camera wouldn't work'. Three weeks
later, Freeman returned and, on this occasion, the sergeant agreed participate, resulting in the making of *Swap Orgy/Degenerate's Orgy*. Both earned £10 for their performance. Freeman visited again another three weeks later, making a second roller featuring his wife having sex with three males, including Freeman. Six months later, he
revisited and made a film featuring the sergeant's wife and a new couple; they were
paid a further £10.[16] The sergeant also purchased two films from Freeman, which he
sold on the RAF base for £24. In his statement, the sergeant claims that he participated because 'my wife said she would leave me with our child if we didn't. I thought
the films would only be sold in Denmark where it was legal'. Legal documents that
contain police interviews with roller performers reveal that this ruse was regularly used
by producers to convince them to take part, allaying fears that family or friends might
discover their involvement. Again, this demonstrates how roller producers were often
unscrupulous in their pursuit of profits and is typical of Freeman's entrepreneurship.
When cross-examined, the RAF officer's wife told the court that money was the motivation for appearing in the films, and also because she 'was bored' with life on the base.

The newspaper articles add a different angle to the case, accusing Freeman of
'espionage' after the RAF sergeant's wife revealed her husband's possible future
manoeuvres. Freeman is alleged to have mentioned that 'he had contacts in Czech-
oslovakia', implying to the wife that he might be interested in purchasing such
information. She told her husband, who immediately reported it to his superiors.
This 'security matter' resulted in him being identified as the performer in the films.
The 14 September 1969 article suspects that Jones' real name is 'Muldoon', Freeman's birth surname, and was one of the men stopped in Brixton. Freeman makes
no mention of this seizure in *I Pornographer* or the interview he gave. At the trial,
the sergeant pleaded guilty to 'five charges of committing disgraceful conduct
by taking part in pornographic films for gain'. He also admitted 'committing an

unnatural act with his wife, aiding and abetting another man in a similar act with her, and behaving disgracefully by acting as an intermediary in the sale of two obscene films to a civilian'. For this, he received a two-year sentence, reduced to 18 months, as well as being demoted 'to the ranks and discharged in disgrace'. In her interview to the *News of the World,* his wife 'sobbed', telling how she had lost her home: 'I wish that I had never got mixed up with the films [...] I was paid a few pounds for my services and look what it has cost me'. In *I Pornographer,* Freeman believes that the *News of the World* concocted the espionage claim and were in league with the police. It is impossible to ascertain such an accusation.

The story behind *Swap Orgy/Degenerate's Orgy* offers a rare glimpse into the experiences of roller performers and how they could also be subject to prosecution. The following chapter also discusses the prosecution of roller performers, particularly for sexual acts such as buggery that were considered 'unnatural' as according to the Sexual Offences Act 1956. Furthermore, this account reveals how the Obscene Publication Squad's attempts to control the economy could fail. For instance, it is not clear why Freeman was stopped and had his films and photographs seized when he was paying for a licence. In *I Pornographer,* he mentions a rogue officer who acted independently, seizing typescripts and photographs and then offering Freeman an opportunity to purchase the stock back for £400. As I have shown in the previous two chapters, the licence only offered limited protection, particularly for activities taking place in and around the West End of London. The reporting of the case is an early example of press interest in the roller trade. Such exposure threatened to undermine attempts made by the Obscene Publications Squad to regulate the economy and safeguard it. Freeman's recklessness and opportunism caused more problems for Obscene Publications Squad, as he began to break the conditions of his licence.

Wanting to increase profits further, Freeman started a mail-order company, despite this being forbidden in his licence. In the 1960s, the Obscene Publications Squad aimed to keep the pornography trade confined to Soho, making it easier to control and police. Legal files relating to Metropolitan Police's anti-corruption unit's investigation into the Obscene Publications Squad show how mail order was a point of contention for them. Local police forces around the country regularly sent the Obscene Publications Squad complaints from the public about receiving unsolicited material in the post. Not all were unsolicited. They may have been requested by previous occupiers of the house or by husbands covertly purchasing pornography via mail-order businesses unbeknownst to their spouse. As part of the Director of Public Prosecutions' investigation into the Obscene Publications Squad's corrupt activities, attention was given to mail-order companies distributing pornography. One such enterprise was operated by the Mansfield family from 1959 onwards. The Mansfields initially supplied in softcore pornography, but as demand for hardcore grew in the early 1960s, they began to sell Soho Postcards.

In a police interview, company director Bernard Mansfield states the Obscene Publications Squad regularly called him into New Scotland Yard where they would make him remove the names and addresses of complainants from his mailing lists.[17] Mansfield mentions how Bill Moody, then head of the squad, 'threatened' him, as public complaints were causing 'a great deal of aggravation'. Several days later, a member of the Obscene Publications Squad contacted Mansfield, warning him to follow their rules and pay for a licence. The Mansfield investigation indicates how the squad attempted to restrict certain entrepreneurial activities in the economy. It is evident that they were deeply concerned about mail order and how the complaints from the public might lead to their superiors questioning the effectiveness of the Obscene Publications Squad and possibly unveiling the corrupt informal licensing system. Because of this, they were reluctant to permit mail-order companies, unless it was under their tight control.

This did not stop Freeman, who advertised his mail-order company – Nestville Photography Ltd – in publications such as *Continental Film Review* (see Figure 3.13) and *Exchange and Mart*. He informed Cheval – his contact at the Obscene Publications Squad – about selling via mail order. Cheval agreed, but wanted an extra payment to be Freeman's inside man, again showing how some officers in the squad had their own independent side-hustles. Freeman used a 'front company' to sell softcore films, such as the glamour films he claims to have produced alongside rollers; these are yet to be discovered.[18] This enabled him to build a mailing list of customers. A few weeks later, he sent a mail-shot in the form of a one-page catalogue offering hardcore pornography to those on the list. Freeman rented office space in dilapidated parts of London under aliases, so that the Obscene Publications Squad would be unaware of his involvement. This also gave him different addresses to use in his mail-shots and, if police raided an address, he still had others to operate from.

One day, Freeman received a tip from Cheval, informing him that one of his addresses in Peckham was about to be searched. Against Cheval's advice, he raced to the location, hoping to catch the postman before he arrived at the premises so that orders and, more importantly, the money could be collected. Another address in Clapham North was obtained via the pornographer Ron 'The Dustman' Davey, who had paid off a local policeman for the location, suggesting that police corruption extended beyond the Obscene Publications Squad. With profits growing, Freeman convinced the Obscene Publications Squad to approve his mail-order business. They agreed, providing that he paid them more money and informed them of the addresses he operated from. It is evident that Freeman enjoyed antagonizing the police rather than maintaining a positive relationship with them.

**GLAMOUR**

A new range of 8mm glamour films in black and white and colour. Send S.A.E. for free list. These superb films are obtainable only from us.

**GLAMOUR**

A new film every month. New. New. New. Avoid disappointment — order now.

**GLAMOUR**

**Nestville Photography Ltd.**
**32 GREAT WINDMILL St. LONDON W.I**

FIGURE 3.13: Advert for Freeman's Nestville Photography Ltd mail-order operation from *Continental Film Review*. Courtesy of 'Phillip Black' and the Erotic Film Society.

Freeman's second breach of the licence occurred when he exported to Amsterdam, Denmark and Sweden. Having previously exported his postcards to Hamburg, Germany, via continental porn smuggler Walter Bartkowski, Freeman wanted to establish his own transnational links to further expand the reach of his enterprise. At first, Freeman tried to deal with Hamburg's bookshops personally, but had little success. Instead, he moved his attention to Amsterdam, where attitudes towards hardcore pornography were more relaxed. After establishing a relationship with a shop in Zeedijk, Freeman claimed that he could earn around £1000 per delivery. Following several successful flights to Amsterdam smuggling pornography, Freeman was arrested at Schiphol Airport and imprisoned for six weeks. An associate made subsequent trips, flying from Amsterdam to Jersey in the Channel Islands – a known tax haven – depositing the money in a bank before travelling back to London. Freeman believes his arrest in Amsterdam resulted in him being 'blackballed' by the Head of the Obscene Publications Squad Leslie Alton due to his disregard for the licence, and a contract on his life was arranged.

In *I Pornographer*, Freeman claims that Alton preferred working with the amenable Evan Phillips, whose status within the economy had now grown. In contrast, Freeman was deemed uncontrollable and volatile. Fearing for his life, Freeman employed a minder named Gerald Hawley, who he had met in prison when serving time for the 1966 offence involving the three 14-year-old girls. According to Freeman and the *Daily Mail* (26 May 1969: 7), Hawley was a former enforcer for the Kray twins, being involved in 'drug peddling and club protection'. Hawley also became Freeman's wholesaler, using his reputation as a hard man to collect money from bookshops across the country. According to Pearson (2015: 250), the Krays had an interest in Soho's pornography business, providing protection to distributors and wholesalers who were importing pornography from Europe. In the interview, Freeman told of how he became concerned that the Krays would deliver the 'hit' on his life on behalf of the police. In Chapter 1 I established that the Obscene Publications Squad often worked with members of the criminal underworld to help police the pornography business. However, I found no evidence to support Freeman's claim of the Krays being in league with the police.[19]

When the Krays were imprisoned in 1968, and no attempt had been made on his life, Freeman assumed the contract to be terminated. He opened his own bookshop and studio at 32 Great Windmill Street, Soho. Freeman named the shop 'Climax Films', going as far as registering the company name Climax Films with Companies House. Adverts placed in *Exchange and Mart* and *8mm Magazine* confirm this: 'CLIMAX FILMS have something different. Send s.a.e. for list of exclusive productions and free photo advertising current film. Climax Films, 32 Great Windmill St W1' (*Exchange and Mart*, 7 November 1968). It is likely that Freeman used the Climax Films brand to provoke Phillips. Moreover, Phillips' warehouse was located at Denham Place, which adjoined Great Windmill Street. Perhaps this was the final provocation that resulted in an attempt being made on Freeman's life?

On the evening of 21 May 1969, Hawley turned up unannounced at Freeman's house and attempted to murder him. Freeman, and his brother-in-law Kenneth Eighteen, resisted Hawley, stabbing him 89 times. Eventually, Freeman, Sandra and Eighteen were arrested for the murder of Hawley, the crime being widely reported in the British tabloid press. The article in the *News of the World* (21 December 1969) details the investigation. Chief Detective Superintendent Bert Wickstead, considered an incorruptible police officer, discovered that Hawley starred in 'blue films', ultimately leading him to identify Freeman as the murderer. A raid on the recently established Climax Films shop on 32 Great Windmill Street uncovered more than '120 canisters of film', implying that the police seized Freeman's films and possibly destroyed them. Although Freeman argued he had acted in self-defence, he was imprisoned for ten years on a charge of manslaughter, as mentioned in the introduction to this chapter. Until his death in 2021, Freeman maintained that this was a conspiracy. While in prison, Sandra, Eighteen and Freeman's father attempted to keep the business running, but it seems to have dissolved in the early 1970s. Freeman returned to the pornography business in 1979 when he was released from prison. I discuss Freeman's move into the home video market in the Epilogue to this book.

## Original Climax Films A/S

With Freeman removed from the economy, Phillips' reputation as the leading producer of rollers grew. No longer involved in their production, Phillips focused his attention on expanding the business. Becoming increasingly frustrated with his inability to meet the demand for Climax rollers and produce a quality product, he explored the potential for moving Climax to Denmark. Dunning and Lundan (2008: 96) describe such transnational opportunities as 'location-specific advantages', which help companies determine where they setup business. They identify transport infrastructure, government policy and a favourable business environment as some of the conditions which attract companies to international locations. With pornography now legalized in Denmark, Phillips could process and print the films without any hassle or the 'threat of competitors discovering where my laboratory was'. Forming a partnership with Walter Bartkowski, the porn smuggler who had established a strong transnational network of bookshops across Denmark, Germany, the Netherlands and Sweden, they registered Original Climax Films A/S as a Danish company in November 1969 (see Figure 3.14). Their plan was to shoot, process and print the films in Denmark then smuggle them back into Britain. This way, they could upscale their production and supply the films internationally.

Fellow pornographer Alberto Ferro – more widely known by his nom de plume Lasse Braun – advised Phillips to improve the quality of his films, shooting and releasing in colour rather than black and white (Hebditch and Anning 1988: 199). Although colour was more costly and complicated to process, Phillips somehow found a solution, possibly paying an employee at a film laboratory for an out-of-hours service, as identified by the reporters from the *Sunday People* (6 February 1972). At this time, colour rollers were scarce and commanded a higher price in Soho's bookshops. According to former bookshop chair Derek Cox, a 200-ft colour roller usually cost £5 wholesale and retailed for around £25, making them a

FIGURE 3.14: Advertisement for Climax Original Films taken from issue 20 of *Chick*, 1971. Author's personal collection.

profitable commodity for producers and distributors.[20] An Original Climax Films catalogue, likely from late 1970, identifies twelve early colour titles produced between 1967 and 1969 prior to their Denmark move; I refer to this period as the second wave of Climax Films' output (see Figure 3.15).

Phillips now employed independent filmmakers to shoot the films. A West End-based contact named Gallwey helped find performers to appear in rollers, and Phillips recruited a filmmaker named Davis to shoot the films. Initially, this

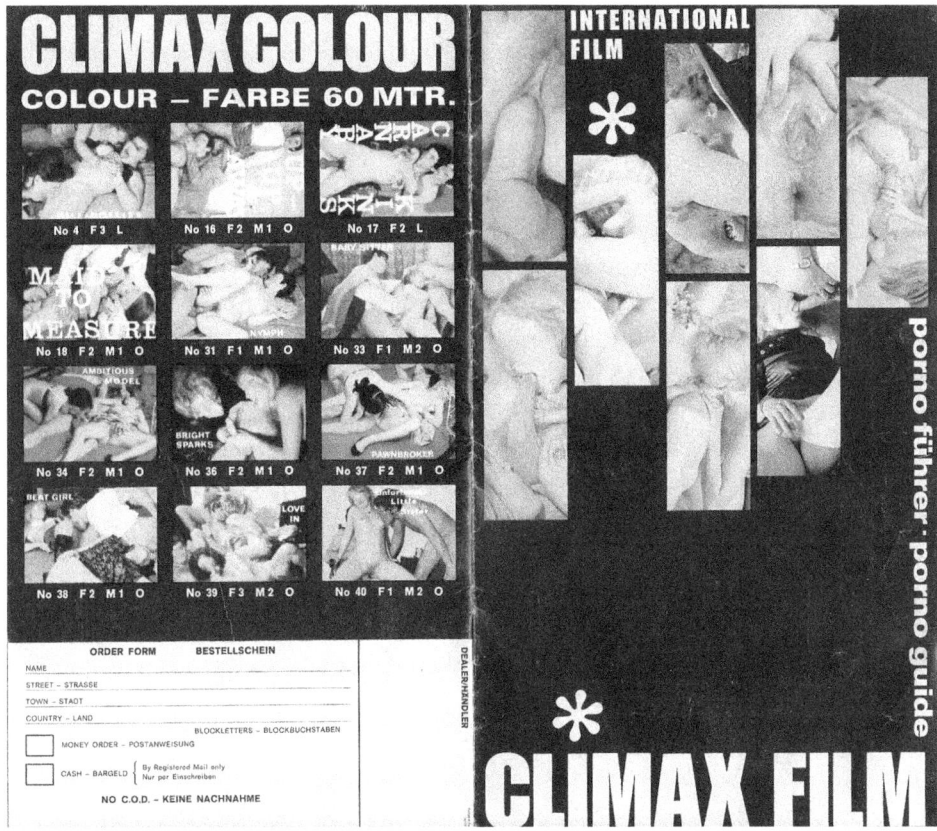

FIGURE 3.15: Extract from Climax catalogue. Author's personal collection. Faces obscured to protect the identity of performers.

'turned out to be very successful' for Phillips, with Davis producing many of the titles released in this second wave and Gallwey arranging the performers and filming locations. Phillips gave them a £200 float for their production budget. He soon discovered that Gallwey and Davis 'wouldn't shoot the required numbers of films and there was a certain amount of monies missing'. Feeling cheated, Phillips employed 'a boy from Orpington, Kent, called Wally – I don't remember his surname' to make films. He later found out that Gallwey had been purchasing film stock from Ilford's using Phillips' account, but not paying for it and selling it on to others in the West End. Phillips claims that Gallwey was arrested for this offence and received a four-year sentence. Some Climax Films' rollers made in the latter half of the 1960s show a move away from a documentary style to including expositions and attempting to tell a simple narrative. The roller *Up, Up and Away* (1968) is an example of this greater ambition.

Shot in colour and available in both colour and black and white versions, *Up, Up and Away* has a notable setup. As illustrated in Figure 3.16, it begins with an establishing shot of a pilot with two female crew members walking away from a plane at an airport. The plane has a distinctive E logo on its tail fin, but the airport is not easily identifiable. Using crowdsourced expertise on the online community *Reddit*, a member of /Aviation identified the plane as a British Eagle 707. British Eagle International Airlines was based at London Heathrow from 1948 to 1968, when it was declared bankrupt, perhaps giving a clue to when this roller was made. It is not clear how the filmmakers gained access to use this location – cutting to the outside of the airport and the exterior of the airline's office. The crew get into a car and drive from the airport to what appears to be a hotel. The camera watches as they enter. Another cut. The camera is now inside the room, focusing on the door as the crew enter. A medium close-up shows them remove their jackets, sit down and enjoy a drink. The pilot clumsily spills his drink on the skirt of one of the flight attendants; a typical set-up in pornographic films. She removes her skirt, which leads to the pilot approaching her from behind and caressing her. They strip, she begins to give him oral. The camera is more still than in the earlier Climax Films' rollers, not moving as frenetically, perhaps indicating the use of a tripod and a filmmaker with technical skill. The other female enters the shot, and they all move to the bed, engaging in

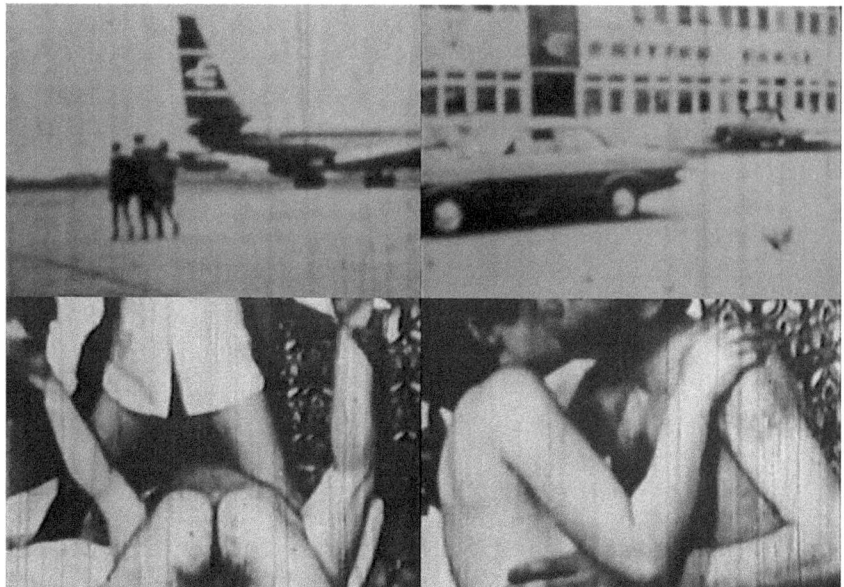

FIGURE 3.16: Screenshots from *Up, Up and Away* (1968). Author's personal collection. Faces obscured to protect the identity of performers.

group sex. The camera focuses on the male, who is on top of the woman, penetrating her. He withdraws, and the other woman gives him oral before climbing on top of him. It cuts to a low-angle close-up of her face, an unusual shot, capturing her pleasure. A cut, and the camera pans down from her face to see the pilot giving the other stewardess oral. The camera pans up to the female's body and then to a close-up of her face. It cut to both women giving the pilot oral, resulting in his climax. The film abruptly ends.

*Up, Up and Away* contrasts with the first wave of Climax Films. The film looks to be competently made, evidencing that Phillips was now outsourcing production to others who had some filmmaking skill. Other films from this second wave were shot on the continent. Issue 20 of the controversial Dutch magazine *Chick* from 1970 reviews several Climax films, *Triangle* (1966–67), *Free for All* (1966–67), *Two's Enough* (1967–68) and *No Mercy for Susan* (1967–68). The latter film is said by the magazine to have been made in Amsterdam, with the opening of *No Mercy for Susan* filmed in Vondelpark. The reviewer also states that other films have been made in Germany without naming any titles. This indicates how Climax had become an increasingly transnational operation, not limiting themselves to films made in Britain and drawing on a network of independent international contacts. It is not clear who produced these titles, though there was an illicit culture of hardcore 8mm film production in the Netherlands. The Venus Tempel Sex Museum in Amsterdam displays the film *Loving Dollies* (Willem de Gier 1966–69), which is said to be one of the first hardcore films produced in the Netherlands. At the first Wet Dreams film festival that took place in Amsterdam between the 26 and 29 November 1970, a selection of Climax Films' rollers were screened on the opening night, highlighting how these films were circulating outside of Britain and receiving recognition.

By 1969, the operation had relocated to Copenhagen, Denmark. At the *Copenhagen Sex Fair*, 1969, Jens Theander is pictured in the newspaper *B.T.* on Friday 24 October, proudly holding a copy of the Climax roller *Lolitas* (1969) to the media. According to Kutchinsky and Snare (1999: 123), *Sex 69* was the 'world's first sex fair'. Instigated by the Theander Brothers and organized by an exhibition company, the purpose of the fair was to promote Denmark's newly commercialized trade in pornography to the world, attracting international visitors and media attention. Kutchinsky and Snare (1999: 124) note that 'pornographic pictures and films' were the most popular articles being exhibited. Jens Theander's displaying of *Lolitas* (1969) demonstrates that Climax rollers were being promoted at *Sex 69* and exhibited to an international market.[21] This is also evident in a documentary covering the event titled *Pornography in Denmark: A New Approach* (Alex De Renzy 1970), where there are several scenes showing Climax rollers being sold and screened.[22] Issue 20 of the Dutch porn magazine from 1970 *Chick* estimates that Phillips' Climax released 175 black and white films and 50 colour rollers by 1970. A Climax catalogue from 1970 indicates that a further 21 titles were to be released from January 1971, many of them produced in Denmark rather than Britain (see Figure 3.15).

I see the period between 1969 and 1972 as the third wave of Climax releases. These show a higher standard of production, being processed and printed in a modern film laboratory, releasing films in colour with higher quality packaging. Interestingly, the Climax catalogue includes a disclaimer:

> The films covering the four last pages of the cataloques [sic] are of an elder [sic] volume but with a content that is quite unique, we want to draw your attention to the fact that the technical quality cannot compete with our latest films, but in spite of this, it is still an article which is highly requested and therefore of cause [sic] has its place in our program.

Despite the technical improvements, the above text demonstrates that customer demand still existed for titles from the first and second wave. In reference to digital pornography, Paasonen (2010: 168) suggests that amateur content is 'somehow more real, raw and innovative than commercially produced'. Although Paasonen is concerned about a format that has different conditions of production, her point about the association between amateurism and authenticity can be related to rollers. Perhaps the earlier Climax Films' titles connote a more authentic or realistic representation of sex for certain viewers, tending to be shot in domestic locations with unsteady cameras by nonprofessionals. Slade (2006) believes that audiences for stags did not seek perfection and their deficiencies reinforced their status as illicit goods. This may explain why Climax's earlier films continued to appeal, regardless of their shift to a professionalized production process.

## Conclusion

By the end of the 1960s, Climax became the most prolific brand in the roller market. A seizure list generated after a search of John Mason's Dean Street Office gives evidence of their dominance (see Appendix 2 for the full seizure list).[23] Of the 83 rollers seized, 41 were Climax, compared to 6 from Freeman's Eros Films label. It is worth pointing out that Phillips maintained a strong relationship with Mason until this seizure and was one of his main suppliers, selling to him directly rather than to individual shops. As most bookshops operated on a sale or return basis, Mason refused to pay Phillips for the seized stock, instructing him to 'stand the loss of the thousand pounds'. Phillips suspected that Mason was attempting to extort money from him and likely reclaimed the stock through his strong relationship with Moody and the Obscene Publications Squad. Following this, Mason and Phillips ceased dealings. Therefore, the number of Climax rollers in this seizure list might be indicative of their earlier arrangement.

The seizure list also shows the emergence of other brands in the economy, such as Playboy and Dolly Films. However, unbranded rollers remained, some of which are likely to have been made by Ivor Cook and were re-released by Blue Scene Films. Other roller labels that appeared during the latter half of the 1960s are the earlier discussed Blue Scene Films, Private Films, Fantasy, Malmo Films, Svensk Films, Global Cinelux, Cherub, Delilah Deluxe and possibly Bunny Films and Steinle Films (see Figure 3.17). Whereas Phillips had one brand, other entrepreneurs followed Freeman's approach, having multiple labels. This becomes more apparent in the following chapter. As the 1960s concluded, rollers were now a popular commodity in the alternative economy, with more entrepreneurs producing and distributing them alongside postcards and typescripts. Furthermore, a new market had opened up following the legalization of pornography in Denmark, creating opportunities for transnational distribution, but also the large-scale importation of pornography into Britain via organized smuggling.

This chapter has explored the expansion of Britain's roller market. It has focused on the entrepreneurship of Mike Freeman and Evan 'Big Jeff' Phillips, providing deeper understanding of the motivations and practices of those who produced and distributed rollers under the Obscene Publications Squad's licensing system. In Chapter 2, I considered how entrepreneurs such as Ivor Cook and Leonard Thorpe might be considered innovators in a Schumpeterian sense, disrupting the economy by making hardcore films using limited technological means. In contrast, Freeman and Phillips can be understood as opportunists, seeking to capitalize on and benefit from the demand for pornographic films. Unlike Cook or Thorpe, Freeman and Phillips had no filmmaking experience and entered the economy as non-professionals who were motivated by the profit potential of pornography. If Cook initially worked within his means, producing small-print runs of his rollers, Freeman and Phillips sought out devices to upscale their output, through purchasing semi-professional machinery or, in the case of Phillips, allegedly bribing laboratory workers to print his films. In many ways, both share similarities with the entrepreneurs who participated in the enterprise culture of early 1980s Britain. Gray (2002: 11) argues that British society in the 1960s and 1970s opposed an entrepreneurial mindset, instead favouring 'collectivism'. However, Freeman and Phillips introduced a commercial approach to manufacture of pornography, solely motivated by profit and success.

FIGURE 3.17: New labels, such as Private Films, Delilah Deluxe and Malmo Films, had appeared by the end of the 1960s. Author's personal collection. Faces obscured to protect the identity of performers.

I argue that the driver for their enterprise was the licensing system introduced by Obscene Publications Squad. In Chapter 1, I suggested that Britain's pornographers were able to legitimize their entrepreneurship through their relationship with corrupt police officers. Throughout this chapter, I have shown how the licensing system was integral to Freeman and Phillips' financial success, with members of the Obscene Publications Squad also benefitting from their enterprise. Although criminality was legitimized, the licensing system also excluded those who refused to work within their institutional framework. Freeman's story is evidence of this. Initially, Freeman succeeded in the alternative economy as he could operate with relatively little threat of arrest. Yet his inability to work within the rules of the economy, and specifically the conditions of the licence, resulted in his removal from it, regardless of whether it was self-inflicted or, as Freeman believes, an arranged assassination attempt.

Conversely, Phillips came to the economy with a background in running a small business. It seems that he applied this mindset to Climax Films and, unlike Freeman, followed the strictures of the licensing system, maintaining good relationships with police officers. Their stories show how entrepreneurship within an alternative economy blurs the lines between criminal and lawful enterprise. At this time, pornography was an illicit commodity, yet the Obscene Publications Act 1959 and how it was enforced by the Obscene Publications Squad legitimized its production and distribution, but within a specific institutional framework. This chapter has shown how the parameters of the licensing system guided the growth of the economy in the latter half of the 1960s. The following chapter explores what happened when this institutional framework began to fall apart, as the corruption in the Obscene Publications Squad and the scale of Britain's alternative economy became public.

# 4

## *House of Mirrors*: Regulating the Roller Trade (1970–73)

### *Introduction*

On 22 November 1972, after a routine stop by local police officers in Harrow, Greater London, an entrepreneur named John Darby was arrested while loading his car with 'obscene material'. At the local police station, they discovered that the boot of Darby's car held 608 pornographic magazines, 35 8mm rollers and the 16mm negatives for 14 films. When searching Darby, several keys were found. One of the officers noted that Darby's car was parked near some garages and returned to the scene, wanting to see whether the keys fit any of the locks. They found a wealth of pornographic material, identifying the base of Darby's mail-order business. The police seized the following materials:

- 4391 magazines (73 titles).
- 354 novels (21 titles).
- 44 typescripts (5 titles).
- 28 records (1 title).
- 16 packets of photographs.
- 601 packets of playing cards.
- 379 titled 8mm rollers (51 titles).
- 346 untitled 8mm rollers (subsequently not deemed to be obscene).
- 17,544 empty film cartons for 37 titles.
- 8 unprocessed film titles.
- a number of 16mm films, including master negatives.

Alongside these were documents relating to his six mail-order operations. Of particular interest to the police was an invoice for 5000 film spools that linked

FIGURE 4.1: *House of Mirrors* (Anthony Collingbourne 1972). Author's personal collection. Faces obscured to protect the identity of performers.

Darby with an 'Anthony Collingbourne' of Watford. The police obtained a search warrant and visited Collingbourne on 29 November 1972, seizing 779 magazines, one typescript and two rollers. At this time, it was not realized that Collingbourne produced many of the titles found in Darby's garage. Further investigation revealed the extent of Collingbourne's operation, ultimately resulting in what would become referred to as the Watford Blue Movie Trial by the popular press.

In the previous chapter, I explored the growth of Britain's profitable trade in hardcore pornographic films. Now I explore how the distribution of pornography by mail order increased in the early 1970s, enhanced by the availability of pornography with higher standards of production imported from Scandinavia, usually via Rotterdam, Netherlands. The economy's growth ultimately resulted in greater regulation, as the Longford Report and the *Sunday People's* investigation into the trade uncovered the corruption endemic in the Obscene Publications Squad. This resulted in the removal of the licensing system, leaving pornographers increasingly vulnerable to prosecution. I draw on the Director of Public Prosecutions' documents relating to the Watford Blue Movie Trial to illustrate how attempts were made to regulate the alternative economy and specially the roller market. I argue that this crackdown on hardcore pornography stunted the market, as the high-profile nature of the Watford Blue Movie Trial and its successful prosecution of its conspirators served as a deterrent for those who were making rollers in Britain.

FIGURE 4.2: John Darby's garage, Rayner's Lane, Harrow. From the National Archives, DPP 2/5303-1.

## A time of crisis

In Chapter 1, I suggested that one of the conditions for the emergence of an alternative economy producing and distributing hardcore pornography was the changing political and cultural attitudes of 1960s. Here, debates relating to permissiveness made sex and morality an oft-discussed topic in the mainstream media and amongst the general public. While these changes have often been overstated, it is difficult to deny that they directly affected sexual culture. Amongst this relative chaos was a growth in hardcore film production, as evidenced in the previous two chapters. Yet, if 1960s' permissive Britain is viewed as a time of optimism and 'controlled hedonism' (Hunt 1998: 20), the 1970s is often 'described as a time of crisis' (Smith 2005: 149), which saw 'a return to moral orthodoxy rectitude and right thinking after the extremely limited liberalisation of the decade before' (Hall 1980: 2). For Hunt (1998: 21), this resulted in a 'commodification of permissiveness' as evidenced by the popular media of the time, particularly the demand for softcore sexploitation films (Sheridan 2005; McGillivrary 2017). However, the early 1970s appear to be a time when society was struggling to come to terms with the changes in morality that occurred during the 1960s. This unease resulted in an increased polarization between those who saw permissiveness as an opportunity for greater liberation and others who felt threatened by a change to the status quo and the corruption of traditional British values. As Weeks (2012) highlights, those who often referred to the term permissiveness used it pejoratively. One such group was the Festival of Light, a Christian organization formed in the early 1970s as a response to permissiveness in British society. Fronted by the infamous activist and moralist Mary Whitehouse, the Festival of Light held a Rally Against Permissiveness in 1971, which Tsaliki (2016: 212) describes as 'an imaginary unification of the voices of various moral stakeholders and advocates who lambast the ills of sexualization and wish for – yet again – a return to "family values"'.

The activities of the Festival of Light regularly featured in the popular press as part of their moral crusade against permissiveness, and it would be one of their members, Frank Packenham, more commonly known as Lord Longford, who in 1970 called for an investigation into the growth of Britain's trade in pornography. As I have shown in previous chapters, the British press regularly reported on the pornography business, their articles providing a rich resource for attempting to uncover Britain's pornography trade. During my research, it became apparent that there was an increase in articles in the 1970s. For instance, a search of the valuable British Newspaper Archive using the word 'pornography' shows 519 hits in 1950–59, 1201 in 1960–69, 3979 for 1970–79 and 1966 for 1980–89.[1] The most significant article in the context of this research was *The People's* exposé of the British trade in hardcore films; this would have a lasting impact. On Sunday,

8 November 1970, the top right of the newspaper's front page stated 'Blue Films' Boom Exposed', alongside the text 'GUILTY MEN NAMED'. Inside, a two-page spread documented their investigation into Original Climax Films, the British label Evan Phillips started in 1966, as discussed in the previous chapter. By 1969, Phillips had moved his roller business to Copenhagen, Denmark, where pornography was fully legalized (Kutchinsky and Snare 1999).

Under section 234 of the Danish Criminal Code, Denmark had clear laws to prevent the production and distribution of obscene writings, pictures or objects, much like many other countries. In 1958, a Danish court declared an imported English version of the book *Fanny Hill* (John Cleland) to be obscene, alongside other erotic literature. Later, in 1964, a Danish version of the same book was brought to trial in the City Court of Copenhagen, but eventually found not to be obscene because of its literary and historical interest. Expert witnesses provided evidence for the defence, speaking to the book's cultural value. The Danish Supreme Court confirmed the verdict in 1965. The *Fanny Hill* trial led to a repeal of the Danish criminal code, removing the phrase 'writings' from the law and permitting the distribution of erotic literature in Denmark. However, it was still legally problematic to produce or distribute obscene pictures or objects. Between 1967 and 1969, Danish pornography's illicitness made it a desirable commodity. Parliament believed that legalizing pornography would lessen its aura and, if the test were deemed successful, the criminalization of all pornography could be repealed. On 30 May 1969, Denmark became the first country to fully liberalize their pornography laws. Now section 234 of the Danish criminal code only had one line: 'Any person who sells obscene pictures or objects to a person under the age of 16 shall be liable to a fine'.

The world watched on with interest, as Denmark commemorated this moment with the *Sex 69* trade exhibition. In a matter of months, Denmark's pornography economy grew, with ten pornography businesses forming companies and at least 120 shops and clubs opening (Kutchinsky and Snare 1999). As I mentioned in the previous chapter, *Sex 69* was a space for these newly established businesses to promote their wares to the world (Madsen 2013). It received significant global media attention, with 300 journalists attending the opening press conference and over 49,000 people visiting the eight-day fair (Lauret 1970; Kutchinsky and Snare 1999). Seeing an opportunity to run his business outside of Soho's alternative economy, where he had to deal with corrupt police, members of the underworld, as well as hiding his makeshift laboratories used to process and print his films, Phillips moved his operation to Denmark. In August 1969, he legally registered the company Original Climax Films AS[2] alongside Walter Bartkowski, a German porn smuggler who helped British pornographers distribute their photographs and films across Europe.[3]

The *People* article tells of how a light aircraft travelling from Denmark made an emergency landing in Belgium and was discovered to be holding 777 boxes in Christmas gift wrapping paper. On opening, it was found that these were not gifts, but rollers from Original Climax Films being smuggled into Britain for distribution. The pilot and an unnamed passenger received a two-month jail sentence for 'smuggling obscene material'. This story caught the attention of reporters at *The People,* prompting an on-going investigation into Britain's pornography trade that was published in their Sunday edition over four weeks. Under the guide of Assistant Editor Laurie Manifold, the reporters planned a 'sting', which involved a 'Middle Eastern businessman' attempting to buy 3000 rollers and have them smuggled into Beirut (Cox et al. 1977: 143). The reporters visited Soho's bookshops, trying to find a potential supplier. One bookshop gave the reporter Ivor Cook's contact details. When contacted, Cook told the supposed agent acting on behalf of the Middle Eastern businessman that he did not have the means to supply such a large amount of stock, further supporting my claim that Cook ran a relatively small-scale business in comparison to more commercially motivated entrepreneurs such as Mike Freeman and Evan Phillips. Instead, Cook gave the reporter contact details for Stuart Crispie, 'Big Jeff's' agent. When speaking to the reporter, Crispie suggested that the films would have to be supplied via Bahrain in the Persian Gulf, where they had an operative working in the post office. Crispie quoted a fee of £1000 for transport, and three-quarters of this needed to be paid in advance. The reporter, acting as the go-between, declined the proposal. Crispie counter-offered, suggesting a delivery of 500 films per week to a location close to Heathrow Airport for £2500 per consignment. The transaction did not go ahead.

Cox et al. (1977: 144) reveal that the reporters also approached James Humphreys, another distributer in the economy who owned eleven Soho bookshops, asking for more information about the mysterious Big Jeff. The reporters also let slip that they had been watching Big Jeff's office in Denman Street, noticing members of the Obscene Publications Squad 'coming in and going out in a friendly fashion with Phillips himself'. Not realizing Phillips was Big Jeff and one of Humphreys' suppliers, the journalists informed Humphreys of the sting, which he then passed on to Phillips. Humphreys was also protecting his own interests, being licensed by Obscene Publications Squad and, like John Mason, he maintained relationships with its officers. According to Cox et al. (1977: 144), Humphreys immediately reached out to one of his police contacts, the high-ranking Commander Wally Virgo, who controlled 'nine specialist detective squads', including the Obscene Publications Squad. In response to the sting, Virgo obtained the address of the fake Middle Eastern businessman from Crispie to uncover the name of the person renting the flat. While this happened,

the Obscene Publications Squad alerted the Soho bookshops, instructing them to be careful what stock they sold as the press planned to expose
the economy.

Following instructions from his police contact, Humphreys gave false information to the reporters, deflecting attention away from Soho. Instead, the ever-
crafty Humphreys used the opportunity to inform the press about those he saw
as competitors, but protected the larger operators like Phillips who had close
ties with the Obscene Publications Squad. Virgo quickly learned that the *Sunday
People* leased the flat, and arranged a counter sting at the Hilton Hotel. When
the businessman and his associates arrived, they were greeted by photographers
taking their pictures. These photographs were distributed to Soho's bookshops for
employees to familiarize themselves with the reporters' faces should they return.
This attempted sting and successful counter sting illustrate the importance of
networks in the alternative economy, with producers, distributors, the police and
the underworld working together to protect it, preserve it and continue benefiting
from it. It was the organization of the economy through the licensing system that
prevented it from being uncovered by the popular press. However, reporters still
learned more about its organization, and on 6 December 1970, in the final article
of their series on Britain's pornography trade, Manifold's team bragged about
how their investigation had slowed down Climax's operations and particularly
their distribution of rollers across Soho's bookshops. This claim was nothing but
a boast as the roller trade continued to expand.

## Universal films

In each of the previous chapters, Soho has been identified as the primary
location for the distribution of pornography in Britain. By the early 1970s,
this distribution network grew, with hardcore pornography readily available
under the counter or in the backrooms of bookshops across Britain's cities.
This is evidenced in legal documents, which describe raids of bookshops in
Southampton, Coventry and Nottingham.[4] At the end of the 1969s, I speculated that there were fifteen labels producing rollers in Britain, with Phillips'
Climax continuing to dominate the market. As the 1970s began, more brands
were established, with entrepreneurs drawn to the high profits that could be
generated through making and selling hardcore pornographic goods. Based
on all the labels I have located, a total of 30 can be identified as emerging in
the early 1970s, almost doubling in little more than a year (see Figure 4.3 for
a list).[5] This growth might also be related to the demand for pornography in
Denmark, where pornography was legalized, and the Netherlands, where it

| Academy | Excelsior | Phoenix |
|---|---|---|
| Amor | Fantasy | Steinle |
| Anglo Continental | Gatsby | Taboo |
| Apollo | International Films | Taboo and Phoenix |
| Blue X | Karl Ordinez | Teenage Productions |
| Bunny Films | Leidibird | United Productions |
| Candy | Look | Universal Films |
| Casanova | New Private | Viking Films |
| Danish Blu | Orchid | Zodiac Films |
| Double X | Pearl Films | |

FIGURE 4.3: List of 1970s roller labels.

was tolerated. However, this was a two-way trade, with bookshop owners importing 8mm films produced by Danish labels, such as Color Climax, Flesh, Topsy Films and Marmalade. In his review of the *Sex 69* trade show, Dahl and Næsby (1970: 165) observed that British distributors were in attendance and placed large orders with the Danish exhibitors. As I show later, by 1972, the number of British roller producers reduced, as it became cheaper for bookshops to import films from Denmark.

One of the most productive labels in this list was Universal Films. Their packaging slightly differentiates from what had become the standard roller box style pioneered by Climax (see Figure 4.4). Instead of having an explicit postcard stuck to a coloured cardboard box with the label name at the top, Universal used a more elaborate type of packaging, with small glamour portraits of women on the left- and right-hand side. This bears a similarity to packaging used by the commercial 8mm label Mountain who released non-pornographic films, their box design displaying small pictures of silent film stars running each side. Might this have been an intentional decision by the producer, attempting to introduce packaging that would be distinct from the increasing number of competing labels? Universal Films released at least 67 titles. Like the previously discussed labels Climax and Mike Freeman's Eros Films, the content of their rollers is diverse and speaks to a wide audience. Although their output is dominated by the depiction of heterosexual group sex, as was typical in rollers, they also issued interracial pornography (*Chinese and Passion*, 1970–72; *Negro*, 1970–72), gay pornography

142

(*Beach Boys*, 1970–72; *Gayland*, 1970–72) and transvestite pornography (*Surprise! TV*, 1970–72). Furthermore, they catered to a range of fetishes, including watersports (*The Toilet Lover*, 1970–72), BDSM (*The Victim*, 1970–72; *Sex Maniac*, 1970–72) and incest (*Sons and Lovers*, 1970–72). Universal Films also released films responding to a perceived market for illegal, extreme or variously taboo sex practices through the use of titles that heavily suggested child pornography, such as *Child's Play* (1970–72), as well as several bestiality films (*Canine Orgy*, 1970–72; *Rex and Rover*, 1970–72).

Universal Films re-released rollers that appeared on other labels. As Figure 4.4 shows, *A Lesson in French* was also issued by Svensk Films in 1969, *Maid-servant* appeared on Dolly Films in 1969 (see Figure 4.5) and, again in 1969, *Late Comer* showed up on the colour label Candy Films. It is difficult to know what to make of this. Either the same producer is simply re-releasing their content on another label, or the person, or persons, behind Universal Films acquired these titles from another producer and reissued them. It could also be a combination of both, given that entrepreneurs in the economy were inclined to favour profit. Unlike the standard white box used by Universal – likely to indicate their earlier releases – purple and black box variants clearly state on

FIGURE 4.4: Links between Universal Films and Dolly Films, Svensk Films and Candy Films
Author's personal collection. Faces obscured to protect the identity of performers.

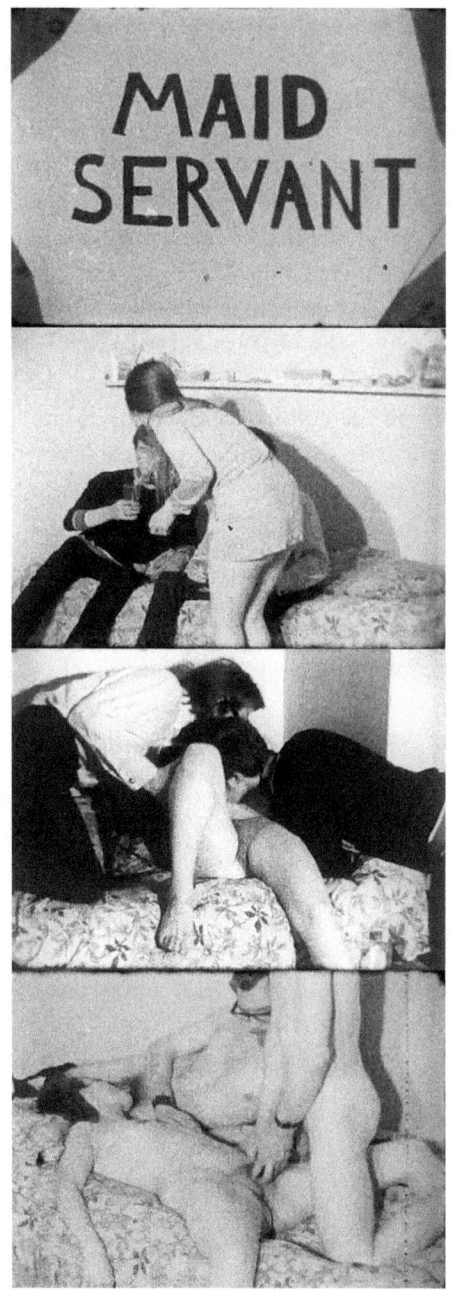

FIGURE 4.5: Screenshots from Universal Films' release of *Maidservant* (1970–72). Author's personal collection. Faces obscured to protect the identity of performers.

the front that the films are 'made in Denmark'. Was this an attempt to disguise their British origins, or were certain titles processed or duplicated in Denmark then imported into Britain for distribution, following a similar model to Original Climax Films?

Evidence points towards Martin Granby being the person behind Universal Films and its related labels. A10, the Metropolitan Police's anti-corruption unit, interviewed him in February 1977 as part of their on-going investigation into the Obscene Publications Squad. Interestingly, a handwritten note in the top left of the opening page of the document states, 'not use [...] info [...] believed to be a Moody plant', implying that Granby was another pornographer to have a close relationship with Chief Inspector Bill Moody. Granby's name first appears in the Ivor Cook investigation of 1962, where he is identified as a delivery driver, transporting pornographic goods to bookshops. In his interview, Granby talks about how he started to manufacture his own Soho Postcards after finding the driving job financially unrewarding. The Obscene Publications Squad carried out their first raid of Granby's premises in 1965. When this happened, Granby was away on his honeymoon, and therefore evaded arrest. A fellow pornographer named Billy Jeal advised Granby to pay for a licence so that he could continue producing postcards without further police harassment, arranging a meeting with Officer Culver of the Obscene Publications Squad.

Granby claims to have paid '£50 or £100' for a licence, again suggesting that the fee was means tested and based on earning power. Later based in Chigwell, Essex, police again raided Granby, discovering a stockpile of postcards that were due to be transported to the north of England for distribution. In his statement, Granby believes that he was framed. When Culver left the Obscene Publications Squad, Granby met with Moody, who advised him to start a mail-order business. Moody assured the inexperienced Granby that he would be given 'all the advice needed' on the condition that Moody knew of the addresses being used and that he took a third of the profits. However, Granby opted to cheat customers, designing 'circulars which suggested I had some photographs of a well-known Hollywood actress performing various acts and circulated the stuff', but had 'no intention of delivering the goods'. On the first day of collecting orders, Granby made '£210 or £220'. The next day, he and his associate were arrested by Leytonstone Criminal Investigation Department. After refusing to give a police statement, Granby was released and got in touch with his police contact.

Angry at being arrested, especially when he had been paying for a licence, Granby threatened the Obscene Publications Squad, telling them that he possessed compromising recordings of his negotiations with officers. An officer named Jones responded: 'this is a very big business that you're involved in. There is a lot of money involved, and they are not going to let any "Johnny Come Lately" upset the apple cart'. Granby understood this as a warning. An agreement was reached where Granby pleaded guilty to the Chigwell raid – fined £50 by the court – and in return, he would not be charged for his mail-order swindle. After leaving the trade for a few months, Granby returned and began making rollers. As mentioned in Chapter 3, Granby's films were initially unbranded, but after seeing the impact the branded label Climax had on the economy, he followed Phillips' lead. Granby is vague about this, but states that he used label names suggestive of 'a Danish or a Swedish origin'.

John Lindsay, a pornographer whose career I discuss in the coming chapter, gives an indication of why such a strategy was used: 'Films are made here that are packaged as if they have come from abroad [...] punters always think they are getting a hotter video if it comes from Scandinavia'.[6] Therefore, roller producers often drew on the myths of 'Swedish sin' (Hale 2003; Schaefer 2014; Arnberg and Marklund 2016; Paasonen 2017) and 'Danish blue'.[7] As Schaefer (2014: 228) highlights, 'the words "Danish" and "Swedish" soon came to signal the hardest material available in the US market in the late 1960s into the 1970s'; it seems that roller makers also used this strategy to achieve the same effect. The naming of these countries on roller boxes may also have been a way to disassociate the films from their illicit origins, particularly for producers who did not pay the Obscene Publications Squad or were breaching licence conditions. Alternatively, and as I speculated earlier, it may point to the films being processed and printed in Denmark then smuggled back into Britain.

When Granby returned to the trade he was unlicensed. After discovering this, Moody advised Soho's bookshops not to stock Granby's films, just as they black-listed Mike Freeman from selling Soho Postcards in the early 1960s. The only shop willing to take them was the Long Shop at 51a Old Compton Street. Granby mentions how Ron 'The Dustman' Davey, acting on behalf of Moody, visited Soho's shops, telling the chairs not to stock them. In keeping with the typical model of distribution described in Chapter 1, Granby's arrangement was sale or return, meaning that unsold rollers were returned. Granby alleges threats of violence, getting 'chinned or knocked out' if he kept wholesaling his rollers to bookshops. To get around this, Granby focused on his non-London contacts, selling to the north of England. He then states that certain members of the Obscene Publications Squad 'granted a partial' licence without Moody's knowledge, costing £200 a month.[8] In 1969, when Freeman was being investigated for Hawley's murder, Granby recalls how police searched his house because of its house's proximity to Epping Forest where Freeman dumped Hawley's body. Granby received no prior warning.

A further raid took place on 9 February 1970 – 'they took several hundred films and a load of negatives at that raid' – which perplexed the now licensed Granby. At his cell in Barkingside Police Station, squad officers told him that 'there was nothing personal in it – there was nothing they could do about it'. On 15 April 1970, he received a six month sentence, suspended for three years, under the Obscene Publications Act 1959. To retrieve the negatives of his films, Granby reached out to the then former Obscene Publications Squad officer Culver, asking him to set up a meeting with his former colleagues. The squad agreed, and officer Fenwick met with Granby at a Soho public house where Granby offered £1000 to buy back the negatives. His offer was accepted and several days later the exchange took place. With the £1000 cash wrapped in a brown paper package, Granby walked up to Fenwick in a lane nearby Denman Street in Soho, gave him the payment and, in return, Fenwick handed Granby a holdall that contained all of the seized negatives. Back in business, Granby continued to make regular payments to the Obscene Publications Squad.

Granby died in October 2018 aged 80 and little is known of his life after 1971. 'Derek', the early roller producer discussed in Chapter 2, remarked that 'Granby was bad news', but did not elaborate why. Granby's police interview provides helpful clues that potentially link him to the labels Svensk Films, Malmo Films, Danish Blu Films, Dolly Films and possibly Candy Films. He claims to have chosen label names that signified 'a Danish or Swedish origin', pointing to Svensk Films, Malmo Films and Danish Blu Films. Rollers released on these labels, Dolly Films and the supposedly German label Candy Films, were re-released by the label Universal Films. Furthermore, the 1970 raid gives some indication of the scale of Granby's enterprise, having 'several hundred films and a load of negatives' seized. Universal Films, and its associated labels, is the only brand to match Granby's description.

Further evidence potentially linking Granby to Danish Blu Films, Dolly Films and Malmo Films can be found in *The People*. As part of their on-going investigation into Britain's blue film trade, a 22 November 1970 article makes mention of a professional photographer named Shakespeare, an associate of the Institute of Incorporate Photographers and the Royal Photographic Society, who 'arranges a do-it-yourself service in pornography'. In addition to selling rollers at his studio in Leytonstone – an area of London where Granby operated – Shakespeare hired out models and equipment for amateurs wanting to make their own blue films. The article also claims that Shakespeare has 'considerable interests in various aspects of the blue film business', selling the rollers *Arabian Nights* (1969) on Danish Blu Films[9] and *Home from School* (1969) on Malmo Films to the reporters. He informs the journalist that he 'printed 50 copies of the cover for the film containers'.

Could Shakespeare have involved in the production of these films, as well as making the postcards for the box covers? Was Universal Films the label Granby

started after the raid, re-releasing many of his older films that he had the negatives for on a new label, as his stock of 'several hundred' was not returned? It is
also likely that Granby eventually moved processing and duplication to Denmark,
with later Universal Films boxes including the text 'made in Denmark'. In his
police interview, Granby appears to follow Phillips' innovations closely – note
how the Malmo Films box resembles a Climax box (see Figure 3.17) – so Granby
moving operations to Denmark is plausible. His approach to entrepreneurship
shares many similarities with that of Mike Freeman's, refusing to comply with
the Obscene Publications Squad. Yet, unlike Freeman, Granby was cooperative
enough to become a significant player in the economy and is likely responsible for
at least five labels and a wealth of unbranded rollers.

## A transnational trade

The legalization of pornography in Denmark meant that its quality of production
was superior to Britain's roller entrepreneurs, who were often using amateur or
semi-professional methods, such as the use of 'garage labs' or the semi-professional duplication machines described in earlier chapters. In a police interview
on 26 November 1975, roller producer Ivor Cook remarks on how 'the bottom
went out' of his business because 'supplies were being brought in from the continent'.[10] An anniversary issue of *Color Climax* magazine from 1986 looks back
at the company's history and details their highly professional approach to film
production. Initially, the Theander Brothers outsourced the processing of their
films to other commercial laboratories, but were dissatisfied with the quality. In
response, they opened their own laboratory, Rodox Color Teknik, investing in
high-end processing and duplicating equipment. Initially, they only had the means
to produce 100 copies of a film per day, struggling to meet market demand for
their films. After improving their workflow, they claim to have made between
3500 and 4000 copies of a film per day, using approximately 200,000 metres of
film and producing over 1 million copies per year. Their machinery consisted of
seven optical copying machines, four developing tanks and an electronic colour
analyser that allowed for each scene of a film to be colour corrected. Such devices
ran continuously and, to ensure that the laboratory ran smoothly, they employed
34 skilled workers.[11] The article brags that Rodox Color Teknik is 'one of the
world's largest Super 8 film laboratories'.

Kodak introduced the Super 8 format in 1965, a response to the large sprocket
holes that took up a large amount of space on standard 8mm film. The purpose
of this new format was to 'increase the area of the film available for the picture'
as well as enhancing the options for having a soundtrack (McKee 1978: 106).
Another benefit of the new format was the film being supplied in a cartridge,

meaning that it could easily be loaded into a camera, making amateur film production more straightforward. However, as a medium for distributing films, Super 8 took a while to be adopted. McKee (1978: 107) surmises that this was due to 8mm having a strong following, but also distributors 'ignoring it', favouring the older format. He also suggests that the smaller sprocket holes of Super 8 were more susceptible to damage. In Britain, rollers were primarily released on standard 8mm. It is not clear why producers did not adopt the new format, though a limited market reach and challenges with processing and printing are likely explanations. Some labels did release rollers on Super 8, as is evident in mail-order catalogues. For example, Blue Scene Films released the roller *Free Sample* (1970–72) in both Super 8 and standard 8mm, while Climax offered titles in both formats following their move to Denmark. This relocation enabled Phillips to enhance his production process, using official film laboratories and industry-standard equipment. However, the large majority of rollers appear on standard 8mm. Super 8 rollers eventually became more commonplace in the mid 1970s when Super 8 replaced standard 8mm as the dominant home film format (McKee 1978: 107), and these were mainly released by John Lindsay.

As a commodity, Danish-produced pornography had a higher material standard than British rollers. Their mass production meant that the unit price for Danish pornography was lower than rollers, especially for retailers. Bookshop owners risked importing films from Denmark, as cheaper wholesale prices meant higher profits. The logistics of smuggling meant that the economy increasingly required casual workers to assist in circulating the goods across Britain.[12] 'Mark' was one of these freelancers, delivering pornography that had been smuggled into the north of England to shops. 'I had a large van', Mark told me, 'a friend of mine had a cousin who lived in the city of Hull. In conversation, it came out that he was looking for someone to help with shifting "goods"'. As Mark's full-time job involved shift work, he often had blocks of days off: 'As I had a bit of free time – especially during the day – I said I would help him out not knowing (at this stage) what it was I had to shift! I agreed to meet him, and we struck a deal'. He then explained how the distribution network operated:

> What used to happen was the porn (Books, 8mm films – mainly Colour Climax stuff) arrived at the port of Hull by ship. I understand that a lot of it came on ships from Scandinavia that brought a lot of timber into the docks. I don't know anything about the Scandinavian end. I also don't know how much came in at any one time. The 'goods' were collected by 'Frank' and possibly other distributors, and he took it back to his house, where he sorted it into large cardboard boxes for distribution to various shops. All I had to do was drive to 'Frank's' house, load up boxes and drive to the shops. I never delivered in the local area. Most of my 'drops' were in

Halifax, Manchester and Newcastle. Sometimes I would combine a drop – Halifax and Manchester, for example – and on other occasions, it would be a single run out. It was simply a matter of driving out, finding the shop, dropping off and coming home. Nothing difficult about it.

Mark never handled any money, with 'the business' taking place 'behind the scenes'.

Payment varied, depending on the distance he travelled and the time it took; 'it was usually just a few quid in my hand [...] and was only a sideline'. I asked him whether he was worried about being stopped:

> I must have carted tons of the stuff across most of the north of England. It got to the point where porn actually got boring as I saw so much of the stuff. Don't know how I would have explained the contents of the back if I had got stopped by the police.

With the trade now stretching out beyond Soho more entrepreneurs were drawn to the profits offered by importing pornography from Denmark. For instance, an article from the 27 June 1972 issue of *The Guardian* reported on the 'biggest consignment of pornography seized by Customs' in Newcastle, which had arrived from Denmark, concealed beneath a carpet in a shipping container. Knudsen, a Danish lorry driver, received a nine-month prison sentence for evading the prohibition of obscene articles after being found to have 'nearly half a ton' of pornography that 'could have been sold for £70,000'. They discovered 'more than 10,000 magazines and more than 300 films and 200 packs of playing cards'. Knudsen worked for a 'Danish organisation smuggling pornography into Britain' and is said to have been paid £270 for delivering the stock 'to two contacts in the London area'. From this, police identified a distribution network operating across the country; their investigation resulted in arrests of men in London and Essex. More significant was the *Birmingham Post's* 12 August 1970 story on John Darby's twelve-month sentence for importing 'blue films' from Denmark. As I show shortly, the police described Darby as a major mail-order distributor of hardcore pornography in Britain, who worked with roller producers to sell their films. With more content now available for distribution, mail-order operations increased, as Figure 4.6 demonstrates. As profits grew, the economy became increasingly uncontrollable for the Obscene Publications Squad who also capitalized on this growth in revenue. Moral crusader and Labour politician Lord Longford took an interest in the economy and set out to uncover its scale, initiating an investigation into Britain's pornography business.

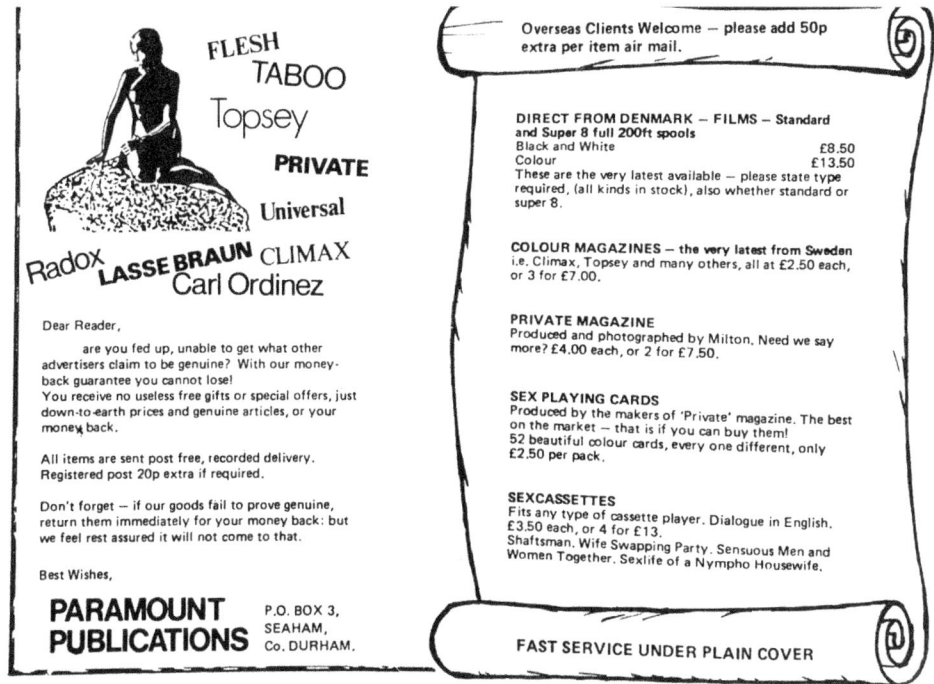

FIGURE 4.6: An advertisement for hardcore 8mm films by Paramount Publications placed in *Film Making* magazine. The Durham post box address demonstrates the growth of the trade outside of Soho. Courtesy of 'Phillip Black'.

## Lord Porn and the fall of the Obscene Publications Squad

*The People's* earlier attempts to expose Britain's illicit trade in rollers had little impact as large quantities of pornography were smuggled in from Denmark via Rotterdam. Other European countries began to expand their production of hardcore pornography. For instance, Walter Bartkowski introduced the brands Tabu and Charlie Brown Produktion to Germany, where hardcore pornography was criminalized. Although Laurie Manifold's team of reporters had succeeded in bringing the hidden business to wider public attention and named some of its minor players, the true identity of 'Big Jeff' remained a mystery. Festival of Light member and Labour politician Frank Packenham, known as Lord Longford, also took an interest in the growth of Britain's pornography trade. Renowned for his moral crusades, on 21 April 1971, Longford raised a debate in the House of Lords that called for an inquiry into the state of pornography in Britain; the government welcomed his intervention but refused to financially support the investigation.

With a committee drawn from his associates, including pop star Cliff Richard and then celebrity Jimmy Saville, Longford set out to investigate the extent of the pornography trade, securing funding from The Dulverston Trust.

In the autumn of 1971, Longford, alongside other committee members, visited Copenhagen to see the impact of legalization in Denmark firsthand. 'Lord Porn', as the tabloids mockingly referred to him, attended two live sex shows and walked out of both. The report was published as a paperback (Anon. 1972), selling well and receiving considerable media attention. Rather than follow the path taken by Denmark or Sweden in fully legalizing pornography, it makes a case for greater regulation in Britain. They recommended that the Obscene Publications Act 1959 be amended, believing that its vagueness had created a loophole for pornographers to thrive. The committee proposed a draft bill for what they termed the Obscenity Act, replacing the Hicklin 'tendency to deprave and corrupt' test with the following:

> For the purposes respectively of the Obscene Publications Acts 1959 and 1964 and section 2 of the Theatres Act 1968, an article or a performance of a play is obscene if its effect, taken as a whole, is to outrage contemporary standards of decency or humanity accepted by the public at large.
>
> (Anon. 1972: 383)

It also proposed the repeal of section 4 – defence of public good – and an 'increase in penalties on summary of conviction' to deter people from participating in the trade (Anon. 1972: 384).

The findings of the Longford Report did not inform any policy relating to pornography or obscenity. Robertson (1979: 231) notes how their proposals 'aroused widespread controversy' and that the 'Home Secretary expressly rejected' them. If anything, it brought further media attention to Britain's pornography trade. However, I argue that the Longford Report was significant in that its research revealed the activities of Obscene Publications Squad, informing yet another tabloid report on the pornography trade by the *Sunday People*. Longford hired a private detective named Matthew Oliver to investigate Soho's porn trade. During his research, Oliver discovered the existence of the alternative economy of hardcore pornography. He quickly learned how it functioned through the Obscene Publications Squad's licensing system and became aware of the police corruption taking place. On 6 February 1972, the *Sunday People* finally named the man they had targeted two years ago, revealing the activities of Evan 'Big Jeff' Phillips and identifying him as Britain's 'FIRST BLUE FILM MILLIONAIRE' (*Sunday People*, 6 February 1972). Acknowledging that they were in league with Longford's moral crusade, Manifold's team reports on the 'full scope and scale that the blue films business has attained in Britain in 1972' in a three-page feature. In the previous chapter, I referred to this article when describing Phillips' growth as an entrepreneur in the economy, but now it has value in its description of Phillips' decline. Manifold's team attempted to ascertain the scale of Phillips' enterprise:

> In all, Phillips' Climax organisation has a range of some 200 pornographic master films. An average of 5000 copies are believed to have been made of each title. On this basis, Phillips has distributed one million blue films throughout the world. Since each copy sells at around £20 each, Phillips' world turnover in the last few years has amounted to approximately £20 millions [sic.]. His profits, allowing for costs of making, processing, smuggling and distributing must have reached the staggering total of £2,000,000.

I have reservations about these numbers, as a black and white roller wholesaled for around £5, and mail order prices were generally lower than those found in bookshops. That said, it is evident that Phillips managed to make a lot of money out of hardcore pornography, owning 'an estate at High Crockett, in the hamlet of Hare Hatch, near Reading, in Berkshire. With its manor house, 10 acres of parkland, swimming-pool, stables and garages, the estate is valued at £80,000'. However, the moving of Climax Films to Denmark had not worked out as well as Phillips intended.

Phillips and Bartkowski's new model of business was based on the exportation of pornographic goods from Denmark to Britain. To achieve this, they arranged for films to be concealed in cars and lorries driven into Britain via ferries – usually hidden in petrol tanks, false boots and roof linings – and via private planes that would drop consignments of films into the sea for boats to collect. According to the German publication *Der Spiegel* (1 November 1971), Bartkowski possessed a list of many small and partially unapproved landing sites in 'Germany, England and other states'. The *Sunday People* reporters also found that 'Danish fishing vessels are also used. They put out into the North Sea and have prearranged rendezvous with fishing boats from Grimsby and North of England ports'. Basu (2013: 316) identifies that the smuggling of commodities is both a 'logistics and transport intensive activity'. Moreover, it is a costly enterprise with significant overheads. With an increasingly competitive market for pornographic films and the added expense of smuggling materials into Britain it is unsurprising that Original Climax Films AS quickly ran into financial troubles. Additionally, the *Sunday People* discovered that the firm was in liquidation as debts had not been paid to the company, with Phillips himself owing DKK 143,427 (£8000). It appears that Phillips mismanaged the growth of the company, being more consumed by his wealth, as the *Sunday People* article suggests. Danish business records show Original Climax Films AS may have been taken over by a company named Spar Sex Corporation, who eventually re-released Climax's third wave titles on 8mm under the brand Climax in Color (see Figure 4.7). The packaging and branding closely imitated the design of the Theander Brothers' popular Color Climax label.

More damningly, the *Sunday People* reported on the corrupt practices of the Obscene Publications Squad, making public that Commissioner Ken Drury of the Metropolitan Police and pornography entrepreneur James Humphreys shared a holiday in Cyprus. The police corruption alleged by *Empire News and Sunday Chronicle* reporter Gerald Byrne in 1959 now proved to be accurate. The newspaper chose not to name any other corrupt police officers but drew on Matthew Oliver's findings into how Soho's economy of pornography operated:

> Police officers in London, in particular some of those attached to Scotland Yard's Obscene Publications Department, are being systematically bribed by dealers in pornography. It is this that largely explains why their businesses flourish; why immense stocks of 'dirty' books, magazines and films are not confiscated.
>
> (*Sunday People*, 27 February 1972)

FIGURE 4.7: Spar Sex Corporation's re-release of Climax's *The Bookworm* 151 (1971–72) following the design of Colour Climax Corporation.

The informer was Charles Julian – actual name Charles Marandola – an American criminal who became engaged in the pornography business. Julian built a relationship with Phillips, arranging for books to be imported from the United States to Denmark for distribution to Britain, but ultimately swindled him. Julian gave the reporters a statement, documenting how he regularly met corrupt police officers through his relationship with Phillips: 'it is common knowledge among overseas dealers such as myself that British porn dealers have to pay the police. If they didn't, they could not operate'. The article states that in 1967, 28 bookshops sold pornography in London's West End and, by 1972, there were 59, almost doubling in the space of five years. Oliver also gave details on the licensing system: 'I am told that a police "tariff" operates in the West End whereby certain police officers between them receive from the pornographic "kings" of £1000 a week'. Oliver refers to an interview he conducted with a mail-order operator who explained the licence's benefits: 'It is far cheaper to pay the police than have the trouble and expense of going to court [...] Now and then the police arrange a raid on my premises, plus the occasional little prosecution, to make things look OK'.

The *Sunday People's* allegations caused a great stir. Robert Mark, the newly appointed Commissioner of the Metropolitan Police, was tasked with rooting out corruption in the force and assigned an officer named Gilbert Kelland to lead the investigation (Mark 1979; Kelland 1986). The institutional framework that facilitated the emergence and the expansion of Britain's trade in hardcore pornographic goods had been removed. With pornography now a subject of national interest, licensed pornographers found themselves vulnerable to arrest and prosecution, as John Darby's arrest, described in the introduction to this chapter, suggests. Darby's detention brought about further arrests, resulting in a significant obscenity trial, referred to as the Watford Blue Movie Trial. Police documents relating to this trial offer more detail on cultures of roller production in the early 1970s, showing how the law was entrepreneurially used to control the trade particularly in the context of police corruption and tabloid interest.

### *The mail-order business*

By the 1970s, mail order became increasingly difficult for the Obscene Publications Squad to control, partly because of an increase in pornography imports from Scandinavia being smuggled into Britain. John Darby was one of many mail-order operators who benefited from the legalization of pornography in Denmark. A police interview from 1977 reveals more about Darby's enterprise, although he is a little economical with the truth.[13] Darby's involvement in the trade dates back to 1969 when he visited Denmark. Discovering that hardcore pornography could legally be purchased over the counter, he bought some and posted it to friends back home. Upon re-entry, Customs and Excise stopped Darby and reported him for attempting to bring indecent material into Britain. Seeing an opportunity to make money, Darby moved from Birmingham to London, starting a mail-order business with two partners who operated from a premises in New Compton Street, Soho. Darby's main contribution to this enterprise was the placing of an advert in *Exchange and Mart* – a weekly magazine containing classified adverts – offering Danish 'scans' for sale.[14] Darby discovered that one of his partners paid a junior officer of the Obscene Publications Squad for a licence to operate the mail-order business, costing £25 per week. They ran their business under four different names from three separate addresses. As part of the licence agreement, officers gave Darby and his partners a list of people who complained to the police about receiving unsolicited mail-shots so they could be removed from the mailing list.

Evan Phillips acted as their main supplier, now based in Denmark, but still maintaining a warehouse on Denman Street, Soho. Phillips suggested that he take over the business, as he had a stronger and more established relationship with senior officers in the Obscene Publications Squad that offered greater protection. Plainclothes officers from Birmingham arrested Darby for the earlier charge of fraudulently evading the prohibition of the importation of indecent or obscene articles from Denmark. At trial, the court ordered a twelve-month prison sentence. While in jail, two officers from the squad visited Darby; one identified themselves as an acquaintance of Phillips. The officer suggested that Darby take the blame for the London mail-order business so that Phillips could continue, and Darby would be looked after. Darby accepted, and the officer wrote a statement on his behalf. On appeal, his sentence was reduced from twelve months to a fine. Undeterred, Darby contacted the officer he had met in prison, requesting permission to restart the business. Darby purchased a mailing list containing 5000 names for £100 from the officer, allowing him to run a number of mail-order operations, providing that he paid a £100 licence fee per month.

Darby now ran six mail-order addresses under different aliases, with one located in Denmark, as Figure 4.8 illustrates. This is an early example of an overseas address being used to take orders from customers, with the order being dispatched from within Britain to avoid customs interference.[15] To do this, Darby paid for a postbox in Denmark and a contact phoned the orders through to to him. It also shows how Darby drew on the notoriety of Denmark's association with pornography to lure customers. With Phillips no longer supplying Darby – it appears that they had some sort of falling out after Darby's earlier arrest – he sourced product from Scandinavia, such as Color Climax, Flesh Films, Lasse Braun, as well as Britain. Darby's mail-order catalogues show that he distributed

Eric Lindstrome,
B.B.C.
Box 37.
Frederikssundsvej 273
2700 Bronshoj
Denmark.

Dear Friend,

I have received your name and address in confidence that you are a mature adult and that you may be interested in adult stag items. If this is not so then please destroy this letter and you will not hear from me again.

If you are interested then perhaps I should introduce myself. I run a Mail Order company here in Denmark, but as you can see by the stamp on the envelope I post all my orders in England. This saves them being stopped by the customs and guarantees that you get your order.

I can supply the very best in colour porno photographic magazines featuring the most beautiful girls in Scandinavia in all types of erotic love positions. I have a good selection of these magazines featuring males only, singles or duos. I have also a good selection of 8mm films in black and white or colour. These films are superb in action and quality and for those of you who like to read I have a very wide range of novels including Gay. Some of these books are illustrated.

If you want a free illustrated list every month would you please fill in the bottom half of this letter with your name and address.

To save offending anyone all these items are very strong hard core porno. So please do not ask for lists then say that you have been shocked.

Cut Here ..................................................................

      Name: ....................................................

      Address: ...................................................

      ................................................................

FIGURE 4.8: Mail-shot from one of Darby's mail-order operations. Author's personal collection.

rollers from the labels International Films, Universal Films, Taboo and Phoenix and Taboo of Sweden. He was again arrested in late 1971, after being stopped by uniformed police with no affiliation to the Obscene Publications Squad, who discovered hardcore pornography in his car. Despite this, Darby, who now paid a £200 monthly licence fee, escaped charge.

However, as outlined in the introduction to this chapter, uniformed police stopped and arrested Darby one year later, charging him with two counts of publication for gain, contrary to section 2 of the Obscene Publications Act 1959 and two counts of sending an indecent or obscene article, namely a brochure, advertising obscene material, contrary to section 11(1) of the Post Office Act 1953. A rough estimate of Darby's seized stock, which is based on the prices found in the mail-order catalogue, suggests that it had a retail value between £250,000 and £400,000, yet again demonstrating the lucrativeness of the trade. The catalogue also illustrates how mail order prices were cheaper than bookshops. For instance, a black and white roller cost £14–£15 in Soho, yet Darby offered them for around £7. He sold colour rollers for £14 or £17. These tended to cost £25 in bookshops. This difference in pricing is likely due to lower overheads of running a mail-order business and their ability to target the national market. It also shows how hardcore pornography became increasingly affordable as the economy grew. In 1972, the average manual male worker took home £32 a week, while non-manual workers earned £43.50. Now rollers were no longer the equivalent of a week's wages and therefore accessible to a larger audience.

The police investigating Darby's enterprise name him as a major mail-order distributor of hardcore pornography in Britain, with many links to active roller labels. This was identified through his possession of 16mm master negatives and having 1200 empty roller boxes for a company named Anglo Continental. Furthermore, the police found an invoice for 5000 film spools, revealing that Anthony Collingbourne of Watford collected half of this order from the supplier. With Darby charged but managing to evade arrest and going into hiding, the police placed their attention on Collingbourne, and carried out a brief investigation. Following a search of Collingbourne's record shop and home, the police found 779 magazines, one typescript and two rollers identical to those sold by Darby. They then searched Collingbourne's previous address, discovering a diary that contained a list of film titles and a drawn diagram of a film processing machine. When interviewed, Collingbourne admitted little, telling officers that all the material was for his personal use, aside from the 779 magazines that he held for a friend. Police did not charge Collingbourne at this point and continued their investigation. Being a licensed pornographer probably helped.

## House of Mirrors

A seemingly unrelated investigation into a company named Fleetwood Films brought police one step closer to arresting Collingbourne. Fleetwood Films was operated by an American named Donald 'Duke' Case and his two partners. Case, whose real name was Nick Valentine, previously ran massage parlours on 42nd Street in New York, fleeing the country after his buildings were fire-bombed. It was alleged that Marty Hodas, a pornography entrepreneur who made his fortune from coin-operated mini-movie machines that showed 8mm pornography (Alilunas 2016: 47–49), instigated the bombings after Valentine undercut the prices of his competitors. Hodas was found not guilty of this crime in 1973 (*New York Times*, 14 July 1973). Fearing for his life, Case fled to Britain and followed Hodas' model of enterprise, introducing mini-movie machines across London's West End, as well as making films for them (see Figure 4.9). As Alilunas (2016: 47) identifies, Hodas' success was not solely due to his introduction of such machines, which were already commonplace in red-light districts such as Times Square, but his ability to defeat the 'legal thickets' that prevented the devices to operate lawfully. Case seems to have had a similar plan, choosing not to produce hardcore films, instead making glamour and softcore pornography. According to Case's police interview, he consulted a solicitor to discuss what films could legally be shown on the machines to avoid obscenity charges. Case described his films as 'mild sex education, well within the law'.[16]

Despite Case's attempt to work within the Obscene Publications Act 1959, he and his partners were still charged with possessing obscene films for publication for gain and publishing by distributing obscene films, pleading guilty at trial. It seems that some of the films went beyond the parameters of acceptability, exposing genitals and showing erect penises. It is also worth noting that two of the films were soft gay pornography: the film *Gay Boys* is named in the court case, supporting Beresford's (2014) claim that the Obscene Publications Act 1959 contains 'norms … as to what constitutes acceptable (heterosexual) and unacceptable pornography (homosexual)'. As the coming chapter shows, prosecutors regularly used gay pornography and BDSM pornography in obscenity cases to increase their chances of a conviction. Case and his partners pleaded guilty, with Case leaving Britain to testify against Hodas (*Daily Telegraph*, 31 October 1973). From the case files, it appears that Case did not pay the Obscene Publications Squad for a licence. When I described the case to Dave, whose family ran many Soho bookshops from the 1960s onwards, he told me that the Obscene Publications Squad did not like outsiders involved in the alternative economy, especially an American with possible Mafia links. However, another American pornography entrepreneur named Reuben Sturman established a partnership with the Soho-based Holloway family, who had been involved in the the pornography business from the 1950s onwards (Schlosser 2004: 130). With Sturman also bringing mini-movie machines into Britain via the Holloways, Case's participation in the economy may not have been welcome, leading to his removal from it.

During the Case investigation, the Obscene Publications Squad linked two of the performers appearing in the 8mm made by Fleetwood Films to rollers seized during raids of Soho bookshops. Following the revelations in the *Sunday People*, the Metropolitan Police carried out 66 raids on bookshops in one January weekend. These were widely reported by the British press, demonstrating the police's new tough stance on the pornography trade (*Daily Mirror*, 29 January 1973).[17] On reviewing the films, they noticed that the performers also appeared in several

# FREE

## THE MACHINE THAT MAKES YOU MONEY:

# MOTION MINI MOVIES
### IN COLOUR & BLACK & WHITE
### *GIGANTIC FILM LIBRARY*

| | |
|---|---|
| Pubs | Cartoons |
| Clubs | Sports |
| Stor... | Shorts & Full Length Features |
| Sch... | Educational Sex ... |
| Adver... ng | All types of F... |
| Super... rkets | Glamour |
| Groc... Shops | Pin-ups |
| or any place | |

100% English Ma...

Completely Automatic

24 Hours Mainte... ...

CALL US TODAY

## FLEETWOOD FILMS LIMI...
### 12 - 14 ARGYLL STREET, LONDON, W.1.
Telephone: 01-437 8320    01-437 8329    01-437 1182

We install the machine FREE!

We supply the films FREE!

We do all the maintenance FREE!

**PLUS You** ...eive 50% of all monies re... ...ed by machine

We buy, sell and trade films of all types.

Telephone:  Office :  01-437 8320
            Factory :  01-986 5227

MACHINES MEASURE :
70″ high     20″ wide     30″ deep
also smaller sizes

If you have this much space in your business
YOU ARE LOOSING A STEADY INCOME

## *CALL US TODAY*

BE THE FIRST TO HAVE SOMETHING NEW!
The only machine that makes you money
AT NO COST TO YOU.

FIGURE 4.9: Promotional brochure for Donald Case's mini-movie machine business Fleetwood Films. Author's personal collection.

Anglo Continental titles and identified one of the filmmakers who had links with Fleetwood Films. With Collingbourne now known to the police, they recognized his face (see Figure 4.10) and also the vehicles and locations used in the films. In a later police interview from 1975, Collingbourne recounted his career of working in pornography.[18] It began in 1962 when Collingbourne was released from prison and soon appeared in rollers made by 'Skinny' Ken Taylor, an early producer discussed in Chapter 2.

By the late 1960s, Collingbourne ran a car dealership in Watford until it mysteriously burnt down. Following an unsuccessful insurance claim, an acquaintance advised Collingbourne to start a photography studio. As back issues of the magazine *Amateur Photographer* show, photography studios were commonplace across Britain. For instance, the classified section of an issue from 23 September 1964 lists eighteen studios. Such enterprises brought together those who had an interest in the practice of photography, allowing them to either rent studio space or, for a fee, take pictures of models paid for by the studio. Glamour and nude photography were not uncommon and openly mentioned in some classified adverts found in *Amateur Photographer*. Studios could be a profitable pursuit for those who owned them, also selling photography equipment as well as offering film processing and developing services. In early 1969, Collingbourne opened Studio Hire in Watford. In addition to taking 'straight' photographs for clients, he also let the studio out for 'club nights', where people could pay to photograph a glamour model; Collingbourne developed and printed the films, as well as selling photography accessories.

FIGURE 4.10: Anthony Collingbourne, screenshot from *Timber* (1970–72). Courtesy of the Erotic Film Society.

Being aware of the studio, Collingbourne claims that Taylor contacted him to ask if he could rent the studio for making rollers. Collingbourne agreed, providing that Taylor showed him and an associate how to produce them. Collingbourne purchased equipment from Taylor, negotiating a deal where Taylor bought any films made by Collingbourne back for a set price. Taylor also sold him an American processing machine so that he could easily develop the films. Again, this relationship illustrates how entrepreneurs within the alternative economy often worked together to share resources and increase profits. Collingbourne also recollects how Taylor advised him to pay for a licence from the Obscene Publications Squad, but as Collingbourne did not operate in London's West End he believed it was not necessary. Later, when selling his rollers to Soho bookstores, he soon realized that he needed police permission to do so. Unlike the other licences discussed in this book, Collingbourne claims that his was a 'pay as you go' licence, with payments ranging between £25 and £1000 depending on the information or protection required. He goes back to the search of his house in late 1972, which resulted in no arrest or charge, despite police discovering 5500 porn magazines in one of the bedrooms. Collingbourne suggests that the two officers ignored these and I found no record of them in the police files. However, after the popular press' exposure of the alternative economy, Collingbourne's protection turned out to be temporary.

Collingbourne admits to releasing rollers on five labels: Anglo Continental, Double X, Apollo, Look, and Academy (see Figure 4.11), although it is likely that he had some involvement in Fantasy given that the same performers often appear.[19] As discussed earlier, roller producers often had a range of brands. This may have been a technique used to confuse the police, with multiple labels implying different producers, but it is more likely that this was also a way for producers to meet the demand for new content, introducing new labels to suggest the availability of fresh material. As the previous examples of Eros Films and Universal Films revealed, some films appear on multiple labels, occasionally under alternate titles. This seems to be a way entrepreneurs maximized the economic return for one film, exploiting customers in an unregulated market. As Gorfinkel (2019: 8) states, the pornography business is a 'fickle profit-driven industry', and unscrupulous tactics are not uncommon in the pursuit of profit. In addition to distributing via mail order through Darby, Collingbourne also sold to bookshops across Britain through a partner named Wyatt. In 1973, police searched a bookshop in Llanelli, Wales. A police statement made by the owner of the shop states that he paid Wyatt between £150 and £200 per month for stock, which included Anglo Continental rollers. Once more, this shows the expansion of the economy beyond Soho, with many towns and cities now having bookstores selling hardcore pornography for sale. With regional police forces interpreting the Obscene Publications Act 1959 in different ways, approaches to

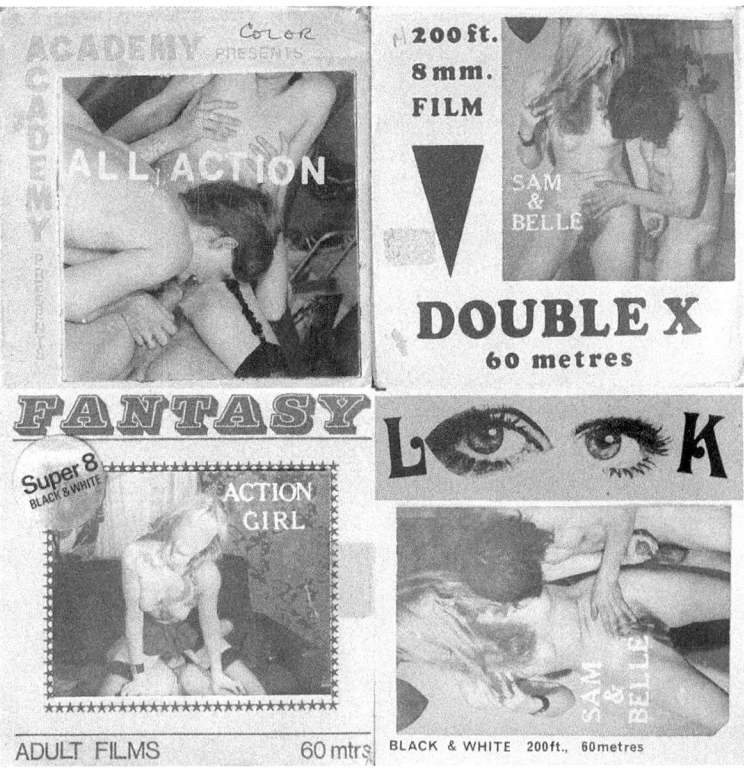

FIGURE 4.11: Other labels associated with Anthony Collingbourne: Academy, Double X, Fantasy and Look. Author's personal collection. Faces obscured to protect the identity of performers.

policing pornography were inconsistent. As Robertson (1979: 5) identifies, some local police forces openly permitted the sale of hardcore pornography.

## The Watford Blue Movie Trial

The police had now linked Collingbourne to the production and distribution of 42 rollers that they considered obscene. Police also identified some of the films' performers, carrying out interviews with them and arresting others involved in producing the films. Many of the performers were in relationships with one another and lived at a home Collingbourne owned, which also served as a studio. A total of eleven arrests were made, with warrants granted for another four performers. The roller to receive the most attention in the police files and the eventual tabloid reportage of the case was *House of Mirrors* (1972). Made in 1972, it features four people engaged in group sex, a common trait of British hardcore pornography from the 1960s and 1970s.

On viewing the film, it is noticeable that the standard of production is not particularly high, offering little narrative or performance. As with the films produced by Climax in the mid 1960, Collingbourne's style is more akin to documentary. *House of Mirrors*, or *House of Mirrows* as the misspelt title reads, was shot on 16mm and printed on 8mm for distribution – the standard process for rollers – and made available in both black and white and colour versions. As the picture of the packaging demonstrates (see Figures 4.1 and 4.2), it was presented in a purple box with the brand at the top and a colour photograph of the front cover containing the title. The title's notoriety is partly due to its setting – the suburban home of Yallop, who also performs in the film. A widowed porn collector from Watford and regular frequenter of Collingbourne's photography studio, Yallop's bedroom had a mirrored ceiling and numerous mirrors placed around the room, giving the roller its title and distinctive setting. The production team made effective use of this location, having the camera operator occasionally film the reflections of the performers (see Figure 4.12). Another film central to the prosecution's case was *Traveller's Rest* (1972). Filmed

FIGURE 4.12: Screenshots from *House of Mirrors* (Anthony Collingbourne 1972). Author's personal collection. Faces obscured to protect the identity of performers.

in Yallop's garden and using much of the same cast as *House of Mirrors*, *Traveller's Rest* features group sex and includes a sequence of anal sex at the conclusion of the film (see Figure 4.13). Following interviews with the performers, the police identified Collingbourne as the director of both films.

Having discussed the police investigation, I now want to focus on the subsequent trial that took place to show how the Obscene Publications Act 1959 was used in combination with other laws to prosecute the majority of people involved in the production and distribution of Anglo Continental rollers. This not only reveals the convolutions of obscenity law, as discussed in Chapter 1, but I argue that this specific case was used to deter pornography production in Britain, following the exposure of the alternative economy by the popular press and its associated police corruption. I suggest that police and prosecutors entrepreneurially combined laws in order to increase the chances of a guilty verdict. It began with a committal hearing that took place on 2 November 1973. The purpose of this was to establish whether there was a case to answer. By 5 December 1973, ten defendants were charged with 'conspiring together and with others to publish obscene films'. Collectively, they faced a total of 30 offences. These included

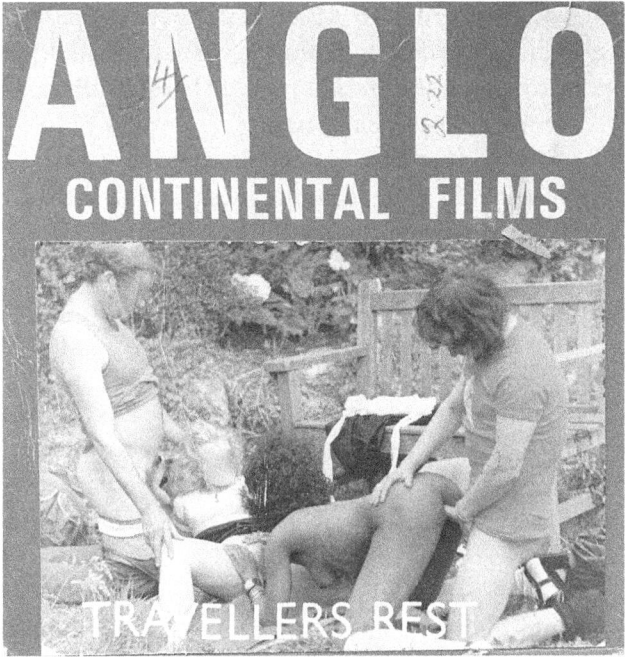

FIGURE 4.13: *Traveller's Rest* (Anthony Collingbourne 1972). Author's personal collection. Faces obscured to protect the identity of performers.

publishing an obscene article and having obscene articles for publication for gain (contrary to the Obscene Publications Act 1959 as amended), sending a postal packet enclosing indecent or obscene articles (contrary to the Post Office Act 1952), and buggery (contrary to the Sexual Offences Act 1956).

Although named in count one along with Collingbourne in a hearing that took place on 26 November, Darby surprisingly escaped the conspiracy charge. After this, he went into hiding, reappearing in a later blue movie case that took place in Birmingham, which I examine in the next chapter. It seems that the strict bail conditions were out of concern for others following Darby's lead.

The case files show that the Director of Public Prosecutions consulted experienced barristers on whether a conspiracy charge would be appropriate in this case, conspiracy being a common law offence that could be used in conjunction with the Obscene Publications Act 1959. According to Robertson (1979: 231–32), common law charges such as conspiracy 'carry a number of tactical advantages unavailable to the prosecution in proceedings brought under the Obscene Publications Act 1959' and that evidence of conspiracy can be 'merely an agreement' between two or more parties. The prosecution questioned whether such a charge might negate a public good defence under section 4 of the Obscene Publications Act 1959. As Robertson (1979: 4) suggests, the public good defence contributed to several high-profile acquittals in the early to mid 1970s, using the opinions of experts to sway the minds of juries. This consultation by the Director of Public Prosecutions implies an attempt to avoid a public good defence for the reasons Robertson identifies, enhancing chances of a conviction, as well as pursuing more substantial sentences and fines through the use of a common law charge. One barrister named Buzzard points out that a conspiracy charge could be highly problematic for the prosecution unless they could show a tangible output resulting from the conspiracy. Otherwise, the defence would have to argue that there was a public good to an article yet to come into physical existence.

It also appears that the Director of Public Prosecutions sought advice on how to try the case, with one barrister suggesting that the prosecution focus their attention on 'three of the worst publications' and warn against trying 'a large number of accused at one time'. This feedback resulted in the Attorney General advising that:

- Conspiracy should only be charged where substantive offences cannot be proved.
- The offence should be worded 'did conspire to contravene the provisions of section 2 of the Obscene Publications Act 1959 by publishing'.

- That the defence should be informed that this does not preclude a section four defence, and should the court not permit a section 4 defence, the conspiracy charge be withdrawn.

The trial commenced on 22 April 1974 and ended on 6 June 1974. It lasted for six weeks and, at that time, was referred to as 'one of the longest pornography trials in Britain' by *The Guardian* (6 June 1974). The defence selected an all-male jury, believing it to be more representative of the audience for the films being prosecuted. This turned out to be a narrow-minded decision that did little in their favour. All the defendants pleaded not guilty to the charges. The trial is not explicitly detailed in the case files, only containing a breakdown of each day's activity, but the summing up from the judge, Marcus Anwyl-Davies, gives an overview of the case, although littered with moralistic assumptions. Further summaries of the trial can be found in the daily reports offered by the tabloid press. These are equally moralistic, focusing on the more sensational and salacious aspects of the case. It is worth mentioning that the case made all the major national papers and included images of the defendants. Articles regularly referred to Yallop's mirrored bedroom where *House of Mirrors* (1972) was filmed, focusing heavily on the suburban location of films and pornography moving out of the confines of the city to a suburban family space. For instance, a headline in the *Daily Mirror* (1 November 1973) reads 'BLUE SECRETS IN ROOM OF MIRRORS', with the introduction to the article stating, 'An innocent-looking house in a quiet lane held some surprises for police working on a pornography case'.

The prosecution took a moral position, arguing that the films produced by the defendants 'debase and defile [an] essential part of human life which ordinary decent standards demand shall remain private' and that they 'defile and debase those who produce them, those who perform in them and similarly, those who view are also defiled and debased'. Davies summarizes the prosecution's overarching argument as 'filth for parties seeking financial gain from the furtive seedy market'.[20] Two of the prosecution's witnesses were involved in the production of the films and had swayed their position, likely for a favourable outcome. One female witness who appeared in several of Collingbourne's films revealed further details of his enterprise and how he sourced female performers from a model agency based in Streatham, South-West London. Initially employed to be photographed by amateur photographers at Collingbourne's studio, female models would later be asked to perform in rollers, being paid anywhere between £25 and £50 per film; men were paid around £10.

Another witness was Yallop, who loaned the use of his house to Collingbourne for filming. A total of ten films are named in the 30 offences; these were screened to the jury to support the prosecution's case. The rollers that received the most attention in the case were those which stood the best chance of being considered obscene by the jury. Both *House of Mirrors* and *Traveller's Rest* were used as they contained instances of anal sex. At this time, heterosexual buggery was an offence in Britain under the Sexual Offences Act 1956, carrying a life sentence. It was not until 1994 that

> the House of Lords accepted an amendment to the Criminal Justice and Public Order Bill which resulted in buggery of a female being partially decriminalised in England and Wales in largely the same way as the law then applied to buggery between males.
>
> (Johnson 2019: 336)

One male performer was charged with two acts of buggery, while the three makers of the two films were charged with aiding and abetting; the prosecution could not trace the female performer. *Dog Lovers* (1971–72) was also referred to by the prosecution and features in many of the newspaper reports. As the title implies, this roller includes scenes of bestiality.[21] According to the police officer tasked with watching the seized films and providing synopses, the male performer has sexual contact with a dog. Yet, newspaper reports state that it is the female performer, highlighting how female performers were castigated for appearing in pornographic films. All involved in these titles were found guilty of the charges, again showing that performers could be prosecuted for making pornography, not just those who produced and distributed it.

The defence's approach was contradictory and chaotic, partly due to circumstances beyond their control. First, Collingbourne fell ill at the beginning of the trial and, like Darby, fled the country. He sought exile in the Netherlands, where he could not be extradited as his charges did not apply due to a loophole in their treaty with Britain. Second, a solicitor's clerk who belonged to a firm representing two of the defendants climbed the court's roof and protested against the protracted nature of the trial, threatening to set off a cylinder of laughing gas into the ventilation system. Finally, four of the defendants married each other. These incidents did nothing more than draw further media attention and made the defence's job more challenging. From the material I collected, it appears that a public good defence was not mounted. However, there is reference in the Director of Public Prosecution files to other trials where it was used, suggesting that the prosecution had prepared for such a tactic. Instead, they focused their attention on limitations of the terms 'deprave and corrupt' and the following key arguments:

1. Those who purchased the films were unlikely to be affected by them.
2. If the activities shown in the films are not depraved and corrupt, but deemed acceptable, how can they deprave and corrupt viewers?
3. While such films may offend some of the population, it does not necessarily mean that they deprave or corrupt.
4. The question of censorship and whether the prohibition of pornography serves a purpose in modern society where attitudes have changed.

The statements from the defendants show that they all sought to minimize their own involvement to lessen their guilt. For example, one male performer said that he took no payment from the films, only appearing in them for the accommodation that Collingbourne provided. One of the assumed filmmakers stated that he also took no payment, acting as a technical advisor in exchange for watching them being made. Both these accounts suggest that the defendants attempted to show that they did not financially gain from the productions, and were therefore not guilty under the Obscene Publications Act 1959. However, the female performers gave more detailed explanations for their involvement. One recounted how she became involved in rollers through meeting someone at the Playland amusement arcade in Piccadilly Circus, having run away from her family in the north to London.[22] She recalls how her relationship with this person led to her making rollers for several years, but is vague about who produced them. Another told of how they performed in rollers to help pay for an abortion. She also described how Collingbourne persuaded her to appear in *Dog Lovers* by offering more money, even though she did not want to be involved. Collectively, all of the defendants and the witnesses for the prosecution who were part of the enterprise did not consider the films to be obscene and believed that hardcore pornography should be legalized. In an interview with the press, one performer declared that her involvement in the trial was far more degrading than performing in hardcore pornography.

Judge Anwyl-Davies' summing up of the case for the jury included a definition of the Obscene Publications Act 1959, an overview of the offences, a reflection on the evidence used in the trial and, finally, a summary of the arguments put forward by the prosecution and the defence. One day later, on 5 June, the jury reached their decision. Out of the ten defendants, seven men and two women were found guilty on a number of charges. A female performer was acquitted of all charges. Although not present, Collingbourne received a five-year prison sentence and a £2223 fine, which he eventually served after being arrested when attempting to re-enter Britain. Wyatt was found guilty on four accounts and sentenced to two years in prison. The court found the male performer charged with buggery guilty and, in line with the other defendants, received a fine and a suspended prison sentence. In his sentencing, Anwyl-Davies described Collingbourne as a 'loathe-some lecher', a term repeated in tabloid newspapers, and told the female who performed in *Dog Lovers* that she was 'a disgrace to womanhood'. He stated the defendants participated in the 'regular production of obscene films of the most horrid and vile nature, hideously crude totally devoid of artistry and deliberately designed for the furtive, filthy and highly lucrative market'. He saw the verdicts as 'a clarion call for reticence and privacy in the matters of personal sexual behaviour' and that they 'condemn the claim that a commercial enterprise of this large nature is acceptable to this Society and [...] the shrill petulant protest of licentious libertines has been resoundingly rejected'.[23]

The defence launched two appeals. The first, by Collingbourne and Wyatt, argued argued that Anwyl-Davies erred in law on four counts, focusing on whether he had misdirected the jury to consider whether a significant proportion of those who were likely to come into contact with the films would be depraved and corrupted. Two performers filed the second appeal, one of whom was found guilty of buggery. Again, it presented four counts, two per appellant, arguing that the performers were not aware of the films being distributed as part of a commercial enterprise. They also argued whether the two-year limit on prosecutions, found in section 2(3) of the Obscene Publications Act 1959, applied, as the offending film was made in 1971. Therefore, the offence did not continue beyond this date, making it inadmissible by the time of the arrest in 1973. The court rejected both appeals, and upheld the original verdicts. The appeal relating to section 2(3) was rejected due to common law charges for conspiracy and aiding and abetting. This made the offence a continuing one that went beyond the two-year limit stated in the Obscene Publications Act 1959.

A reporter from the *News of the World* (23 June 1974) eventually tracked down Collingbourne, finding him in Amsterdam. Collingbourne told the reporter: 'I admit I am no saint. And I've made a small fortune out of blue films. But over the years my associates and I have had to pay about £250,000 in bribe money to policemen'. Collingbourne also bragged about repeatedly returning to Britain without being arrested. He was eventually arrested in May 1975 and began serving his prison sentence. It is not known what happened to him once he was released in 1979. He died in 2007.

## Conclusion

The Watford Blue Movie Trial was a long, complex and, at times, chaotic obscenity trial that resulted in the convictions of nine people. At the appeal hearings, Prosecutor Richard Du Cann described it as the 'first of its kind'. Beyond this, I argue that it has significance for two reasons. First, it provides yet another window into how the alternative economy was organized. The Director of Public Prosecution files reveal the entrepreneurial practices of the producers and the experiences of performers, the latter being a voice that is absent in histories of the British pornography business (Bowring et al. 2018). Although the files pertain to only one instance of roller production and distribution in Britain, it demonstrates the development of the trade beyond Soho and increase in mail-order enterprises selling rollers at cheaper prices. Second, it shows how pornography was regulated when it was becoming a subject of national interest. The Watford case began when the trade regularly featured in the popular press and the limitations of the Obscene Publications Act 1959 for controlling the trade were being called into question. This is echoed in an article from *The Guardian* in which Lord Denning, then Master of the Rolls (President of the Court of Appeals and Head of Civil Justice), recognized that 'the test of obscenity was too restricted and had been interpreted by courts too narrowly' and that the public good defence has 'opened a door through which many a pornographer could escape' (*The Guardian*, 28 November 1972).

From looking at the case files, it appears that the prosecution was conscious of this context, entrepreneurially combining the Obscene Publications Act 1959 with the Sexual Offences Act 1956, Post Office Act 1952 and common law offences, such as conspiracy and aiding and abetting, to strengthen their chances of prosecution and introduce stronger penalties and fines than those that are possible under obscenity law. The files suggest that they also explored whether a public good defence would be possible in light of a conspiracy charge, perhaps not wanting to prejudice the trial in any way, as well as being aware of it providing a potential escape route for the defence. Also significant is performers being prosecuted for their involvement in the production of hardcore pornography. Under the Obscene Publications Act 1959, making pornography was not an offence. However, introducing a conspiracy to contravene section 2 of the Obscene Publications Act 1959 by publishing material enabled all of those involved in the production and distribution to be prosecutable; the buggery conviction and the aiding of abetting the act under the Sexual Offences Act 1956 are further evidence of this.

Following this trial, the production of rollers slowed and, for the remainder of the 1970s, John Jesner Lindsay dominated the trade, who, despite being named three times in the case files, was not implicated in the conspiracy. It would appear that the profile of this trial, a stricter approach to policing the trade following revelations about corruption within the Obscene Publications Squad and the increase of cheaper, but higher material quality, pornographic commodities from

Europe contributed to this decline. Suddenly, the alternative economy was left with no institutional framework, and entrepreneurs now had to find new loopholes in the law to allow them to operate. In the coming chapter, I refer to other obscenity trials to further illustrate the battle between pornographers and the legal system, as the economy increasingly shifted from producing pornographic films to distributing them.

# 5

## *Strip Poker*:
## Distributing Hardcore Films
## in Britain (1973–83)

### Introduction

On 28 October 1973, one year after the Longford Report, the British television channel ITV aired an episode of *The Frost Programme* titled 'Sex and Pornography'. Hosted by the well-known personality David Frost, the episode brought together pornographers, authors, politicians, activists and a general audience to debate the morality of pornography. At the heart of the episode was a conversation with Lord Longford, who reflected on the findings of his report. As the previous three chapters have shown, British hardcore pornography entrepreneurs operated in the shadows, actively avoiding the limelight unless arrested and named by the popular press. *The Frost Programme* shows hardcore pornographers openly speaking about their practices on national television and, more specifically, their moral boundaries. The two people who stand out amongst this debate are David Waterfield and John Jesner Lindsay. Waterfield, who owned two North London cinema clubs that screened hardcore pornography, speaks of showing the film *Deep Throat* (Gerald Damiano 1972). When asked by Frost what effect this had on his audience, Waterfield cheekily responds 'well, all I can say is that they walk out a lot happier than when they came in', resulting in laughter from the audience.

Lindsay joins the debate, similarly stating that those who attend his cinema choose to do so:

> at my instance, my film is showing with the title only and for adults only, no sexy film posters, nothing. Now, the only person who pays 75p and walks into that cinema is a person who knows that's a sex film and wants to see it. Nobody here is forced to go into that cinema.

FIGURE 5.1: *Strip Poker* (1970–72) on International Films. Author's personal collection. Faces obscured to protect the identity of performers.

After interviewing Longford, who claims that pornographers lack moral boundaries, Frost asks Lindsay and Waterfield where they 'draw the line'. Lindsay responds, 'under no circumstances will I ever use a child in a pornographic film', while Waterfield declares that he screens no films 'with violence in it or sadism at all, because I don't like it personally, but I don't object to anyone wanting to see it if they want to do that, that's their business, it's not your business'. Also present are Labour politician Raymond Blackburn, who made a number of unsuccessful private prosecutions during the 1970s, with one attempting to order the Commissioner of the Metropolitan Police to push for greater powers to seize material and prosecute pornographers,[1] and Peter Thompson, representing the Festival of Light who introduced their Nationwide Petition for Public Decency in 1972. This called for stronger obscenity laws, resulting in 1.35 million signatures by 1973, which made it 'the most successful petition since the peace campaigns of the 1930s' (Sanbrook 2011: n.pag.).[2]

*The Frost Programme* is significant as it demonstrates that pornography had become a subject of open public discussion, but still marked by prurience. Although presented as an entertaining spectacle, the debate illustrates the surfacing of a moral battlefield that later dominated the latter half of the 1970s, with pornographers like Waterfield and Lindsay openly calling for the legalization of pornography, while anti-pornography activists campaigned for stricter regulation. If the other pornography entrepreneurs discussed so far in this book can be considered 'pariah capitalists' (Gertzman 1999) who shunned the limelight to continue profiting from their enterprise, Lindsay and Waterfield represent a shift in the economy. Instead, they positioned themselves as what Becker (1966: 47) describes as 'moral entrepreneurs', a term I unpack shortly. In this chapter, I show how Lindsay and Waterfield placed themselves amongst this moral battlefield, justifying their pornography enterprises as moral in an attempt to establish a new legal framework for pornography and consequently benefit from it. Drawing on legal documents and media reportage relating to their extensive legal battles, I demonstrate how the Metropolitan police aggressively responded to their attempts to find loopholes in the law and therefore legitimize their enterprise. Finally, the chapter reflects on how both pornographers and the police entrepreneurially used inconsistencies in the Obscene Publications Act 1959 and other laws to control Lindsay's enterprise, ultimately resulting in the introduction of new legislature to control the hardcore pornography trade.

## The moral battlefield

'Lawless' was the word 'Steve' used to describe the state of the alternative economy in the mid 1970s. Steve entered the business after the crackdown on police corruption that resulted from the *Sunday People's* exposé, opening his first sex shop in Soho. With most of the economy's key operators facing legal action, prison sentences or simply lying low, control of Soho was 'up for the taking' (Manchester 1986: 45). Manchester (1986: 41) identifies the opening of the first Ann Summers shop in 1970 as a significant moment in sex-related entrepreneurship. Whereas Soho's bookshops specialized in selling pornography, Ann Summers, named after the secretary of founder Michael Caborn-Waterfield, sold various sex-related artefacts, including underwear and sex toys. After a year of business, David and Ralph Gold purchased the company, noticing that the shop attracted women, a marked difference to the bookshops of Soho (Gold 2012: 236).

As Smith (2005: 53) identifies, the mid 1970s saw a growth in Britain's pornography business with the potential high economic benefits attracting other entrepreneurs who focused on the lucrative and relatively safer softcore market.[3] The Gold brothers and David Sullivan exemplify this new type of pornography entrepreneur. The Golds had been in the bookshop business since the early 1960s, moving into publishing in the mid 1960s and starting the successful softcore magazine company Gold Star Publications.[4] Ann Summers has become a staple fixture of the British high street, and the brand now markets itself as celebrating sex and female empowerment. For Manchester (1986: 41), the opening of Ann Summers made Soho's bookshops realize that they could move away from using the bookshop alibi. Instead, the title of 'sex shop' gave a 'ready indication of the nature of the material stocked' and provided a 'legitimate "front"'. Now above-the-counter softcore pornography could be displayed in shop windows, with bright neon lights attracting the attention of customers.

David Sullivan also exploited the demand for pornography, using confidence tricks to hoodwink consumers who wanted to obtain hardcore. Born in Cardiff and graduating with a degree in economics from the University of London, Sullivan started his pornography business by selling nude photographs through mail order. He placed adverts in adult magazines and *Exchange and Mart*, offering customers twenty nude images for just £1. After receiving little interest, Sullivan and his partner re-strategized and decided to offer 200 nude images for £1. Their change in direction proved to be a success, although customers were no doubt disappointed when they received the same nude image 200 times. Such scams became a feature of Sullivan's unethical entrepreneurship. For instance, he purchased old magazines, but printed new covers that were suggestive of hardcore – they were not – and sold them at high prices. This resulted in large profits and a mailing list of 60,000 customers to repeatedly exploit (Killick 1994: 12–14).[5] His eventual chain of sex shops was branded 'Private Shops', a reference to Sweden's well-known hardcore magazine *Private*, but only sold softcore pornography. Killick (1994) believes that

Sullivan brought a Soho sex shop-style experience to provincial towns, expanding Britain's soft market for pornography by deceiving customers into thinking they were buying hardcore.[6]

Hardcore pornography was now primarily imported from Scandinavia, where its large-scale production, higher material quality and pricing increased the margins of profit for sex shop owners and mail-order operators. It was no longer a high-priced commodity exclusive to the wealthy. From 1972, the domestic production of rollers contracted significantly. In the previous chapter, I argued that this was due to the high-profile nature of the Watford Blue Movie Trial, and also the removal of the Obscene Publications Squad's informal licensing system that underwrote the economy. Few domestic producers of hardcore pornography remained. Mike Freeman and Anthony Collingbourne were both serving prison sentences while Evan 'Big Jeff' Phillips was jailed in 1974 for conspiracy under the Obscene Publications Act 1959 and committed suicide in 1975. John Lindsay, who had been named several times during the police investigation into Collingbourne and John Darby, became the dominant producers of rollers in 1970s. Along with another entrepreneur named David Waterfield, they shifted from the production of hardcore films to distributing them through cinema clubs and sex shops.

Previousuly, the Obscene Publications Squad's licensing system created a stable framework for pornographers to operate within. Its removal created disorder. Responding to the allegations of corruption made by the popular press, the Metropolitan Police assembled a 'new police squad to handle cases of obscene publications' (*Daily Mail*, 18 November 1972). Now pornographers received limited protection, as Gilbert Kelland's team of anti-corruption investigators set their sights firmly on the Obscene Publications Squad. According to Soho sex shop owner Steve, the rebuilt squad's response to the pornography trade was heavy-handed, resulting in what he described as a 'lawless economy' with stricter policing. Soho sex shop owner Dave also recalled these changes: 'they recruited PCs from the beat to the vice squad and changed them every six months so that they could not build relationships with the bookshops'.[7] Because of this new approach to policing the trade, pornography entrepreneurs like Lindsay and Waterfield found new ways to evade the police and escape prosecution. In Chapter 1, I suggested that evasive entrepreneurship is a key element of pornography entrepreneurship. With the alternative economy now lacking an institutional framework, Lindsay and Waterfield positioned themselves as moral entrepreneurs, claiming that their actions were for the public good and part of a commitment to changing Britain's regulatory framework for pornography through their entrepreneurship. By doing so, they situated themselves amongst other moral entrepreneurs, such as MPs Lord Longford and Raymond Blackburn, Mary Whitehouse of the Festival of Light and the Metropolitan Police, who enforced the law.

Becker (1966: 148) used the term moral entrepreneur to describe 'rule creators' who seek reform for the greater good. The moral entrepreneur is motivated by change, either preventing the 'exploitation of one person by another' or endeavouring to 'provide the conditions for a better way of life'. To do this, they seek to bring change to a prohibitive regulatory system by introducing new legislation. Becker uses the example of prohibitionists as moral entrepreneurs, attempting to improve people's lives by removing alcohol consumption. Typically, activists opposing pornography have been described as moral entrepreneurs. Strub (2011: 6) finds that moral entrepreneurs played a pivotal role in promoting 'pornography as a source of social consternation' in America. Strub observes that an 'absence of moral entrepreneurs' results in a public and political 'ambivalence' to pornography, highlighting how morality is often used as 'political capital' (295). Yet, I want to suggest that the pornographers too can use morality for their own political gain. I am not suggesting that pornographers are moral. Instead, I wish to show that they often adopt moral positions in order to strengthen their own self-interests and use it as an alibi.

Arnberg and Marklund (2016: 193) consider how Swedish pornography entrepreneur Berth Milton contributed to a 'discursive reframing of pornography – from something sinful and dangerous to something liberating and radical'. In his *Private* magazine, Milton used an editorial column titled 'Morals' to promote his permissive philosophy, calling for sexual policy change and the legalization of pornography. Arnberg and Marklund note that one of Milton's editorials was cited by Swedish lawyer in 1969 as evidence for 'the deregulation of pornography' in Sweden. This, I argue, illustrates how pornography entrepreneurs can take a moral position to enhance their own economic position. North (1990: 83) suggests that entrepreneurs can be agents of change who seek to transform institutional frameworks in order to benefit from doing so. In later work, North (2005) added that entrepreneurs must also convince others that such change is worthwhile and advantageous by taking an ideological outlook to their enterprise. The examples I use in this chapter illustrate how pornography entrepreneurs struggle to make change in the face of regulators but take a moral stance to bring wider attention to their efforts and sway public opinion. Ultimately, their goal was to formalize the alternative economy by legalizing the distribution of hardcore pornography.

Becker (1966: 146) defines moral entrepreneurs as 'rule creators' or crusading reformers because of their commitment to changing the law. He also proposes a second type of moral entrepreneur – 'rule enforcers' (155). For Becker, rule enforcers police the new laws that emerge out of moral crusades. His idea of the moral entrepreneur has limitations. As Müller (2015) argues, Becker does not offer a thorough unpacking of their motivations, particularly for rule enforcers. Yet, I find it a useful framework for thinking about the motivations for pornographers, activists and rule enforcers during the latter half of 1970s Britain. In this section, I have suggested that the morality of pornography had become a subject of public debate and dominated by moral entrepreneurs calling for stronger controls, or for legalization. Controlling the trade were the newly constituted Obscene Publications Squad – the rule enforcers – who took a heavy-handed approach to policing the economy, requiring pornographers to find loopholes in laws to evade arrest. I argue that morality was one of the justifications they used for their practices, claiming that they served a public good, a defensive tactic available under the Obscene Publications Act 1959. This, I show, was used an alibi to justify their entrepreneurship. David Waterfield is an example of a pornographer who assumed this moral position.

## Members only

Pictured in Figure 5.2, David Waterfield first became involved in the adult entertainment business in the mid 1960s, working as a stage manager at a strip club in Soho, London.[8] He later joined the Merchant Navy as a commis waiter, serving first-class passengers on trips from Southampton to New York and back. On one visit to New York, Waterfield observed crowds flocking to see *Deep Throat* (Gerald Damiano 1972), a film which is considered to be the 'most financially successful hardcore pornographic film ever produced' (Barnett 2018: 15). According to

FIGURE 5.2: David Waterfield, 1972. Courtesy of Patricia Clark.

Patricia Clark, Waterfield's ex-wife, who gave a detailed interview about his life and their relationship, he purchased a copy of the film in New York, either a commercial 8mm release or 16mm print, and smuggled it back into Britain.[9] This made Waterfield aware of the transnational opportunities for sourcing and distributing pornographic materials across borders. Around this time, Waterfield read Napoleon Hill's book *Think and Grow Rich*. First published in 1937, this self-help book claims to have drawn on an analysis of financially successful Americans, resulting in a list of 'thirteen steps to riches'. It became particularly influential in depression-era America and spoke to Waterfield's ambition to make money. According to Patricia Clark, Waterfield closely followed each of these steps, especially Hill's advice to 'engage in no transaction which does not benefit all whom it affects'; this would be a guiding principle for his entrepreneurship.

Having witnessed the demand for hardcore pornography in New York, Waterfield sensed an opportunity in Britain. Around 1972, he opened two cinema clubs in North London, The Exxon[10] and Archibalds, the latter ironically named after the *Archbold's Justice Manual*, a guide on updates to legislation that is often referred to by legal professionals or those choosing to defend themselves and requiring an understanding of the law. Using this name suggests that Waterfield was aware of his new enterprise's legal implications and was not afraid of provoking authority. Private, members-only cinema clubs typically screened films that were either banned or cut by the then named British Board of Film Censors (BBFC). As Simpson (1983: 14) points out, the Cinematograph Act 1952 did not apply to 'all film shows', therefore cinema clubs 'fell outside any effective control'. Additionally, 'films in general were exempted from the 1959 [and 1964] Obscene Publications Act in order to avoid the extension of censorship to cinema exhibition on licensed premises' (Cocks 2016: 274). Providing owners followed the law carefully, having new members 'wait an obligatory hour for their membership applications to be processed', they could operate legally (Hebditch and Anning 1988: 216).

Perhaps the most well-known exponents of this enterprise were Michael Klinger, Bernard Samuels and Tony Tenser, who established The Compton Cinema Club in October 1960 (Spicer et al. 2013). The majority of cinema clubs, such as The Compton Club (see Figure 5.3), avoided showing hardcore pornography, instead screening uncensored European feature films that pushed the boundaries of sexual representation. Non-cinema clubs based in Soho often used lurid advertisements, promising 'Scandinavian Uncensored Sex Films'. More often than not, these were a scam, only realized by the customer once they had paid the entrance fee and walked inside the establishment, being shown softcore nudist films and charged high prices for refreshments. Referred to as 'clip joints', these public cinemas were subject to police enquiry, but their success did little to discourage their owners (Trevelyan 1973: 124). As I discussed in Chapter 2,

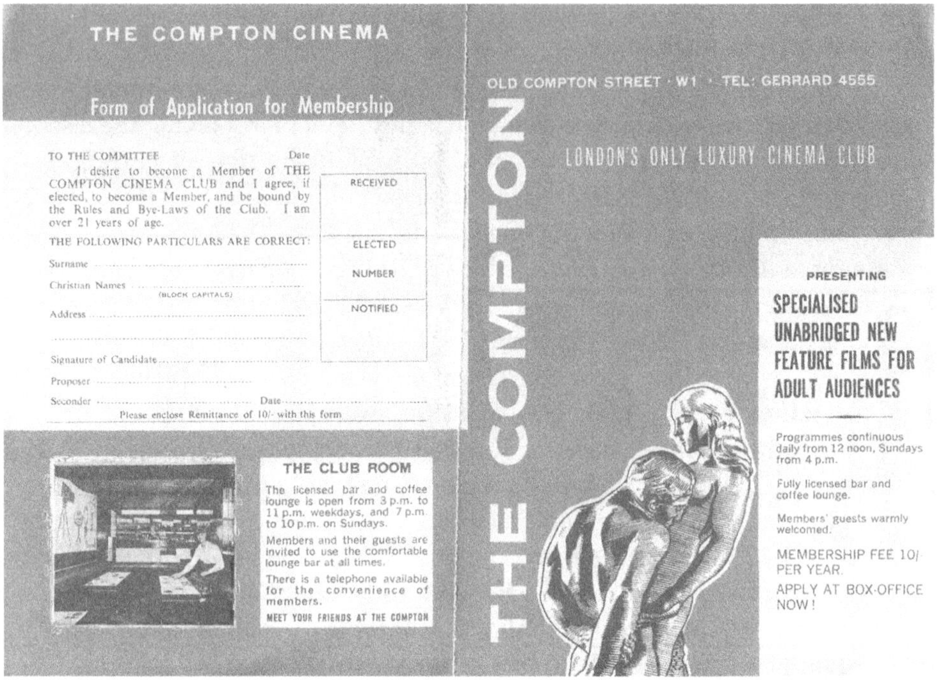

FIGURE 5.3: Flyer promoting the Compton Cinema Club and including membership application form. Author's personal collection.

the screening of hardcore pornography was either confined to the home or through blue movie shows.

Waterfield's innovation was to offer an experience somewhere in between, exploiting the loophole in the law for showing hardcore pornography in a private members club. A feature on Waterfield found in the adult magazine *Experience* states that the Exxon is the 'only place in Britain where you can genuinely see blue movies', claiming that Waterfield is 'a pioneer in running the first blue cinema club in Britain'.[11] In the article, Waterfield comments on his competitors and how they disappoint their customers by not showing what they promise, stating that he 'built up a regular clientele – people who know that they're not going to be conned or cheated, but will get value for money'. Again, following Napoleon Hill's advice, adverts for the Exxon Cinema Club promised a full money-back guarantee (see Figure 5.4). This became a regular feature of Waterfield's enterprises, seeking to operate ethically in an economy that was subject to exploitation by more unscrupulous entrepreneurs, such as David Sullivan and his confidence tricks. Clark told me that Waterfield believed he ran a legitimate business within

FIGURE 5.4: Advert for the Exxon Cinema Club. Author's personal collection.

the boundaries of the law and never paid the police for protection. Given that Waterfield opened his clubs outside of Soho, this may have been an attempt to avoid police corruption.

According to *R v. Waterfield* (1975), the clubs were a financial success, earning Waterfield between £400 and £700 per week, at least ten times the average weekly wage for a male manual worker in 1973. The *Sunday People* (6 February 1972) revealed that he charged a £3 entry fee and each show lasted for 90 minutes with no interval. Waterfield regularly adopted a moral discourse when discussing the motivations for his entrepreneurship. For instance, in the *Experience* article, the author claims that Waterfield is campaigning for sexual freedom 'not just for himself, but for everyone'. Further evidence of these claims can be found in an article from the November 1975 issue of the magazine *Forum*. It tells of how Waterfield used some of the profits generated by his cinema clubs to fund 'community ventures', such as the alternative magazine *Up Against the Law*, a publication offering legal advice to counter-cultural groups who found themselves in breach of the law, providing guidance on how to legally represent yourself in court, as well as revealing corrupt police officers and solicitors. He was also a 'leading donor' to the Community Levy for Alternative Projects (CLAP), 'an experiment in alternative economics', where alternative projects could be funded through a 'community levy' on the incomes of donors (Button 2019: 87). This suggests that Waterfield had a social conscience much like Beate

Ushe, a female pornography entrepreneur who ran a successful erotic mail-order business in post-war Germany (Heineman 2011).

Moreover, Waterfield made his views on pornography public, being interviewed on *The Frost Programme* and in magazines. Furthermore, on 6 February 1972, the *Sunday People* named his cinema clubs in their exposé of Britain's pornography business. This contrasts with other pornography entrepreneurs discussed in this book who, out of self-preservation, avoided any form of media attention that could jeopardize their business. Interviews and legal documents indicate that Waterfield positioned himself as a legitimate businessman, but one situated amongst the radical movement of the early 1970s, rejecting the dominant hegemonic values of 'straight society' and wanting to challenge them, especially through opposing censorship. The *Forum* article posits that his involvement in such radical activities ultimately led to his arrest. For Clark, it was a plan to open a third cinema club in Kings Cross that stirred the authorities into taking action.[12]

### Regina *v.* Waterfield

Waterfield's use of loopholes in the Cinematograph Act 1952 and the Obscene Publications Act 1959 prevented the police from closing his profitable cinema clubs. To apprehend him, the police explored other legal options. As discussed in Chapters 1 and 4, common laws offered a number of 'tactical advantages' for policing pornography (Robertson 1979: 231). Robertson (1979: 210) notes that rule enforcers use 'elastic' common laws 'to punish conduct which they dislike, but Parliament had declined to make specifically illegal'. This illustrates how the law could be used entrepreneurially to patch up holes in other legislation. Waterfield was initially charged under the Disorderly Houses Act 1751, 'a relic of eighteenth-century attempts to curtail cockfighting and bear-baiting [...] refurbished by the Court of Appeal in 1961' to control strip clubs operating through a similar ambiguity (Robertson 1979: 211). The case, reported in considerable detail by *Forum*, relied on the assumption that pornography encouraged masturbation. Therefore Waterfield could be charged with running a disorderly house. Yet, to pursue such a charge, it is necessary to catch someone in the 'act'. A costly two-year operation started, with police officers acting as planning inspectors in order to access The Exxon Cinema without a warrant. Additional officers were stationed in a flat on the opposite side of the street, observing the members entering and leaving club. A further ten plain-clothed officers used public money to become members of the club in an attempt to spot masturbators, eventually witnessing a cinema club member pleasuring himself and using a green tweed hat to disguise the act. They also followed members to the toilets in order to ascertain whether they had ejaculated, documenting their findings in police notebooks.

Statements from the police officers give accounts of the 8mm films screened at the clubs, which were of German, American, but mainly Scandinavian origin, from labels such as Color Climax and Lasse Braun productions (see Figure 5.5). It appears that Waterfield favoured screening these films rather than ones made in Britain as they were cheaper to purchase and of a higher material quality, being professionally duplicated on the Super 8 format. Also, unlike rollers, such films regularly featured soundtracks, rather than being silent. In addition to the police investigation, Her Majesty's Customs and Excise (HMCE) also took an interest in Waterfield's enterprise, questioning how he obtained the films shown in his cinema clubs. As McClister (1994) identifies, customs laws, such as the the the Customs Consolidation Act 1857, were used alongside the Obscene Publications Act 1959 to regulate the distribution and sale of obscene materials in Britain. Whereas the Obscene Publications Act 1959 is based on the test of obscenity, customs law uses indecency. For Robertson (1979: 178), both terms 'convey the same idea', but indecency has been perceived as a lower offence than obscenity, leading to a higher chance of conviction.

In 1972, HMCE seized a consignment of 7647 films and 72,429 magazines,[13] which were subsequently linked to Waterfield. According to Clark, Waterfield sold these materials to club members, but could have wholesaled them to others in the economy. Due to the risk of seizure when importing hardcore pornography from the continent, entrepreneurs favoured large consignments. They ordered through transnational agents such as Charlie Geerts, a Dutch-based pornography entrepreneur who acted as a representative for the Danish company Color Climax in the early 1970s (Ferris 1993: 261). As court records and files from the Director of Public

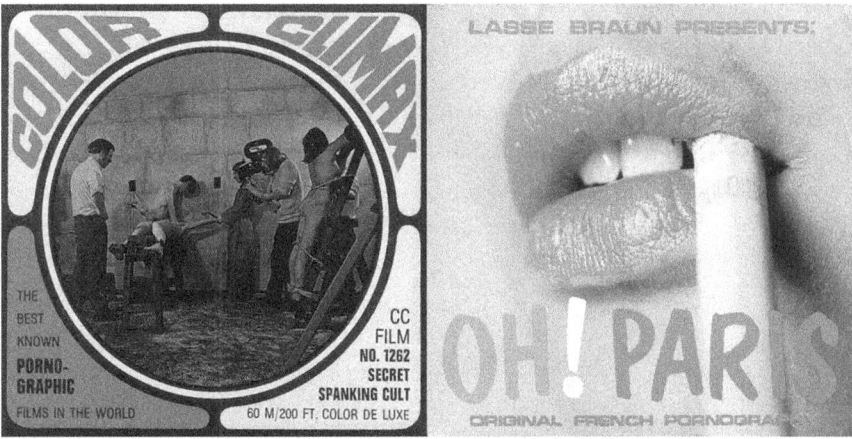

FIGURE 5.5: Releases from Color Climax Corporation and Lasse Braun. Author's personal collection.

Prosecutions show, pornography was regularly hidden in lorries containing meat products such as bacon or chicken and smuggled into Britain; couriers on commercial flights or ferries carried smaller orders in their luggage (Hebditch and Anning 1988). As established in Chapters 2 and 3, Britain was a substantial exporter of hardcore photographs and films prior to the legalization of pornography in Denmark. After legalization, these roles reversed, it being cheaper to import professionally produced material, despite the risk of seizure. Evidently, Waterfield had established trade relationships with Danish pornography entrepreneurs and Netherlands-based agents who specialized in smuggling goods via Rotterdam.

The exact details of the transaction are difficult to decipher from the Director of Public Prosecution files. In short, Waterfield arranged for a delivery of 8mm films and magazines to his storage from Color Climax. This was to come via Rotterdam, smuggled in a lorry containing chicken meat. The files show that another pornography entrepreneur with strong links to the Netherlands – James Humphreys – became aware of the large shipment and used his contacts within the Obscene Publications Squad to arrange for it to be confiscated once it arrived in Britain. On 3 July 1972, a courier named Mulder delivered 15 of the 70 boxes to Waterfield; the remainder were put into storage but confiscated by the police on 5 July after Mulder's arrest. However, the legal files show discrepancies in the number of seized boxes and those formally logged by the police. It appears that an additional 30 boxes of pornography were left in the van and made available to Humphreys to sell in his Soho bookstores, 'bringing in £67,500 in clear profit' (Kelland 1986: 186–88). In a police interview, Humphreys claims that he did not receive the stock, as he could not agree on a price with the Obscene Publications Squad officer. Instead, he believes that it went to a rival named Gerald Citron, a wholesaler of mainly pornographic magazines and another major player in the economy. However, it seems that both Citron and Humphreys benefited from the seizure. Issue nine of *Up Against the Law* states that this whole affair was intended to put Waterfield out of business, further indicating how entrepreneurs ruthlessly pursued profit. As I have shown throughout this book, British pornographers were open to collaboration, providing that it was to their economic benefit, but equally willing to deceive.

On 4 July, police raided Waterfield's premises, arresting him and his staff. He was later indicted on four charges:

1. Keeping a disorderly house.
2. Outrage to public decency.
3. The fraudulent evasion of a prohibition on the importation of indecent articles, contrary to section 304(b) of the Customs and Excise Act 1952.
4. Dealing with prohibited goods contrary to section 304 (a) of the Customs and Excise Act 1952.

Waterfield's trials are difficult to decipher, as the original indictment was severed from one to two – a strategy used by the prosecution to attempt to secure a conviction – resulting in two separate trials.[14] In the first, which took place on 30 June 1974, Waterfield was tried for charges one and two, with the jury being only shown the American films seized from the cinema clubs, suggesting that he also had trade links with North America as well as Europe. Waterfield initially chose to defend himself, no doubt following the guidance available in *Up Against the Law*, and on 24 June 1974 was acquitted of both charges. He called a club member as a witness for the defence, who swore to seeing no masturbation at the cinema club. The trial made the national press; an article in the *Daily Mirror* on 24 June 1974 featured the headline 'DEEP THROAT SEVEN CLEARED'. The jury foreman congratulated Waterfield on his successful defence and for taking a stand against censorship.

Waterfield's second trial on 27 June 1974 focused on charges three and four, which directly related to the transnational aspects of his enterprise – importing pornographic materials for sale and exhibition at his clubs. Waterfield again framed his enterprise as a moral act in the interests of public good, arguing that he was attempting to change Britain's overly restrictive laws against pornography. Unconvinced, the judge dismissed Waterfield's claims as 'humbug', declaring that he was purely motivated by the profit of selling or screening imported material, which the police estimated to have a sale value of £30,000. The jury, who viewed 22 of the seized films, found him guilty, and the judge, who had a reputation for issuing harsh sentences, sentenced him to three years in prison and fines totalling £7000. Waterfield appealed his conviction, this time employing council. His defence focused on the severity of his sentence, arguing that indecency is a lesser charge than obscenity, which gives a two-year sentence. Therefore, the three-year sentence should be reduced. The judge agreed, determining that the films were in 'touching distance of the border between indecency and obscenity',[15] both highly problematic, subjective terms that have received much criticism (Robertson 1979; Woozley 1982). Because of this, the court reduced Waterfield's sentence from three years to eighteen months, the judge wanting to ensure that a 'deterrent sentence' was still given to dissuade others from participating in the trade.

The debts from Waterfield's court cases led to him selling both of his clubs. When released from prison, he and his partner started an ethical company that manufactured bean bag chairs, which he sold to high-street retailers. Although Clark claimed this was financially 'successful', Waterfield found the business uninspiring. Waterfield moved back to Southampton, opening the Oslo Club. He became a silent partner in the Exxon Cinema Club's eventual reopening, this time in his birth town of Southampton rather than North London. It opened in October

1976; police raided the premises in February 1977. This was used as a test case on cinema clubs showing pornographic films, with three men eventually being found guilty of keeping a disorderly house and keeping premises for the purposes of showing an indecent exhibition; Waterfield escaped prosecution (*The Journal*, 8 November 1977). By 1977, the Obscene Publications Act 1959 'was extended to cover all film exhibitions' (Robertson 1979: 258) in an attempt to close the loophole that enabled Waterfield's enterprise. Further laws were subsequently introduced to control cinema clubs showing hardcore pornography, as discussed later in this chapter. Waterfield later returned to the pornography business, starting the mail-order distribution company Your Choice in the late 1980s, which specialized in supplying hardcore pornography to British customers (Carter 2022).

Waterfield's entrepreneurship was evidently informed by radical politics, as evidenced by his links with the 1970s counter culture. However, framing his enterprise within this political context was also advantageous to his own financial position. I have shown how the police and the courts entrepreneurially used the law to prosecute Waterfield. Although their initial attempt to use common law charges was unsuccessful, a lesser charge of indecency, contrary to the Customs and Excise Act 1952, resulted in Waterfield's prosecution. This further illustrates the shortcomings of the Obscene Publications Act 1959, requiring other laws to achieve guilty verdicts in pornography cases.

### *For export only*

Another entrepreneur involved in running cinema clubs was the Scottish pornographer John Jesner Lindsay (see Figure 5.6). Of all discussed in this book, Lindsay is perhaps the most widely known, having been discussed in academic and non-academic work (Kerekes 2000; Flint 1999; Sheridan 1999; Sheridan 2005; Thompson 1994; Hunt 1998; Hunter 2013). This is likely because of his outspokenness, innumerable legal battles and the amount of media attention he received, leaving a more accessible trail for researchers to uncover. However, other than a highly exaggerated claim made in 1976 that he had single-handedly been involved in the production of 3824 films, little is known about his early years in the business and his lengthy legal struggles.[16] Given the attention that Lindsay continues to generate, it is surprising to find that no one has identified that Lindsay passed away in 2006, dying in relative anonymity after moving away from the pornography trade in the mid 1980s. To trace Lindsay's enterprise, I draw on a range of sources. This includes newspaper reportage, the files relating to a police investigation into Lindsay's making of hardcore pornographic film funded by the BBC obtained from the National Archives[17] and an interview he gave to *Penthouse*

FIGURE 5.6: John Jesner Lindsay, image taken from his magazine *The Sexorcist*. Courtesy of Rambooks.

magazine in 1976, which outlines his entry into the business. Like Waterfield, Lindsay also presented himself to the public as an anti-censorship campaigner, seeking to reform obscenity law and legalize pornography. His activities and many trials drew further attention to the morality of pornography, with other moral entrepreneurs joining the debate and calling for stricter control. By the end of the 1970s, the legalization of pornography seemed a possibility, as Lindsay won a high-profile obscenity trial, and and the then in power Labour government instigated a review of Britain's pornography laws. However, as I now show, entrepreneurial policing, changes in policy and a shift in political agenda, with Margaret Thatcher's Conservative government taking control in 1979, resulted in tighter regulation of Britain's pornography business.

John Lindsay was born in Glasgow, Scotland, on 19 April 1935. In an interview for *Penthouse* magazine, Lindsay describes himself as a heretic, equating the persecution of pornographers like himself to the witches, wizards and warlocks of years past and the moral guardians, such as Mary Whitehouse and Lord Longford, to witch hunters. He declares that he 'works for sexual freedom and permissiveness' and this, the article argues, has made him 'enemy incarnate' to those who believe he undermines 'the very foundations on which our society is built'. Lindsay maintains that he questioned authority from a young age, leaving school aged 18 and then studying at the Glasgow School of Art. Unlike other pornographers I have discussed, Lindsay appears to have had a formal arts education and received professional photography training. He found himself drawn to life studies, sketching his first nude model in the bedroom of his parent's house. After art school, Lindsay took a job as a press photographer at the *Daily Record* newspaper in Glasgow, eventually being sent to London to work for the *Daily Mirror* and the *Daily Express,* doing fashion and pin-up photography. He also claims to have worked for the fashion magazine *Vogue,* and the adult men's magazines *Penthouse* and *Playboy.* Dissatisfied with this work, Lindsay changed professions, working as a disc jockey for the pirate station Radio Nord on a ship stationed off the Essex coast. This occupation led to an early encounter with the law, resulting in him being arrested along with others at the station. Afterwards, he returned to glamour photography.

Lindsay claims that his reputation as a glamour photographer led to him making rollers. Initially, he had taken nude photographs of an unnamed 'world-famous model' and sold them abroad 'for good money, of which I got 60%. So, I thought, if that kind of money is to be made from pictures of girls without their clothes on, why I am shooting fashion?'. Lindsay opened a fashion advertising studio in Covent Garden, near the West End of London, next to a premise owned by two men. One of these men was John Darby, the distributor I discussed in the previous chapter. Lindsay recalls seeing women frequently visiting Darby's premises, eventually learning that he was involved in the production of hardcore films. At first, Lindsay purchased films from Darby to show to his clients on Friday afternoons, again highlighting Waugh's (2001) observation on how stag movies were typically screened in male-dominated, homosocial spaces for male pleasure. While Darby produced rollers, Lindsay shot photographs for softcore English men's magazines, alongside harder content for 'Dutch and Scandinavian' firms. This is confirmed by the Dutch magazine *Chick,* which names John Lindsay as a contributing photographer from the 1970s onwards. Lindsay states that Darby asked him if he would be interested in making rollers: 'I told him that as long as it was legal, I'd do it'. Lindsay then recounts how he conferred with his lawyer about whether it was lawful, leading him to meet with members of the Obscene Publications Squad:

> I explained the proposition that had been put to me and asked what the legal position was. They said that six weeks previously, a new law had been passed legalising homosexuality. But the Act just said that 'consenting adults in private' can do what they like sexually. As far as they could see, this meant that I was at liberty to shoot blue films in private as long as I used consenting adults. They went on to say that, however, if I published or sold the films in this country, they'd come down like a ton of bricks on me.

With the legal position confirmed, Lindsay agreed to shoot films for Darby, but have no responsibility for what Darby chose to do with them, 'churning them out every weekend'. The Sexual Offences Act 1967 was enacted in the July of that year, making it likely that Lindsay began producing rollers around then, rather than the 1966 date he gives in the *Penthouse* article. This calls into question the truthfulness of Darby's 1977 testimony given to Gilbert Kelland's anti-corruption unit. He gives 1969 as the year he first entered the business, attending the *Sex 69* fair in Denmark. To further complicate matters, Lindsay's self-published magazine states he began in 1970, 'shooting over 100 films [...] 35 of these [...] were for the export market'. Such sources again demonstrate the challenges of researching pornography's history relying on 'unstable' and 'slippery material' (Larsson 2018: 13). Therefore, it is difficult to ascertain when Lindsay began making rollers, though it would have been in the latter half of the 1960s.

Lindsay's oddly exact estimate of producing 3824 rollers seems far-fetched. Yet, it is evident that he made films on a large scale for a range of distributors. The first Darby label to release Lindsay's films was named Excelsior (see Figure 5.7). Lindsay may have also been involved in two other early brands with links to Darby – Steinle Films and Leidibird – both of which used German/Scandinavian sounding

FIGURE 5.7: *Nympho Artist* (John Lindsay, 1969–72) on Excelsior Film. Author's personal collection. Faces obscured to protect the identity of performers.

names. In Chapter 4, I suggested that this was a marketing strategy used by roller producers, drawing of representations of 'Swedish sin' and 'Danish blue' to signify stronger content. As Figure 5.8 shows, films released on Steinle and Leidibird also appear on another label named Academy, which links to Darby, Collingbourne and Lindsay, such as the film *Joyride* (1969–71) and *We Had to Do It* (1969–71). Legal documents relating to the Watford Blue Movie Trial name Lindsay at least three times, but the police assumed that 'Lindsay' was one of Darby's many pseudonyms. The files reveal that Darby released films made by Lindsay, having 16mm colour negatives that stated Lindsay's name or his alias 'John Linden', some of which had not yet been developed.

FIGURE 5.8: *We Had to Do It* (1970–72) on Leidibird and *Joyride* (1970–72) on Steinle Films. Both were re-released by Academy. Courtesy of private collectors. Faces obscured to protect the identity of performers.

Excelsior Films issued around twenty titles. The early box covers have a very basic appearance, following the usual style that had become commonplace in the economy following the inception of Phillips' Climax brand – a blank box with a label name at the top and a sexually explicit photograph on the front, usually with a Letraset title. However, as a twist on this style, the boxes for *Nympho Artist* (John Lindsay 1970–71) and *The Builders* (John Lindsay 1970–71) include a hand-written title next to a small sketch. Lindsay's films were released and re-released on many Darby labels. For instance, Excelsior's *Kinky Vicar* (John Lindsay 1970–72), a roller featuring a necrophiliac vicar and identified as a personal favourite by Lindsay in his *Penthouse* interview, also appears on Anglo Continental and Taboo & Phoenix. Similarly, *And the Rain Came* (John Lindsay 1970–72) was issued on both Academy and Orchid. Numerous other titles appear across labels that include Phoenix International, Taboo of Sweden, Teenage Productions and Zodiac Films, as indicated in the labelography found in Appendix 1.

I have linked over 200 rollers to Lindsay. As with other labels, it is highly plausible that there were more, but are yet to resurface or have been lost to time. The majority of the titles are shot across the United Kingdom, particularly the south of England, although there are titles claiming to be filmed on the Continent. For instance, *Alpine Lust* (John Lindsay 1970–72), *Artic Fuck* (John Lindsay 1970–72), *High Society* (John Lindsay 1970–72) and *Tyrollean Love* (John Lindsay 1970–72) were filmed in the Alps (see Figure 5.9). Like the travelling Italian pornography entrepreneur Lasse Braun, who Paasonen (2017: 127) refers to as a 'markedly translocal operator' due to his use of exotic filming locations, Lindsay likely shot these films while on other assignments for European producers (Sheridan 1999: 51). Lindsay's reputation reached Germany, where now-former pornography smuggler Walter Bartkowski hired him to shoot the earlier mentioned *Miss Bohrloch* (John Lindsay 1972–73) for his label Tabu de Luxe starring British glamour model Mary Millington (see Figure 5.10). The film was praised in reviews and is said to have sold nearly 300,000 copies (Sheridan 1999: 52), winning a Golden Phallus award at the Frankfurt Pornographic Film Festival sometime in the early 1970s.[18]

Lindsay's professionalism is evident in the equipment he used. Whereas the other filmmakers discussed in this book tended to favour the semi-professional Bolex 16mm camera, Lindsay preferred an Arriflex ST 16mm cine camera, a device typically used for television drama and newsgathering. The documentary *Naughty!* (Stanley Long 1972) includes behind the scenes footage of Lindsay making a roller. In this footage, he can be seen operating the heavy Arriflex while directing three performers. According to the *Penthouse* interview, Lindsay shot on colour film, recording 60 minutes of footage and then edited it down to 20 minutes or less for printing. Sound, if necessary, was added later during post-production; on-set audio was not used. Although little is known about how his films were

FIGURE 5.9: A selection of John Lindsay's European shot films: *Tyrollean Love* (1970–72), *Artic Fuck* (1970–72), *High Society* (1970–72) and *Alpine Lust* (1970–72). Author's personal collection. Faces obscured to protect the identity of performers.

developed, the files from the Watford Blue Movie Trial offer a clue. One of the untitled 16mm masters seized from Darby's lock-up is recorded as having '24.11.71. John Linden. Swedish Doc. Studio Film Laboratories' written on the can. The police officer inspecting the film confirms that it is hardcore, describing it as a 'very good quality film' and 'very well produced'. Studio Film Laboratories, based in Soho, located on Meard Street, appears to have developed some of Lindsay's films, likely as an out-of-hours service.[19] Lindsay's relationship with Stanley Long, the established Soho-based filmmaker and director of *Naughty!* might have helped get access to such laboratories. It is not clear how the films were printed for release on

FIGURE 5.10: Produced for the German market, *Miss Bohrloch* (John Lindsay 1972–73) star-ring Mary Millington on Walter Bartkowski's Tabu de Luxe label. Author's personal collection.

the standard 8mm format, but the police involved in the Watford case suspected that a non-professional system was used (*Evening Echo*, 3 June 1974), perhaps a device similar to the Uhler, as utilized by Mike Freeman.[20]

Following his appearance in *Naughty!*, Laurie Manifold's team of reporters published an article on Lindsay as part of their ongoing investigation into Brit-ain's pornography economy (*Sunday People*, 5 March 1972). Like Waterfield, Lindsay did not care about revealing his trade. In the article, Lindsay 'admits to being Britain's leading producer', making 'some 60 pornographic films in Britain, in addition to those he has made in Denmark and Sweden', earning him profits of 'about £50,000'. Lindsay presents himself as a jobbing filmmaker to 'the order of pornographic businessmen overseas', charging £250 for his services, paying female performers £25 a scene, with men getting 'even less'. He claims that his films are shot in 'opulent homes', with a 'member of the nobility' permitting the use of his home to shoot four films on the condition that he could watch. It names Lindsay's professional company as Mayfair Productions Ltd, having premises on Margaret Street in the West End of London, and states that he entered the business of hard-core filmmaking around 1968. The article identifies Lindsay as making films for export outside of Britain.[21] For Lindsay, his working for European distributors was as an alibi to evade the Obscene Publications Act 1959. Initially, this strategy seemed to work well, distancing himself from their distribution and not getting embroiled in the Watford Blue Movie Trial. However, a series of rollers shot at a Birmingham school came to the attention of the police, leading to an investigation into Lindsay's enterprise.

## Sex at school

*The Pornbrokers* (Laurence Barnett and John Lindsay 1973) represents an attempt by Lindsay to move into feature film production (see Figure 5.11). Numerous media interviews indicate his frustration with making rollers, finding them 'dull and boring', limiting him as a professional filmmaker (Kerekes 2000: 194). According to Kerekes (2000: 193), Lindsay's first became involved with features in 1969 when he worked as a stills photographer on the softcore film *The Wife Swappers* (Derek Ford 1969).[22] The early 1970s saw a growth in the release of soft core 'sexploitation' films, particularly sex comedies (Hunter 2013: 110). These low-budget films offered high economic returns from an audience eager to see sex on screen. Lindsay briefly participated in this lucrative market, producing and contributing the original story for *The Love Pill* (Ken Turner 1972) and scripting, producing and directing *The Hot Girls* (John Lindsay 1974). *The Pornbrokers* (1973) differs in that it was an attempt at a serious documentary. The film explores the transnational trade in pornography, featuring interviews with Lindsay's network of European pornography entrepreneurs and performers, such as Lasse Braun, the publisher of *Chick* Joop Wilhelmus, *Private's* Berth Milton, amongst others. In the interview found in his own magazine, Lindsay states that he made the documentary as a retort to the Longford Report. Although the British version did not contain any hardcore footage, the BBFC refused to certify the film. Greater London Council approved the film for showing in cinemas and it was later allowed by the BBFC in 1977, albeit heavily cut.[23] While dabbling with feature films, Lindsay still produced rollers for John Darby, who managed to escape the Watford Blue Movie Trial.

Lindsay became entangled in the Metropolitan Police's crackdown on the alternative economy. His films were seized in raids on bookshops taking place across the country, as Scotland Yard brought in a new eighteen strong squad in late 1972 (*Daily Mail*, 18 November 1972). Kerekes (2000: 193) also posits that Lindsay's releasing of *The Pornbrokers* and his appearance on *The Frost Programme* brought unwanted attention from the authorities. On 8 December 1973, the *Daily Mail* reported that 'vice squad detectives' were investigating how the science laboratory and art room at Aston Manor secondary school in Birmingham came to be used as the location for a series of rollers. The article tells of how the seized colour films showed 'orgies involving scantily clad "schoolgirls" and men dressed in gowns and

MILTON        JOHN LINDSAY       JOOP WILHELMUS       ULRICH GEISMAR

## Meet the Men . . . And Women . . . behind the European Porno-scene
## THE PORN-BROKERS

The broker is an essential middleman operating between the market forces of Supply and Demand.

With the worldwide demand for Pornography rapidly increasing for both "soft" and "hard" varieties – the supply increases proportionately to satisfy it.

And so it is that the middlemen, with their collective finger on both sides of the market, have grown into the controllers and entrepreneurs of an extremely lucrative business. These, then, are the PORN-BROKERS . . .

Their basic stock-in-trade consists of blue films, "dirty" books, erotic magazines and the shock live shows which have become part of the entertainment scene in many European capital cities.

Their clients are legion : men and women from all walks of life and all social levels, but with one vital common interest. To promote, exploit and enjoy the act of sexual intercourse and its associated deviations to an ecstatic degree, without the necessity of actual participation. Such is the true present day meaning of pornography which, like beauty, rests to a large degree in the eye of the beholder.

THE PORN-BROKERS is a daring report on the whole scene, through the perceptive eyes of British fashion photographer turned movie-maker John Lindsay, whose uninhibited comments add much to the stark realism of the film. We follow the complete production of a "blue" movie, from casting to copulation : look in on some of the sex clubs of Hamburg and Copenhagen ; hear the matter-of-fact views of some of the biggest operators in the business : visit the affluent homes of porno-magazine editors and listen to their realistic, even philanthropic, approach to their lucrative vocation.

This is a film that will shock many people with its utter frankness. Nothing shocks like the truth, and in this sense THE PORN-BROKERS can justly be described as the first TRUE blue movie!

### CREDITS

Produced and directed by JOHN LINDSAY and LAURIE BARNETT

Cameramen : JOHN LINDSAY and MIKE KUBICKI

Sound : DAVID JONES    Lighting : BILL SUMMERS

Production Secretary : PENNY COTTON    Editor : JOHN PIPKIN

Dubbing Editor : TONY ANSCOMBE    Commentary : ROGER HEATHCOT

### WORLD SALES

DIETER-WAHL-FILM
Poccistrasse 3, 8 München 2. W. Germany
TARGET INTERNATIONAL PICTURES LTD.
National House, 60-66 Wardour Street.
London W.1. England

FIGURE 5.11: Advertisement for *The Pornbrokers* (Laurence Barnett and John Lindsay 1973). The face of the female model has been obscured.

mortarboards'. Police interviewed Staff and pupils, with two men and two women arrested for 'conspiring to publish obscene material'. As with many obscenity cases, Director of Public Prosecution files appear to have not been archived, leaving newspapers as the only documented source. The obscenity case – *R* v. *Lindsay*

(1974) – received much attention in the British national and local press, making it possible to establish a chain of events.

The *Daily Mail* (17 October 1974) summarizes how Scotland Yard determined Lindsay's involvement. Twenty-nine rollers, including *Kinky Schoolgirls* (1971–72), *Schoolgirl Incest* (1971–72), *Sex Lessons at School* (1971–72), *Jolly Hockey Sticks* (1971–72), *A Hundred Lines* (1971–72) and *Convent of Sin* (1971–72), were seized during a raid in Portsmouth, Southampton, and others taking place across the country. Upon viewing the films, the police noticed that they used the same school location. On closer inspection, a towel was spotted and, when magnified, the words 'gham Corp' were revealed. Police eventually determined that this stood for 'Birmingham Corporation' and showed the images to a Birmingham school inspector who recognized the location – Aston Manor. The school's headmaster of the school confirmed this and, when doing so, noticed that the caretaker and former Head Boy appeared in the films. The headmaster is said to have been 'shocked' as he spotted the science laboratories, girls' changing rooms, class-rooms and even the deputy head's study. The caretaker admitted to being paid £200 for access to the school over three weekends. When the police searched his premises, they found an outline for a film titled *Charity Begins at Home*, demon-strating that some rollers were, to some extent, pre-planned. The *Birmingham Post* (17 October 1974) printed the brief outline:

> *Charity Begins at Home*
> Location: Flat; Personnel: one male, one female; Clothes: frumpy type clothes, glasses, charity collection box (Imagine good looking girl with old-fashioned but good clothes, spectacles and hair done in a bun). Opening: girl arrives at flat of rampant bachelor collecting for charity. He invites her in. Begins to make [...] [the newspaper states that the remainder of the text was 'obliterated'].

Lindsay and Darby – identified as the director of the films – were charged along with a total of five performers for conspiring to publish obscene films between 1 November 1972 and 30 November 1973. Originally from Birmingham, it appears that Darby arranged for the films to be made. Lindsay claims that he was just the cameraman, paid £25–50 per film, and that his 'gross income was about £2000 a year' (*The Times*, 19 October 1974). This amount is remarkably lower than the £750,000 he claimed to have earned in 1972 as a 'freelance producer director' (*The National Insider*, 30 September 1973). As with the Watford Blue Movie Trial, Darby fled the country to evade arrest. The police named him as 'the kingpin of the "blue movie" industry in England' (*Daily Telegraph*, 21 November).

The trial began at Birmingham Crown Court on 16 October 1974. The performers all pleaded guilty to charges; Lindsay pleaded not guilty. The prosecution presented Lindsay as a major player in the economy, using his film *The Pornbrokers* as evidence of his transnational network and status. Lindsay denied this, explaining that he was a cameraman for hire and had been commissioned by Dutch pornography entrepreneur Joop Wilhelmus to shoot the films. The prosecution asked Lindsay if he was genuinely surprised by his films being sold in Britain; 'very surprised', he replied. He claimed that his motivation for producing them was not financial, but part of a moral crusade, making 'a stand for adult liberty and against censorship' (*Birmingham Post*, 19 October 1974). When asked about his involvement in *The Frost Programme*, Lindsay told the court that five women contacted him for work after discovering that he made pornographic films and that he had recruited a total of 'forty to fifty' women, 'thirty of them in Britain' (*Daily Mirror*, 22 October 1974). These performers were obtained through his reputation as a photographer, while others were recommended by those who had taken part in his films.[24] One of the performers – the former Head Boy – took the stand. He told the court that he received £15 per film and appeared in four of them. Another female performer who was not one of the defendants stated that she received £20 for each one. According to the *Birmingham Post* (19 October 1974), 'Lindsay did the filming and John Darby told them what to do' (*Birmingham Post*, 24 October 1974). By identifying himself as a cameraman working for foreign producers, Lindsay sought to distance his involvement, using this as an alibi.

From a legal perspective, the trial was significant for the judge's decision to screen seven of Lindsay's films to the court, including the press and the public. This contrasted with the earlier discussed *R v. Waterfield* (1975) and the Watford Blue Movie Trial case, where the judge refused to screen the films to members of the public.[25] The *Daily Mirror* (18 October 1974) reports that over 50 people were present during the screening of Lindsay's *Convent of Sin* (1972–73),[26] *Temptation* (1972–73, pictured in Figure 5.13), *School Sex Lessons* (1972–73), *Anal Rape* (1972–73), *White Hunter* (1972–73), *School Art Lesson* (1972–73) and *Jolly Hockey Sticks* (1972–73), which is said to have been filmed in the girls' changing rooms at Aston Manor. These were issued on labels related to Lindsay, such as Karl Ordinez,[27] Orchid Films and Teenage Productions. The titles of these films are typical of themes present in Lindsay's work, including the use of schoolgirls and references to religion, specifically Catholicism. As Hunter (2013: 117–18) points out, the 'schoolgirls' in Lindsay's films appear to be 'well over eighteen', and use of the school 'is a staple of porn stories, a regimented setting ripe for power play, the transgression of generational boundaries and fantasies of educational curricular sex'. For Jones (2007: 124), the motif of the schoolgirl is a 'market of the exploitative elements of permissiveness'. Like Mike Freeman, Lindsay seemed to be aware of the demand for such content, hence why much of his output is devoted to it.

Similarly, Lindsay's attention to religion is another common pornographic trope that dates back to the eighteenth century, when representations of monks and nuns 'typified the anti-societal exploration of sexual pleasure for its own sake' (Saunders 2020: 7). Considering how the press adopted a moral position when discussing pornography, it seems remarkable, particularly in contemporary society, that the articles reporting the trial do not pass judgement on the representation of schoolgirls or girl guides in Lindsay's pornography, let alone the reference to rape in many of his titles. Today, it is likely that such titles would draw ire from the press and the public, while the films featuring such acts could potentially fall foul of the Criminal Justice and Immigration Act 2008, a concern highlighted by Jones and Mowlabocus (2009). However, in the context of the 1970's post-permissive culture, Lindsay and Darby's 'emotive titles and risqué themes' (Kerekes 2000: 196) are indicative of attitudes to sex and sexuality in that period, highlighting the types of pornography then in demand.

Returning to the trial, Lindsay's defence argued that the films shown to the court were of a public good, under section 4 of the Obscene Publications Act, providing sexual education to those who watch them. To support this, they called Dr Lionel Hayward, a psychiatrist with an expertise in psychological sexual disorders and marriage guidance, whose research showed that 'married couples who had the opportunity of seeing sex films showed their sex life had been improved by seeing them' and there was no evidence of 'mental illness having been caused by such films or by pornography generally' (*The Times*, 22 October 1974). Another expert witness, Maurice Yaffe, a research psychologist, told how hardcore pornography offered more benefits than softcore, producing 'a more stimulating effect' in the viewer's mind, and did no harm (*Birmingham Post*, 22 October 1974). The prosecution's expert witness, Dr Myre Sim, said that pornographic films 'could be upsetting and harmful to some' though 'some scenes could be used for treating people with psycho-sexual problems' (*Birmingham Post*, 23 October 1974). In his summing up, Justice Wien referred to Lindsay's claim that the police told him that 'anything that took place between consenting adults in private was legal' was 'hopelessly wrong'. He instructed the jury to consider whether 'the films were obscene in the sense that they were intended to deprave and corrupt such persons who were likely to see the film'. On 23 October, after almost five hours, the jury gave their verdict. They were 'hopelessly divided' on whether Lindsay was guilty, leaving the judge to discharge the jury and order a retrial. The five others who pleaded guilty to charges were sentenced on 26 October 1974. The man who arranged the making of the films received a nine month prison sentence, suspended for two years and fined £200 or two months in jail. The school caretaker was fined £350 or six months prison. Of the performers, one female was given a three-month sentence, suspended for a year and the couple were each given a fine of £150 or two months in jail (*The Times*, 26 October 1974).[28]

# Blue Movies

This is on of the most exciting offers ever published in a magazine because these are genuine blue movies featured in the John Lindsay blue movie case in Birmingham last year.

These are beautifully produced 200 ft. Karl Ordinez movies. All are Super 8mm and in full colour.

We guarantee you won't be disappointed with these selected films. They are the real thing – not simulated sex films.

*We have chosen sex titles which provide exciting variety. They are:*

Price £20 each

**Safari.** The sound of the drums throb through the jungle as the hot sun burns out of the sky to reveal a Landrover on expedition. Why has it stopped? A beautiful blonde and a man fucking on the bonnet! And that's not the whole story. They've left their sexy colleagues back at camp . . . .

**Schoolgirl Seduction.** Schoolgirl Caroline alone at home answers the door to the milkman. Mummy hasn't left any money to pay the bill so Caroline is left to her own devices to keep the visitor happy. Caroline is no innocent teenager.

**Girl Guide Rape.** Two lovely 16-year-old girl guides are invited into a flat by two men. Drinks come first, sexy games follow. The four enjoy the most fantastic sex scene you have ever seen.

**Dr. Zego.** The sinister Dr. Zego and his lovely black nurse specialise in helping beautiful women overcome their sexual problems. In his laboratory is the ultimate sex aid – the world's only computerised fucking machine!

**Frustration.** Two guys patiently wait for the girls to get ready. An unexpected view in the mirror starts off a frenzied foursome of exciting sex acrobatics.

You may still not be convinced that we are offering you completely genuine blue movies and may feel £20 is too much to gamble. If that is so we have arranged for one black and white film *(Schoolgirl Seduction)* to be made available to you for the bargain price of just £8. This is the only black and white movie available and is Standard 8mm. Why not take this opportunity of proving to yourself that we are as good as our word?

FIGURE 5.12: Mail-order advert for Lindsay's 8mm rollers, referring to the Birmingham Trial. Author's personal collection.

FIGURE 5.13: Screenshots from *Convent of Sin* (John Lindsay 1972–73). Author's personal collection. Faces obscured to protect the identity of performers.

The retrial commenced on 14 November 1974. Lindsay refused to give evidence, instead offering a statement from the dock, summarizing some of the points he made during his stand at the earlier trial, repeating his moral stance:

> I believe films showing sexual behaviour between happily consenting adults are not obscene, nor they harm those who wish to watch them [...] I believe sincerely the films I have made are not obscene [...] I have filmed acts between consenting adults which are universal practice. If you call these acts obscene you are calling humanity obscene.

He again claimed he did not make large sums of money from making the films, only being employed as a cameraman (*Daily Mirror*, 15 November 1974). Mounting a public good defence, medical expert Dr Christine Pickard told the court that she had 'treated hundreds of patients with sexual problems and she recommended some of them to watch blue films'. She also added that the films were 'instructional', freeing 'people from their fears' and making them 'more able to give pleasure rather than demand it' (*Daily Mirror*, 16 November 1974). Days later, the prosecution countered with their own expert witness, psychiatrist Dr Anton Stephens, who attempted to disprove Pickard's statement by saying that pornographic films can have the opposite effect: 'I know of marriages which have broken up through sexual expectations not being fulfilled' (*Daily Mirror*, 19 November 1974). On 20 November, the and after a four-hour deliberation, the court found Lindsay not guilty of conspiring to publish obscene films.

As Hunt (1998: 38) observes, the constantly shifting 'sexual climate' of the 1970s left the Obscene Publications Act 1959 'floundering in a sea of inconsistences', which Lindsay's legal team exploited through a public good defence. *R* v. *Lindsay* (1974) is also significant for implying that 'good clean pornography' would no longer be found obscene by juries (Robertson 1979: 4), seemingly legalizing heterosexual pornography. For the *Daily Mail* (21 November 1974), the verdict set a precedent, throwing 'Britain's obscenity laws into confusion', affecting future definitions of the law and having implications for the production of pornography. In his statement to the press, Lindsay presented himself as an activist who 'made these films as part of my campaign against adult censorship'. Analysis of the two trials suggests Lindsay manipulated the Obscene Publications Act 1959 for his own benefit, using his ongoing position as a jobbing professional filmmaker hired to shoot films that, to his knowledge, were being exported for distribution. Lindsay stood to economically gain if his films were found not to be obscene. Following the trials, the opening of Lindsay's films included a disclaimer referencing the Birmingham Trial, stating that they were cleared of obscenity charges (see Figure 5.14). This became a regularly used promotional device for Lindsay (Smith 2007: 56) and another legal alibi (see Figure 5.12).

As sources show, the trial received daily coverage in both national and local press, drawing greater awareness to Lindsay's role as a producer of hardcore pornography. Seizing on this publicity, Lindsay opened a shop – the London Blue Movie Centre – in Soho, moving further towards the distribution of hardcore pornography. According to an article in the *Sunday People* (31 August 1975), Lindsay believed that the acquittal in Birmingham now made him immune from further prosecution. It describes how the shop, located at 37 Berwick Street, had a sign placed in the window: 'The films under this counter are the films which were prosecuted with John Lindsay at Birmingham Crown Court November 1974. They are pornographic'. On entering the London Blue Movie Centre, customers had to sign a form, declaring that they did 'not disapprove of pornographic films and will not bring a prosecution', further showing how Lindsay saw himself as working within the scope of the Obscene Publications Act 1959. Customers could pay 50p to preview excerpts from the films on a viewer to confirm they were hardcore. The following week, the *Sunday People* (7 September 1975) describes how customers queued outside the shop when it opened, purchasing films 'at £10 and £20 each'. On the following day, the Obscene Publications Squad raided the shop and seized all of the stock. This triggered an ongoing legal battle with the police, as Lindsay became implicated in another criminal investigation, this time for making a hardcore film funded by the British Broadcasting Corporation.

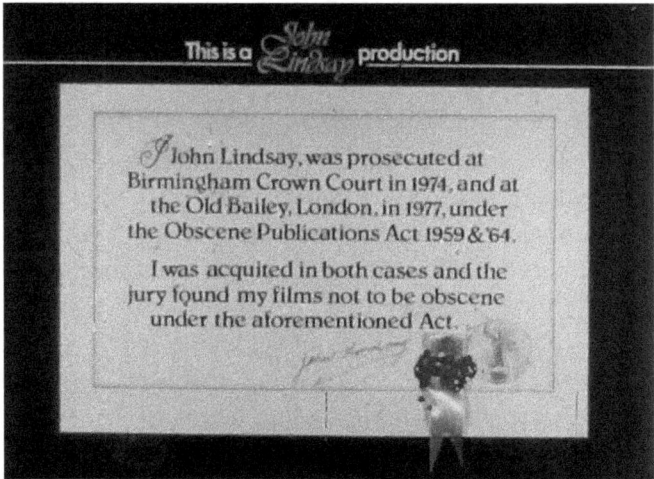

FIGURE 5.14: Lindsay's disclaimer used at the beginning of his rollers referring to the Birmingham Trial. Author's personal collection.

## *Dirty work*

Lindsay expanded his enterprise to include cinema clubs (see Figure 5.15), opening one in the basement of the building next to his shop on Berwick Street in 1975. In a rare interview for the television documentary *History of Hardcore* (Martin Morrison 2002), Lindsay spoke of his move into the lucrative cinema club business:

> So, I went to see this lawyer. I said I've got this idea to open a private cinema club. You need to become a member, and you can't become a member unless you're proposed and seconded and you have to wait 24 hours before you become a member […] I say,

Figure 5.15: Advertisement for Lindsay's Taboo Cinema Club, 15–18 Great Newport Street, London. Author's personal collection.

well, can my manager propose them? 'Oh yes'. Can the assistant manager second them? 'Oh yes'. And I did it officially, I didn't want my collar felt or to go to jail, but they get you anyway. I opened the first Taboo Cinema on Great Newport Street, Leicester Square, opposite the Odeon [...] and they were queueing around the block [...] it was unbelievable, and the money was unbelievable.

He eventually opened other cinema clubs under the Taboo brand, with one on Frith Street in Soho, two in Birmingham and another in Blackpool. These became a profitable venture for Lindsay, allowing him to move away from filmmaking as his primary income and benefit from his large catalogue of films. He also appears to have licensed his films to European labels. The Danish company Flesh and the German label CD-Film re-released a selection of his early 1970s titles. His growing status as a pornographic filmmaker led to his involvement with a television programme made by the BBC as part of their collaboration with the Open University, a relationship that would eventually result in a scandal known as the BBC Blue Movie Case. The case is documented in a Director of Public Prosecutions file that can be accessed at the National Archives in Kew, London.[29] It was also reported by the national press. Before computers and internet access transformed the delivery of online education, the BBC screened educational programmes for Open University students to watch. One such series was titled *People and Work* and based on the research of a sociologist named Geoff Esland. An episode named 'Dirty and Deviant' intended to have a BBC crew present during the making of a softcore pornographic film, interviewing the people involved in its production.

While being interviewed by a reporter from the *News of the World* for a feature article titled 'Marriage in a Permissive Age', Lindsay spoke of his participation, instigating a police investigation. The police viewed the unedited footage for the programme, finding that it depicted 'actual, not simulated, intercourse with a number of close-up shots [...] the kind of "hardcore film" which is generally thought to be obscene'. They interviewed the BBC producer, Gwynn Pritchard, and Lindsay under caution. Pritchard told the investigator how he first met Lindsay in January 1975, later attending the filming of one of Lindsay's films at a London Penthouse flat on 31 January 1975. Pritchard alleges that he told Lindsay not to shoot hardcore while his camera crew were present, a request Lindsay agreed to. Filming took place on 8 February 1975 at a London Penthouse belonging to movie producer Stanley Long. The performers were paid £10 each for the interviews in advance. After filming started, the BBC crew discovered that Lindsay was shooting hardcore. Coming back from holiday early, Long returned to his flat and found Lindsay using it to make the film.[30] Long dismissed the people present and refused to let the BBC take the footage away from the flat, passing it on to a 'neutral' film laboratory – Kay's Laboratory in North London – for safekeeping. The contract between Lindsay and the BBC included in the file states that he was to be paid £75 for his involvement.

Lindsay's interview provides a slightly different chain of events. He claims Pritchard and Esland specifically asked to film the making of a hardcore film, as a 'simulated movie' did not offer the same 'atmosphere'. As with the Birmingham Trial, Lindsay told the police that the financier for the hardcore film was a Dutch distributor of pornography, but this time it was Ari Van Der Heul investing £400, not Joop Wilhelmus.[31] Lindsay defers to his usual 'for export only' defence, stating that Van Der Heul agreed to buy the completed movie from Lindsay to sell on the 'Continent'. The police sided with Pritchard's version of events, believing Lindsay double-crossed him to make a film that he could 'sell for a profit'. However, the investigators acknowledge that Pritchard may have been involved in deliberate deception, although it was likely because of an 'error in judgement'. Police notes exhibit a willingness to prosecute Lindsay and reveal how they explored the variety of legal options available to them. First, a charge under the Obscene Publications Act 1959 was considered. However, as Pritchard commissioned Lindsay to make the film, they recognized that a jury might find him not guilty. Second, as Lindsay admitted to sending the film to Van Der Heul in the Netherlands, the police contemplated an alternative charge of sending indecent articles through the post, under the Post Office Act 1953. To make this viable, the documents state that evidence of postage was necessary. A common law charge of conspiracy to corrupt public morals was deemed inappropriate and, finally, investigators decided on a charge of 'conspiracy to publish abroad an obscene article', only to find it not possible under English law. The Obscene Publications Squad had no other choice but to close the case, recognizing that the newspaper coverage of the case had affected the public 'image of the BBC'.

This coverage brought unwanted public attention, as Lindsay sold his story to the *News of the World*. On 14 September 1975, the paper devoted a full page to the case, including some of the stills taken during the filming of a roller named *Strip Poker*. A BBC spokesperson interviewed for the article is evasive when commenting on the content of Lindsay's film but admitted that an error of judgement had been made. In response to this and other articles featured in the national press, Hugh Watts of the Action Group on Abuse of Law wrote a letter to the then Director-General of the BBC, expressing his disgust at the matter, recommending that they seek charges of offence to corrupt public morals, conspiracy to debauch and indict Lindsay for living on immoral earnings as if he were a pimp.[32] Despite such calls from anti-pornography activists, police took no further action. On 6 May 1976, the BBC and the Open University representatives visited Kay's Laboratory to identify the film before it was incinerated under police supervision. The interviews shot for *Dirty Work* are said to have survived. But what happened to *Strip*

*Poker*, the film Lindsay shot while being observed by the BBC production team? Lindsay claims he made three films, one softcore for the movie machine market, another hardcore film that ended up being stolen along with his car, and *Strip Poker*. Evidently, Lindsay is deceiving the police, just as he did with the prosecution during the Birmingham trials. However, in his police statement, he does associate Dutch producer Van Der Heul with a British label named International Films, which coincidentally released a film called *Strip Poker* (see Figure 5.1).

International Films released around 31 titles and were seemingly active between the years 1970 and 1972, as indicated by one of Darby's mail-order catalogues. A promotional poster in the film *Euston Capture* (1972) dates its making to 1972. Lindsay is associated with the label as titles also appear on Academy, a brand linked to Anthony Collingbourne and John Darby, who likely is the distributor. The content of *Strip Poker* does not match the photographs printed in the *News of the World*, nor does it feature the same performers.[33] Furthermore, the dates of production do not match, so it is plausible that this was another ruse on behalf of Lindsay, again using the 'for export only' alibi to evade arrest. Judging from the police's deliberations, this once more proved to be an effective tactic. By the mid 1970s, Lindsay's making of rollers subsided. He appears to have diverted attention to his cinema clubs and shops, but also his role as a father, after his wife Penny gave birth to twin daughters in 1975. In an interview for the *Evening News* (25 February 1982), he declares that the cinema clubs earned £2500 each week, a potential £130,000 per year.

Throughout Lindsay's career as a roller producer, the material quality of his films became increasingly lavish, moving from the generic 'Soho style' box to glossy, higher quality boxes with full cover printing during the Karl Ordinez period. When he established the brand Taboo, in keeping with his cinemas and shops, the packaging was now akin to that used by Walter Bartkowski's German label Tabu de Luxe. The development of the packaging used for 8mm hardcore pornography is further indicative of its over-supply, as entrepreneurs found ways to make their product stand out amongst the numerous other labels populating the shelves of sex shops and mail-order catalogues. Tabu de Luxe releases, such as *Miss Bohrloch*, used larger boxes containing a 100 m (328 ft) or 150 m (492 ft) reel – longer than the usual 200 ft roller – housed in a plastic inlay tray with the Tabu brand embossed. Unlike roller packaging, the boxes feel strong and feature bright, colourful printing of a distinctive still taken during filming, indicating Bartkowski's commitment to offer a quality product. Lindsay presented Taboo releases, such as *Health Farm* (John Lindsay 1975–77) and a remake of *Jolly Hockey Sticks* (John Lindsay 1975–77), in similar superior packaging. For example, *Health Farm* was distributed in a red, plastic gatefold case with a full cover colour image placed inside a plastic cover, similar to the style of VHS, DVD and

Blu-ray cases (see Figure 5.16). The Taboo brand was also distinctive, featuring a drawing of a woman enveloped by a snake-like penis. Given the challenges of producing a quality product in a clandestine market, Lindsay's strive for professionalism and quality stands out, suggesting that he kept a close eye on developments in the international market.

## *A wanted man*

The BBC Blue Movie Case exemplifies Lindsay's growing celebrity after his acquittal in the Birmingham Trial. The investigation also shows that the police actively sought his prosecution, concerned that his enterprise threatened the moral fabric of British society. Following the not guilty verdicts of *R v. Lindsay* (1974) and *R v. Hatiatt* (1976),[34] it appeared that heterosexual, hardcore pornography would be decriminalized. Thompson (1994: 26) saw the latter trial as a landmark for printed pornography, suggesting that it 'would rarely be prosecuted again'. In response, anti-pornography moral entrepreneurs voiced their concerns about the harm of pornography. Joining the Festival of Light were the Soho Society, who set-out to eradicate the growing sex industry, which became unwieldy after the

FIGURE 5.16: *Health Farm* (John Lindsay 1975–77) on Taboo Films. Courtesy of 'Ken'. Faces obscured to protect the identity of performers.

downfall of the Obscene Publications Squad and, in 1977, the London Revolutionary Feminist Anti-Pornography Consciousness-Raising Group carried out their first London Reclaim the Night March through the streets of Soho, collaborating with the Rape Action Group to picket a sex shop (Long 2012: 43–44). Pro-pornography groups also emerged, such as the National Campaign for the Reformation of the Obscene Publications Act (NCROPA), founded by actor David Webb as a response to the activities of Mary Whitehouse and the inadequacy of obscenity law.

According to Thompson (1994), a moral panic around pornography was prompted by the activities of David Sullivan, who expanded his sex shop empire across provincial Britain, and a growing concern about the availability of child pornography. Thompson (1994) outlines how Mary Whitehouse's moral entrepreneurship around child pornography resulted in the Protection of Children Act 1978. Such pressure from activists and opposing politicians led to the Labour government instigating a committee investigation into obscenity and film censorship, and Margaret Thatcher's Consvervative party made morality a central focus of their campaign for leadership, openly detesting 'permissiveness' assault on tradition' (Collins 2007: 27). The Obscene Publications Squad's licensing system brought some semblance of order to the alternative economy of hardcore pornography, but now it was uncontrolled, spreading from the confines of Soho across Britain. In response to the growth of cinema clubs, the Obscene Publications Act was amended in 1977 under section 53 of the Criminal Law Act 1977 to include film exhibitions. This was intended to modify 'the law relating to the crime of conspiracy but retained the much-criticised common-law offences of conspiracy to corrupt public morals and conspiracy to outrage public decency' (Simpson 1983: 1). It also granted the police power to search and seize material from cinema clubs, removing the need for extended surveillance as was necessary when pursuing a disorderly house charge.[35]

As Simpson (1983: 54) observes, the amendment did little to stop entrepreneurs from running cinema clubs with prosecutions becoming unworkable. I asked Soho sex shop owner Dave why this was so:

> It was difficult to shut them down. Like the shops, they used a frontman and only kept one print [of a film] on the premises at a time. So, if the police raided them and seized the projector and the film, all they had to do was get another projector and another film, and they'd be up and running again. It just wasn't worth the hassle.

At the same time, plans were also being made to implement further regulation of pornography trade through the licensing of sex shops and controlling sex shop displays. These changes to legislation are discussed in the conclusion to this chapter.

Despite this shifting political landscape, Lindsay continued to distribute hard-core pornography through his shops and cinema clubs. In 1977, Lindsay was tried under obscenity law for selling rollers at his London Blue Movie Centre shop, with the same films from the Birmingham Trial being used as evidence of obscenity.[36] The hearing took place on 13 July 1977 at the Old Bailey in London. Lindsay's barrister, Brian Capstick, admitted that the offending films were pornographic, but reminded the jury of five women and seven men that Lindsay could only be found guilty if 'the sale of the films tended to corrupt or deprave' those who had purchased them (*The Guardian*, 15 July 1977). Using the same approach as he did in Birmingham, Lindsay told the court that his films featured consenting adults who engaged in sexual behaviour that 'could not be termed obscene'. The defence called a 23-year-old customer of the shop as a witness, who recalled purchasing four films for his own use: 'For the reason of being overweight, my sex life is very difficult indeed. I get a lot of pleasure from sex films. You feel that by watching a sex film once or twice a week you can lead a normal life'.

By the time of this trial, *DPP* v. *Jordan* (1976) amended the public good defence, closing a loophole that enabled the defence to call experts to claim that pornography benefited people's sexual health. Now, the public good defence was limited to 'material with intrinsic merit as literature or learning' (Robertson 1979: 4), again showing how rule enforcers constantly revised the law to control the economy. Prosecutor David Tudor Price, referred to this amendment, asking the jury to discount the verdict of *R* v. *Lindsay* (1974). The jury found Lindsay not guilty, who brazenly declared to the press that he had made 'pornographic films legal in this country at last'. He added,

> the establishment in this country are out of touch with ordinary people. They went to single-sex public schools and have no idea what ordinary people think about sex. Sooner or later they will realise you can't legislate against the popular past time.
>
> (*Evening Post*, 15 July 1977)

He also provocatively revealed the next focus of his moral crusade – to abolish the BBFC.

While the police attempted to prosecute Lindsay, the then Labour government instigated a review of 'the laws governing of obscenity, indecency and violence in publications, displays and entertainment in England and Wales, except in the field of broadcasting, and to review the arrangements for film censorship in England and Wales; and to make recommendations' (Simpson 1983: 1). They introduced the Home Office Committee on Obscenity and Film Censorship on 13 July 1977. Chaired by Bernard Williams, a Professor of Philosophy in Cambridge and Provost of Kings College, London, it was referred to as the Williams Committee.

In contrast with the Longford Report, this was officially sanctioned by the Home Office. It consisted of thirteen members – a former police officer, film critic, youth and community worker, a reverend, a psychotherapist, amongst others. After almost two years of research, the Williams Report made a total of 56 proposals, finding pornography not to be harmful and recommending that adults should be permitted access to hardcore pornography, providing it was inaccessible to children.

Like the Longford Report, they too saw the Obscene Publications Act 1959 as unfit for purpose. Yet, instead of simply amending it, the committee first, and rather progressively, recommended that 'the existing variety of laws in this field should be scrapped and a comprehensive new statute should start afresh' (Williams 2015: 212). They advised that only a 'small class of material' be prohibited,[37] and the printed word should be exempt from control. Instead, the committee proposed a system of restriction, limiting access to hardcore pornography through licensed sex shops or cinemas where those under 18 years of age were not permitted. The only material the committee recommended be controlled was that which would have likely caused harm to their participants, such as child pornography and extreme sexual violence. This, however, would have criminalized the representation of specific sexual acts, namely fetishes, such as urolagnia, coprophilia and potentially a range of bondage, discipline and sadomasochistic (BDSM) practices. Despite this, the findings of the Williams Committee were remarkably liberal and represented a marked political and philosophical change to the control of pornography in Britain. As Petley identifies (2011: 131), the research was 'ditched by the incoming Tories as unacceptably liberal'. The report was leaked to the media, many of whom welcomed their common-sense approach, but for Thatcher's newly elected Conservative government, who made Victorian family values a cornerstone of their election campaign, it was viewed as too permissive. Instead, the Conservatives instituted further controls on the pornography trade.

Lindsay became entangled in this 'symbolic battle over permissiveness' (Thompson 1994: 26). In 1981, he was again prosecuted at Ealing Magistrates Court for the same films that were acquitted of obscenity charges in 1974 and 1977. Once more, the court found him not guilty, and the trial's judge 'severely criticised the police's actions, ordered the films to be returned, and awarded him costs' (*Time Out*, 6–12 November 1981). In response to these failed attempts, Thompson (1994: 46) claims that police raided Lindsay's premises repeatedly 'to close him down'. According to Soho sex shop owner Dave, police regularly used this tactic to put pornographers out of business. As warrants lasted for 24 hours, the vice squad could raid and seize stock more than once. A 1981 Thames television news feature titled *Soho: People Live Here Too* captures police raiding one of Lindsay's cinema clubs, seizing the projector and films, and the Taboo sex shop. Chair of the shop and Lindsay's business partner, an Australian named Chuck Sloman, quips 'jeez, you're a bunch of happy bastards today' as the police remove stock. On the same day of this raid, Lindsay attended Knightsbridge Crown Court for five separate obscenity trials alongside some of his unnamed associates. According to a document sent to NCROPA by Lindsay's solicitor R. H. Brown, the first trial consisted of two video tapes – titled *Intensive Care* (David Sear 1974) and *Thrilling Drilling* (Stan Sobel aka Leon Gucci 1974) – and one 8mm reel containing an assortment of six films.[38] The medium of video tape now superseded small-gauge film formats like 8mm and Super 8.

Pleading not guilty, Lindsay and his colleagues were acquitted in the first trial as the jury failed to reach a decision. In the second, a jury spent five hours examining a sample of the accused films, returning a not guilty verdict after just one hour of deliberation. The prosecution decided to withdraw the final three trials and did not re-try the first case. Lindsay's defence requested for their legal costs be paid and asked the judge for his view on the further fifteen planned indictments involving Lindsay. Justice Babington regretted that he did not have the authority to stop 'vexatious prosecutions' and proclaimed that obscenity cases were a 'shocking waste of public money' (*New Law Journal*, 21 January 1982). He asked to personally hear all future prosecutions involving Lindsay, a request that did not come to fruition. Interviewed at the beginning of the Knightsbridge Trial by Thames Reports for *Soho: People Live Here Too*, Lindsay comments on his battle with the police:

> Every film that I have or *had* prior to the raid this morning has been acquitted of all obscenity charges by a Crown Court jury. The latest one was in 1977 at the central criminal court – the Old Bailey – where the jury not only acquitted the films of obscenity, they actually spelled out why they were acquitting them […] the police, not the police who are conducting the raids who are nice enough blokes they are only doing their duty. Whoever is ordering the raids is completely disregarding a high Crown Court jury's decision. I will restock, and I will be raided again, with legal films, so, they are obviously attempting to close me down, not through a due process of law, but hitting me financially.

NCROPA supported Lindsay during this period, writing a press release identifying the persecution of Lindsay and how such investigations and trials were of great cost to the taxpayer. David Webb, Honorary Director of NCROPA, adds, 'this is a typical example of covert totalitarianism at work: it demonstrates just one of the ways in which the present government and its agencies are waging a war of attrition against vital civil liberties on many fronts. Who can predict who, and in what circumstances, may be their next arbitrary victim?'

Lindsay also faced charges at Preston Crown Court in the north of England, and another trial at Birmingham Crown Court – both related to raids of his cinema clubs (Manchester 1986: 208). Furthermore, a second series of police prosecutions were scheduled for 10 May 1982, again at Knightsbridge Crown Court, for the raid filmed during Thames Reports segment. With the police unable to successfully prosecute Lindsay, they planned to limit his ability to earn and eventually drive him out of the economy. The 1981 Knightsbridge Trial cost Lindsay £28,000 and his annual legal bills were said to be £50,000 (*Evening News*, 25 February 1982). In 1981, he had a tax bill for £3 million as well as paying almost £200,000 on corporation tax and VAT (*Daily Mirror,* 21 April 1981). Company records show that he ran at least five different companies: Screentime Ltd, Streamone Ltd, Taboo, Karl Ordinez Films Ltd and Mayfair Film Productions. In an interview with the Aberdeen newspaper *Evening News* (25 February 1982), Lindsay defiantly announced plans to open another Taboo cinema club in Aberdeen, which no doubt would have likely made the police more determined to put him out of business.

According to McGillivray (2017: 144), Lindsay 'received a tipoff from a friendly detective at New Scotland Yard that orders had been received from the highest authority to put Lindsay out of business by any means necessary'. After learning this, he left Britain for the more liberal Netherlands, following Darby and Collingbourne's example. His exile was brief, returning after missing his twin daughters. This is where Lindsay's legal history becomes hazy due to the lack of preserved legal documents and, oddly, little mention of his ongoing legal battles in the national press. With the press attention he received in the past, might this absence from the national media indicate an attempt to limit his publicity? The only source to document what may have been his final legal battle can be found in a local newspaper named the *Barnstead Herald* (17 February 1983) which details how police and customs officials collaborated to unearth a 'massive pornography racket' after they raided the house of Geoff Gold,[39] a business partner of Lindsay's and father of the Gold brothers who ran the softcore pornography magazine business Goldstar.

The *Barnstead Herald* details the arrest. In February 1980, police watching one of Lindsay's Soho cinemas witnessed another squad – West End Central – raid the building, seizing the projector and films. Rather than leave, the surveillance team stayed and observed Gold's company secretary arrive to replace the films. The article also tells of HMCE investigating Lindsay for tax evasion after carelessly telling the police that that he paid cash to the Danish Bacon lorry drivers who smuggled pornography into Britain. By June 1980, HMCE developed an operation in collaboration with the police and raided Lindsay's cinemas. On leaving one of the cinemas, police followed Lindsay to his storage facility, which was opposite to Gold's Roydock Books Ltd offices; this company is said to have paid the rent on Lindsay's cinemas. The raid on the storage facility found 800 films; more were discovered in Lindsay's white van, in Gold's Mercedes car and at Gold's home. The raids also uncovered 'voluminous correspondence' detailing their business. They faced a total of eleven charges, including 'keeping illegally imported indecent films' and 'having obscene articles for publication for gain'. Unlike previous trials, which prosecuted Lindsay under the Obscene Publications Act 1959, he was now being tried for indecency contrary to the Customs Consolidation Act 1876, a lesser offence than obscenity. Coincidentally, this was the same method used to successfully prosecute David Waterfield. Lindsay and Gold pleaded not guilty, though Gold later admitted to three charges of 'sending indecent books through the post'. They were found guilty on nine charges; Lindsay was given a twelve-month prison sentence, Gold received nine months and a fine of £8000. After nine years and numerous attempts trials, the police finally put Lindsay in jail, but not using the Obscene Publications Act 1959.

This did not stop the police from pursuing further convictions. An NCROPA document from September 1983 mentions Lindsay standing trial at Preston Crown Court for films publicly screened at the Blackpool branch of his Taboo cinema club. McGillivray (2017: 146–47), who co-wrote the Lindsay-produced softcore sex comedy *I'm Not Feeling Myself Tonight* (Joseph McGrath 1976) and knew him personally, recalls this final trial. Four counts of obscenity were based on four videotapes that 'thirteen policemen swore had been found at one of Lindsay's clubs'. These tapes 'featured homosexual rape' and representations of 'graphic violence', atypical of the normative genres of pornography routinely screened at his clubs. Lindsay alleged that the police planted them to strengthen their chances of an obscenity conviction. At first glance, this might seem at best an unlikely claim. However, given that three separate interviewees for this book, Mike Freeman, Lindsay Honey and Terry Stephens,[40] made similar allegations about the police planting hardcore BDSM pornography during searches of their premises that resulted in their eventual convictions, perhaps there is a grain of truth to this? As Beresford (2014: 386) argues, the implementation of the Obscene Publications Act 1959 through case law cumulatively normalized what she describes as heterosexual 'acceptable pornography' while determining 'unacceptable pornography', such as gay pornography or even hardcore BDSM. Therefore, the prosecution's choosing of articles depicting non-normative sex acts as evidence in obscenity trials was a strategic decision designed to result in a de facto guilty verdict from a jury and prosecution. In Lindsay's case, he was sentenced to a further twelve months imprisonment, serving three (Manchester 1986: 208). According to Manchester (1986: 208), Lindsay faced his eleventh obscenity trial at Birmingham Crown Court in 1984 where he was found not guilty of conspiring to publish obscene video tapes.

McGillivray (2017: 146–47) notes that Lindsay sold his clubs once the Cinematograph (Amendment) Act 1982 came into effect in October 1983, now requiring all films shown in cinema clubs to be certificated by the BBFC. The law did not deter entrepreneurs from screening hardcore pornography, but Lindsay chose to end his pornography business, either running out of money or no longer having the desire to fight the authorities. According to McGillivray, the final coup de grâce was a £3.5 million tax bill from the Inland Revenue. Although they were 'willing to settle for £100,000', Lindsay 'refused to pay a penny'. After serving his sentence, Lindsay appeared on the television debate show *Central Weekend* (20 June 1986), and commented on the legality of pornography in Britain:

> Pornography in England is totally illegal. When I was running cinema clubs – private cinema clubs showing hardcore pornography – Mrs. Thatcher changed the law and said that if you saw a hardcore pornographic film in your cinema club, you will be fined £20,000 per day, for every day your cinemas opened [...] so the myth is, which with respect, Mrs. Thatcher likes to promote the myth [...] that pornography is available in England. It's not. If you show hardcore pornography in England, or if you sell hardcore pornography in England, you are doing a prison sentence. I've done one.

## Conclusion

The 1980s saw the introduction of further laws, giving the police new powers to combat the cinema clubs, sex shops and other sex-related enterprises that made hardcore pornography available to the British public. First came the Indecent Displays (Control) Act 1981, addressing 'the increased public display of pornographic material and the inability of the existing law to exercise any effective control' (Manchester 1986: 93). A key motivation of its passing was the expansion of David Sullivan's sex shop empire across Britain, leading to opposition from from anti-pornography activists, particularly when some opened in close proximity to schools (O'Toole 1999: 133; Smith 2005: 152). Moreover, politicians raised concerns about the displays of Soho's sex shops and sex cinemas. With the growth in sex establishments came greater competition, seeking to entice customers through explicit displays. The Indecent Displays (Control) Act 1981 'restricted public display and introduced warning signs' (Thompson 1994: 74). Now sex shops had blacked out windows, creating 'a fear of what lurked within for many female consumers' (Hubbard 2012: 173) and making them look more furtive than they actually were.

The expansion of sex shops also contributed to the Local Government (miscellaneous provisions) Act 1982, giving local authorities the power to control sex establishments – sex shops, sex cinemas or sexual entertainment venues – through, ironically, a licensing system. As Manchester (1986: 103) observes, many local councils did not see the need to implement such controls, especially when sex establishments in their locality caused no public nuisance. Yet Westminster Council – the district where Soho is located and then home to 62 shops – adopted the law in December 1982, with a licence application costing £5000.[41] Some entrepreneurs chose not to pay the fee, selling hardcore pornography and risking fines and/or arrest. Others used a loophole in the act, where owners could declare they had no knowledge of their premises being used as sex establishment and therefore not be liable for prosecution. Some circumvented the law by operating as 'pseudo-sex shops', ensuring that they stocked no more than 10 per cent of 'sex-related stock' (Manchester 1986: 195).[42] In the first instance, Westminster Council approved nine applications and rejected eighteen. In 1984–85, the annual licence renewal fee cost £11,000, much to the annoyance of their proprietors. For Thompson (1994: 31), the Greater London (General Powers) Act 1986 Section 12, amending the Local Government (miscellaneous provisions) Act 1982 had the biggest impact on Soho, leading to the further closure of sex shops and shifting the distribution of softcore pornography to newsagents; this inadvertently expanded the softcore market.

Brought in alongside the Local Government (miscellaneous provisions) Act 1982 was the Cinematograph Amendment Act 1982, extending the original 1909 Act to other exhibitions of moving pictures. Coming into effect on 13 October 1983, its purpose was to 'licence all commercial cinema clubs' and close the loophole that enabled them to operate (Petley 2011: 130). Additionally, the BBFC and the Home Office introduced the R18 certificate for films shown in a restricted, licensed cinema where children could not be admitted (Petley 2011: 130).[43] Yet, the R18 certificate did not legalize hardcore pornography, it instead permitted 'straight forward heterosexual or homosexual activity between consenting adults [...] so long as the scene does not focus solely or dominantly upon the genital organs' (Petley 2011: 130). R18-rated video tapes could only be sold in licensed sex shops.

Furthermore, the Cinematograph Amendment Act 1982 gave enhanced powers to police, allowing them to arrest a suspect without a warrant if a name and address are not offered, and if armed with a warrant, they could seize equipment. If found guilty, the manager(s) of the club, the licence holder (if showing uncertified material) and any other person involved were liable for a fine not exceeding £10,000. It also brought in safety checks, targeting poorly maintained cinema clubs that could be potentially hazardous to public safety. Greater London Council hired thirteen inspectors to assess the many premises. However, prosecutions remained a challenge as cinema clubs were resilient enterprises that could be quickly restarted after a police raid. An article in *Sight and Sound* (Winter 1982/83) states that cinema clubs kept a low profile after 1983 and became increasingly tolerated by the police. The Cinemas Act 1985 consolidated the Cinematographic Acts 1909 and 1952 and the Cinematograph (Amendment) Act 1982, leading to the further marginalization of cinema clubs, especially in London.

In combination with the Video Recordings Act 1984, which I discuss in the epilogue to this book, these laws ostensibly pushed the distribution of hardcore pornography into a black market. Ambiguities still existed but the mess of overlapping laws provided rule enforcers with a patchwork of legal options to exercise, making it tricky for entrepreneurs to do business. In this chapter, I have shown how David Waterfield and John Lindsay attempted to take advantage of the political value of morality, using it to benefit their own economic positions. Whereas activists and politicians used morality as a vehicle for the stricter regulation of pornography, Waterfield and Lindsay utilized it for the opposite, seeking to reform Britain's restrictive pornography laws through their enterprise and establish a formal institutional framework for distributing hardcore pornography. Although Waterfield demonstrates a commitment to wider social causes, investing profits into subcultural enterprises, both stood to profit from the legalization of pornography. Therefore, I have suggested that morality was used as an alibi. For instance, Lindsay claimed his films served a public good and used the publicity generated by his obscenity trials and self-proclaimed war on censorship as publicity for his sex shops and cinema clubs.

I have also shown how police and prosecutors responded to their attempts by entrepreneurially using the law, often contentiously, to control their activities. It proved increasingly difficult to prosecute Waterfield and Lindsay under the Obscene Publications Act 1959. However, their use of transnational networks to obtain hardcore pornography enabled prosecutors to successfully employ customs law, which involved the lesser charge of indecency. Lindsay's eventual prosecution under the Obscene Publications Act 1959 also calls into question the issue of continuing police corruption in the pursuit of a guilty charge. The late 1970s were undoubtedly a period of moral struggle, with hardcore pornography entrepreneurs losing the battle to anti-pornography activists. Seeing 'the value of morality votes' (Thompson 1994: 26), the views of these activists were absorbed by Thatcher's newly elected Conservative government and informed the changes in regulation discussed above. As Smith (2007: 56) suggests, these changes resulted in Britain's pornography market becoming 'stagnant' and dominated by softcore entrepreneurs. It took another twenty years for Britain to permit the sale of hardcore pornographic films, but only under strict conditions.

# Conclusion

This book has explored the cultural and economic development of Britain's hard-core pornography business, focusing specifically on the production and distribution of rollers from the 1960s to the early 1980s. I have shown how entrepreneurs created a new market for hardcore films within an alternative economy. I used the term alternative economy to indicate a separate, distinct economic space from the formal or the informal, where entrepreneurs find loopholes in regulation to create their own institutional framework. Central to the economy was the Obscene Publications Act 1959, a deeply flawed legislation with subjective terminology that was open to interpretation. Tasked with policing the act, the Metropolitan Police's Obscene Publications Squad were particularly entrepreneurial with this law, devising a corrupt licensing system in the 1950s that permitted producers and distributors of hardcore pornography to do business. In the early 1960s, the trade began to grow, and a culture of domestic hardcore production took over from imported pornography, with goods sold in Soho's bookshops and through mail order.

Throughout *Under the Counter*, I have investigated the development of the roller market, initially through innovative entrepreneurs using small-gauge film-making equipment and then expanded further by opportunists with little or no filmmaking skill but the means to upscale their business. Following the British tabloid press' exposure of the corrupt licensing system, the alternative economy's institutional framework crumbled and the Obscene Publications Act 1959 was regularly combined with other laws to prosecute pornographers. Because of this, the domestic production of hardcore pornography declined and, by the mid to late 1970s, the economy shifted from production to distribution. Entrepreneurs like John Lindsay and David Waterfield became agents of change (North 1990; 2005), attempting to legalize pornography through their enterprise and establish a formal institutional framework for hardcore pornography in Britain. Against a backdrop of shifting morality, I discussed how the police entrepreneurially used the law to remove Lindsay and Waterfield from the economy. I concluded the last chapter by demonstrating how a change in the political landscape resulted in stronger regulation that plugged the holes in the Obscene Publications Act 1959 but, in turn, created a black market (Petley 2011: 142). In conclusion, I want to bring together some of the key findings that have emerged out of this work and consider their implications for studying the pornography business and its historical foundations.

First, despite a restrictive legal framework, Britain was a significant player in the development of commercial hardcore pornography. Sutherland (1982: 4) believes that the 'British domestic production of pornography' operated on a 'cottage industrial scale', particularly in the 1960s. Yet, by the end of the decade, Britain upscaled their production of hardcore, establishing a relatively organized and functioning roller market with transnational links. In North America, Shelby (1970: 13) observes that rollers were in 'greater demand' than stag films, identifying how they were smuggled in through customs, copied and advertised for sale in the back pages of men's magazines. Like Knight and Alpert (1967), Shelby (1970: 13) equates the appeal of British hardcore films with the zeitgeist of 1960s swinging London and their representation of this cultural moment.

During the 1960s, Britain took a crucial role in developing the hardcore pornography business before Denmark legalized all pornography in 1969. For Slade (2000: 105–06), roller makers 'outpaced' American stag makers in the 1960s but were overtaken by Denmark and the rise of porno chic in the United States. By the mid 1970s, Britain's roller trade declined due to tighter policing and and a growth in imported pornography from Denmark and Germany. It has proved impossible to ascertain the economic value of the roller market. Police documents and newspaper reports indicate that vast amounts of money exchanged hands. Although some of these figures are questionable, arrest records and seizures lists demonstrate the profitability of the economy, particularly for distributors. It is the material conditions of the pornography business that make its history difficult to ascertain. My approach has been to focus on the activities of entrepreneurs to help build a picture of Britain's trade in hardcore films.

Second, the research contributes to debates around pornography entrepreneurship, an area of pornography studies gaining increasing traction (Deslandes 2015; Johnson 2019; Pezzutto 2019; Freibert 2021). It also furthers understandings of British entrepreneurship in 1960s' and 1970s' Britain. In this period, it is generally regarded that entrepreneurship and innovation declined (Gray 2002; Godley and Casson 2012). Therefore, the activities of British pornography entrepreneurs evidence the hidden enterprise cultures of this moment, perhaps providing a link between the opportunistic spivs of the 1940s and 1950s, who traded in black and grey market goods (Roodhouse 2013), and the 'greed is good' enterprise culture of the early 1980s (Dodd and Anderson 2001). I have also discovered that pornography entrepreneurship is multifaceted. For instance, early innovators like Ivor

Cook disrupted the economy and, along with others, created a market for rollers, which was developed by opportunistic entrepreneurs (Kirzner 1973) such as Mike Freeman, Evan Phillips, Anthony Collingbourne and John Darby with little or no filmmaking skill. These characters exploited the demand for hardcore films and expanded the market through scaled production and distribution. Pornography entrepreneurs can also adopt a moral stance to justify their practices, positioning themselves in opposition to other moral crusaders, such as anti-pornography activists, politicians and 'rule enforcers' (Becker 1966). I do not claim that pornography entrepreneurs are moral; instead, I argue that a moral position can be advantageous for legal and economic reasons.

Throughout this book, entrepreneurs demonstrate the ability to identify inconsistencies or loopholes in the law, legitimizing their practices and minimizing the risks of prosecution. This process has been described as 'evasive entrepreneurship' (Leeson and Coyne 2004; Elert and Henrekson 2016) and is an important feature of the pornography business, which operates in uncertain legal contexts. While writing this book, one question that constantly came to mind is whether the pornographers I discuss are criminals? In many ways, their practices share similarities with others who produce or trade illicit goods. However, their evasiveness blurs the boundaries between criminal and lawful enterprise, allowing them to mitigate risk. The alternative economy also appears to have offered social mobility to a number of working-class men with criminal backgrounds. For example, Mike Freeman's criminality initially benefited him, facilitating his success in the alternative economy. But it also proved to be his downfall, as he refused to operate within the economy's institutional framework. The pornography entrepreneurs I have studied were undoubtedly motivated by money, displaying an entrepreneurial spirit that shares similarities with the culture of Thatcher's Conservative Britain in the 1980s. Amusingly, Freeman part-financed his later return to the pornography business through one of Thatcher's enterprise initiatives; I discuss this in the epilogue of this book.

If the alternative economy offered social mobility for working-class males, what opportunities were there for women? Women were primarily employed as performers, appearing in rollers for a one-off payment. The payments identified in police documents suggest that roller work was roughly the equivalent of two to three times the average weekly wage of an adult female. It is also clear that male pornography entrepreneurs heavily exploited women, taking advantage of an increasingly sexualized cultural landscape where sex without the possibility of pregnancy was now a possibility thanks to the contraceptive pill. Many entrepreneurs showed little regard for the age of consent and they often used uncomfortable, persuasive techniques to convince women to appear in their films, saying they were only made for the European market. Appearing in rollers carried risk. Both male and female performers were prosecuted for performing in rollers, even though it was legal to make pornography in Britain. Common and sexual offence laws allowed prosecutors to achieve guilty verdicts against roller performers, usually when 'unnatural acts' occurred.

Female hardcore pornography entrepreneurs appear to have been a minority. Freeman claimed his wife Sandra was involved in the economy before and after his arrest. In her book *Knock Down Ginger* (Joyce 2011), Sandra confirms that she ran Freeman's business while served prison sentence between 1966 and 1967, but her story ends with the murder of Gerry Hawley in 1969. Following his interview for *Hardcore Guaranteed* (Simon Fletcher 2018), Freeman gifted a 16mm colour reversal film that included Sandra's name and address on the tin. This softcore film looks to have been made in the early 1970s, implying that Sandra moved into production. Also, in the early roller *The Rent Man* (1963–65), a female figure accidentally appears in the frame, standing behind a tripod, alluding to her involvement in making the film. The voice of female producers and performers has become an important part of the Porn Studies conversation (Abbott 2010; Bakehorn 2010; Taormino et al. 2013), making it even more conspicuous that the women I discuss in this book are silent, relying heavily on secondhand sources. Clearly, there is a need for more work on female participation in the British pornography business, particularly during its formative years.

Another idea prominent in the book is the entrepreneurial aspects of policing. The notion of police being entrepreneurs emerges out of Becker (1966) and Hobbs (1988: 194). Typically, literature discussing entrepreneurial policing focuses on its positive features (Smith 2020). Yet, as Hobbs (1988) recognizes, entrepreneurial detectives often bend the rules of what is deemed lawful in order to benefit themselves. The actions of the Obscene Publication Squad demonstrate entrepreneurial traits: first, in their implementation of the licensing system and, second, through their interpretation of the law, particularly in the latter half of the 1970s when police took a stricter approach to control the pornography trade. The licensing system can be seen as entrepreneurial because of how they found loopholes in the Obscene Publications Act 1959 to make money, just as pornographers did. This inadvertently caused the growth of an alternative economy of hardcore pornography by providing an institutional framework that set the 'rules of the game' for pornographers to make money (North 1990). The application of the law can also involve entrepreneurial tactics. For instance, police and prosecutors regularly combined laws to enhance their chances of prosecution, plugging up the ambiguities of the Obscene Publications Act 1959. Therefore, entrepreneurship offers a helpful framework for understanding the political, economic and cultural conditions pornographers operate in.

Third, I have shown how the Obscene Publications Act 1959 was an inadequate legal instrument for regulating pornography. In the early 1980s, it was eventually determined that further regulations were necessary to regulate pornography in Britain, creating a mess of overlapping laws that not only defined pornography but also formulated the 'boundaries which impact on producers and their products' (Smith 2007: 16). Furthermore, the inadequacy of the Obscene Publications Act 1959 lay in its use of subjective terminology, namely the terms 'deprave and corrupt'. This became increasingly apparent during the 1970s when juries began to doubt the 'corrupting potential' of pornography and its effect on society's 'moral fabric' (Robertson 1979: 2). Juries increasingly found normative heterosexual pornography not guilty of obscenity and, in turn, othered non-normative sexual practices, such as gay sex or BDSM (Beresford 2014), which were regularly found guilty. The past twenty years have seen a reduction in obscenity cases. A Freedom of Information request to the Ministry of Justice reveals a considerable drop, with 429 convictions in 1984, compared to just 10 in 2014.[1] It is also interesting to note that the use of the Obscene Publications Act 1959 significantly fell from 2001 onwards, following the re-evaluation of the R18 certificate in 2000 and the effective legalization of hardcore in Britain. It dropped even further after the introduction of the Criminal Justice and Immigration Act 2008, which criminalized the possession of extreme pornography.

In 2019, following a consultation process, the Crown Prosecution Service (CPS) modified prosecution guidelines for the Obscene Publications Act 1959. A number of non-normative sexual acts once declared as obscene by CPS guidance were removed (Petley 2019). The CPS now recommend that prosecutors contemplate a list containing fourteen potentially applicable laws before considering the Obscene Publications Act 1959:

> real caution must be exercised when assessing the tendency to deprave or corrupt of acts which Parliament has not provided should be subject to the criminal law, provided the likely audience is not under 18 or otherwise vulnerable. That is particularly so because whilst they may well be construed to be 'repulsive', 'filthy', 'loathsome' or 'lewd', and so fall under ordinary language to be classified as obscene, that will not suffice for obscenity under the Act.[2]

Although this implies that obscenity law has little purchase today, a more likely explanation for this change is regulators shifting attention from production to consumption and focusing on the harmful impacts of pornography (Smith 2018), particularly in the context of pornography's digital turn. Here, emphasis is placed on online harms and the dangers of young people accessing pornography via the internet, resulting in calls for age verification to access pornography and stricter measures on platforms. Studying the legal histories of pornography offers a context for how regulators approach and implement new legal instruments to control pornography as its material conditions evolve, but also how people find ways to evade the law.

Finally, there is something to be said about methodology and the challenges of researching clandestine economic activity. Out of the 38 primary interviews I conducted, only 3 of these participants were directly involved in the period I have studied. Many people involved in the formative years of the alternative economy have died, are uncontactable or are unwilling to share their experiences. Therefore, I relied heavily on other primary sources that offered secondhand information via media reportage and legal documents. Such archival materials are undoubtedly a rich resource for pornography historians, yet their reliability must be questioned. For example, legal documents specific to obscenity or pornography can be either closed, be heavily redacted or, and perhaps most frustratingly, have not been archived. Furthermore, the contents of such documents can be problematic. Police statements lack detail, and interviewees are evasive, intentionally vague or economical with the truth. Also, certain areas of practice are not discussed or deemed pertinent to the police investigation. An example of this is a lack of interest in the processing and printing of films, suggesting that this aspect was of little concern, despite being an essential part of the distribution chain.

To counter this, I attempted to corroborate all information where possible. For instance, Mike Freeman's interview and series of autobiographies were triangulated using legal documents pertaining to the murder of Gerald Hawley and the anti-corruption investigation into the Obscene Publications Squad, together with newspaper articles reporting his activities. However, it must be recognized that legal documents and media reportage can potentially provide a 'skewed picture' (Kane 2019: 44) of events. Legal files are from the perspective of those who regulated the pornography trade and, given the corruption that was endemic in the Obscene Publications Squad, their validity must be questioned. Similarly, newspaper reports, particularly those from tabloids, are heavily editorialized, often with an unhelpful moralistic tone and potential bias. Larsson (2016: 13) encountered similar challenges in her research on Swedish 8mm pornography, recognizing the fragility of her findings. However, Larsson sees this as 'unavoidable' when documenting the history of a pornography business that has clandestine beginnings.

Locating and engaging with pornographic materials became an essential part of my ethnohistorical approach. European porn magazines like *Chick*, *Ero* and *Vue* contained evidence of Britain's transnational trade, while British magazines occasionally carried interviews with pornographers and performers. The rollers themselves were of immense value. Although these films often circulate in digital forms via online fora, having access to the physical objects proved vital, finding that they offered clues about their origins; I elaborate on this in the labelography (see Appendix 1).

As Waldroup (2020: 17) observes, objects from the past 'tell us things if we are willing to listen (and look, and touch)'. Film stock, packaging design and traces of processing are all signs that point to the signatures of different pornography entrepreneurs. But to draw any meaningful conclusions, a broad sample of rollers is vital.

The challenge here is the lack of formal archives preserving rollers, particularly in Britain. The Kinsey Institute in Indiana, USA, houses the most extensive collection of rollers (Slade 1984: 161), yet the British Film Institute hold none. Therefore, personal archives of pornography are valuable resources, and it would be remiss of me to not acknowledge the important contribution collectors made to this book by granting access to their films and related ephemera. Analysing a larger sample of these objects, particularly from their early, unbranded period, may tell us more about how these films were produced and circulated. Furthermore, examining other illicit pornographic materials from the same period, such as Soho Bibles and Soho Postcards alongside rollers, might reveal how these commodities inter-relate and crossover. Could specific styles, tropes or other clues hidden in these goods unearth more about the faceless entrepreneurs who made them? Without archives of these under-the-counter materials, we will never know.

# Epilogue:
## *Truth or Dare*

## *Introduction*

In the conclusion to his study of the American adult video industry, Alilunas (2016: 208) notes how the 'struggles and tensions' he discusses 'have played out before and will play out again, albeit with their contours occasionally reshaped and relocated and with new technologies [...] substituted for old'. As I end this first volume of *Under the Counter*, I want to explore the shift from small-gauge film to the video cassette recorder (VCR). In doing so, I show how the debates from the previous chapters transferred to this new technology. Here, similar themes repeat themselves – entrepreneurs spot an arbitrage opportunity and attempt to capitalize on it by finding loopholes in regulation. Again, I focus on the entrepreneurship of Mike Freeman, drawing on his interview, self-published autobiographies (Freeman 2012a, 2012b, 2013a, 2013b) and contextual information from magazines such as *Late Night Video* and *Video World* to demonstrate the relationship between pornography entrepreneurs and the law. Once more, the outcome of these legal battles was increased regulation, pushing the trade out of an alternative economic space and into a black market.

### From 8mm to video

As John Lindsay moved from making rollers to distributing them via his cinema clubs and sex shops, the domestic production of hardcore pornographic films in Britain slowed. The British porn business went from being a pioneer of hardcore film production, distributing transnationally, to finding themselves unable to compete with the wealth of material generated in Denmark, Sweden, Netherlands, Germany, France and the United States. Many of these countries legalized the distribution of hardcore pornography, but in Britain the trade remained under the counter until 2000. However, hardcore films were still made in Britain for the

FIGURE E.1: Title card from *Truth or Dare* (Mike Freeman 1981). Courtesy of Mike Freeman.

export market. During the course of gathering research for this book, I spoke to the German entrepreneur Gerd Wasmund – better known by his nom de plume Mike Hunter – who produced films in Britain and distributed them in Germany on Super 8.[1] In collaboration with the transnational Italian pornography entrepreneur Lasse Braun, Wasmund produced twelve of the British films directed by Braun in 1977; these are known as Braun's 'London Series'.

Many of the performers in these films also appear in titles made for Walter Bartkowski in Germany.[2] Given that some of these performers took part in John Lindsay's productions, it is likely that they were hired via his Ragdolls modelling agency. A familiar face appears in *Tit Friction* (Lasse Braun 1977). As highlighted in chapter two, 'Big' John English regularly appeared in British-made pornography from mid 1960s onwards, working for most of the major roller producers. English's career continued into the early 1980s, employed by European producers such as Wasmund and Denmark's Theander Brothers. Wasmund described Braun's London series as a frustrating experience due to Braun's cocaine abuse and general unreliability. For this reason, Wasmund did not trust Braun with money and ended up compiling the London series into two stand-alone features – *Sex Maniacs* (Gerd Wasmund 1977) and *Sin Dreamer* (Gerd Wasmund 1977). He commissioned the shooting of extra footage to help create a tenuous narrative link between each scene.[3] After parting ways with Braun, Wasmund introduced his Mike Hunter brand and continued to use Britain as a production location.

I asked Wasmund why he went to the bother of making films in Britain. He concisely responded: 'the teams were reliable'. Wasmund described the production process – his production manager hired a British independent production team who specialized in news and documentary but shot hardcore pornography as a sideline. Wasmund repeatedly referred to the professionalism of this outfit and how 'he never got ripped off', unlike his later experience of working in the United States.[4] One of the most unusual films made in Britain by this production team for Wasmund is *School-Girl träumt von King-Kong* (Gerd Wasmund/Anon. 1977–79).[5] As the box cover image shows (see Figure E.2), it explores the lead female's fantasy of having sex with King Kong, with one memorable scene showing the performer – a British glamour model who occasionally featured in hardcore films – tied to a large prosthetic gorilla penis. Wasmund remembered nothing about this film, stating that his production team made any creative decisions; he just distributed them. Now in his early 80s, Wasmund could not recall any further details about the team. Clues suggest that one of the camera operators associated with Braun and Wasmund later worked on many popular British feature films. Wasmund also mentioned how the production team made their own films, which he purchased for distribution. Britain now became an exporter of hardcore, its

FIGURE E.2: *School-Girl träumt von King-Kong* (Gerd Wasmund/Anon. 1977–79). Courtesy of Gerd Wasmund. Faces obscured to protect the identity of the performer.

market subsumed by the thriving European pornography business. For a brief moment, home video technology changed this situation.

The VCR was introduced to Britain in 1977. The new technology enjoyed an accelerated level of adoption, with people having the opportunity to watch films in the privacy of their own homes and record television broadcasts (Carter 2018a). Furthermore, 'the VCR allowed a greater amount of personal interaction with adult films than had ever been previously available, with users having the ability to pause, rewind and fast-forward as they watched' (Alilunas 2016: 25). In comparison, small-gauge formats were cumbersome and inconvenient. Films could get stuck in projectors, particularly those at the lower end of the market, resulting in burned film, lost footage and other irretrievable damage. The greater accessibility of the VCR appealed to a broader audience, signalling the end of the 8mm and Super 8 era. Films were housed in a plastic cassette and easily slotted into the VCR for playback. As Alilunas' (2016) study of the introduction of adult video in the United States shows, the medium transformed the production and distribution of adult film. Shooting pornography on video was cheaper than using 16mm or 35mm film and involved a simpler, more cost-effective workflow. Films no longer needed to be developed and duplication was more straightforward. Major Hollywood studios were initially apprehensive about releasing their movies on home video, fearing an impact on cinema attendance. In Britain, opportunistic entrepreneurs saw an opportunity to fill this and meet public demand for content by cheaply licensing low-budget films, often in the horror and exploitation (Brewster et al. 2005: 5).

According to 'Dave', who worked in Soho sex shops around this time, the first hardcore pornographic videos arrived in Soho sometime in the late 1970s via the distributor Ben's Books. Ran by Ben Holloway and his family, Ben's Books had been an integral part of Soho's economy from the 1950s onwards, wholesaling books and magazines to the bookshops. In 1971, Ben Holloway forged a partnership with the American distributor Reuben Sturman. A key player in the American pornography business, Sturman started in publishing but diversified his enterprise to include profitable peep show booths before moving into the home video market and establishing General Video (Alilunas 2016: 77). The money from his early enterprise enabled him to 'enter overseas markets', forming partnerships with Charlie Geerts in the Netherlands and the Holloway family, giving them 'capital and expertise' (Schlosser 2004: 130). Sturman's Doc Johnson brand of sex toys led to the creation of the Holloway-ran Doc Johnson's sex shop in Soho. 'Dave' supposes that it was this transnational relationship with Sturman that gave them access to the six videotapes that circulated in Soho.[6] By this time, Dave's family's shops no longer dealt in hardcore, selling softcore magazines and softcore Super 8 films, such as those produced by Aventura and George Harrison Marks. He told me that the police permitted representations of straight sex, but bondage-related material could result in seizure and forfeiture under section 2 of the Obscene Publications Act 1959. This again shows how the police entrepreneurially interpreted the law, changing the boundaries of acceptability at their whim.

Dave's uncle stocked the videotapes provided by Ben's Books, assuming they were softcore films. One day, during a routine visit from the Obscene Publications Squad, a friendly officer told Dave that the videotapes were actually hardcore and advised that they be removed from the shop. One of Dave's uncle's shops was located at 45 Old Compton Street in Soho. In the early 1980s, they experienced many visitors asking for the whereabouts of 55 Old Compton Street. This was the base for the Holloways' video labels Rippledale and the Video Collection Exchange, selling hardcore videotapes via mail order. Their business involved importing hardcore master tapes from the United States and the Netherlands via Sturman, duplicating them, packaging them and advertising their catalogue of titles in newly established publications dedicated to home video, such as *Late Night Video* and *Video World* (see Figure E.3). Other companies distributing pornography on VHS, such as CalVista and Mistral, released softcore content. One label, Russell Gay's Mistral, pushed the boundaries of acceptability, occasionally showing open-legged female performers (Upton 2016). However, the Holloway family

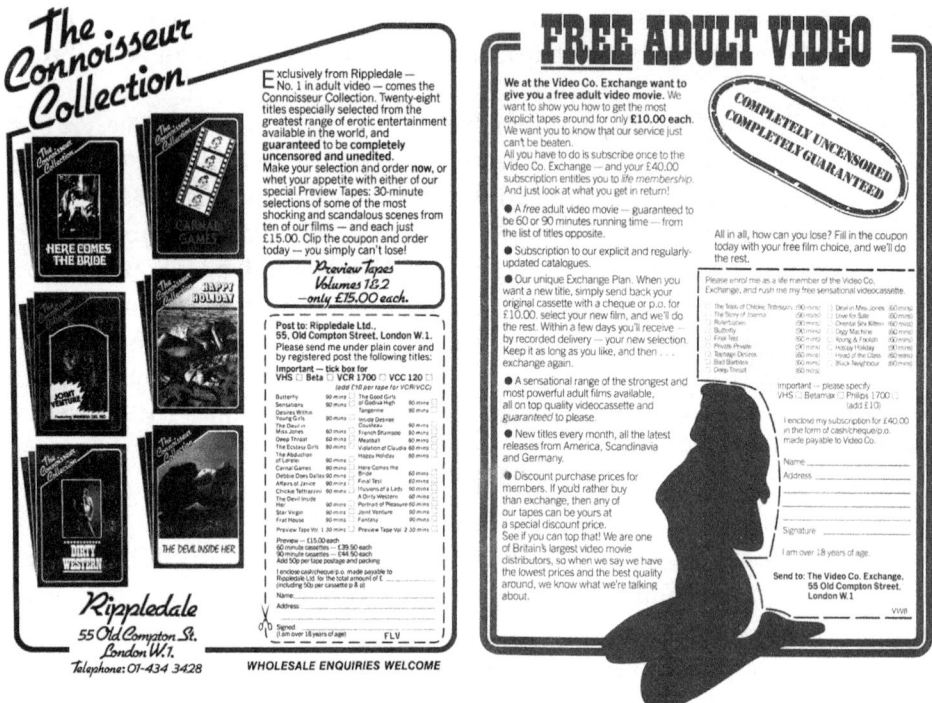

FIGURE E.3: Adverts for the Holloway's hardcore video label Rippledale and the Video Co. Exchange. Author's personal collection.

focused on the hardcore market (see Figure E.4), offering customers two sample tapes at £15 each. Otherwise, films cost £39.50–£44.50, roughly a third of the average weekly male wage in 1980. As mentioned in Chapter 5, John Lindsay also entered the video market, re-releasing his films on the VHS, Betamax and V2000 formats under the brand Taboo. He sold them in his Soho sex shops and through mail order, advertising in the same video magazines. Like the Holloways, he also offered a preview tape to customers, undercutting their price by £2.50, showing how entrepreneurs kept a close eye on the economy and competed with one another to expand their market share.

In the early years of home video, there was some legal confusion about whether video could be considered an article under the Obscene Publications Act 1959, hence why Lindsay, the Holloway family and others openly sold hardcore pornography. After being released from prison in 1979, Mike Freeman also sought to profit from this legal confusion. While serving his sentence, Freeman followed developments in film and video by reading magazines. Now free and changing his surname from Muldoon to Freeman, he quickly re-entered the alternative economy

FIGURE E.4: Holloways' VHS release of *Butterfly* (Joe Sarno 1972) on the Rippledale label. Courtesy of the Erotic Film Society.

of hardcore pornography.[7] It appears that no other person made hardcore pornography in Britain at this time, other than those who produced it for the export market. Freeman planned to shoot hardcore films for distribution on videotape, differentiating himself from the Holloways and John Lindsay, who released older or American made content. Freeman formed the company Videx, identifying that he needed a working capital of at least £10,000 to buy the necessary Electronic News Gathering Umatic cameras, recording deck, lighting and sound equipment. A childhood friend – and former bank robber – offered £20,000 and £1000 came from the Department of Trade via the London Chamber of Commerce.[8] Freeman's free-market approach to entrepreneurship fit well with Thatcher's enterprise ethos of the early 1980s, and this funding was one of several initiatives aimed at kickstarting new businesses. After purchasing the necessary equipment, Freeman placed an advertisement in *The Stage*, a publication devoted to the British entertainment industry. The listing read: 'Beautiful Girls 18 and upwards wanted for a series of erotic films, top rates of pay, ring […] now with your details'. Freeman registered the company Videx Ltd with Companies House in 1980, believing that he could legally make and sell hardcore pornography.

By 1980, the courts determined that a video cassette was an obscene article contrary to section 1(2) of the Obscene Publications Act 1959.[9] According to *The Times* (2 September 1980), an indictment charged three people and a company with 'publishing an obscene article, namely a video cassette, contrary to section 2 of the Obscene Publications Act 1959, at a date prior to the coming into force of the [...] Criminal Law Act 1977'. The judge directed the jury to deliver a not guilty verdict 'on the ground that a video cassette was not an obscene article', declaring that videotape was 'not of the same genus as film' and therefore 'publication' was not possible. When debating this verdict in court, the prosecution argued that the statute's broad terms were 'intended to embrace any article that could be used to show an obscene image', and the only articles excluded were explicitly identified. In response, the defence countered that video cassettes were still in an experimental phase when the Obscene Publications Act 1959 was passed, and therefore exempt. The judge now determined section 1(2 and 3) were 'sufficiently wide to embrace a video cassette' and it could be considered an article under the law. Another loophole had been closed, making entrepreneurs producing and distributing hardcore on videotape liable for prosecution.

After making two films, *Erotic Images* (1980) and *Lesbian Model Agency* (1980), Mike Freeman placed an advert in the classified magazine *Exchange and Mart*: 'Send an SAE for our list of uncensored adult videos. Money-back guarantee if your video film is not hardcore', using an address provided by his financier. Freeman recalled the 'hundreds of letters' received, all sending money for films, and a phone call from who he believes to have been a member of the Obscene Publications Squad, warning him to 'keep it soft'. Believing hardcore to now be legal, Freeman carried on regardless. As he built up a catalogue of films, Freeman took out full-page colour advertisements in *Video World* and *Late Night Video*, amongst others, selling tapes for £40.25 each or two for £70 (see Figure E.5). Freeman claims that Videx became a highly profitable business in a short space of time.[10] The most significant film made during the Videx period was *Truth or Dare* (Mike Freeman 1981), arguably the first heterosexual hardcore feature produced for the British market. It is also important for its cast, starring Royal Academy of the Dramatic Arts trained actress Paula Meadows and Simon Lindsay Honey (see Figures E.1 and E.2), who later became Britain's most successful hardcore pornographer with his Ben Dover character (Flint 1999; Hunter 2013).

Meadows contacted Freeman through the advert in *The Stage*, and, after working with him, she later appeared in several American hardcore films. Honey met Freeman at a photography shoot in Soho; he was a male model, usually appearing alongside his partner, glamour model Linzi Drew. Tuppy Owens, sex activist and occasional hardcore performer, told me that she appeared in one of Freeman's films – *Lady Victoria's Training* (Mike Freeman 1981–82) – because of *Truth or Dare's*,

FIGURE E.5: Two adverts for Videx titles. Author's personal collection. Some faces are obscured to protect the identity of performers.

cinema verité like qualities.[11] Her experience of working with Freeman did not live up to her expectations. She felt his overuse of marijuana clouded his judgement as a filmmaker, refusing to follow the script or any planned structure. In interview, Honey offered similar memories: 'Mike's modus operandi on set was to basically smoke loads and loads of pot and just make stuff up as he went along, which was kind of interesting'. Freeman's style of filmmaking has led to him being labelled 'a fucking terrible filmmaker' (Rupert James cited in Hebditch and Anning 1988: 234), and his films described as 'painful to watch' (Flint 1999: 98). Honey sees it differently, believing that Freeman invented the genre of 'gonzo porn by mistake […] Mike was shooting gonzo on this massive, big breeze block of a camera, which weighed about 40 pounds'.[12]

Meadows suggested to Freeman that he make gay pornography. The challenge appealed to Freeman, particularly when Meadows told him that the Obscene Publications Squad forbode it. As Watney (1997: 59) identifies, 'raids and prosecutions of shops and clubs selling gay magazines and periodicals […] occurred with grim and monotonous regularity throughout the United Kingdom'. This may explain why

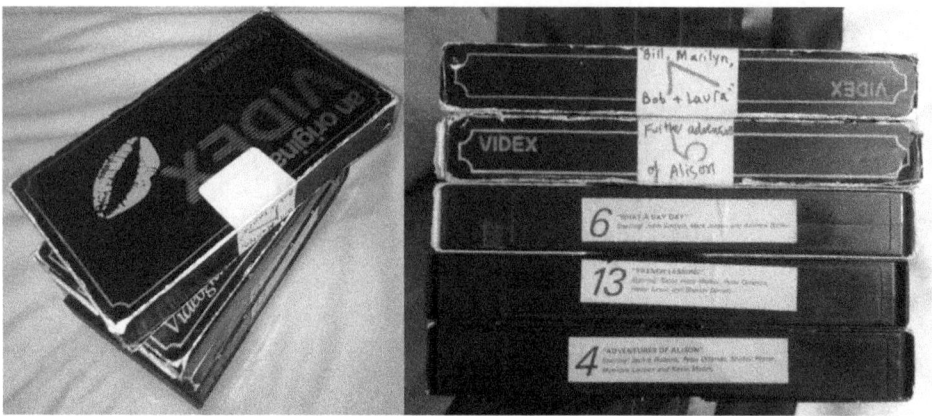

FIGURE E.6: A selection of Videx releases on the VHS format. Courtesy of Dale Lloyd.

British hardcore gay pornographic films were a scarce commodity. Out of all the rollers I have located, less than 1 per cent depict gay sex, indicating that such material was produced, but on a small scale. As pictured in Figure E.7, the first feature-length hardcore gay film to be made in Britain appears to have been the 60-minute *Hard Dollar Hustler* (Alan Purnell 1977), a compilation of Super 8 films produced by people involved in publishing the magazine HIM (Deslandes 2015). Four years later, Freeman made two gay hardcore films, *What a Gay Day?* (Mike Freeman 1981–82), as shown in Figure E.6, and *Dial a Guy* (Mike Freeman 1981–82). Freeman advertised them in *Gay News* and, after doing so, he claims that Videx profits 'rose 40% overnight'. The Obscene Publications Squad raided him shortly after producing these two titles, seizing his filmmaking equipment and the masters. His solicitor advised him to take the two gay films off the market. Freeman refused, declaring that they were part of his stance against censorship, adopting a similar discourse to John Lindsay and David Waterfield. Given that Freeman claimed that the films accounted for 40 per cent of his overall takings, it seems more likely that he was conscious of their economic value, hence why he kept on selling them.

To grow Videx further, Freeman attended the MIPCOM film and television trade show in Cannes, France, drawing international attention to the company. This resulted in his largest individual order yet – £78,000 from Hong Kong. He also claims that the British high street electronics retailer Rumbelows placed a speculative order of 100 VHS and 50 Betamax tapes. Freeman believes that these orders, along with a deal he had cut with the British Videogram Association to give their members £10 off the Videx retail price, indicated that hardcore pornography was about to be legalized. To capitalize on this, Freeman lowered prices from

FIGURE E.7: Advert for *Hard Dollar Hustler* (Alan Purnell 1977). Courtesy of Joe Rubin. Faces obscured to protect the identity of the performers.

£40.25 to £30 and spent 'thousands of pounds worth of advertising per month' to attract more customers. The *Daily Star* tabloid newspaper also provided free advertising, devoting a double-page spread to the making of a Videx film starring Ian Mitchell, a former member of the successful popular music band the Bay City Rollers. Freeman's activities took place in the context of a growing moral panic around video nasties and the damaging effect of video violence (Barker 1984;

Kerekes and Slater 2000; McKenna 2020). The *Sunday Times* (30 May 1982) vaguely reported that 'sexual pornography' accounted for all seizures made in the London Metropolitan district between 1979 and 1982, with just 125 videotapes seized in 1979, growing to 5000 in the first three months of 1982.

In December 1981, the Holloways appeared at Knightsbridge Crown Court, which saw many obscenity trials around this time, such as those involving John Lindsay. Their case is significant, as it decided 'what should be sentencing policy in regard to the commercial exploitation of pornography'. It related to two searches and seizures of cinema clubs in Soho, the first on 5 March 1980 and the second on 23 April 1980. The second raid took place at 55 Old Compton Street, the location of the Holloways' hardcore video business. Under two indictments, they were found guilty of having obscene articles for publication for gain on 22 January 1982; the first indictment concerned 'homosexual practices', while the second indictment related to three hardcore videotapes. Christopher Holloway claimed to have made £25,000 a year from two shops, leading the judge to recommend harsher prison sentences for all connected with the trade, imposing 'very substantial fines' as a deterrent. This, the judge declared, is the only way to put the 'front men' out of business, making it a 'hazardous occupation'.[13] By January 1984, all but two of the Holloways were imprisoned on obscenity charges after customs officials stopped one of Reuben Sturman's agents at London Heathrow with an undeclared £24,149 in cash. The agent was eventually charged with conspiracy to import obscene material while Sturman was 'charged in absentia' (Schlosser 2004: 154–55). The *Daily Mirror* (12 January 1984) reported that the Holloways turned over at 'least £1 million a year' from their enterprises.

By 1984, Freeman was indicted with conspiracy to publish obscene articles for *What a Gay Day?* (Mike Freeman 1981–82), *Dial a Guy* (Mike Freeman 1981–82) and the rape-themed *Sex Slave* (Mike Freeman 1981–82), further supporting Beresford's (2014) observation that the Obscene Publications Act 1959 othered non-normative sexual practices. Freeman also faced a second obscenity trial for *The Videx Video Show* (Mike Freeman 1982). *The Videx Video Show* was intended to be a monthly video series, not too dissimilar to the popular softcore *Electric Blue* series, containing a string of vignettes and short features intertwined with hardcore pornography. According to *I Pornographer*, Freeman and his crew visited the Eureka Nudist Camp after discovering that the BBC were in attendance, filming for the television programme *Game for a Laugh*. Freeman planned to use this as a marketing gimmick, including the BBC presenter Sarah Kennedy in the cast list for *The Videx Video Show*. While there, he filmed a nudist competition, which involved naked underage children, and chose to include this footage in the final edit. Shortly after its release, the Obscene Publications Squad raided the Videx offices in Wimbledon, London. Their warrant permitted them to enter and search the premises, citing *The Videx Video Show* as an allegedly obscene video. Freeman had already prepared for such an event and attempted to destroy the stock of videotapes and documents containing customer details before the police gained access. Following his arrest, the police charged Freeman with offences under the Obscene Publications Act 1959 and the Protection of Children Act 1978.

As with John Lindsay, no formal records of Freeman's trials appear to have survived, and they received little, if any, coverage in the national press. In *I Pornographer*, Freeman states that *What a Gay Day?* (Mike Freeman 1981–82), *Dial a Guy* and *Sex Slave* were found to be obscene, resulting in a fifteen-month prison sentence in 1982. During this first trial, he agreed to liquidate Videx in exchange for a reduced sentence. After serving ten months, he was released but placed on remand until the second trial for *The Videx Video Show*. Freeman defended himself and was found not guilty. However, Freeman faced yet another trial for the common law offence of perverting the course of justice. This charge related to Freeman's ownership of a videotape eraser machine. He attempted to use this device during the Videx office raid, wiping the content of his stock of videos. However, it failed to work. Now Freeman found himself being tried under a law that was not used against any of the other pornography entrepreneurs discussed in this book, again demonstrating how police and prosecutors used common laws to achieve convictions. The jury reached a guilty verdict, and the judge sent Freeman to prison; the duration of this sentence is not detailed in *I Pornographer*. By 1984, most of the British entrepreneurs engaging in producing or distributing hardcore pornography were either in prison or had retired.

The final nail in the coffin for Britain's domestic trade in hardcore pornographic films was the introduction of the Video Recordings Act 1984. A cornerstone of Thatcher's Conservative Party re-election campaign in 1983, the Video Recordings Act 1984 became a political tool, bringing control to the unregulated home video market and, specifically, the video nasties. It was rooted in a moral panic fuelled by moralist Mary Whitehouse and the British tabloid press. They focused on children's access to violent and pornographic films and the harmful effects these might cause. Petley (2011: 34–35) describes its introduction as 'a multi fronted attack on civil liberties in Britain' and notes how it was poorly received by the industry. The Conservative government made the now rebranded British Board of Film Classification the statutory body for film censorship in Britain, effectively privatizing censorship. All films released on any physical home video format require a classification from the BBFC, a cost borne by the distributor. According to the Video Recordings Act 1984, the penalty for supplying uncertified films, or possessing uncertified films for the purposes of supply, was a fine not exceeding £20,000. In 1995, an amendment to the Video Recordings Act 1984 added the option of a six-month prison sentence (see Petley 2011: 92–97). A video with an R18 certificate could only be sold in a licensed sex establishment, such as a sex shop or cinema. The distribution of hardcore pornography was strictly forbidden.

The Video Recordings Act 1984 joined the other laws instituted in the early 1980s – the Indecent Displays Control Act 1981; the Local Government (miscellaneous provisions) Act 1982 and the Cinematograph Amendment Act 1982. Weeks (2012: 376) notes that these changes in legislation were crafted by 'Christian moral entrepreneurs' like Mary Whitehouse in the late 1970s. Yet, by the early 1980s, morality had become a cornerstone of 'the New Right and neo-Conservatism', not just in Britain but also in the United States with Ronald Reagan's Republican Party. According to Strub (2011: 294), the New Right weaponized 'moral issues such as abortion, gay rights and pornography' for political capital. In Britain, the result of this was a 'flurry of legislation concerning the representation of sex' (Watney 1997: 67), becoming home to perhaps the strictest film censorship in Western Europe (Petley 2011: 1). A thriving black market took over from the

FIGURE E.8: Early adverts for David Waterfield and Patricia Clark's Netherlands-based company Your Choice. Courtesy of Patricia Clark.

alternative economy, generating multiple pirate copies of videotapes smuggled in from Western Europe and sold via mail order or under the counter in sex shops. However, entrepreneurs still spotted legal loopholes.

In the late 1980s, David Waterfield and his then-wife Patricia Clark founded the company Your Choice in Amsterdam, Netherlands, specializing in distributing hardcore pornography to British customers (Carter 2022). They smuggled master tapes into Britain, where a series of agents copied them and dispatched them, circumventing potential customs interference (see Figure E.8). In the early 1990s, entrepreneurs offered decryption cards that enabled British customers to access European hardcore satellite television feeds (O'Toole 1999: 156). The BBFC permitted hardcore sex in eighteen certified 'educational' videotapes, such as *The Lover's Guide* (Simon Ludgate 1991). Mike Freeman's protégé Lindsay Honey created the internationally successful Ben Dover brand in the mid 1990s, kickstarting a new culture of British hardcore pornographic film production (Hunter 2013). Hardcore films were effectively legalized in 2000, following a review of the R18 certificate (Petley 2011; Perkins 2012). Yet, it was placed under tight constraints. All films required BBFC certification and could only be sold in licensed sex shops. The path to liberalization is yet another story of entrepreneurship, legal battles, the circumvention of the law, transnational networks and new technologies, as the second volume of *Under the Counter* will reveal.

# Appendix 1:
# Labelography

Rather than simply present a long filmography, I have instead opted to produce a labelography. Its purpose is two-fold. First, it offers some indication of the scale of roller production in Britain, identifying over 1000 titles being made between the years 1960 and 1980. Second, it serves as a resource for future scholarship in this area. My listing is by no means exhaustive. As this book has shown, the conditions in which rollers were produced and distributed make it difficult to ascertain just how many were created in this period. With limited print runs, due to the use of amateur or semi-professional processing and printing techniques, particularly before 1969, many rollers have likely been lost to time. The rollers in this labelography have been identified through a combination of sources.

My starting point was Di Lauro and Rabkin's (1976: 125–58) filmography and title index. According to them, this was generated from film catalogues, films seen by the authors, the Kinsey Institute for Sex Research and the *Postif* filmography (Kyrou 1964). Another named source of information is a mysterious American collector whom they refer to as their 'very own "Deep Throat"'. Kinsey and Di Lauro's filmography is especially valuable as they give possible production dates. Their dating system is based on 'the authority of their sources' and how the titles and content of some films refer to cultural moments. For example, the dress of performers, cars, locations and even magazines, newspapers or music records can help give an approximate period of production. Of course, this accuracy is questionable, but I have built on their dating by cross-referencing with primary sources generated through my research. Because of this, the dates I give are an informed estimate of when they were likely produced and should not be treated as exact. All titles marked as having a British origin were extracted from Di Lauro and Rabkin's list – 261 in total – and then others were added from the Kinsey's Institute's archive catalogue.

According to Slade (1984: 161), a private collector donated a significant number of rollers to the Kinsey Institute for Sex Research in Bloomington, Indiana. Their online catalogue lists approximately 367 titles marked as English. The Kinsey Institute also attempt to date their collection by identifying when the film stock was issued. However, the accuracy of this method is questionable, with different film stocks being used to reprint or re-release earlier titles. Helpfully, Kinsey regularly named labels, a detail missing from Di Lauro and Rabkin (1976: 125–58), although the archivist appears to have only reached titles beginning with the letter 'S', suggesting that this is still work in progress.

Another helpful resource was the Adult Loop Database, providing titles missing from Di Lauro and Rabkin (1976) and the Kinsey Institute. This crowdsourced website catalogues international releases of adult 8mm films, organizing them by label. It is not as exhaustive as the other sources I used, but it is valuable for its list of Climax rollers and rare labels, such as Global Cinelux. Many labels are missing and there are inaccuracies, such as John Lindsay being associated with Blue Scene Films. Furthermore, there is no attempt to date rollers.

The COVID-19 pandemic interrupted my plans to visit Kinsey's archive and view their collection of rollers. However, I gained access to seven private collections, ranging from physical contact with the collections to virtual contact, with collectors willingly sharing images of box covers. This helped to identify further titles, but also enabled me to discover links between labels. For example, one collector pointed out that John Lindsay's titles were re-released on the Danish Gatsby label belonging to Flesh Film. Three collectors shared original catalogues relating to specific labels, such as Climax, International Films, Viking Films and New Private, as well as providing mail-shots and catalogues from mail-order companies. Over half of the titles included in this labelography were sourced from these private collections. Their contribution to this study was invaluable.

Finally, part of the methodology involved the collecting of a physical sample of rollers. Following an object-based material culture approach (Wickstead 2020), I attempted to locate a roller from each label so that I could identify the types of film stock used and examine the packaging to see if any further clues of their origin could be determined from their physicality. Through this approach, I linked the film *Lavabora* (1960–63), an early unbranded British roller, to three other titles – *Hotel Sexi* (1960–63), *La Dolce Vita* (1960–63) and *Chez Mrs Pirgeon* (1960–63) – as the style of the handwritten title card was the same. *Chez Mr Pirgeon* was also the source for the cover image of this book, where a second cameraman accidentally comes into the frame for a split second or two, again showing how these films can occasionally offer hints at how and when they were made. At my own expense, I collected over 100 individual titles, but did not achieve the desired sample. Other titles included in the labelography were discovered in newspaper articles and police seizure lists found in the Director of Publication Prosecution files at the National Archives.

As the term suggests, the labelography is organized by label. I give a brief background for each label, before listing titles in alphabetical order. Films are 200ft/60m and standard 8mm, unless otherwise indicated. Estimated dates of production are given where possible and I also identify when a title has been re-released by another label. I have listed titles in full, and not corrected any spelling errors. As Kerekes (2000: 196) acknowledges, these films often have 'emotive titles and risqué themes'. For Slade (1984: 160–61), British rollers contain 'some of the most maladroit scenarios ever committed to celluloid' and use 'eloquent' titles. This, he believes, is due to the producers having 'no idea what consumers wanted and were willing to offer them anything'. I question whether this was the case, and the emotive titles are likely more of an attempt to attract customers' attention in what was becoming an increasingly crowded market, particularly in the early 1970s when the legalization of hardcore pornography in Denmark led to an influx of content. Titles also offer some clues to dates of production, referencing certain cultural moments, such as Climax's *Sex Olympics*, which can be dated to the Mexican Olympics of 1968. It is also possible to spot trends/themes, including the regular reference to 'schoolgirls' and the casual use of the word rape. Today, some of these titles may offend and, as I posited in Chapter 5, could potentially foul the law, particularly the Criminal Justice and Immigration Act 2008. They are included here in verbatim, revealing attitudes towards sex and sexuality during this overlooked period of filmmaking.

## Unbranded

In Chapter 2, I identified 1960–65 as the unbranded period of rollers. Before Evan 'Big Jeff' Phillips introduced Climax in 1966, rollers were typically distributed in generic boxes or 'photo-boxes' featuring an explicit photograph on the front, usually taken during filming, and the title of the roller Letraset onto the image. Some of the titles here go beyond 1965, and could possibly be re-boxes of branded titles by bookshops, replacing a damaged original box before reselling it, or short-lived operations seeking to profit from the demand for hardcore films. Unbranded titles contrast with the 'unknown' films I list at the end of the labelography, as I am unable to confirm whether these titles were unbranded or not.

| Title | Year | Notes |
|---|---|---|
| *The Adulterer* | 1965–67 | Same green cardboard box as *Flatmates*, *Kinky Les*, *The Perverts*, *The Swingers* and *Surprise Reward*. |
| *Afternoon Lust* | 1964–67 | Same red cardboard box as *Sisterly Lust*. |
| *Babs and the Burglars* | 1966–70 | |

| Title | Year | Notes |
|---|---|---|
| *Bachelor's Thoughts* | 1968 | |
| *Black Magic* | 1963–67 | |
| *Black Maid* | | |
| *Boys Orgy* | | |
| *The Casting Couch* | 1963–66 | |
| *Chez Mrs Pirgeon* | 1960–63 | Same producers as *Hotel Sexi, La Dolce Vita* and *Lavabora*. |
| *Close Investigation* | | |
| *Couch Vibe* | | |
| *Double Diamond* | 1964–65 | Also issued on 16mm. |
| *Double Number* | | |
| *Double Sex Party* | | |
| *Dream Orgy* | | |
| *Duet* | 1968 | Same orange cardboard box as *Incestral Home, The Seduction of Susan* and *Turkish Delight*. Re-released later by Blue Scene Films, shot in Victorian flat. |
| *Erotica* | 1960–64 | |
| *Exposure* (parts 1 and 2) | | |
| *Fanny* | 1967 | Re-released by Blue Scene Films, shot in Victorian flat. |
| *Fisherman's Luck* | 1965–67 | Also issued on 16mm. Re-released by Blue Scene Films. |
| *The Flabs* | 1966–68 | |

(Continued)

| Title | Year | Notes |
|---|---|---|
| *Flatmates* | 1966–67 | Same green cardboard box as *The Adulterer*, *Kinky Les*, *The Perverts*, *The Swingers* and *Surprise Reward*. Possibly very early Climax, same performers appear in *Jealous Sisters*. |
| *Forest Friends* | | |
| *Free Sample* | 1969 | Re-released by Blue Scene Films. |
| *Good Time Girls* | 1965–66 | Re-released by Blue Scene Films. |
| *Hair* | | |
| *Happy Nurses* | | |
| *Hotel Romance* | | |
| *Hotel Sexi* | 1960–63 | Same producers as *Chez Mrs Pirgeon*, *La Dolce Vita* and *Lavabora*. |
| *Incestral Home* | 1967 | Same orange cardboard box as *Duet*, *The Seduction of Susan* and *Turkish Delight*. Re-released later by Blue Scene Films, shot in Victorian flat. |
| *Invitation Sex* | 1969 | Re-released by Blue Scene Films. |
| *Join In* | | |
| *Just Like a Woman* | | |
| *Kinky Couples* | 1966–67 | Same performers appear in Climax's *Schoolgirl Nightmare*. |
| *Kinky Les* | 1966–67 | Same green cardboard box as *The Adulterer*, *Flatmates*, *The Perverts*, *The Swingers* and *Surprise Reward*. Possibly very early Climax, same performers appear in *Jealous Sisters*. |
| *La Dolce Vita* | 1960–63 | Same producers as *Chez Mrs Pirgeon*, *Hotel Sexi* and *Lavabora*. |
| *Lavabora* | 1960–63 | Same producers as *Chez Mrs Pirgeon*, *Hotel Sexi* and *La Dolce Vita*. |

| Title | Year | Notes |
|---|---|---|
| *The Lesbian Trio* | | Re-released by Blue Scene Films. |
| *Lonely But Happy* | 1965–66 | Produced by the same people behind *Private Nursing Home, Sexuality, Sex School* and *Up the Junction*. |
| *Lucky Boys* | 1967–68 | Re-released by Blue Scene Films. |
| *Lucky Girl* | 1968 | Re-released by Blue Scene Films, shot in Victorian flat. |
| *Lucky Prowler* | | |
| *Lust* | | |
| *Misadventure* | | |
| *The Mistress* | 1969 | |
| *The Music Masters 1* | 1965–67 | Uses the Victorian flat location where many rollers were filmed and later re-released by Blue Scene Films. |
| *The Music Masters 2* | 1965–67 | Uses the Victorian flat location where many rollers were filmed and later re-released by Blue Scene Films. |
| *A Natural Break aka TV Man* | 1965–67 | Re-released by Blue Scene Films. |
| *Ordeal* | | |
| *Part Time Job* | 1962–66 | |
| *Peak Performance* | | |
| *The Perverts* | 1966–67 | Same green cardboard box as *The Adulterer, Flatmates, Kinky Les, The Swingers* and *Surprise Reward*. Possibly very early Climax, same performers appear in *Jealous Sisters*. |
| *Private Nursing Home* | 1965–66 | Produced by the same people behind *Lonely But Happy, Sex School, Sexuality* and *Up the Junction*. |
| *Rear Admiral* | 1969 | Re-released by Blue Scene Films. |

*(Continued)*

| Title | Year | Notes |
|---|---|---|
| *The Rent Man* | 1963–65 | |
| *Room Service* | 1962–66 | |
| *Sado Trio* | 1967–69 | |
| *Scrabble* | | |
| *Secret Meeting* | 1964 | |
| *The Seduction of Susan* | 1967–69 | Same orange cardboard box as *Duet*, *Incestral Home* and *Turkish Delight*. |
| *Session with Dave* | | |
| *Sex and Suds* | | Possibly the same film as *Suds and Sex*. |
| *Sex School* | 1965–66 | Produced by the same people behind *Lonely But Happy*, *Private Nursing Home*, *Sexuality* and *Up the Junction*. |
| *Sexuality* | 1965–66 | Produced by the same people behind *Lonely But Happy*, *Private Nursing Home*, *Sex School* and *Up the Junction*. |
| *Sisterly Lust* | 1964–67 | Same red cardboard box as *Afternoon Lust*. |
| *Spy for Love* | | |
| *Stage Struck* | 1962–66 | |
| *Stick Up* | | |
| *Surprise Reward* | 1966–67 | Same green cardboard box as *The Adulterer*, *Flatmates*, *Kinky Les*, *The Perverts* and *The Swingers*. Possibly very early Climax, same performers appear in *Jealous Sisters*. Also seems to have been re-released by Playboy Films. |
| *The Swingers* | 1966–67 | Same green cardboard box as *The Adulterer*, *Flatmates*, *Kinky Les*, *The Perverts* and *Surprise Reward*. Possibly very early Climax, same performers appear in *Jealous Sisters*. |

| Title | Year | Notes |
|---|---|---|
| *Take My Daughter!* | 1966 | |
| *Turkish Delight* | 1967–68 | Same orange cardboard box as *Duet*, *Incestral Home*, *The Seduction of Susan* and re-released later by Blue Scene Films, shot in Victorian flat. |
| *Unexpected Guests* | 1962–65 | Re-released by Blue Scene Films. |
| *Up the Junction* | 1965–66 | Produced by the same people behind *Lonely But Happy*, *Private Nursing Home*, *Sex School* and *Sexuality*. |
| *The Visit* | | |
| *What the Butler Saw and Did* | 1965–67 | Re-released by Blue Scene Films, shot in Victorian flat. |
| *Worth Waiting For* | 1969 | This was released in two parts, giving a total of 400ft. |

## *Academy*

In a police interview, Anthony Collingbourne admitted to his involvement with Academy. This was likely a collaboration with distributor John Darby and John Lindsay, who could have produced some of the titles listed here. The boxes have a distinctive appearance and the branding printed in a colourful font, but can vary between titles. For instance, *Cinzano*, a nod to the popular alcoholic drink, was issued in three different boxes, with one having a tartan masthead. Might this refer to Scottish pornographer John Lindsay? Academy has links to other labels, with titles also appearing on Climax, International Films, Leidibird, Orchid Films and Steinle.

| Title | Year | Notes |
|---|---|---|
| *All Action* | 1970–72 | Also released on International Films. |
| *And the Rain Came* | 1970–72 | Also appears on Orchid Films. |
| *Brown Bomber* | 1970–72 | |

| Title | Year | Notes |
|---|---|---|
| *Cinzano* | 1970–72 | |
| *Home Perm* | 1970–72 | |
| *Joyride* | 1970–72 | Also appears on Steinle. |
| *Lechers Dream* | 1970–72 | |
| *Pick Up* (part 1) | 1970–72 | Part 2 appears on Fantasy, another label linked to Collingbourne and Darby. |
| *Psycho Sex* | 1970–72 | |
| *Ring for Sex* | 1970–72 | |
| *Timber* | 1970–72 | |
| *Turks Delight* | 1970–72 | |
| *We Had to Do It* | 1970–72 | Also appears on Leidibird. |

## Action Films

The last roller label introduced by Mick Muldoon aka Mike Freeman, likely appearing in 1969 and re-releasing titles previously issued on his earlier labels Eros Films and Venus Films. I have only been able to identify five films on this label.

| Title | Year | Notes |
|---|---|---|
| *Degenerates Orgy* | 1967–69 | Also released on Venus Films. |
| *Schoolgames I* | 1969 | |
| *Schoolgames II* | 1969 | |
| *Schoolgirl Initiation* | 1967–69 | Also released on Eros Films. |
| *Young Sexpot* | 1967–69 | |

## Amör Films

A label re-releasing films originally produced and distributed by Climax between 1967 and 1968. It is possible that Amör was either a bootleg outfit, or an offshoot of Climax. Films are presented in distinctive yellow boxes for black and white prints and red boxes for colour prints; the latter are difficult to come across. Amör claims to be a Danish label, but this is likely used as a synonym for hardcore. The reference to Denmark also suggests this label emerged in 1969 or 1970, following legalization.

| Title | Year |
|---|---|
| *Ambitious Model* | 1970–72 |
| *Good Deal* | 1970–72 |
| *The Milkman* | 1970–72 |
| *No Mercy for Susan* | 1970–72 |
| *Pussy Galore* | 1970–72 |
| *Sailor's Delight* | 1970–72 |
| *Staff Room* | 1970–72 |
| *Teacher* | 1970–72 |

## Anglo-continental

Another Anthony Collingbourne label, featuring heavily in the Watford Blue Movie Trial discussed in Chapter 4. This listing is based on police documentation relating to the trial. Films were available in colour and black and white. *Kinky Vicar* is a re-release of a John Lindsay roller, previously issued on the Excelsior label, and other titles appeared on Taboo & Phoenix/Orchid, again revealing a working relationship between Collingbourne, John Darby and John Lindsay.

| Title | Year | Notes |
|---|---|---|
| *All I Want for Christmas* | 1970–72 | |
| *Carry On Cowboy* | 1970–72 | |
| *Dog Lovers* | 1971–72 | |
| *First Night* | 1970–72 | |
| *Fun and Games* | 1970–72 | |
| *Hotel (aka Lady Jane)* | 1970–72 | |

| Title | Year | Notes |
|---|---|---|
| *House of Mirrors* | 1972 | |
| *Kinky Capers* | 1970–72 | |
| *Kinky Vicar* | 1970–72 | Also appears on Excelsior Films. |
| *Midnight Cowboy* | 1970–72 | |
| *Paradise Bay* | 1970–72 | Also appears on Taboo & Phoenix. |
| *Pisss* | 1970–72 | |
| *Private Practice* | 1970–72 | |
| *Randy Tea Party* | 1970–72 | |
| *Satisfaction* | 1970–72 | Also appears on Taboo & Phoenix. |
| *Seduction* | 1970–72 | |
| *Sex Adviser* | 1970–72 | Also appears on Orchid. |
| *Sock It to Me* | 1970–72 | |
| *Surprise* (part 2) | 1970–72 | |
| *Surprise Visitor* | 1970–72 | Also appears on Taboo & Phoenix. |
| *Three in a Boat* | 1970–72 | |
| *Travellers Rest* | 1972 | |

## Apollo Films

Another likely collaboration between Collingbourne, Darby and Lindsay. One collector confirmed two titles in this list and others are taken from police files relating to the Watford Blue Movie Trial.

| Title | Year |
|---|---|
| *Daughter's First Lesson* | 1970–72 |
| *Dog Fashion* | 1970–72 |
| *Hayride* | 1970–72 |
| *Pick Up Part Two* | 1970–72 |

## *Blue Scene Films*

Discussed at length in Chapter 2, I posited that Ivor Cook was the likely person behind Blue Scene Films due to the label re-releasing rollers dating back to the mid-1960s, but also producing new content shot in Scandinavia. Blue Scene Films appear to have started releasing titles around 1969. Some of the later films are printed in colour, and two titles – *Free Sample* and *Pussy Lovers* – were released on both standard 8mm and Super 8. Blue Scene Films appears to have been well distributed, as the titles are regularly auctioned online. Many of the titles below have been taken from a Blue Scene Films mail-order catalogue.

| Title | Year | Notes |
|---|---|---|
| *After Sales Service* | 1969 | Shot in Scandinavia. |
| *All Action Number 1* | | |
| *Bound for Pleasure* | 1970–72 | |
| *Bunny Girls* | 1971–72 | |
| *Call Boys* | 1968 | |
| *Dinner and Dessert* | 1969 | |
| *Duet* | 1968 | Re-release of an unbranded roller. |
| *Family Affair* | 1969–72 | Re-release of an unbranded roller. |
| *Fanny* | 1969–72 | Re-release of an unbranded roller. |
| *Fisherman's Luck* | 1969–72 | Re-release of an unbranded roller. |
| *Forest Fantasy* | | |
| *Free Sample* | 1969 | Released on 8mm and Super 8. Shot in Scandinavia. |
| *Friends and Neighbours* | 1970–72 | |
| *Good Time Girls* | 1969–72 | Re-release of an unbranded roller. |
| *Gratis* | 1969 | |
| *Homework* | | |
| *The Hunter* | 1969 | Shot in Scandinavia. |
| *I Spy* | | |

| Title | Year | Notes |
|---|---|---|
| *Incestral Home* | 1969–72 | Re-release of an unbranded roller. |
| *Invitation Sex* | 1969–72 | Re-release of an unbranded roller. |
| *The Lesbian Trio* | | Re-release of an unbranded roller. |
| *Love Affair* | 1970–72 | |
| *Lucky Boys* | | |
| *Lucky Girl* | 1969–72 | Re-release of an unbranded roller. |
| *Man Hunt* | 1969 | Shot in Scandinavia. |
| *The Mistress* | | Re-release of an unbranded roller. |
| *More Suds and Sex* | 1967 | Re-release of an unbranded roller. |
| *Morning Lust* | 1965–69 | |
| *A Natural Break aka TV Man* | 1965–66 | Re-release of an unbranded roller. |
| *No Hiding Place* | 1967–72 | |
| *Part Time Job* | | Re-release of an unbranded roller. |
| *Pussy Lovers* | 1970–72 | |
| *Rear Admiral* | 1969 | Re-release of an unbranded roller. |
| *Sex Pets* | 1967–72 | |
| *Seduction of Susan* | 1969–72 | Re-release of an unbranded roller. |
| *Take Five* | 1967–72 | |
| *The Treatment* | | |
| *Turkish Delight* | 1969–72 | Re-release of an unbranded roller. |
| *Unexpected Guests* | 1969–72 | Re-release of an unbranded roller. |
| *What the Butler Saw and Did* | 1969–72 | Re-release of an unbranded roller. |

## Blue X

Discovered amongst a batch of other rollers from the early 1970s, it appears that Blue X issued only one title – *The Waiter* – in an oversized green box with the title of the film and the label written on to the photograph on the front of the box. The film itself is the usual 200ft and is shot in a hotel room. It is plausible that the film was made between 1969 and 1972, being indicative of the opportunists who made hardcore for the potential quick profits.

## Bunny Films

Presented in distinctive foil-like gold boxes, the two Bunny Films rollers I found do not appear to have titles on the film itself or the cover of the box. The box covers include film length in both metre and feet, suggesting that they were also sold on the continent. This could be a Scandinavian label, but one title looks to a reissue of the New Private roller *Dream Orgy* (1970–72).

## Candy Films

Another distinctive box with pink and white candy striping. Like Bunny Films, Candy Films shows how roller makers began to think more carefully about branding, differentiating from other labels. The label claims to originate from Germany, but the imperial 200ft measurement suggests otherwise. Titles indicate a predilection for BDSM-themed pornography (*The Hole Story* and *A Taste for Leather*), and the Letraset used on the cover images often takes a gothic style. In Chapter 4, I suggested that Martin Granby is a potential candidate for this and other labels, as *Anal Sex* and *Late Comer* also appear on Universal Films, possibly being re-released. The gothic-style Letraset also features on the covers of Universal Films, offering further evidence of this association.

| Title | Year | Notes |
|---|---|---|
| *Anal Sex* | 1969 | Also appears on Universal Films. |
| *Cum On* | 1969 | |
| *Gagged and Bound* | 1969 | |
| *The Hole Story* | 1969 | |
| *Late Comer* | 1969 | Also appears on Universal Films. |
| *A Taste of Leather* | 1969 | |

## Casanova Film

Casanova Film released titles in elaborate felt-covered boxes with gold-embossed text, more akin to the packaging typically used to hold jewellery. Fashions and haircuts suggest this label was active in the early 1970s, possibly 1972; the title *Teasy Rider* is likely a reference to the film *Easy Rider* (1969). Markings on the film *Office Party* indicate that the film was developed by a professional laboratory, and therefore could have been made in Europe rather than Britain.

| Title | Year |
|---|---|
| *Barbershop* | 1970–72 |
| *Fashion* | 1970–72 |
| *Office Party* | 1970–72 |
| *Pleasure Drive* | 1970–72 |
| *Prefect's Prize* | 1972 |
| *Teasy Rider* | 1970–72 |
| *The Thief* | 1970–72 |

## Cherub

I was only able to locate *More La More II* from this label, which stars 'Big' John English in the Victorian flat that was regularly used in several unbranded titles, later reappearing on Blue Scene Films. *Poor Old Man* was also released by Delilah Deluxe, making a link between Blue Scene Films, Delilah Deluxe and Cherub a possibility. Fantasy's release of *A Small Hotel* includes a Cherub title card at the beginning of the film, pointing to a relationship between these labels. The dates of release suggest that Cherub came before Blue Scene Films, Delilah Deluxe and Fantasy. Given the elusive 'Skinny' Ken Taylor's connection to Anthony Collingbourne and Ivor Cook, I do wonder if he was responsible for Cherub, Delilah Deluxe and Fantasy.

| Title | Year | Notes |
|---|---|---|
| *Let's Stay Home* | 1968 | |
| *More La More I* | 1968 | |
| *More La More II* | 1968 | |

| Title | Year | Notes |
|---|---|---|
| *Off the Beat* | 1968 | |
| *Perchance to Dream* | 1968 | |
| *Poor Old Man* | 1969 | Also appears on Delilah Deluxe. |
| *Quality Street* | 1969 | |

## *Climax Films/Climax Original*

Started by Evan 'Big Jeff' Phillips and Bob Byrne in early 1966, possibly with assistance from Ivor Cook, Climax was the first British roller label to brand their releases. At least 196 titles were released by Climax. Issue 20 of the Dutch magazine *Chick* specifies a total of 225 productions: 175 in black and white, 50 in colour. As I suggested in Chapter 3, there appears to be three waves of Climax releases. The first wave is 1966–67, when the films usually had handwritten titles and were mainly produced by Phillips, Byrne and possibly Cook. The year 1967–69 saw the second wave, when Phillips moved away from making the films, outsourcing production. Rollers from this period appear to have been shot on 16mm colour film, but mainly printed on black and white; some of these titles were made available in colour. Several second-wave films were filmed on the continent, for instance *No Mercy for Susan* was shot in the Netherlands. Climax are also important as they became a transnational concern, particularly during their third wave (1970–72) when the operation moved to Denmark and now a collaboration between Phillips and Walter Bartkowski. Films from this wave had a higher production standard, mainly shot in Denmark and printed in a formal film laboratory.

It seems that the label began as Climax Films, changing name to Climax Original. It is plausible that this change was made to differentiate from the Theander brothers' growing Color Climax brand that emerged in 1968. Boxes differ considerably. I have found around seven variants. Orange boxes are the dominant style, usually indicating first- and second-wave titles, but red boxes were also used. Green boxes are indicative of colour releases, increasing during the third wave. Climax experimented with shorted 100ft/30m films under the label Climax Mini. A purple box variant exists with a $50 price printed on the front, signifying that these were likely intended for the American market. At least five titles in the list appear to be re-releases, such as International Films'

*Geisha* and *Euston Capture*. These are presented in an orange box with a slightly different box design and could be an attempt to associate with the brand due to its dominance, or are bootlegs. The field 'CAT' includes numbers taken from a 1970 Climax mail-order catalogue. The volume of titles here demonstrates their dominance of the market.

| Title | Year | Cat | Notes |
|---|---|---|---|
| *100% Lust* | 1966 | | |
| *44 in Action* | 1966–67 | | |
| *A Cosy Evening* | 1971–72 | 236 | |
| *A Length for Two* | 1968 | | |
| *Ad-Vice* | 1967–68 | | |
| *After the Party* | 1967–68 | | |
| *Aladdin's Lamp* | 1971–72 | 223 | |
| *All Action* | 1968 | | |
| *All in Black* | 1967–68 | | |
| *Ambitious Model* | 1967–69 | 34 | Also available in colour. |
| *Anything Goes* | 1967–68 | | |
| *Apartment Sex* | 1967–69 | | |
| *Auto Sex* | 1968 | | |
| *Baby Doll* | 1966–67 | | |
| *Baby Sitter* | 1967–69 | 33 | Also available in colour. |
| *Bang Bang* | 1966–67 | | |
| *Bathing Time* | 1970-72 | | Also appears on New Private, possibly a bootleg. |
| *Beach Girls* | 1969–70 | 214 | |
| *Beat Girl* | 1967–69 | 38 | Also available in colour. |
| *Beatnik Bedlam 1&2* | 1966 | | |
| *Beauty and the Beast* | 1967–68 | | |
| *Bed Geisha* | 1969–70 | 216 | |

| Title | Year | Cat | Notes |
|---|---|---|---|
| *Bed Set* | 1968–69 | 111 | |
| *Bicycle-Accident* | 1971–72 | 229 | |
| *Big Prick* | 1970–72 | | |
| *Big Surprise* | 1969–70 | 213 | |
| *Birthday Present* | 1968–69 | 112 | |
| *Birthday-Present* | 1971–72 | 235 | |
| *Bondage* | 1967 | 62 | |
| *The Bookworm* | 1971–72 | 219 | |
| *Bright Sparks* | 1967–69 | 36 | Also available in colour. |
| *Car Accident* | 1971–72 | 230 | |
| *Carnaby Kinks* | 1968 | 17 | Also available in colour. |
| *Carry on Sheik* | 1970–72 | | Likely not an official Climax release, produced by Collingbourne/Darby. |
| *The Cat Burglar* | 1966 | | |
| *Caught in the Act* | 1967 | | |
| *Club X* | 1969 | 208 | Available with soundtrack. |
| *Cock a Spaniel* | 1967–68 | | |
| *Come On Over* | 1971–72 | 222 | |
| *Country Cousins* | 1970–72 | | Likely not an official Climax release, produced by Collingbourne/ Darby. |
| *Cum Clean* | 1967 | 92 | |
| *Desire* | 1967 | | |
| *Dill-Dollies* | 1966–67 | 4 | Also available in colour. |
| *Doctor in Bed* | 1969 | 201 | |
| *Dog Friend* | 1969 | | |
| *Dream Lovers* | 1967–68 | | |
| *Eastern Promise* | 1969 | | |

*(Continued)*

| Title | Year | Cat | Notes |
|---|---|---|---|
| *Easy Meet* | 1967 | | Appears to have the same performers as *Tonight at 8*. |
| *End of Term* | 1967–68 | 78 | |
| *Equal to Mummy* | 1967–68 | 83 | |
| *Escort Agency* | 1966 | | |
| *Euston Capture* | 1970–72 | | Likely not an official Climax release, possibly produced by Lindsay/Darby. Also on International Films. |
| *Exhibition* | 1967–68 | 74 | |
| *False Pretences* | 1966–67 | | |
| *Fantasy* | 1971–72 | 233 | |
| *Fantasy Morning* | 1971–72 | 239 | |
| *Filthy Schoolgirls* | | | |
| *First Audition* | 1966–67 | 38 | |
| *First Time* | 1966–67 | 43 | 100ft (30m). Also released in colour. |
| *Fixing to Fuck* | 1969 | | |
| *Flagellation* | 1966–67 | 11 | |
| *Forced Entry* | 1969–70 | 209 | |
| *Foursome* | 1970 | 202 | |
| *Free for All* | 1966–67 | 49 | |
| *Fruit Salad* | 1967–68 | | |
| *Full Recovery* | 1968–69 | 90 | |
| *Full Treatment* | 1966–67 | | |
| *Fun at Lunch* | 1967–68 | | |
| *Geisha* | 1970–72 | | Likely not an official Climax release, possibly produced by Lindsay/Darby. Also on International Films. |
| *Geisha* | 1971–72 | 224 | |
| *Gigs and Boys* | 1969–70 | 217 | |
| *Gigs and Guys* | | | |

| Title | Year | Cat | Notes |
|---|---|---|---|
| *Gin and Lime* | 1971–72 | 237 | |
| *The Girlfriend* | 1967 | 63 | |
| *Girls & Boys* | | | |
| *Good Deal* | 1968–69 | 114 | |
| *Good Knight* | 1968–69 | 107 | 100ft (30m). |
| *The Good Life* | 1966–67 | | |
| *Great Love* | 1969 | | |
| *Gruppen Sex* | 1969–70 | 211 | |
| *Guessing Games* | 1967 | | |
| *The Gynaecologist* | | | |
| *H.P Man* | 1966–67 | | |
| *Happy Family* | 1967–68 | | |
| *Hell-Fire Club* | 1969–70 | 203 | |
| *Hippy Sex* | 1969–70 | 200 | Available with soundtrack. |
| *Hot-line* | 1967–68 | 84 | Original catalogue number was 24. |
| *Hotel* | 1966–67 | | |
| *In Drag* | 1967 | | |
| *Incest* | 1966 | | |
| *Intoxication* | 1971–72 | 231 | |
| *Jealous Sisters* | 1966 | | |
| *Judo Lesson* | 1969–70 | 205 | |
| *Kinky Lovers* | 1966–68 | | Also released unbranded. |
| *Kinky Spender* | 1966–67 | 41 | 100ft (30m) Also released in  colour. |
| *Lady Lovers* | 1967–68 | | |
| *Lesbian Girls* | 1971–72 | 232 | |
| *Lesbian Sister* | 1967–68 | | |

(*Continued*)

| Title | Year | Cat | Notes |
|---|---|---|---|
| *Little Girl Lost* | 1966 | 31 | |
| *Live Show* | 1967–68 | | |
| *Living for Kicks* | 1967–68 | | |
| *Lolitas* | 1969 | | |
| *Love for Sale* | 1967–68 | | |
| *Love Game* | 1969–70 | 300 | 100ft (30m). Also released in colour. |
| *Love In* | 1967–69 | 39 | Also available in colour. |
| *A Lovely Game* | 1969–70 | | |
| *Lucky Draw* | 1967–68 | 99 | |
| *Lusty Au-Pair* | 1968 | 89 | |
| *Magic Lust* | 1968 | | |
| *Maid to Measure* | 1967–68 | 18 | Also available in colour. |
| *Maid's Delight* | 1966–67 | | |
| *Man Crazy* | 1967 | | |
| *Man Hungry* | 1966 | | |
| *Massage* | 1966 | | |
| *Massage Treatment* | 1966 | | |
| *Medieval Masochist* | 1968–69 | 101 | |
| *Men* | 1966–67 | 48 | Original catalogue number was 16. |
| *Miss Conduct* | 1967–68 | | |
| *Mixed Feelings* | 1967–68 | 76 | |
| *More Arts and Crafts* | 1966–67 | | |
| *More Beatnik Bedlam* | 1966–67 | | |
| *More Than He Can Handle* | 1968–71 | | |
| *Naughty Girl* | 1967 | | |
| *Nelson's Column* | 1966 | | |

| Title | Year | Cat | Notes |
|---|---|---|---|
| *Nightspot* | 1967–68 | 86 | |
| *No Mercy for Susan* | 1967–68 | 87 | |
| *Nymph* | 1967–69 | 31 | Also available in colour. |
| *Nympho Nurse* | 1969 | | |
| *O My Pussy* | 1969–70 | 302 | 100ft (30m). Also released in colour. |
| *Orgy Trip* | | | Also appears on New Private, possibly a bootleg. |
| *Outnumbered* | 1968–69 | 96 | |
| *P* | 1966-69 | | |
| *Party Kicks* | 1967 | 32 | |
| *Patient* | 1966 | | |
| *Pawnbroker* | 1967–69 | 37 | Also available in colour. |
| *Pay the Man* | 1968 | | |
| *The Phantom* | 1966–67 | | |
| *Plateing Is an Art* | 1968 | | |
| *Playboys* | 1968 | 71 | |
| *Porno Poker* | 1971–72 | 234 | |
| *Private Patient* | 1969 | 108 | |
| *Pussy Club* | 1966–67 | | |
| *Pussy Galore* | 1966–67 | 39 | |
| *Randy* | 1966–67 | | |
| *Randy Intruder* | 1968–69 | | |
| *Rape* | 1966 | | |
| *Rare Capture* | 1968 | 95 | |
| *Real Lovers* | 1967–68 | | |
| *Rent Collector* | 1966–67 | 41 | |
| *Ring Up for Love* | 1966–67 | | |

(*Continued*)

| Title | Year | Cat | Notes |
|---|---|---|---|
| *Room Service* | 1967–68 | | |
| *Sailor's Delight* | 1969 | 98 | |
| *Satan's Children* | 1967–68 | 82 | |
| *Schoolgirl Dream* | 1970-72 | | Likely not an official Climax release, possibly produced by Lindsay/Darby. Also on International Films. |
| *Schoolgirl Nightmare* | | | Same title appears on New Private, but is possibly a different film. |
| *Schoolgirls Raped* | 1966 | | |
| *A Seasoned Dinner* | 1971–72 | 225 | |
| *Secret Weapon* | 1969–70 | 207 | |
| *Seduction '68* | 1968 | 64 | |
| *Services Rendered* | 1967–68 | | |
| *Sex and Lust* | 1969–70 | 301 | 100ft (30m). Also released in colour. |
| *Sex Bomb* | 1970–72 | | |
| *Sex Campus* | 1969–70 | 215 | |
| *Sex Holdup* | 1970–72 | | |
| *Sex in Colour* | 1967–69 | | |
| *Sex Olympics* | 1968 | 100 | |
| *The Sex Orgy* | 1966–67 | | |
| *Sex Service* | 1971–72 | 228 | |
| *Sex Study* | 1968–69 | 109 | |
| *Sextet* | 1968–69 | 97 | |
| *Short Time* | 1968–69 | 106 | 100ft (30m). |
| *Sixty Nine* | 1971–72 | 226 | |
| *Sixus* | 1969–70 | 212 | |
| *Skin Skin Skin* | 1971–72 | 220 | |
| *Skov* | 1970–72 | | |

| Title | Year | Cat | Notes |
|---|---|---|---|
| *Sleeping Beauty* | 1968–70 | | |
| *Something Special* | 1966–67 | | |
| *Spanish Lust* | 1968 | | |
| *Speedy Love* | | | |
| *Speedy Saloon* | 1969–70 | 204 | |
| *Staff Room* | 1967–68 | 105 | |
| *Sudden Sex* | 1967 | 94 | |
| *Sunday at Simons* | 1971–72 | 221 | |
| *Surprise* | | | |
| *Swedish Massage* | 1968–69 | 113 | |
| *Teacher* | 1967–68 | 103 | |
| *The Teen Scene* | 1966–67 | | |
| *Telephone-Service* | 1971–72 | 227 | |
| *Three Roses* | 1969–70 | 206 | |
| *Three Times Animal* | 1969–70 | 218 | Available with soundtrack. |
| *Threesome* | 1968–69 | 110 | |
| *Tonight at 8* | 1966–67 | | I have found no evidence to support that this is a Climax title but it is included on other lists. |
| *Triangle* | 1966–67 | 50 | |
| *Twisted* | 1968 | 238 | |
| *Two Plus One Makes Three* | 1971–72 | 238 | |
| *Two's Enough* | 1967–68 | 104 | |
| *Unfortunate Little Sister* | 1967–69 | 40 | Also available in colour. |
| *Up, Up and Away* | 1968 | 16 | Also available in colour. |
| *Young and Lusty* | 1969–70 | 210 | |

## *Danish Blu Films*

Releases from Universal Films, Candy Films, Dolly Films and Svensk Films also appear on this label. The packing is glossy, unlike the basic designs used for Dolly Films, Svensk Films and, to some extent, Universal Films, indicating that Danish Blu Films came to the market later and were re-releasing content from these other labels. In Chapter 4, I suggested that the likely culprit for this label was Martin Granby.

| Title | Year | Notes |
|---|---|---|
| *6 for Sex* | 1970–72 | Also appears on Universal Films. |
| *8 for Sex* | 1970–72 | Also appears on Universal Films. |
| *Anal Sex* | 1970–72 | Also appears on Candy Films and Universal Films. |
| *Anchors Away* | 1970–72 | Also appears on Dolly Films. |
| *Arabian Nights* | 1970–72 | Also appears on Dolly Films. |
| *Bashful* | 1970–72 | |
| *Chinese and Passion* | 1970–72 | Also appears on Universal Films. |
| *Keep It Clean* | 1970–72 | Also appears on Universal Films. |
| *Lesbo* | 1970–72 | Also appears on Universal Films. |
| *A Lesson in French* | 1970–72 | Also appears on Svensk Films and Universal Films. |
| *Maidservant* | 1970–72 | Also appears on Dolly Films and Universal Films. |
| *Randy Chick* | 1970–72 | Also appears on Universal Films. |
| *Savage Intruder* | 1970–72 | |
| *Sex Lift* | 1970–72 | |
| *Single X* | 1970–72 | |
| *Spunky Trio* | 1970–72 | Also appears on Universal Films. |
| *Young Lust* | 1970–72 | |
| *Young Virgin* | 1970–72 | |

## Delilah Deluxe

Delilah Deluxe was likely the second label from the people behind Cherub, releasing films in bright yellow boxes with the typical postcard on the front. A blue version of the same style box was used by Global Cinelux, making it possible that this was another label from the same team.

| Title | Year | Notes |
|---|---|---|
| *Beat Girl* (part 1) | 1970–72 | |
| *Beat Girl* (part 2) | 1970–72 | |
| *Beloved Lover's* (part 1) | 1970–71 | |
| *Beloved Lover's* (part 2) | 1970–71 | |
| *Mirror Girl* | 1969–72 | |
| *Order Me Male* | 1969–72 | |
| *Out of the Night* | 1969 | |
| *Passionate Housewife* | 1969 | |
| *Peter the Painter* | 1969 | |
| *Plate My Foot* | 1969–72 | |
| *Poor Old Man* | 1969 | Also appears on Cherub. |
| *Rise Sir Pee Wee* | 1969 | |
| *Roof Rider* | 1970–71 | |
| *Two Can Play* | 1969–72 | Also released in colour. |
| *What's That Darling?* | 1970–71 | |

## Dolly Films

Appearing at the end of the 1960s, Dolly Films released films in basic bright yellow boxes with the brand 'Dolly Films' stencilled at the top above the usual postcard image. Titles were later re-released by Svensk Films, Danish Blu Films and Universal Films, possibly being one of Granby's early attempts at branding. A distinctive male performer who bears an uncanny resemblance to Charles Manson features in many Dolly Films rollers, but also performed in Climax rollers, such as *Hell Fire Club* and *Judo Lesson*.

| Title | Year | Notes |
|---|---|---|
| *Anchors Away* | 1969 | Also appears on Svensk Films. |
| *Arabian Nights* | 1969 | Also appears on Danish Blu Films. |
| *Close Up* | 1969 | |
| *Contract* | 1969 | |
| *Maidservant* | 1969 | Also appears on Danish Blu Films and Universal Films. |
| *The Masseur* | 1969 | |
| *Pick Up* | 1969 | |
| *Plaything* | 1969 | Also appears on Universal Films. |
| *Rear View* | 1969 | |
| *Sex Pots* | 1969 | Also appears on Universal Films. |
| *Sheik's Pleasure* | 1969 | |

## Double X

Another of Collingbourne's labels. Around the same time, there was a softcore label from Mountain Films named Impact Double X, and Collingbourne's Double X could have been a reference to this.

| Title | Year | Notes |
|---|---|---|
| *Baby Doll* | 1970–72 | |
| *Chicks Do-lay* | 1970–72 | Also appears on Fantasy. |
| *Currant Affair* | 1970 | |
| *Home from School* | 1970–72 | |
| *Les Teacher* | 1970–72 | |
| *My Dog Blue* | 1970–72 | |

| Title | Year | Notes |
|---|---|---|
| *Sam and Belle* | 1970–72 | Also appears on Look. |
| *Schoolgirl Lark* | 1970–72 | |
| *Schoolgirl Rave* | 1970–72 | Also appears on Look. |
| *Shag Happy* | 1970–72 | |
| *Tour de Love* | 1970–72 | Also appears on Look; same performers as *Country Cousins*. |
| *Welcome Home* | 1970–72 | |
| *Woodpecker* | 1970–72 | |

## Eros Films

The first label from Mick Muldoon/Mike Freeman. Early titles are sub-branded 'Pornographer at the Pictures', which appears before the film's title. Boxes for early titles have a 'cut and paste' appearance, with the Eros Films branding being stuck on to generic boxes alongside the usual postcard image. Some early titles – *Homework* and *Perversion* – have no branding on the front of the box, just a large postcard. Later titles have the branding printed on the box, following the style of other labels, and many films were made available in colour. The list of titles shows Muldoon's tendency towards 'taboo' themes, such as incest, bestiality and schoolgirl/teenage sex. Some films were later re-released on Muldoon's other labels Action Films and Venus Films.

| Title | Year | Notes |
|---|---|---|
| *After School* | 1966–67 | #8 in the 'Pornographer at the Pictures' series. |
| *Bath Games* | 1968 | |
| *Beach Buggery* | 1967 | #27 in the 'Pornographer at the Pictures' series. |
| *Bum-fun* | 1967–68 | Available in colour. |
| *Corruption* (part 1) | 1968 | Available in colour. Part two likely exists. |

| Title | Year | Notes |
|---|---|---|
| *Cuntry Girls (on a Day Off)* | 1966–67 | #2 in the 'Pornographer at the Pictures' series. |
| *Dirty Girls* | 1966–67 | #12 in the 'Pornographer at the Pictures' series. |
| *Dirty Perverts 1* | 1967–68 | Available in colour. |
| *Dirty Perverts 2* | 1967–68 | Available in colour. |
| *Dog Orgy* | 1966–67 | #15 in the 'Pornographer at the Pictures' series. |
| *Dogfun* | 1967 | Available in colour. |
| *Family Fun* | 1967–68 | Available in colour. |
| *Five for Sex* | 1967 | #22 in the 'Pornographer at the Pictures' series. |
| *French Maid* | 1967 | |
| *Get Fucked!* | 1966–67 | #16 in the 'Pornographer at the Pictures' series. |
| *Handy Man* | 1966–68 | #17 in the 'Pornographer at the Pictures' series. |
| *Home Work* | 1966–67 | Also identified as #2 in the 'Pornographer at the Pictures' series by the Kinsey Institute. |
| *Humiliation* | 1966–67 | #10 in the 'Pornographer at the Pictures' series. |
| *Incest* | 1967–68 | Available in colour. |
| *Intoxication (part 1)* | 1967 | |
| *Intoxication (part 2)* | 1967 | Available in colour. |
| *Keep It Kinky* | 1967–68 | |
| *Kinky Fun* | 1967–68 | Available in colour. |
| *Kinky Sisters* | 1967–68 | Available in colour. |
| *Legs Up for Sex* | 1967–68 | |

| Title | Year | Notes |
|---|---|---|
| *Luscious Lesbians* | 1967 | #28 in the 'Pornographer at the Pictures' series. |
| *Navy Larks* | 1966–67 | #21 in the 'Pornographer at the Pictures' series. |
| *The Nymphettes* | 1966–67 | #7 in the 'Pornographer at the Pictures' series. |
| *Nympho Nurses* | 1966–67 | #20 in the 'Pornographer at the Pictures' series. |
| *Peeping Jane* | 1968 | |
| *Perversion* | 1966–67 | #6 in the 'Pornographer at the Pictures' series. |
| *Phallus '68* | 1968 | Available in colour. |
| *Satisfied* | 1968 | #34 in the 'Pornographer at the Pictures' series. |
| *School Holiday* | 1967 | Available in colour. |
| *Schoolgirl Buggery* | 1967–68 | |
| *Schoolgirl Initiation* | 1967 | Re-released on Action Films. |
| *Schoolgirl Lust* | 1966–67 | #13 in the 'Pornographer at the Pictures' series. |
| *The Schoolgirls* | 1966–67 | #9 in the 'Pornographer at the Pictures' series. |
| *Sex* | 1966–67 | #18 in the 'Pornographer at the Pictures' series. |
| *Sexation* | 1967 | Re-released on Venus Films. |
| *Sex Hostess* | 1967 | #25 in the 'Pornographer at the Pictures' series. |
| *Sexual Reflections* | 1966–67 | |
| *Swap Orgy* | 1968 | Re-released as *Degenerates Orgy* on Action Films and Venus Films. |

*(Continued)*

| Title | Year | Notes |
|-------|------|-------|
| *Teenage Sex* | 1966–67 | |
| *TV Sex* | 1968 | |
| *Two Times Two* | 1966–67 | #26 in the 'Pornographer at the Pictures' series. |
| *Wife Swoppers* | 1967 | #23 in the 'Pornographer at the Pictures' series. Part two likely exists. |
| *Wife Swoppers 3* | 1967 | #32 in the 'Pornographer at the Pictures' series. |
| *Wrens at Play* | 1967 | #24 in the 'Pornographer at the Pictures' series. |
| *Young Couple* | 1966–67 | Available in colour. |
| *Young Girl Lost* | 1967 | Available in colour. |
| *Young Love* | 1967–68 | |
| *Young Lust* | 1967 | #11 in the 'Pornographer at the Pictures' series. |

## Excelsior Films

The earliest label associated with Scottish pornographer John Jesner Lindsay. A collaboration with John Darby, Excelsior Films likely first appeared around 1969. Like Eros Films, early boxes have a 'cut and paste' appearance with the branding being stuck on to generic purple or pink boxes. In a twist to the usual Letraset, postcards feature hand-drawn titles, often with a small drawing. *Nympho Schoolgirl* is released in a different box, with the brand printed on it – 'Excelsior Films of Denmark' – and a full colour postcard. Most titles appear to have also been released on 16mm in addition to standard 8mm, and at least two titles were re-released on the later Lindsay/Darby collaboration Taboo & Phoenix, but also the Collingbourne/Darby label Anglo Continental.

| Title | Year | Notes |
|-------|------|-------|
| *The Builders* | 1969–72 | |
| *The Carpet Fuckers* | 1969–72 | |

| Title | Year | Notes |
|-------|------|-------|
| *Continental Instruction* | 1969–72 | |
| *Dick Decimal* | 1969–72 | |
| *A Fair Cop* | 1969–72 | |
| *Go Go Dancer* | 1969–72 | |
| *Kinky Vicar* | 1969–72 | Also appears on Anglo Continental and Taboo & Phoenix. |
| *Night Shift* | 1969–72 | |
| *No Service Charge* | 1969–72 | |
| *Nympho Artist* | 1969–72 | Also appears on Taboo & Phoenix and Zodiac Films. |
| *Nympho Schoolgirl* | 1969–72 | |
| *The Peeping Policewoman* | 1969–72 | |
| *Plumber* | 1969–72 | |
| *Prick Laying* | 1969–72 | |
| *Sailor's Ahoy* | 1969–72 | Also appears on Taboo and Phoenix. |
| *School Day* | 1969–72 | |
| *Sexy Babysitter* | 1969–72 | |
| *Special Treatment* | 1969–72 | |
| *Up Your Kilt* | 1969–72 | |
| *Window Wanker* | 1969–72 | |

## *Fantasy*

I question whether this label belonged to 'Skinny' Ken Taylor, due to his links with Anthony Collingbourne – many Watford performers appear in Fantasy rollers and *Pick Up* (part 2) could be a follow-on to Academy's *Pick Up* (part 1) – and Ivor Cook. *A Small Hotel* uses a Cherub title card and is possible a re-release. *Action Girl* was issued on Super 8, making it one of the few rollers available in this format until John Lindsay's later labels. 'Big' John English appears in *Making Whopee*.

| Title | Year | Notes |
|---|---|---|
| *Action Girl* | 1968–72 | Also available on Super 8. |
| *Bed Sitter* | 1968–72 | |
| *Chicks Do Lay* | 1968–72 | |
| *Making Whopee* | 1968–72 | |
| *Pick Up* (part 2) | 1968–72 | |
| *Ritual* | 1968–72 | |
| *Sewing for Pleasure* | 1968 | |
| *She's Mad* | 1968–72 | |
| *A Small Hotel* | 1968 | |
| *Turkish Delight* | 1968–72 | |

## Gatsby

Not a British label, but Danish, mainly re-releasing John Lindsay and possibly George Harrison Marks' titles so worth mentioning here. Gatsby was one of the many labels from Flesh Films, who were one of the biggest Danish competitors to the Theander's Color Climax Corporation.

| Title | Year | Notes |
|---|---|---|
| *no title* | 1972–75 | Re-release of John Lindsay's *Hay Ride*, formerly released by Phoenix International. |
| *Man Eater* | 1972–75 | |
| *Spanking* | 1972–75 | |

## Global Cinelux

Global Cinelux has similar packaging to Delilah Deluxe, using blue colouring rather than Delilah's yellow, suggesting a link between these labels. Only one of the collectors I met owned a Global Cinelux roller. This label could be associated with Cherub, given its possible relationship with Delilah Deluxe.

| Title | Year |
|---|---|
| *Cupboard Love* | 1969 |
| *Dance Don't Sleep* | 1969 |
| *He Done It, Daddy* | 1968 |
| *Racing, Yes* | 1969 |

## International Films

In his police interview, Anthony Collingbourne associates International Films with Ivor Cook, but it is more likely that this label was the work of John Lindsay and John Darby, given the links to Academy and its inclusion in Darby's mail-order catalogues. Early titles were released in black cardboard boxes with printed white text and a black and white postcard, eventually replaced with two-part thick cardboard boxes, embossed gold lettering and usually a small colour postcard. Some titles were made available in colour. A billboard promoting the film *Mary Queen of Scots* (Charles Jarrot 1971) is shown in *Euston Capture*, dating this film to 1971. Other films could be later than this. Two films are re-released on Climax, but their boxes are slightly different from the usual Climax style, possibly indicating bootlegs. Seventeen of these rollers have been identified from an International Films catalogue. 'Big' John English appears in *Strip Poker*.

| Title | Year | Notes |
|---|---|---|
| *Action 1* | 1970–72 | |
| *Action 2* | 1970–72 | |
| *All Action* | 1970–72 | Also released on Academy. |
| *Beatnik Bandits* | 1970–72 | |
| *The Boyfriend* | 1970–72 | |
| *Change Partners* | 1970–72 | |
| *Crazy Pickup* | 1970–72 | |
| *Dog Scene* | 1970–72 | |
| *Euston Capture* | 1971 | Also released on Climax. |

| Title | Year | Notes |
|---|---|---|
| *Flogged & Raped* | 1970–72 | |
| *Geisha* | 1970–72 | Also released on Climax. |
| *Jag Puller* (part 2) | 1970–72 | |
| *Les Bisex* | 1970–72 | |
| *Like Father Like Son* | 1970–72 | |
| *Male Bisex* | 1970–72 | |
| *Panther Kidnap* | 1970–72 | |
| *Psychic Sex* | 1970–72 | |
| *Randy Picnic* | 1970–72 | |
| *Ring for Sex* | 1970–72 | Also released on Academy. |
| *Schoolgirl Dream 2* | 1970–72 | |
| *Schoolgirl Nymphs* | 1970–72 | |
| *Sex Pool* | 1970–72 | |
| *Sexy Session* | 1970–72 | |
| *A Splendid Night* | 1970–72 | |
| *Strip Poker* | 1970–72 | Available in colour. |
| *Table for Two* | 1970–72 | |
| *Vice Sex* | 1970–72 | |
| *Whip Rape* | 1970–72 | |
| *Wife Swop* | 1970–72 | |
| *Windowclean Rape* | 1970–72 | |
| *Windowcleaner* | 1970–72 | |

## Karl Ordinez

John Lindsay's Karl Ordinez label seems to appear following the Watford arrests in 1973. It was another collaboration with John Darby who, according to the Birmingham court case discussed in Chapter 5, directed the films. The name Karl

Ordinez is still subject to debate. Sheridan (1999: 149) refers to Karl Ordinez as Lindsay's 'mysterious "German Backer" (sometimes referred to as Swedish too)' and 'the elusive faceless film producer [...] there is some doubt as to whether he existed'. Company records show that Karl Ordinez Films became a limited company in 1978, although films were being made from 1973 to 1977. It is possible to date some films by the Birmingham court case, which identifies dates of production. Films were available in colour and Super 8 formats, and the boxes come in a range of different styles. As the list shows, titles from other Darby/Lindsay labels – Orchid, Taboo & Phoenix and Taboo of Sweden – were re-released as Karl Ordinez titles. Sheridan also suggests that Lindsay shot some of these titles in Germany and in the Netherlands, such as *Special Assignment*.

| Title | Year | Notes |
|---|---|---|
| *100% Nymph* | 1973–77 | Re-release, also available on Taboo & Phoenix and Taboo of Sweden. |
| *Anal Rape* | 1972–73 | Also released on Teenage Productions. |
| *Anticipation* | 1973–77 | |
| *Beatnik Orgy* | 1973–77 | |
| *Boarding School* | 1973–77 | |
| *Convent of Sin* | 1972–73 | |
| *Counterfeit* | 1973–77 | |
| *Danger Route* | 1973–77 | |
| *Doctor Zego* | 1973–77 | |
| *Espionage* | 1973–77 | |
| *Fruits of Sin* | 1973–77 | |
| *Frustration* | 1973–77 | |
| *Gangsters Mole* | 1973–77 | |
| *Girl Guide Rape* | 1973–77 | |
| *Ground Bait* | 1973–77 | |
| *Gypsy's Curse* | 1973–77 | |
| *Hay Ride* | 1973–77 | Re-release, also appears on Phoenix International and Gatsby. |

| Title | Year | Notes |
|---|---|---|
| *Hot Sensations* | 1973–77 | |
| *Illusions* | 1973–77 | |
| *The Intruders* | 1973–77 | |
| *Jamboree* | 1973–77 | |
| *Man Hunters* | 1973–77 | |
| *Misadventure* | 1973–77 | |
| *Naughty Girl Guides* | 1973–77 | |
| *Oh Doctor* | 1973–77 | |
| *Oh Nurse* | 1973–77 | |
| *Oral Connection* | 1973–77 | |
| *Oral Lust* | 1972–74 | |
| *The Payoff* | 1973–77 | |
| *Private Agent* | 1973–77 | |
| *Pursued* | 1973–77 | |
| *Riding Stable* | 1973–77 | |
| *Safari* | 1973–77 | |
| *Schoolgirl Seduction* | 1973–77 | Re-release, also appears on Taboo & Phoenix, Orchid and Teenage Productions. |
| *Sensuous Introduction* | 1973–77 | |
| *Sex Ahoy!* | 1973–77 | |
| *Sex Angle* | 1975–76 | |
| *Sexational* | 1973–77 | |
| *Special Assignment* | 1973–77 | |
| *Spellbound* | 1973–77 | |
| *Temptation* | 1972–73 | |
| *Triangle of Lust* | 1973–77 | |

| Title | Year | Notes |
|---|---|---|
| *Wet Nymph* | 1973–77 | |
| *White Hunter* | 1972–73 | |

## Leidibird

One of the many British labels attempting to pass themselves off as European. Leidibird rollers were issued in brown boxes with gothic-style lettering. The spelling of 'Standard' is incorrect and the text 'Svensk Meid' appears on the side of the box, again evidence of the makers trying to disguise the origin of the label. Only two titles have been located on this label. *My Cue* features a male crossdresser having sex with two other males. *We Had to Do It* also appears on Academy, indicating a possible link with Collingbourne, Darby and Lindsay.

| Title | Year |
|---|---|
| *My Cue* | 1970–72 |
| *We Had to Do It* | 1970–72 |

## Look Films

A Collingbourne label with distinctive branding; the two 'o's' in Look are represented as eyes. Inclusion of both feet and metres suggests that this label may have been distributed internationally or was presented to look as if it originated from Europe. Two titles appear on another Collingbourne label – Double X – and *Carry on Sheik* and *Country Cousins* were also released in Climax boxes, but are likely bootlegs.

| Title | Year | Notes |
|---|---|---|
| *200 Lust* | 1970–72 | |
| *Carry on Sheik* | 1970–72 | Also appears on Climax. |
| *Country Cousins* | 1970–72 | Also appears unbranded and on Climax. |
| *Go Go* | 1970–72 | |

*(Continued)*

| Title | Year | Notes |
|-------|------|-------|
| *I Spy* | 1970–72 | |
| *Miss Whip* | 1970–72 | |
| *Riding Hood* | 1970–72 | |
| *Sam and Belle* | 1970–72 | |
| *Schoolgirl Fun* | 1970–72 | Also appears on Double X. |
| *Schoolgirl Rave* | 1970–72 | Also appears on Double X. |
| *Sexy Sisters* | 1970–72 | |
| *Tour de Love* | 1970–72 | Same performers as *Country Cousins*. |

## Malmo Films

Another late 1960s British label presenting itself as Swedish. Malmo Films followed the same box style as Climax, but used the colour blue instead of orange or green, likely trying to associate themselves with Climax. In Chapter 4, I suggested that Martin Granby could have been involved in this label.

| Title | Year |
|-------|------|
| *Brotherly Love* | 1969–71 |
| *Close Up Orgy* | 1969–71 |
| *Easy Come* | 1969-71 |
| *Fuck My Bum* | 1969–71 |
| *Home from School* | 1969–71 |
| *In My Mouth* | 1969–71 |
| *Office Rape* | 1969–71 |
| *Sarah's Secret* | 1969–71 |
| *School Tramp* | 1969–71 |
| *Sex Machine* | 1969–71 |

## New Private

This list was drawn from a New Private catalogue. The postcards attached to the boxes often use collage, contrasting with other labels. As the list demonstrates, many have emotive titles, referencing rape and focusing heavily on schoolgirls, the latter a common trope in British hard and soft pornography. *Boy Friends* is one of the few instances of hardcore British gay pornography. The label is likely associated with Private Films, which was started in 1966 or 1967, with boxes using a similar red and black colour scheme. Some titles were released in unbranded photo-boxes.

| Title | Year | Notes |
| --- | --- | --- |
| *All Action (Anal) Rape* | 1970–72 | |
| *All Action Sex Orgy* | 1970–72 | |
| *Bathing Time* | 1970–72 | |
| *Black & White Kittens* | 1970–72 | |
| *Boy Friends* | 1970–72 | |
| *The Captive* | 1970–72 | |
| *Close Up Action* | 1970–72 | |
| *Colour Fantasy* | 1970–72 | |
| *Filthy Schoolgirls* | 1970–72 | |
| *Orgy Trip* | 1970–72 | Also appears on Climax; a likely bootleg. |
| *Schoolgirl Dream Orgy* | 1970–72 | |
| *Schoolgirl Dream Orgy No. 2* | 1970–72 | |
| *Schoolgirl Flogged & Raped* | 1970–72 | |
| *Schoolgirl Lesbians* | 1970–72 | |
| *Schoolgirl Lesbians No. 2* | 1970–72 | |
| *Schoolgirl Nightmare* | 1970–72 | Also appears on Climax; a likely bootleg. |
| *Schoolgirls Raped* | 1970–72 | |
| *Schoolgirls Spanked* | 1970–72 | |

(*Continued*)

| Title | Year | Notes |
|-------|------|-------|
| *Two's Company* | 1970–72 | |
| *The Whipping* | 1970–72 | |

## Orchid Film

Another John Darby and John Lindsay collaboration, with Anthony Collingbourne also possibly involved. Orchid appears to have specialized in schoolgirl-themed films, judging from the titles. The rollers are presented in a colourful pink box with the text 'for the discerning collector and connoisseurs' underneath the 'An Orchid Film' brand. As the list shows, titles reappear on other Darby, Lindsay and Collingbourne labels. The version of *Jolly Hockey Sticks* is different to the one later issued on Taboo Films.

| Title | Year | Notes |
|-------|------|-------|
| *And the Rain Came* | 1970–72 | Same performer as Joyride. |
| *Ball on the Lawn* | 1970–72 | |
| *Jolly Hockey Sticks* | 1970–72 | Also appears on Taboo & Phoenix. |
| *My Little Sis* | 1970–72 | |
| *Schoolgirl Incest* | 1970–72 | Also appears on Teenage Productions. |
| *Schoolgirl Seduction* | 1970–72 | Also appears on Taboo & Phoenix, Teenage Productions and Karl Ordinez. |
| *Schoolgirls Seduced* | 1970–72 | Also appears on Teenage Productions. |
| *Sex Adviser* | 1970–72 | Also appears on Anglo Continental. |

## Pearl Films

Like Malmo Films, Pearl Films used the same box design as Climax, but with the colour red. Only two films have been identified on this label; both have no titles.

On one box, the image is directly printed on to the front and is a collage of images taken from what appears to be a number of different films, similar to the style of New Private. The title I viewed was issued in Super 8, suggesting an early 1970s date, and looked to have been filmed in a cottage in Europe.

## Phoenix International

A collaboration between John Darby and John Lindsay, Phoenix International represents a move to a more ambitious box design, with a colour image printed on to the front of the box. The branding is printed on the rear, and the text 'Produced in Germany' features on the side of the box. A German description of the film is provided on the rear, underneath the English description. Four of the titles – *Alpine Lust*, *Artic Fuck*, *High Society* and *Tyrolean Love* – were filmed in or around the Alps, and an edit of *High Society* later appears on the German label Amorette Film under the title *Alpenglühen* (*Alpine Glow*), with sound. Another label named 'Euro-Vision Associates' issued *High Society*, while *Dr No* was also released by 'Blue Boy Films'. Both of these are likely bootleg outfits or further attempts at branding. Most titles were also published on the other Darby and Lindsay label Taboo & Phoenix.

| Title | Year | Notes |
|---|---|---|
| *Alpine Lust* | 1970–72 | Also appears on Taboo & Phoenix. |
| *Artic Fuck* | 1970–72 | Also appears on Taboo & Phoenix. |
| *Black Magic* | 1970–72 | Also appears on Taboo & Phoenix. |
| *Convent School* | 1970–72 | Also appears on Taboo & Phoenix. |
| *Dr No* | 1970–72 | Also appears on Taboo & Phoenix. |
| *Hay Ride* | 1970–72 | Also appears on Karl Ordinez and Gatsby. |
| *High Society* | 1970–72 | Also appears on Taboo & Phoenix. |
| *Jungle Beat* | 1970–72 | Also appears on Taboo & Phoenix. |
| *Live Bait* | 1970–72 | Also appears on Taboo & Phoenix. |
| *Two's Up* | 1970–72 | Also appears on Taboo & Phoenix. |
| *Tyrolean Love* | 1970–72 | |

## Playboy Classic

Only three titles on this label were discovered. Kinsey dates Playboy Classic to 1966–67, making it one of the early attempts to follow Climax in branding their releases. Unlike other roller labels, Playboy Classic printed directly on their boxes, giving them a more professional look. 'Big' John English appears in *Caught*.

| Title | Year |
|---|---|
| *Black and White Frolics* | 1966–67 |
| *Caught* | 1966–67 |
| *Country Watcher* (parts 1 and 2) | 1966–67 |

## Playboy Films

Seemingly unrelated to Playboy Classic, Playboy Films shares similarities with Blue Scene Films, re-releasing older rollers and producing newer films that were likely made in Denmark. The brown-coloured outer sleeve has 'Playboy Film' printed at the top in red, while the reel is held in a plastic flip box. Length of film is given in both imperial and metric, indicating British and European distribution. Titles are listed on the rear of the box in English, German and French. A Lyngby, Denmark post box address is also given. The Adult Loop Database suggests that this label could be related to Sven Nielsen's Danish 8mm label 'Delhi', which first appeared in 1963. The Lyngby-based Nielsen, who published the glamour magazines *Vue* and *Varieté*, also owned a film laboratory and is said to have 'helped the gentlemen of Soho' to 'process and duplicate' rollers (Hebditch and Anning 1988: 78). Given that Playboy Films re-released some early British rollers, it seems plausible that Nielsen had some involvement with this label.

| Title | Year | Notes |
|---|---|---|
| *no title* | 1967–71 | |
| *Big John Cocker* | 1967–71 | Appears to be a re-release of an American loop starring a young John Holmes. |
| *Caught!* | 1966–67 | |
| *A Date in Bed* | 1969–71 | |

| Title | Year | Notes |
|-------|------|-------|
| *The Doctor Treatment* | 1967–71 | |
| *The Hotel Room* | 1971 | |
| *Initiation* | 1969–72 | |
| *The Loved Ones* | 1967 | |
| *More Suds and Sex* | 1967–68 | Also appears on Blue Scene Films. |
| *The Piano* | 1971 | |
| *Rape* | 1969–72 | |
| *Ring Me* | 1968 | |
| *Romantic Maid* | 1967–71 | Box feature shows same performers as *Surprise Reward*. |
| *A Walk in the Woods* | 1968 | |
| *The Whip* | 1967–71 | |
| *The Wild Lovers* | 1967–71 | |
| *The Youngsters* | 1969 | |

## Private Films

According to the Kinsey Institute, Private Films began releasing in 1966, making them one of the earliest labels to brand. They issued films in red and white boxes. *Shower Nymph* is presented in a different style of box, closely resembling the design of Amor, Climax and Malmo Films, but having a red background and featuring the text – 'Made in Sweden'. This could possibly be a different label, attempting to reference Berth Milton's *Private* magazine that was published in Sweden. New Private appears to be a later incarnation, also using the same colour scheme for their boxes. 'Big' John English stars in *Kinky Scene*.

| Title | Year |
|-------|------|
| *Behind Bars* | 1966–69 |
| *Black & White Kittens* | 1966–69 |
| *Kinky Scene* | 1966–69 |
| *The Maid's Lover* | 1969 |
| *Nurse's Delight* | 1969 |
| *The Patient* | 1969 |
| *Severe Mistress* | 1966 |
| *Shower Nymph* | 1968 |
| *The Young Nurse* | 1969 |

## Pussy Film

The Kinsey Institute identify the film *Office Sex* as British, naming the label as Pussy Films and dating it as 1970–72. This is not a label I have discovered, but include it here for posterity.

## Queen of Hearts

An interviewee named 'Derek' claimed that he made rollers in the early 1960s under the brand Queen of Hearts. As mentioned in Chapter 2, he stated that his films were issued in a box with a queen of hearts playing card on the front, making them an early attempt at branding. Unfortunately, Derek was vague with dates and only recalled one title – *Peeping Tom* – out of six. No rollers on this label have yet been uncovered.

## Royal Film Productions

Royal Film Productions appear to be a British-based production team making hardcore films for distribution on the continent. With Mike Hunter (aka Gerd Wasmund) and Lasse Braun using British crews for their productions around the same period, it could be that the same teams were producing for Royal Films. When I interviewed Wasmund, he explained how he employed professional freelance British crews to make the films he released through his Mike

Hunter brand, many of whom were making documentaries and other productions, but having a side-line in hardcore. Issue 12 of the Swedish pornography magazine *Ero* documents the making of a hardcore film in London. Photographs show the location – the Hotel Sheraton, London – and the performers. These match the film *Friendly Flatmates*, with the accompanying text naming the producer as 'Ralph' and noting that the lighting expert also worked for the BBC. This dates the film to 1975. The performers in Royal Film Productions also feature in John Lindsay rollers, indicating that the same modelling agency was used to source talent. All films are presented in colour and on the Super 8 format.

| Title | Year |
|---|---|
| *The Burglars* | 1975–78 |
| *The Cream* | 1975–78 |
| *Friendly Flatmates* | 1975 |
| *The Heats On* | 1975–78 |

## Steinle Filme

Similar to Leidibird, Steinle Filme attempts to disguise themselves by using a European sounding name. Compared with other roller boxes, Steinle Filme used a flimsier cardboard box. Only two titles have been identified. *Joyride* also appears on Academy, indicating a possible link to Collingbourne, Darby and maybe Lindsay, being an early attempt at a label.

| Title | Year |
|---|---|
| *Joyride* | 1970–72 |
| *My Dad* | 1970–72 |

## Svensk Films

Appearing towards the end of the 1960s, Svensk Films follows Malmo, Leidibird and Steinle in using European sounding name. In Chapter 4, I proposed that Martin Granby was likely involved with this label, as he admitted in a police interview to using labels with Scandinavian sounding names. The boxes are generic red photo boxes, similar to the basic presentation used by Dolly Films, which also issued *Anchor's Away*. The postcard for *Rear End* uses a collage-style image, contrasting with others.

| Title | Year | Notes |
| --- | --- | --- |
| *Anchors Away* | 1968–69 | Also appears on Dolly Films. |
| *Groovy* | 1968–69 | |
| *A Lesson in French* | 1968–69 | Also appears on Danish Blu Films and Universal Films. |
| *Rear End* | 1968–69 | |

## Taboo

It seems that Taboo was John Lindsay's final label, recalling the branding he and Darby used in the early 1970s, his sex shops and cinema clubs and possibly referencing Walter Bartkowski's (aka Charlie Brown) 'Tabu' brand for which Lindsay shot several films. As I mentioned in Chapter 5, the label shows a move towards higher quality packing, generally using gatefold style boxes with a plastic wallet containing the cover. I have only located three titles on this label, but there are likely to be more. *Jolly Hockey Sticks* is a remake of an earlier Lindsay film that appeared on Orchid and Taboo & Phoenix. Taboo Films releases are sought after by collectors and rarely appear on the second-hand market. All releases are colour, Super 8.

| Title | Year |
| --- | --- |
| *Boarding School* | 1973–78 |
| *End of Term* | 1973–78 |
| *Health Farm* | 1973–78 |
| *Jolly Hockey Sticks* | 1973–78 |

## Taboo & Phoenix Productions

Another John Darby and John Lindsay collaboration, Taboo & Phoenix followed Excelsior Films, appearing alongside Anglo Continental, Orchid, Phoenix International, Taboo of Sweden and Teenage Productions. Taboo & Phoenix titles reappear on all of these labels, showing Darby's intent to dominate the growing economy. Films are presented in the typical photo-boxes, but always use colour photographs.

| Title | Year | Notes |
|---|---|---|
| *100% Nymph* | 1970–72 | Also appears on Karl Ordinez and Taboo of Sweden. |
| *Alpine Lust* | 1970–72 | Also appears on Phoenix International. |
| *Artic Fuck* | 1970–72 | Also appears on Phoenix International. |
| *Black Magic* | 1970–72 | Also appears on Phoenix International. |
| *Bound, Whipped and Raped* | 1970–72 | |
| *Caged, Bound and Raped* | 1970–72 | |
| *Convent School* | 1970–72 | Also appears on Phoenix International. |
| *Dr No* | 1970–72 | Also appears on Phoenix International. |
| *Family Planning* | 1970–72 | |
| *Hi Fi Sex* | 1970–72 | |
| *High Society* | 1970–72 | Also appears on Phoenix International and Amorette Films. |
| *HP Man* | 1970–72 | Also appears on Taboo of Sweden. |
| *Jail Bait* | 1970–72 | |
| *Jolly Hockey Sticks* | 1970–72 | Also appears on Orchid. |
| *Jungle Beat* | 1970–72 | Also appears on Phoenix International. |
| *Kinky Vicar* | 1970–72 | Also appears on Anglo Continental and Excelsior Films. |
| *Lingerie Party* | 1970–72 | |
| *Live Bait* | 1970–72 | Also appears on Phoenix International and Amorette Films. |
| *Maneaters* | 1970–72 | |
| *Monks Orgy* | 1970–72 | Also appears on Taboo of Sweden. |
| *Nurses Orgy* | 1970–72 | |

| Title | Year | Notes |
|---|---|---|
| *Nympho Artist* | 1970–72 | Also appears on Excelsior Films. |
| *Nympho Nurses* | 1970–72 | |
| *Paradise Bay* | 1970–72 | Also appears on Anglo Continental. |
| *Pussy* | 1970–72 | |
| *Riding School* | 1970–72 | |
| *Sailor's Ahoy* | 1970–72 | Also appears on Excelsior. |
| *Satan and the Virgin* | 1970–72 | |
| *Schoolgirl Pussy* | 1970–72 | Also appears on Teenage Productions. |
| *Schoolgirl Seduction* | 1970–72 | Also appears on Karl Ordinez, Orchid and Taboo & Phoenix. |
| *Schoolgirl Sex* | 1970–72 | |
| *Seduction* | 1970–72 | Also appears on Anglo Continental. |
| *Sultan's Haram* | 1970–72 | |
| *Surprise Visitor* | 1970–72 | Also appears on Anglo Continental. |
| *Two's Up* | 1970–72 | Also appears on Phoenix International. |

## Taboo of Sweden/Taboo Films of Sweden

Darby and Lindsay issued at least nineteen titles on this label. Like Phoenix International, colour images are printed on to the box, which uses a yellow and black colour scheme. The text 'Eastman Colour' is presented on the one side of the box, indicating that the films were shot on this film stock, and 'Pornography for the Connoisseur' on the other. A description of the film is given on the rear of the box, as well as a catalogue number, and is accompanied by the text 'Taboo Films are made by professionals with some of the most beautiful girls in Scandinavia giving you lots of action and very good close-ups'. From the content of two films I have seen, it appears that the films were usually shot in Britain with British performers. *HP Man* was later reissued by the German label Amorette as *Herrenbesuch* (*Men's Visit*).

| Title | Year | Cat | Notes |
|---|---|---|---|
| *100% Nymph* | 1970–72 | 19 | Also appears on Taboo & Phoenix and Karl Ordinez. |
| *Bound, Whipped and Raped* | 1970–72 | [no cat] | Also appears on Taboo & Phoenix. |
| *Family Planning* | 1970–72 | 9 | Also appears on Taboo & Phoenix. |
| *HP Man* | 1970–72 | 8 | Also appears on Taboo & Phoenix and Amorette Film under the title *Herrenbesuch*. |
| *Lingerie Party* | 1970–72 | 10 | *Also appears on Taboo & Phoenix.* |
| *Monks Orgy* | 1970–72 | 3 | Also appears on Taboo & Phoenix. |
| *Nympho Nuns* | 1970–72 | 1 | |
| *Sultan's Harem* | 1970–72 | 6 | Also appears on Taboo & Phoenix. |
| *Vicar's Fantasy* | 1970–72 | 4 | |

## Tarantula

A label initially discovered in the Kinsey archive, Tarantula appears to be an early attempt at branding, but without boxes. Only two Tarantula titles have surfaced, belonging to one collector. They were not in original boxes and printed on Gevaert stock, prior to them becoming Agfa-Gevaert in 1964, suggesting that they were produced around this period. It is also possible that the films were printed on older stock and could have appeared later. Two titles imply a French origin, though Kinsey identifies *Eve and the Serpent* as British.

| Title | Year |
|---|---|
| *Eve and the Serpent* | 1965–67 |
| *La Maitresse Cruelle and Sa Esclaf* | 1960–65 |
| *La Service Privee* | 1960–65 |

## Teenage Productions

Jones (2007: 123) notes that 'the depiction of schoolgirls as sexual agents' was a common theme in British pornography of the late 1960s and early 1970s. Teenage Productions, yet another collaboration between Darby and Lindsay, specialized in releasing schoolgirl-themed pornography. As Hunter (2013: 117) points out, the performers appear to be well over 18, although some of the films were shot in a Birmingham school for added verisimilitude, which led to Lindsay's eventual arrest and a well-publicized obscenity trial (see Chapter 5). The early green boxes are in keeping with Darby's typical brightly coloured packaging with colour photography on the front. Later boxes moved to a black box with colour photograph printed on the front, the brand 'Teenage Productions' presented in a small box at the top. English text on the rear of the box describes the title, with French and German translations also provided, indicating that this may have been transnationally distributed. Titles appear on other Darby and Lindsay labels.

| Title | Year | Notes |
|---|---|---|
| 100 Lines | 1970–73 | |
| Anal Rape | 1970–73 | Also appears on Karl Ordinez. |
| Collection Day | 1970–73 | |
| College Rape | 1970–73 | |
| Juvenile Sex | 1970–73 | |
| Lust after School | 1970–73 | |
| School Art Lesson | 1972–73 | |
| School Teacher's Pussy | 1970–73 | |
| Schoolgirl Gym Lesson | 1970–73 | |
| Schoolgirl Incest | 1970–73 | Also appears on Orchid. |
| Schoolgirl Joyride | 1970–73 | |
| Schoolgirl Medical | 1970–73 | |
| Schoolgirl Pussy | 1970–73 | Also appears on Taboo & Phoenix. |
| Schoolgirl Seduction | 1970–73 | |
| Schoolgirls Medical | 1970–73 | |
| Schoolgirls Seduced | 1970–73 | Also appears on Orchid. |

| Title | Year | Notes |
|---|---|---|
| *Sex Kitten* | 1970–73 | |
| *Sex Lessons at School* | 1970–73 | |

## United Productions

Discovered in Kinsey's catalogue, United Productions is identified as a British title with listings for three titles. This label did not appear in any private collection.

| Title | Year |
|---|---|
| *Friendship* | 1971 |
| *Opening Night* | 1971 |
| *Out Late Again* | 1971 |

## Universal Films

Next to Climax, Universal Films released the second most titles under an individual label. I discussed Universal Films at length in Chapter 4, associating it with Martin Granby. Rollers appear in three different coloured boxes – white, purple and black – with the latter two colours having the text 'Made in Denmark' on the front of the box. The box design contrasts with all other boxes, featuring small glamour portraits on the left- and right-hand sides and is more akin to type of boxes used by commercial 8mm distributor Mountain Films. Universal re-released titles issued by Candy Films, Dolly Films and Svensk Films. Danish Blu Films also issued some of the titles, possibly being a later iteration of Universal Films given the quality of the boxes used. As the list shows, Universal Films released a diverse range of content.

| Title | Year | Notes |
|---|---|---|
| *77* | 1970–72 | |
| *81* | 1970–72 | |

*(Continued)*

| Title | Year | Notes |
|---|---|---|
| *3 for Sex* | 1970–72 | |
| *6 for Sex* | 1970–72 | |
| *8 For Sex* | 1970–72 | Also appears on Danish Blu Films. |
| *Anal Sex* | 1970–72 | Also appears on Danish Blu Films and Candy Films. |
| *Anal-fuck* | 1972 | |
| *Asian Lust* | 1970–72 | |
| *Beach Boys* | 1970–72 | |
| *Bed & Breakfast* | 1970–72 | |
| *The Boy Friend* | 1970–72 | |
| *Butch and Bitch* | 1970–72 | |
| *Canine Lust* | 1970–72 | |
| *Canine Orgy* | 1970–72 | |
| *Child's Play* | 1970–72 | |
| *Chinese and Passion* | 1970–72 | |
| *Drunken Whore* | 1970–72 | |
| *Exclusive Love* | 1970–72 | |
| *Fantasia* | 1972 | |
| *Gayland* | 1970–72 | |
| *Gymslip* | 1970–72 | |
| *Heavy Hippy* | 1972 | |
| *Hot Stuff* | 1970–72 | |
| *Keep It Clean* | 1970–72 | Also appears on Danish Blu Films. |
| *Kinky Bit* | 1970–72 | |
| *Lady Without Washer* | 1972 | |
| *Late Comer* | 1972 | Also appears on Candy Films. |
| *Lesbo* | 1970–72 | Also appears on Danish Blu Films. |
| *A Lesson in French* | 1970–72 | Also appears on Danish Blu Films and Svensk Films. |

| Title | Year | Notes |
|---|---|---|
| *Maidservant* | 1970–72 | Also appears on Danish Blu Films and Dolly Films. |
| *Mixed-Doubles* | 1972 | |
| *Negro* | 1970–72 | |
| *No Time for Tea* | 1970–72 | |
| *Orgasmic Scene* | 1972 | |
| *Peek a Boo* | 1970–72 | |
| *Play* | 1970–72 | |
| *Plaything* | 1970–72 | Also appears on Dolly Films. |
| *Porno Plunge* | 1970–72 | |
| *Randy Chick* | 1970–72 | |
| *Rape!* | 1970–72 | |
| *Rear Guard Action* | 1970–72 | |
| *Rex and Rover* | 1970–72 | |
| *Romeo and Juliet* | 1970–72 | |
| *Session* | 1970–72 | |
| *Sex Maniac* | 1970–72 | |
| *Sex Pots* | 1970–72 | Also appears on Dolly Films. |
| *Sextet* | 1970–72 | |
| *Snatch* | 1970–72 | |
| *Sons and Lovers* | 1970–72 | |
| *Spank Spank* | 1970–72 | |
| *Spunky Trio* | 1970–72 | Also appears on Danish Blu Films. |
| *Stolen Climax* | 1970–72 | |
| *Strip for Sex* | 1970–72 | |
| *Surprise! TV* | 1970–72 | |
| *The Toilet Lover* | 1970–72 | |

*(Continued)*

| Title | Year | Notes |
|---|---|---|
| *The Trespass* | 1970–72 | |
| *Violent Wedding* (part 1) | 1970–72 | |
| *Violent Wedding* (part 2) | 1970–72 | |
| *The Victim* | 1970–72 | |
| *A Walk in the Wood* | 1970–72 | |
| *Women in Love* | 1972 | |
| *Young Dream* | 1970–72 | |

## Venus Films

Mick Muldoon/Mike Freeman's second label, appearing in 1967. Venus Films seems to have mainly put out new titles, but only in black and white. Boxes were issued in purple, bright pink and red colours, with a distinctive font and the usual postcard glued to front. 'Big' John English appears in *Perverts Party 2*.

| Title | Year | Notes |
|---|---|---|
| *Buggery Unlimited* | 1967–69 | |
| *Daughter Defiled* | 1967–69 | |
| *Degenerates Orgy* | 1967–69 | Also released on Action Films. |
| *Dr No* | 1967–69 | |
| *Dr No 2* | 1969 | |
| *More Three's Company* | 1969 | |
| *Perverts Party 1* | 1967–69 | |
| *Perverts Party 2* | 1969 | |
| *Schoolgirl Fuck* | 1967–69 | |
| *Sex School* | 1967–69 | |

| Title | Year | Notes |
|---|---|---|
| *Sex Triangle* | 1967–69 | |
| *Sexation* | 1967–69 | Re-release of an Eros Films title. |
| *Sexgirls* | 1967–69 | |
| *Sexy Susan* | 1967–69 | |
| *The Snatchers* | 1967–69 | |
| *The Snatchers 2* | 1967–69 | |
| *Three's Company* | 1967–69 | |

## Viking Films

This list has been generated from a catalogue provided by a collector. Police files pertaining to the Watford Blue Movie Trial identify this label as belonging to Collingbourne and Darby. Rollers from Viking Films rarely appeared in collections, suggesting limited circulation. It is worth noting that the titles are often highly emotive, as were the descriptions of the films in the catalogue. The catalogue states that titles were available on 8mm and Super 8, and the use of metres before feet implies that the catalogue was intended for European retailers. Boxes are dark green with the usual black and white postcard image on the front. On the back of the box, a list of nine titles is given.

| Title | Year |
|---|---|
| *Nazi Brutality* | 1970–72 |
| *Nurse Buggery* | 1970–72 |
| *Pervert's Mass Orgy* (part 1) | 1970–72 |
| *Pervert's Mass Orgy* (part 2) | 1970–72 |
| *The Plummers and the Schoolgirl* | 1970–72 |
| *Repetitional Lessons in Sex* | 1970–72 |

*(Continued)*

| Title | Year |
|---|---|
| *Schoolgirl Anal Initiation* | 1970–72 |
| *Schoolgirl Kidnapped* | 1970–72 |
| *Swinging Schoolgirls* | 1970–72 |
| *The Young Ones* | 1970–72 |

## Zodiac Films

Another John Darby and John Lindsay enterprise, as indicated in the files relating to the Watford Blue Movie Trial. Only two films have been located – *Nympho Artist* and *Sex Hit*. The packaging looks professional and more similar to those used on the continent, having a black box with the brand 'Zodiac Films' in green text above a colour image printed directly on to the box. The rear contains a summary of the film and a catalogue number ('No. 4' for *Nympho Artist*).

## Unknown

What follows is a list of British titles identified in Di Lauro and Rabkin (1976) and Kinsey's archive that I have not personally discovered in any of the collections I accessed. Some of these could be branded titles. I have excluded seven nameless rollers that did not have headers or a title from the list. Note that two titles can be dated back to the 1930s and 1940s, possibly being early examples of British hardcore. Both of these 16mm films can be accessed at the Kinsey Institute.

| Title | Year | Notes |
|---|---|---|
| *100% Desire* | 1966–68 | |
| *2nd Hand Rose* | 1967 | |
| *AC/DC* | 1969 | |

| Title | Year | Notes |
|---|---|---|
| *Action Man* | 1970–79 | Same producer as *In the Woods*, *Nightshift*, *Passionate Girl*, *Teaching Pleasure* and *Difficulties Overcome*. |
| *African Intruder* | 1966–67 | |
| *After School Earnings* | 1963–66 | |
| *After the Wedding* | 1968 | |
| *All at Once* | 1970–72 | |
| *Amorous Lesbians* | 1966 | |
| *An Evening at Home* | 1960–66 | |
| *Art Show* | 1970–72 | |
| *Au Pair Rape* | 1965–66 | |
| *Auto Sapho* | 1965–66 | |
| *Bad Session* | 1965–67 | |
| *Banana Split* | 1966–67 | |
| *Barber's Shop* | 1969–71 | |
| *Bathing with the Boys* | 1968 | |
| *Be Prepared* | 1966–67 | |
| *Bed Session* | 1965–67 | |
| *Beyond the Sunset* | 1965–67 | |
| *Bi-Sexuals* | 1967 | |
| *Big Nose* | 1969–71 | |
| *The Big Tip* | 1969 | |
| *Bisexual Buggery* | 1969 | |
| *Black and White Orgy* | 1969 | |
| *Black Beast* | 1967–68 | |
| *Black Bubbles* | 1964–67 | |
| *Black Mac* | 1964–67 | |

*(Continued)*

| Title | Year | Notes |
|---|---|---|
| *Black Power* | 1968–70 | |
| *Blackmail* | 1966 | |
| *Blackpussy* | 1969 | |
| *Bottle Me Darling* | 1966–67 | |
| *The Boyfriend* | 1969 | |
| *Bridgette* | 1969 | |
| *Captive* | 1965–67 | |
| *Carpet Layer* | 1968 | |
| *Christmas Dreams* | 1970–71 | |
| *Closely Related* | 1965–66 | |
| *Coloured Rainbow* | 1964–66 | |
| *Daddy* | 1970–71 | |
| *Dancing Teacher* | 1966 | |
| *Difficulties Overcome* | 1970–79 | Same producer as *In the Woods*, *Nightshift*, *Passionate Girl*, *Teaching Pleasure* and *Action Man*. |
| *Dildo Delight* | 1969–71 | |
| *Do-It-Yourself* | 1966 | |
| *Doctor's House Call* | 1970–72 | |
| *Dog Fun* | 1968 | |
| *Domination of Justine* | 1965–67 | |
| *Don't Come Back* | 1966–67 | |
| *Double Dildo* | 1969–71 | |
| *Dress Maker* | 1968 | |
| *Dusky Maid* | 1969 | |
| *E Plonkit (Masseur)* | 1969 | |

| Title | Year | Notes |
|---|---|---|
| *Easiest Way* | 1930–35 | 16mm. Di Lauro and Rabkin identify this as British and from the 1920s, though Kinsey dates it at 1930–35. |
| *English Joys* | 1940–43 | 16mm. |
| *English Model* | 1962–66 | |
| *Erotica* | 1966–67 | |
| *Evening at Home* | 1960–66 | |
| *Evening in June* | 1968 | |
| *Fake Rape* | 1967–68 | |
| *A Family Affair* | 1964–66 | |
| *Father and Daughter* | 1966 | |
| *Four's Company* | 1968 | |
| *Friend of the Young One* | 1964–66 | |
| *Fun and Games* | 1968 | |
| *Giant killer #1* | 1963–65 | |
| *Giant killer #2* | 1963–65 | |
| *Girl Farm* | 1968–70 | |
| *Girlfriends* | 1969 | |
| *Good Neighbours* | | |
| *Her Daughter Raped* | 1964–66 | |
| *Her Maid Raped* | 1966–67 | |
| *Her Victim* | 1966–67 | |
| *Hitch Hiker* | 1965–67 | |
| *Home from School* | 1963–66 | |
| *Home Type* | 1969 | |
| *Hungry* | 1968 | |
| *I Like Monday* | 1968 | |
| *I Want Two* | 1967–68 | |

(*Continued*)

| Title | Year | Notes |
|---|---|---|
| *In the Woods* | 1970–79 | Same producer as *Passionate Girl*, *Teaching Pleasure*, *Difficulties Overcome* and *Action Man*. |
| *Indian Giver* | 1958–62 | |
| *Inventation* | 1968 | |
| *Invitation* | 1968 | |
| *Just Sex* | 1969 | |
| *Kinky Lovers* | 1966–67 | |
| *Ladies Night* | 1969 | |
| *Last Exit* | 1966–68 | |
| *Legs First* | 1967–68 | |
| *Les Delight* | 1967 | |
| *Lesbian Desires* | 1966–67 | |
| *The Lesbian Trio* | 1965–66 | |
| *A Little Bird Told Me* | 1962–68 | |
| *Love Expert* | 1964–66 | |
| *Love In* | 1969 | |
| *Lucky Break* | 1964–66 | |
| *Lunch in the Wood* | 1970–71 | |
| *Making the Maid* | 1965–66 | |
| *More Black and White Orgy* | 1969 | |
| *More Fucking and Sucking* | 1968 | |
| *More Fun and Games* | 1964–66 | |
| *Mother and Daughter* | 1960–66 | |
| *Mother and Daughter* | 1965–67 | |
| *Mr Pilgrim's Progress* | 1966–67 | |

| Title | Year | Notes |
|---|---|---|
| *My Love* | 1969 | |
| *My Young Sister* | 1966 | |
| *Nightshift* | 1970–79 | Same producer as *Nightshift, Passionate Girl, Teaching Pleasure, Difficulties Overcome* and *Action Man.* |
| *No Short Measure* | 1968 | |
| *No Viewing* | 1968 | |
| *Nurse Penny and Co.* | 1966–67 | |
| *Nymph* | 1969 | |
| *One for Two* | 1966 | |
| *Orgy* | 1967 | |
| *The Other Young Ones* | 1964–66 | |
| *Our Thing* | 1970–72 | |
| *Out of Town* | 1966–67 | |
| *Passionate Girl* | 1970–79 | Same producer as *In the Woods, Nightshift, Teaching Pleasure, Difficulties Overcome* and *Action Man.* |
| *The Payoff* | | |
| *Penny's Birthday Party* (part 1) | 1966–67 | |
| *Penny's Birthday Party* (part 2) | 1966–67 | |
| *Personal Touch* | 1966–68 | |
| *Phantom Fucker* | 1965 | |
| *Photo Session* | 1964–66 | |
| *Pick of the Crop* | 1968–72 | |
| *Playboy Love* | 1970–71 | |
| *Poodled* | 1968 | |
| *Private Sec* | | |

(*Continued*)

| Title | Year | Notes |
|---|---|---|
| *Private Tutor* | 1960–64 | |
| *Private Tutor* | 1965–66 | |
| *Punishment* | 1966 | |
| *Punishment* | 1964–66 | |
| *Punishment for Naughty Girls* | 1968 | |
| *Rape in the Dark Wood* | | |
| *Round Robin* | 1962–66 | |
| *The Sacrifice* | 1964–67 | |
| *Saturday Night* | 1970–71 | |
| *Schoolgirl* | 1965–67 | |
| *Schoolgirl Fucked I* | 1968 | |
| *Schoolgirl Fucked II* | 1968 | |
| *Schoolgirl Holiday* | | |
| *Schoolgirl Rape* | 1964–66 | |
| *Schoolgirl Rape 2* | 1964–66 | |
| *Schoolgirl's Dream* | 1964–66 | |
| *Scrabble* | | |
| *Second Hand Rose* | 1966–68 | |
| *The Secretary* | 1966–67 | |
| *Seducing Susan* | 1966–67 | |
| *Seduction* | 1964–66 | |
| *Sex Flight* | 1968 | |
| *Sex for Three* | 1964–66 | |
| *Sex Plantation* (part 1) | 1965–67 | |
| *Sex Plantation* (part 2) | 1965–67 | |

| Title | Year | Notes |
|---|---|---|
| *Sex Plot* | 1966 | |
| *The Sex Pot* | 1966 | |
| *Sex Therapist* | 1965–66 | |
| *Sexy School 2* | 1969 | |
| *Sexy School I* | 1969 | |
| *Sister-in-Law* | 1965–67 | |
| *Slave Girls* | 1968 | |
| *Slave of the Beast* | 1965–67 | |
| *Sock It to Me* | 1966–68 | |
| *Spanking for Three* | | |
| *Spunk Orgy* | 1968–70 | |
| *Stallion* | 1966–67 | |
| *Strange Love* | 1966–67 | |
| *Suds and Sex* | 1966–68 | May be linked to the unbranded *More Suds and Sex*. |
| *Surprise* | 1964–66 | |
| *Take It Down* | | |
| *Teaching Pleasure* | 1970–79 | Same producer as *In the Woods*, *Nightshift*, *Passionate Girl*, *Difficulties Overcome* and *Action Man*. |
| *Teaching the Teacher* | 1968 | |
| *Teenage Ecstasy* | 1965–66 | |
| *Teenage Orgy* | 1968–70 | |
| *Teenage Party* | 1966–67 | |
| *Teenage Rape* | 1968–70 | |
| *Thank You Girl* | 1966–67 | |
| *Tillie* | 1966–67 | |
| *Tom and Jerry* | 1966–67 | |

| Title | Year | Notes |
|---|---|---|
| *Tomboy* (parts 1 and 2) | 1958–63 | |
| *Tri-sexual* | 1966–67 | |
| *Two for the Price of One* | 1968 | |
| *Two Holes in One* | 1968 | |
| *Two Into One* | | |
| *Voyeurs Only* | 1968 | |
| *The Waiter* | 1966–67 | |
| *Wake Up to Sex* | | |
| *Water Babe* | 1969 | |
| *Wedding Night* | 1963–66 | |
| *Wedding Night for Three* | 1969 | |
| *Welcome Stranger* | 1966 | |
| *The Whore* | 1966–68 | |
| *Wrong Room* | 1965–67 | |
| *Young Lovers* | 1968 | |

## Unknown John Lindsay titles

I have been unable to associate nine John Lindsay films with labels. Most of these films were named in newspaper coverage of the Birmingham Obscenity Trial. Given that the titles relate to schoolgirls, I expect that these were issued on the Teenage Productions label. Other possible labels are suggested below.

| Title | Year | Notes |
|---|---|---|
| *Desire* | | Possibly a Karl Ordinez title. |
| *Girl Guide Temptation* | | Possibly a Teenage Productions title. |

| Title | Year | Notes |
|-------|------|-------|
| *Girl Guides Misfortune* | | Possibly a Teenage Productions title. |
| *Naughty Schoolgirls* | | Possibly a Teenage Productions title. |
| *No Man's Land* | | Possibly a Karl Ordinez title; the photograph on the unbranded box suggests that this could have been filmed at the same location as *Safari* and *White Hunter*. |
| *School Sex Lessons* | 1972–73 | Possibly a Teenage Productions title. |
| *Sex after School* | | Possibly a Teenage Productions title. |

## *Continental market*

This list attempts to collect titles made by British filmmakers for different European labels. In Chapter 5, I considered how continental labels regularly employed British filmmakers such as John Lindsay and George Harrison Marks to produce content. John Fortune is another Brit who appears on this list and the name may be a pseudonym for filmmaker Russell Gay, whose label Venus Films released glamour in the 1960s. In the late 1970s, his Mistral and Astral labels released 'near beer' Super 8 pornography for the British market. It appears that some of these titles were also issued as hardcore versions on the continent. For example, the Astral film *Black Desire* appears as *Black Mystique* (John Fortune 1979–80) on Walter Bartkowski's label Tabu de Luxe. I have also included films made in Britain by European pornographers such as Lasse Braun and Gerd Wasmund (aka Mike Hunter). Films made in Europe with British performers have not been included. It has been constructed by drawing on information found at the Adult Loop Database and the George Harrison Mark's website www.thekameraclub.co.uk. It is by no means exhaustive. For instance, John Lindsay claims that he filmed for numerous international labels, including working in North America, though there is little evidence to support this. An issue of the Dutch magazine *Chick* names Lindsay as the maker of their line of films.

| Title | Year | Label | Cat | Country | Filmmaker | Notes |
|---|---|---|---|---|---|---|
| *Aktmalerei* | | Amorette Film | AM-1 | Germany | John Lindsay | |
| *Alpenglühen* | | Amorette Film | AM-3 | Germany | John Lindsay | Colour re-release of *High Society*. |
| *Herrenbesuch* | | Amorette Film | AM-11 | Germany | John Lindsay | Re-release of *HP Man*. |
| *Petri-Heil* | | Amorette Film | AM-4 | Germany | John Lindsay | Colour re-release of *Livebait*. |
| *Primanerliebe* | | Amorette Film | AM-3 | Germany | John Lindsay | |
| *Turnstunde* | 1978 | Amorette Film | AM-9 | Germany | John Lindsay | |
| *Wäsche-Party* | 1975 | Amorette Film | AM-8 | Germany | John Lindsay | |
| *Big Cook – Big Tits* | | Beauty Film | 1425 | Sweden | Unknown | |
| *Big Tit Dreamer* | 1981 | Beauty Film | 2452 | Denmark | Unknown | Produced by the Theander Brothers. |
| *Lusty Lechers* | 1981 | Beauty Film | 2441 | Denmark | Unknown | Produced by the Theander Brothers. |
| *At the Office* | 1971–73 | Chick Films | | Denmark/ Netherlands | John Lindsay | Produced by Joop Wilhelmus. |
| | | | | | | Published in Denmark by Topsy Forlaget. |
| *Café Sex* | 1971–73 | Chick Films | | Denmark/ Netherlands | John Lindsay | Produced by Joop Wilhelmus. |
| | | | | | | Published in Denmark by Topsy Forlaget. |

| Title | Year | Label | Cat | Country | Filmmaker | Notes |
|---|---|---|---|---|---|---|
| *Chick Mix of Sex* | 1971–73 | Chick Films | | Denmark/Netherlands | John Lindsay | Produced by Joop Wilhelmus. Published in Denmark by Topsy Forlaget. |
| *Chick-Club Orgy (part 1)* | 1971–73 | Chick Films | | Denmark/Netherlands | John Lindsay | Produced by Joop Wilhelmus. Published in Denmark by Topsy Forlaget. |
| *Having a Sexy Drink* | 1971–73 | Chick Films | | Denmark/Netherlands | John Lindsay | Produced by Joop Wilhelmus. Published in Denmark by Topsy Forlaget. |
| *Playing the Guitar* | 1971–73 | Chick Films | | Denmark/Netherlands | John Lindsay | Produced by Joop Wilhelmus. Published in Denmark by Topsy Forlaget. |
| *Sexy Young Lesbians* | 1971–73 | Chick Films | | Denmark/Netherlands | John Lindsay | Produced by Joop Wilhelmus. Published in Denmark by Topsy Forlaget. |
| *Surprise Visitor* | 1971–73 | Chick Films | | Denmark/Netherlands | John Lindsay | Produced by Joop Wilhelmus. Published in Denmark by Topsy Forlaget |

(Continued)

| Title | Year | Label | Cat | Country | Filmmaker | Notes |
|---|---|---|---|---|---|---|
| *Young and Sexy* | 1971–73 | Chick Films | | Denmark/Netherlands | John Lindsay | Produced by Joop Wilhelmus. Published in Denmark by Topsy Forlaget. |
| *Arabian Nights* | 1979 | Color Climax | 1429 | Denmark | George Harrison Marks | Produced for the Theander Brothers. |
| *Big Boobed Lady* | 1978 | Color Climax | 1427 | Denmark | George Harrison Marks | Produced for the Theander Brothers. |
| *Black and White Orgy* | 1979 | Color Climax | 1354 | Denmark | Unknown | Produced for the Theander Brothers. |
| *Busty Baller* | 1979 | Color Climax | 1359 | Denmark | George Harrison Marks | Produced for the Theander Brothers. |
| *Cunt Casino* | 1981 | Color Climax | 1441 | Denmark | Unknown | Produced for the Theander Brothers. |
| *Hypno Humpers* | 1981 | Color Climax | 1445 | Denmark | Unknown | Produced for the Theander Brothers. |
| *London Lust* | 1978 | Color Climax | 1343 | Denmark | Unknown | Produced for the Theander Brothers. |
| *Non Stop Spunker* | 1979 | Color Climax | 1431 | Denmark | John Fortune | Produced for the Theander Brothers. |
| *Video Fuckers* | 1980 | Color Climax | 1365 | Denmark | Unknown | Produced for the Theander Brothers. |
| *Hippy Orgy* | 1971–75 | Diamant | | Netherlands | John Lindsay | Produced for Walter Bartowski or Ari Van Der Heul. |

| Title | Year | Label | Cat | Country | Filmmaker | Notes |
|---|---|---|---|---|---|---|
| *Sexy Salesman* | 1971–76 | Diamant | | Netherlands | John Lindsay | Produced for Walter Bartowski or Ari Van Der Heul. |
| *A Splendid Night* | 1971–74 | Diamant | | Netherlands | John Lindsay | Produced for Walter Bartowski or Ari Van Der Heul. |
| *Taken by Surprise* | 1971–77 | Diamant | | Netherlands | John Lindsay | Produced for Walter Bartowski or Ari Van Der Heul. |
| *London Love* | | Explora Film | 2 | Germany | Unknown | Same footage as *Picadilly 6*. |
| *Huge Tit Service* | 1980 | Expo Film | 110 | Denmark | Unknown | Produced for the Theander Brothers. |
| *Swopping Sweethearts* | 1978 | Expo Film | 87 | Denmark | Unknown | Produced for the Theander Brothers. |
| *Die Autogrammstunde (Teil 1)* | | Exstase-Film | EX5 | Germany | George Harrison Marks | |
| *Die Autogrammstunde (Teil 2)* | | Exstase-Film | EX6 | Germany | George Harrison Marks | |
| *Kurzschluss* | | Exstase-Film | EX7 | Germany | George Harrison Marks | |

(*Continued*)

| Title | Year | Label | Cat | Country | Filmmaker | Notes |
|---|---|---|---|---|---|---|
| *Die Lüsterne Gräfin* | | Exstase-Film | EX3 | Germany | George Harrison Marks | |
| *Penistipistin & Sweet 16* | | Fortuna Film | 1 | Germany | Unknown | Produced for Walter Bartkowski. |
| *Hexenfett* | | Insiders | 48 | Germany | George Harrison Marks | Produced for Walter Bartkowski. |
| *Die Lollos* | | Insiders | 47 | Germany | George Harrison Marks | Produced for Walter Bartkowski. |
| *Blondie's Lessons in Statistics* | 1977 | Lasse Braun | LB26 | Germany | Lasse Braun | Produced with Gerd Wasmund included in the film *Sex Maniacs*. |
| *Call Girls* | 1977 | Lasse Braun | LB27 | Germany | Lasse Braun | Produced with Gerd Wasmund included in the film *Sin Dreamer*. |
| *Country Life* | 1977 | Lasse Braun | LB17 | Germany | Lasse Braun | Produced with Gerd Wasmund included in the film *Sin Dreamer*. |
| *English Schoolgirl* | 1977 | Lasse Braun | LB19 | Germany | Lasse Braun | Produced with Gerd Wasmund included in the film *Sex Maniacs*. |
| *Jealousy* | 1977 | Lasse Braun | LB18 | Germany | Lasse Braun | Produced with Gerd Wasmund included in the films *Sex Maniacs* and *Sin Dreamer*. |

| Title | Year | Label | Cat | Country | Filmmaker | Notes |
|---|---|---|---|---|---|---|
| *Locked Out* | 1977 | Lasse Braun | LB20 | Germany | Lasse Braun | Produced with Gerd Wasmund included in the film *Sex Maniacs*. |
| *Nazi Games* | 1977 | Lasse Braun | LB21 | Germany | Lasse Braun | Produced with Gerd Wasmund included in the film *Sin Dreamer*. |
| *Satin Party* | 1977 | Lasse Braun | LB22 | Germany | Lasse Braun | Produced with Gerd Wasmund included in the film *Sin Dreamer*. |
| *Tit Friction* | 1977 | Lasse Braun | LB23 | Germany | Lasse Braun | Produced with Gerd Wasmund included in the film *Sex Maniacs*. |
| *Uncle Roger* | 1977 | Lasse Braun | LB25 | Germany | Lasse Braun | Produced with Gerd Wasmund included in the film *Sin Dreamer*. |
| *Blondes Haar* | | Lolita | 26 | Germany | George Harrison Marks | Produced for Walter Bartkowski. |
| *Goldene Berge* | | Lolita | 28 | Germany | George Harrison Marks | Produced for Walter Bartkowski. |
| *Moralpisser* | | Lolita | 27 | Germany | George Harrison Marks | Produced for Walter Bartkowski. |

(*Continued*)

| Title | Year | Label | Cat | Country | Filmmaker | Notes |
|---|---|---|---|---|---|---|
| Zum Knutschkeller | | Lolita | 26 | Germany | George Harrison Marks | Hardcore version of *Bistro Bordello*. |
| Bus Stop | | London Film | LF2B | Germany | Unknown | Gay pornography. |
| Dream and Reality | 1977–79 | Mike Hunter | 11 | Germany | Unknown | Made by a British freelance crew for Gerd Wasmund (aka Mike Hunter). |
| Lolitas geile Titten | 1977–79 | Mike Hunter | 12 | Germany | Unknown | Made by a British freelance crew for Gerd Wasmund (aka Mike Hunter). |
| Magic Club | 1977–79 | Mike Hunter | 13 | Germany | Unknown | Made by a British freelance crew for Gerd Wasmund (aka Mike Hunter). |
| School-Girl träumt von King-Kong | 1977–79 | Mike Hunter | 16 | Germany | Unknown | Made by a British freelance crew for Gerd Wasmund (aka Mike Hunter). |
| Les Mamelles de Lola | | Miroir Films | | Unknown | Unknown | |
| Estate Agent | | NaNa Films | 42 | Germany | Unknown | Produced for Walter Bartkowski. |
| Turniermiezen | | Obszön Film | 3 | Germany | Unknown | Produced for Walter Bartkowski. |
| Bratwurst-Reigen | | Pfiff Film | 60 | Germany | Unknown | Produced for Walter Bartkowski. |

| Title | Year | Label | Cat | Country | Filmmaker | Notes |
|-------|------|-------|-----|---------|-----------|-------|
| *Dr. Ficke* | | Pfiff Film | 57 | Germany | Unknown | Produced for Walter Bartkowski. |
| *Fussball Porno* | | Pfiff Film | 56 | Germany | Possibly John Lindsay | Produced for Walter Bartkowski. |
| *Guter Fick ist ... Goldes Wert* | | Pleasure-Film | 1001 | Germany | George Harrison Marks | |
| *Das Vögeln ist des Mannes Lust* | | Pleasure-Film | 2 | Germany | George Harrison Marks | |
| *Die diebische Elster* | | Porno-Film | R629 | Germany | George Harrison Marks | |
| *Picadilly 6* | | Professional Film | PF/5A3 | Germany | Alan Vydra | Same footage as *London Love.* |
| *Barmaid Pleasures* | 1978 | Rodox | 676 | Denmark | George Harrison Marks | Produced for the Theander Brothers. |
| *Big Tit Riders* | 1979 | Rodox Film | 679 | Denmark | Unknown | Produced for the Theander Brothers. |
| *Cockpit Cunts* | 1979 | Rodox | 688 | Denmark | George Harrison Marks | Produced for the Theander Brothers. |
| *Big 'n' Busty* | | Sex Orgy | 239 | Denmark | George Harrison Marks | Produced for the Theander Brothers. |

*(Continued)*

| Title | Year | Label | Cat | Country | Filmmaker | Notes |
|---|---|---|---|---|---|---|
| Busty Chicks | 1978 | Sexorama | 866 | Denmark | Unknown | Produced for the Theander Brothers. |
| Sommer Fantasie | 1978–79 | Starlight Film | 1516 | Germany | John Fortune | |
| London Lust | 1978 | Swedish Erotica | 232 | United States | Unknown | Re-release of Color Climax's *London Love.* |
| Happy Nurses | | Tabu | 21 | Germany | George Harrison Marks | Produced for Walter Bartkowski hardcore version of *Goodnight Nurse.* |
| Schwarzes Fieber | | Tabu | 22 | Germany | George Harrison Marks | Produced for Walter Bartkowski. |
| Wotzi-Wotzi | | Tabu | 24 | Germany | George Harrison Marks | Produced for Walter Bartkowski. |
| Black Mystique | 1979–80 | Tabu de Luxe | 140 | Germany | John Fortune | Produced for Walter Bartkowski. |
| Camera Club | | Tabu de Luxe | 124 | Germany | Unknown | Produced for Walter Bartkowski. |
| Carmen und ihre Nichten | 1972–73 | Tabu de Luxe | 72 | Germany | John Lindsay | Produced for Walter Bartkowski. |
| Crème Delight | | Tabu de Luxe | 108 | Germany | Unknown | Produced for Walter Bartkowski. |

| Title | Year | Label | Cat | Country | Filmmaker | Notes |
|-------|------|-------|-----|---------|-----------|-------|
| *Gurken Club* | 1979–80 | Tabu de Luxe | 137 | Germany | Unknown | Produced for Walter Bartkowski. |
| *Miss Bobrloch* | | Tabu de Luxe | 103 | Germany | Unknown | Produced for Walter Bartkowski. |
| *Nina & Tina auf Männerfang* | | Tabu de Luxe | 114 | Germany | Unknown | Produced for Walter Bartkowski. |
| *Obsession X* | | Tabu de Luxe | 125 | Germany | Unknown | Produced for Walter Bartkowski. |
| *No Morals* | 1980 | Tabu de Luxe | 138 | Germany | Unknown | Produced for Walter Bartkowski. |
| *Pop Concert* | 1980–81 | Tabu de Luxe | 141 | Germany | Unknown | Produced for Walter Bartkowski. |
| *Schoolgirl Holiday* | 1978 | Teenage Sex | 709 | Denmark | George Harrison Marks | Produced for the Theander Brothers. |
| *Vor Geilheit kochen* | 1973–74 | ZaZa | 68 | Germany | George Harrison Marks | Produced for Walter Bartkowski hardcore version of *Dolly Mixture*. |

# Appendix 2:
# List of Rollers Seized from John Mason's Dean Street Office, 1 July 1969

Taken from The National Archives, Records of the Central Criminal Court, CRIM 1/5218, Vinn, George Samuel. Charge: Having obscene articles for publication for gain, 1969.

| Title | Label |
|---|---|
| *100% Lust* | Climax |
| *Acts of Cunninglitis, Fellatio, Lesbianism, Sexual Intercourse* | Unknown 16mm. |
| *Acts of Sexual Intercourse and Fellatio* | Unknown |
| *Ambitious Model* | Climax |
| *Amorous Lesbians* | Unknown, possibly unbranded. |
| *Au Pair Rape* | Unknown |
| *Baby Sitter* | Climax |
| *Barbara* | Unknown (Glamour) |
| *Beatnik Bedlam* | Climax |
| *Birthday Present* | Climax |
| *Bright Sparks* | Climax |
| *Cat Burglar* | Climax |
| *Close Investigation* | Unknown, possibly unbranded. |
| *Close Up* | Dolly Film |
| *Country Watcher* | Playboy Classics |
| *Cum Clean* | Climax |

| Title | Label |
|---|---|
| *Dirty Perverts* | Eros Films |
| *Double Number* | Unbranded |
| *Easy Meet* | Climax |
| *End of Term* | Climax |
| *Escort Agency* | Climax |
| *Fisherman's Luck* | Unbranded, later re-released by Blue Scene Films. |
| *Free for All* | Climax Films |
| *French Maid* | Eros |
| *Full Recovery* | Climax |
| *Full Treatment* | Climax |
| *Girlfriends* | Unknown |
| *Good Deal* | Climax |
| *Hot Line* | Climax |
| *Hotel Sexi* | Unbranded |
| *Incestral Home* | Unbranded, later re-released by Blue Scene Films. |
| *Just Like a Woman* | Unbranded |
| *Kinky Lovers* | Climax |
| *Kinky Spender* | Climax |
| *Lucky Draw* | Climax |
| *Lucky Prowler* | Unbranded, later re-released by Blue Scene Films. |
| *Lusty Aupair* | Climax |
| *Man Crazy* | Climax |
| *Miss Conduct* | Climax |
| *Mixed Feelings* | Climax |
| *More Beatnik Bedlam* | Climax |

(*Continued*)

| Title | Label |
|---|---|
| *More Suds and Sex* | Unbranded, later re-released by Blue Scene Films. |
| *Morning Lust* | Unbranded, later re-released by Blue Scene Films. |
| *Nightspot* | Climax |
| *Outnumbered* | Climax |
| *Pawnbroker* | Climax |
| *Peak Performance* | Unbranded |
| *Personal Touch* | Unknown, possibly unbranded. |
| *The Perverts* | Unbranded |
| *Photo Session* | Unknown, possibly unbranded. |
| *Playboys* | Climax |
| *Private Patient* | Climax |
| *Pussy Galore* | Climax |
| *Rape in the Dark Wood* | Unknown, possibly unbranded. |
| *Rare Capture* | Climax |
| *Rear Admiral* | Unbranded, later re-released by Blue Scene Films. |
| *Sailor's Delight* | Climax |
| *Satan's Children* | Climax |
| *Schoolgirl* | Unknown, possibly unbranded. |
| *Seduction of Susan* | Unbranded, later re-released by Blue Scene Films. |
| *Services Rendered* | Climax |
| *Sex Oympics* | Climax |
| *Sex-Tet* | Climax |
| *Sexpots* | Dolly Films |
| *Shower Nymph* | Unknown |
| *Spanish Lust* | Climax |

| Title | Label |
|---|---|
| *Sudden Sex* | Climax |
| *Surprise Rewards* | Unbranded |
| *Swedish Massage* | Climax |
| *Take It Down* | Unknown, possibly unbranded. |
| *The Patient* | Climax |
| *Three for Sex* | Unbranded, later re-released by Blue Scene Films. |
| *Three's Company* | Venus Films |
| *Threesome* | Climax |
| *TV Man* | Unbranded, later re-released by Blue Scene Films as *A Natural Break*. |
| *TV Sex 1968* | Eros Films |
| *Twisted* | Climax |
| *Two Into One* | Unknown, possibly unbranded. |
| *Unfortunate Little Sister* | Climax |
| *Wake Up to Sex* | Unknown, possibly unbranded. |
| *What the Butler Saw and Did* | Unbranded, later re-released by Blue Scene Films. |
| *The Wife Swappers* | Eros Films |
| *Worth Waiting For* | Unbranded, 400ft. |

# Notes

## Introduction: *Tonight at 8*

1. 'Blue movie' was also used to describe hardcore pornography and this term was regularly used in British newspapers. According to Flexner (1982), the word 'blue' was used in 1864 to connote obscene talk.

2. In the book *Tonight at 8*, author Chrissie Bentley (2013) gives what might be described as a semi-fictional, biographical account of the career of Elizabeth Smart, who she claims produced a number of Climax rollers between the years 1967 and 1969. The blurring of fact and fiction makes it difficult to ascertain whether Bentley's claim of Smart being the hand behind these films is accurate. Frustratingly, Bentley's use of pseudonym further muddies the water. The research I have conducted for this book indicates that there were no female filmmakers involved in the Climax films, but it is likely that some females were involved behind the camera of rollers, such as the mysterious female briefly seen in *The Rent Man* and Mike Freeman's wife Sandra (see Chapter 3). I did contact Bentley to find out more about the research for *Tonight at 8*, but did not receive a response.

3. The aforementioned *Tonight at 8* (Bentley 2013) is an example of the 'twisting path' of which Alilunas speaks. Inaccuracies are common and are inevitable when researching a largely undocumented illicit industry. For instance, Sheridan (2005) claims that John Lindsay's film *Miss Bohrloch* received the Golden Phallus award at the 1970 Wet Dreams Festival in Amsterdam, when it was actually awarded at a later Frankfurt Porn Film Festival.

4. Chibnall's misspelling of Cook's surname is likely to have originated from an article in *The People* newspaper (8 November 1970), which attempted to identify the people behind Climax, and implicated Ivor Cook in the development of the business (see Chapter 4). The Cooke spelling is also used by Hebditch and Anning (1988: 212).

5. http://vintage-erotica-forum.com/.

6. https://adultloopdb.nl.

7. Kinsey's system appears to be based on dating the film stock, giving a rough time period, or even an exact year to when the film was likely distributed. While useful, the system should also be treated with caution as certain films may have been reprinted or even re-released, so not giving an accurate year of production. In the labelography at the end of this book

I have attempted to build on Kinsey's dating system, identifying likely dates of production based on my primary research. Di Lauro and Rabkin's (1976) film and title index has also been a helpful source in attempting to date production.

8. Non-anglophone sources were translated using AI translation software, such as Google Translate and sent to willing native speakers for review.

9. https://www.britishnewspaperarchive.co.uk/.

10. https://www.ukpressonline.co.uk/.

11. https://www.infotextmanuscripts.org/ncropa/.

# 1. *Carnaby Kinks*:
## Obscenity, Permissiveness and the Dirty Square Mile

1. This was repealed in 2010, correcting an error made in 1984 which ostensibly meant that the Video Recordings Act was not enforceable by law, despite a number of people being prosecuted for distributing films that can now be legally purchased from retailers. See Petley (2011: 197–206).

2. Edward Goodman, interview, 22 May 2020.

3. See Manchester (1982).

4. Jean Straker was the subject of a number of obscenity trials in the 1960s.

5. 'Steve', interview, 22 June 2020.

6. According to the Index on Censorship's guide on obscene publications, 'there is a slightly different 'public good' defence for performances, films and soundtracks. Here it applies if publication of the film or soundtrack is justified as being for the public good because it is in the interests of drama, opera, ballet or any other form of art, literature or learning' (https://www.indexoncensorship.org/2016/02/art-law-obscene-publications/).

7. See Marcus' (2017) work on sexuality and pornography in the Victorian period.

8. Martin Tomkinson, interview, 22 February 2017.

9. Aidan McManus, interview, 8 June 2016.

10. The National Archives, UK, Director of Public Prosecutions, DPP2/5760, Virgo, Wallace Harold and others: corruption offences between 1 January 1964 and 24 October 1972.

11. 'Colin', interview, 27 June 2016.

12. The National Archives, UK, Director of Public Prosecutions, DPP2/5786, Virgo, Wallace Harold and others: corruption offences between 1 January 1964 and 24 October 1972.

13. This murder is detailed in a number of newspaper articles, such as the *Liverpool Echo* (29 October 1956) and the *Daily Herald* (30 October 1956). A Canadian sailor named Richard Henley was accused of shooting Dean Street bookshop worker Alan Robinson, known also as 'Big Bill' in the trade. Henley had intended to steal photographs and films from the shop.

When given access to the backroom, Henley drew his gun, telling Robinson that he was leaving. Robinson rushed at Henley, who panicked and discharged his weapon.

14. Mike Freeman, interview, 3 and 6 April 2016, Italy.
15. 'Rob', interview, 12 August 2016.
16. 'John', interview, 11 October 2018.
17. See Hammond (1976) for a definition and history of French postcards.
18. Average weekly earning data taken from the Office of National Statistics: https://tinyurl.com/ywe3hcrn.
19. The National Archives, UK, Director of Public Prosecutions, DPP2/5800, Virgo, Wallace Harold and others: corruption offences between 1 January 1964 and 24 October 1972.
20. See Short (1990: 268–90) for a discussion of the Obscene Publication Squads' links with Freemasonry.

## 2. *Fisherman's Luck*: Making the Roller Market (1960–65)

1. McCabe was interviewed by Bernard Braden and his wife Barbara Kelly in 1968 for what became an unfinished TV series titled *Now and Then*. McCabe is identified as the owner of a Soho strip club named The Doll's House, but it is likely that he was a 'front'. The interview is an extra feature found on the British Film Institute's Blu-ray release of Arnold L. Miller's *Primitive London* (1965).
2. Cook's police interview was conducted 26 October 1975 and can be found in The National Archives, UK, Director of Public Prosecutions, DPP2/5786, Virgo, Wallace Harold and others: corruption offences between 1 January 1964 and 24 October 1972.
3. Murray Goldstein's (2005) autobiography reflects on his career as a strip club owner in 1960s Soho and gives a sense of the zeitgeist of this period.
4. See Wood (2017) and Long and Sheridan (2008), for more detail on Marks and Long's early careers as glamour photographers in Soho.
5. This interview can be found on the American Blu-ray release of *For Men Only* (Pete Walker 1967).
6. Peter Walker, interview, 9 November 2018.
7. Norman J. Warren, interview, 8 November 2019.
8. The General Post Office's Film Unit specialized in making documentaries promoting the organisation between 1933 and 1940. For more information, see: https://www2.bfi.org.uk/films-tv-people/4ce2b94268cf8.
9. 'Philip Black', interview, 3 September 2021.
10. 'RonnieX', interview, 4 October 2021.
11. Willem van Batenburg, interview, 13 October 2019.
12. Taken from the Rialto Report's interview with Lasse Braun: https://www.therialtoreport.com/2015/03/01/lasse-braun-the-early-years-of-a-trailblazer-his-last-interview/.
13. Brian Pritchard, interview, 13 December 2019.

14. Glamour model and occasional roller performer Mary Millington commented on why Lindsay occasionally filmed in Europe: 'it was agreed that we could go over to Holland to make the film. We did this for two reasons; firstly the studio facilities for making blue films are much better over there and there is no hassle about getting the film processed; and second, the moral climate in that country is much more advanced and adult than it is in the UK' (*Adult Fantasy Magazine*, number 6, 1985: 31).

15. Introduced in 1959, Letraset were a company who specialized in the manufacture of typeface transfer sheets, which could be rubbed on to photographs, adding text to an image.

16. See: The National Archives, CRIM 1/4360, 'R v. *Murray* and others'. 1965–66.

17. 'Derek', interview, 22 February 2020.

18. The National Archives, UK, Director of Public Prosecutions, DPP 2/5301-2, Collingbourne, Anthony and others: offences committed under the Obscene Publications Act 1959 on dates between 1 June 1971 and 14 May 1973.

19. Dave Wells, interview, 17 October 2018.

20. Mike Freeman, interview, 3–6 April 2016.

21. The National Archives, UK, Director of Public Prosecutions, DPP2/5786, Virgo, Wallace Harold and others: corruption offences between 1 January 1964 and 24 October 1972.

22. This claim is also included in Anthony Frewin's (2000) fictional book *London Blues*, which tells the story of Tim Purdom, a pioneer of rollers who was implicated in the Profumo Affair. The titles of actual rollers, such as *100% Lust*, are included in the book, blurring the boundaries between fiction and reality.

23. Pornography collector 'Mal Mallister' claims to own two hardcore 16mm films that feature Keeler, one having a BDSM theme. These were purchased in the 1980s from an antique shop outside of Soho. The owner also showed Mal an album of non-pornographic photographs featuring himself, Keeler and the other woman implicated in the Keeler Affair, Mandy Rice Davies. Mal did not offer access to these films, making it impossible to determine whether his claims are genuine ('Mal Mallister', interview, 12 September 2019). Farmer (2017: 467) makes mention of two American nudist films starring Keeler: 'Christine Keeler Goes Nudist (a black and white picture that, its distributor claimed, "really shows Christine Keeler – in the nude!") and The Naked Tales of Christine (a "naughty-nudie movie – in color!")'. Research reveals that these did not star Keeler, being nothing more than instances of exploitation marketing techniques. However, both of these examples highlight the enduring myth that surrounds Keeler and how the Profumo Affair sexualized her.

24. Copenhagen's antique bookshops sold pornography, just as those based in Soho.

25. It is also worth mentioning that Keeler was a popular figure in Denmark. The Danish produced *The Christine Keeler Affair* (Robert B. Spafford 1963) featured a pre-credit sequence with the actual Keeler. The BBFC refused to certify the film (see Trevelyan 1973: 175–77). A British pornography collector I name 'Ken' told me that he used to frequent

Denmark's bookshops, purchasing 8mm films ('Ken', interview, 14 October 2019). He recounted a story about one Copenhagen bookshop owner who claimed to have a Christine Keeler 8mm pornographic film in his safe; it was not for sale. When I hosted the research event '*Sex 69*: Denmark London and Beyond' in Copenhagen, an elderly Danish man came up to me at the end, wanting to talk about Keeler, further showing her lasting status as an international symbol of permissiveness.

26. Cook had strong links to Germany, having a German wife and the Cornwall Gardens case reveals that he had a German associate named Von Elison.

27. This claim is made by a Danish blogger known as 'Mike' who posts about the history of Danish pornography: https://www.hmpmovie.dk/ivor-cooke-rodox-film. Some of his entries are based on newspaper research, but it is not clear whether this particular story is accurate. In an attempt to corroborate it, I wrote to Peter Theander, but did not receive a response.

28. Arnberg (2010) also identifies a distributor named 'Valter' who was involved in distributing pornography on behalf of Danish producers to Sweden. It is plausible that Valter was also Walter Bartkowski, indicating that he was not just a distributor for British pornographers, but Danish producers too.

29. Another roller re-released by Blue Scene Films is *Rear Admiral* (1969), whose opening sequence is filmed on a river, which is likely to be the same location to use to shoot *Fisherman's Luck*.

30. In this catalogue, the letters 'KTC' are handwritten below some of the titles. 'Ken', another roller collector, owns several Blue Scene Films titles that are presented in plastic cases with the text 'KTC' printed on the spine. KTC likely refers to a shop named Kentish Town Cine who sold 8mm films on Kentish Town main street and distributed glamour films. Other collectors claimed to have no knowledge of Kentish Town Cine dealing in rollers or hardcore pornography. 'Philip Black', who regularly frequented the shop, believes that KTC could have distributed Blue Scene Films titles under the counter, but doubts that the company had any involvement in their making.

31. Simon Sheridan has written a blog post summarizing English's career in pornography: https://www.marymillington.co.uk/?p=675.

32. This roller is implied to be a sequel to an earlier film titled *Suds and Sex* (also known as *The Handyman*) which is likely to be British and made during the early 1960s.

33. The photograph on the cover of *Duet* includes a copy of Observer magazine, which is dated to 23 June 1968, hinting at a possible date of production.

34. *More La More I* and *II* (both 1968) released by the label Cherub Films also stars John English and is filmed in the same Victorian flat, suggesting a possible link with the person, or persons, behind Blue Scene Films.

35. An American poster on the *Vintage Erotica Forums* shared a collection of postcards that his late father had purchased in New York during the late 1960s. Amongst these are photographs that were also published in *Seduction Susan* in 1970–71.

## 3. *Up, Up and Away*:
## Entrepreneurship in Britain's
## Expanding Roller Trade (1966–69)

1. Sandra refused to be interviewed for this book.
2. The National Archives, UK, Records of the Criminal Court, CRIM 1/5203, Muldoon, Michael John and others. Charge: Murder, 1 January 1969–31 December 1972. Sadly, one of Freeman's remains closed, despite repeated Freedom of Information requests. This led to the closure of a second file. I was told that the files were closed to 'protect the mental health of the victim's family and the personal, sensitive information of a number of identified individuals'. Fortunately, I accessed the second file before its closure and draw on its contents throughout this chapter.
3. The Protection of Children Act 1978 criminalized indecent images of children under 16. The Sexual Offences Act 2003 defined a child as 18 years old, criminalizing indecent pictures of under 18s (Gillespie and Ost 2016).
4. 'Paula' is the pseudonym Sandra uses for Tony's wife in *Knock Down Ginger*.
5. 'Soho George', interview, 5 September 2018.
6. Another pornographer, Martin Granby, described in a police interview how he too was blacklisted by Soho shops for not having a licence. See: The National Archives, UK, Director of Public Prosecutions, DPP2/5809, Virgo, Wallace Harold and others: corruption offences between 1 January 1964 and 24 October 1972.
7. The National Archives, UK, Director of Public Prosecutions, DPP2/5773, Virgo, Wallace Harold and others: corruption offences between 1 January 1964 and 24 October 1972.
8. The National Archives, UK, Director of Public Prosecutions, DPP2/5778, Virgo, Wallace Harold and others: corruption offences between 1 January 1964 and 24 October 1972.
9. See the blog *Climax Story* for a well-researched summary of the early years of the Theanders' enterprise: http://climaxstory.com/.
10. At this point, it is worth mentioning that I personally never encountered any instances of British-produced child pornography during my research. One unnamed interviewee with experience of Soho's bookshops confirmed that it did circulate in the form of postcards and typescripts, but in small amounts. This is confirmed in a mail-shot from 1963 purporting to sell postcards of 9- and 11-year-old 'schoolgirls' involved in sexual acts (see The National Archives, UK, Records of the Central Criminal Court, CRIM 1/4082, Pritchard, Arthur Finlay Lindsay-Fynn, Caroline, May 1963). Freeman (2011) writes about how postcards of 'juves' (juveniles) were available in Soho's bookshops, though does not clarify whether this was underaged material. Like Stoops (2018), I also believe that the circulation of this material was very small scale and perhaps involved different economies of exchange.
11. It seems that the brand Climax Original signifies later re-releases of the earlier Climax Films' titles when Phillips moved operations to Denmark and increased duplication. This

may explain why few Climax Films' titles currently circulate, perhaps due to smaller print runs, yet Climax Original releases regularly appear.

12. I have attempted to contact Peter Theander to confirm this claim, but he did not respond to my letter. Theander has a reputation for not giving interviews (see Tate 1990: 45).

13. The National Archives, UK, Director of Public Prosecutions, DPP2/5809, Virgo, Wallace Harold and others: corruption offences between 1 January 1964 and 24 October 1972.

14. This person refused to be interviewed and would have likely added further information on Freeman's practice. They died in 2021.

15. It is possible that Freeman took the name Venus Films from Russell Gay who had an established glamour label with the same title.

16. *Bisexual Buggery* (Mike Freeman 1968) is likely the title of this third film.

17. The National Archives, UK, Director of Public Prosecutions, DPP2/5778, Virgo, Wallace Harold and others: corruption offences between 1 January 1964 and 24 October 1972.

18. A collector showed me a mail-shot that is likely to be Freeman's glamour 'front company' under the name 'Climax Films'. The Clapham North addressed document offers three glamour films – *Miss Mini Skirt*, *Cindy* and *Teengirls*. These 200ft titles sold for £4 each. The use of the name 'Climax Films' was likely done to anger Evan Phillips.

19. In legal files relating the Krays, a police interview with a Kray associate named Teale alleges that the twins had something called the 'dreaded list', which contained names of people to be 'executed'. Teale states that 'a fellow connected with blue films in the West End' was on this list, though this is likely to be George Cornell, a member of the Richardson gang who is said to have been involved in distributing blue films. See The National Archives, Records of the Metropolitan Police, MEPO 2/11406, Statements re Cornell, 1966–68.

20. Cox was interviewed for the Channel 4 documentary *The Porn King, the Stripper and the Bent Coppers* (Simon Berthon and Daniel Korn 1998).

21. For further information on the Danish sex fairs, see Dahl and Næsby (1970) and Lauret (1970).

22. It is also plausible that Jens and Peter Theander had some involvement in Phillips and Bartkowski's Original Climax Films, especially given that they too used the same brand name and had previously sold Climax Films' rollers at their Copenhagen bookshop.

23. The seizure list is taken from The National Archives, Records of the Central Criminal Court, CRIM 1/5218, Vinn, George Samuel. Charge: Having obscene articles for publication for gain, 1969.

## 4. *House of Mirrors*:
### Regulating the Roller Trade (1970–73)

1. While there are limitations when searching the British Newspaper Archive, mainly relating to the inconsistent results of the Optical Character Recognition software used to make the scans of old newspapers searchable, it still serves as a useful indication of the column inches devoted to the subject in the 1970s, as the trade grew, and a moral panic began to emerge.

2. AS stands for Aktie Selskab and identifies that it is a formally registered company in Denmark.

3. I assume that the name Original Climax Films instead of Climax Films was used to either differentiate the brand from the popular Danish magazine Color Climax published by Rodox or perhaps a response to Mike Freeman's attempts to distribute as Climax Films in 1969.

4. The National Archives, UK, Director of Public Prosecutions, DPP2/4960, Whyte and others, 1971–72; The National Archives, UK, Records of the Supreme Court of Judicature and related courts, J 192/50, Pitblado, Mary and Kelly, John: charged with having an obscene article for publication for gain, 1974–75; The National Archives, UK, Director of Public Prosecutions, Budworth, Trevor and Parker, Charles: publishing and possessing obscene articles, 1968.

5. It is worth pointing out that a number of labels would belong to one producer, a way for them to saturate the market with seemingly new product. I discuss this later in the chapter, using the example of John Darby and Anthony Collingbourne.

6. Lindsay's comments are taken from an interview printed in an article found in the Aberdeen newspaper *Evening News*, 25 February 1982.

7. American film critic Vincent Canby used the term 'Danish blue' to describe documentaries such as *Pornography in Denmark: A New Approach* (Alex de Renzy 1970), *Pornography: Copenhagen 1970* (Jorgen Lyhne 1970) and *Sexual Freedom in Denmark* (John Lamb 1970) which all focused on Denmark's legalization of pornography. See the *New York Times*, 21 June 1970.

8. A red marker on the police report seems to suggest that this statement might be untrue, and Granby is attempting to protect Moody.

9. I suspect that *Arabian Nights* may have been first released by either Svensk Films or Dolly Films in 1969, given the set used and the performers who are linked to both labels. Danish Blu Films could have been introduced between 1970 and 1973, its glossy colourful box contrasts with others from this period and are demonstrative of more professionalized production, possibly taking place in Denmark.

10. The National Archives, UK, Director of Public Prosecutions, DPP2/5786, Virgo, Wallace Harold and others: corruption offences between 1 January 1964 and 24 October 1972.

11. Such was the Theander brothers' commitment to high-quality production that when they moved from Super 8 to video in the early 1980s they opened 'one of the most sophisticated video facilities houses in northern Europe'. Not only were these facilities used to duplicate pornographic video tapes, other companies utilized them to duplicate video releases of popular Hollywood films such as *Raiders of the Lost Ark* and *Terms of Endearment* (Hebditch and Anning 1988: 60).

12. There were a range of casual roles in the alternative economy, ranging from drivers like 'Mark' through to the bookshop workers and general gofers ('Mark', interview, 1 November 2018). Another interviewee named 'Ernie' was a casual supplier of hardcore pornography to South Wales. This involved him regularly visiting Soho, picking up goods and transporting them back to his hometown. Ernie claimed that he was asked by his Soho supplier to temporarily store a large amount of rollers, postcards and typescripts: 'in those days

they had informants inside the police. And if they were going to be raided [...] they were always pre warned they were given about a week notice that they were going to be raided. And he said is there any chance of me looking after the stock [...] for a few months? [...] I went to London, picked it up in the van'.

Ernie said that he held the stock for a surprisingly long six months, until his Soho contact collected it. Ernie could not recall exact dates, though it is possible that this took place in 1972 or 1973 when a high number of raids occurred following the exposure of corruption in the Obscene Publications Squad ('Ernie', interview, 21 January 2021).

13. The National Archives, UK, Director of Public Prosecutions, DPP2/5789, Virgo, Wallace Harold and others: corruption offences between 1 January 1964 and 24 October 1972.

14. 'Scans' was the trade term for hardcore Scandinavian pornography magazines.

15. This model of distribution was used to great effect from the late 1980s onwards by a British company based in the Netherlands named Your Choice. The company took orders in the Netherlands, but dispatched from within the United Kingdom, having a network of people across the country duplicating smuggled video master tapes.

16. The National Archives, UK, Director of Public Prosecutions, MEPO 26/352, Donald Case alias Duke Case and others: convicted of possessing obscene articles for gain and publishing obscene articles by distributing films following police raids at 12–14 Argyll Street, London W1, and 81 Belgrave Road, London SW1, on 21 February 1973.

17. See Chapter 8 of Kirby (2018) for a detailed overview of the raids of Soho bookshops that took place in 1972 as part of the Metropolitan Police's investigation into police corruption.

18. The National Archives, UK, Director of Public Prosecutions, DPP2/5789, Virgo, Wallace Harold and others: corruption offences between 1 January 1964 and 24 October 1972.

19. Fantasy could be a label belonging to 'Skinny' Ken Taylor. The film *Action Girl* (1968–72) features performers who regularly appeared in Collingbourne and Darby productions, while *A Small Hotel* (1968–72) includes a title card for Cherub Productions. This suggests a link between Fantasy and Cherub, which issued the film *More La More II* (1968) that was shot in the Victorian flat possibly used by Ivor Cook (see Chapter 2). Given Taylor's associations with Cook and Collingbourne, I do wonder if these labels belonged to him.

20. The National Archives, UK, Director of Public Prosecutions, DPP 2/5301-2, Collingbourne, Anthony and others: offences committed under the Obscene Publications Act 1959 on dates between 1 June 1971 and 14 May 1973.

21. The commercial production of bestiality pornography became common in Scandinavia when competing labels such as Color Climax diversified their production to include performers having sex with animals. Bestiality appears in rollers, with many of the larger labels having at least one title. This appears to slightly increase in the early 1970s as British labels such as Anglo Continental, International Films and Universal Films competed with European material, but out of the 1000 plus rollers made in Britain, around 2 per cent depict bestiality.

22. The Playland amusement arcade was the subject of a vice investigation in September 1975, focusing specifically on the sexploitation of teenage boys. The arcade attracted youngsters and was frequented by pimps who attempted to exploit them. This interview suggests that some roller performers were also recruited through Playland. One of the male survivors of Playland, Anthony Daly (2018), has written a book recounting his traumatic experience.

23. The National Archives, UK, Director of Public Prosecutions, DPP 2/5301-2, Collingbourne, Anthony and others: offences committed under the Obscene Publications Act 1959 on dates between 1 June 1971 and 14 May 1973.

## 5. *Strip Poker:*
## Distributing Hardcore Films in Britain (1973–83)

1. See *R v. Commissioner of Police of the Metropolis*, Ex parte Blackburn and Another (1972).

2. The Nationwide Petition for Public Decency in 1972 was introduced after the *Oz* obscenity trial. A counter-cultural magazine, *Oz* published the 'School Kids' issue, which, as the title suggests, had been guest published by school children between the ages of 14 and 18. According to Carlin (2007: 134), it included 'teenagers' thoughts on sex, drugs, rock 'n' roll, corporal punishment and institutionalized abuse'. On appeal, the publishers were found not guilty, though Mary Whitehouse and the Festival of Light seized the moment and introduced this petition.

3. Softcore pornography entrepreneurs were also prone to 'periodic raids' and prosecution (Thompson 1994: 28).

4. The Golds offer further background on their enterprise in their autobiographies (Gold 1997; Gold 2012).

5. One of Sullivan's many confidence tricks was to produce adverts implying bestiality, such as a woman with a horse, and the paying customer would discover they received what the advert stated, in the form of a copy of the equestrian magazine *Horse and Hound*. The customer was unlikely to complain, for obvious reasons.

6. Sullivan angered European pornographers Berth Milton and the Theander Brothers for his unauthorized use of the brands Private and Color Climax and producing censored bootlegs of their magazines. Both attempted to pursue legal action against Sullivan but did not take it any further (see Hebditch and Anning 1988: 347–53).

7. 'Dave', interview, 1 December 2017 and 12 October 2018.

8. David Waterfield did not respond to several interview requests. His story comes second-hand, told by his ex-wife Patricia Clark and her son Jayson Pannell, who ran the business Your Choice alongside Waterfield. I also draw on magazine interviews, newspaper articles and legal documents.

9. Patricia Clark, interview, 16 July 2018.

10. Clark informed me that the American petroleum company Exxon Mobil attempted to sue Waterfield for using their trade name. Exxon lost the case when the judge ruled in

Waterfield's, favour, declaring that there was a clear distinction between the business interests of each party. According to Clark, this is why Exxon trade in the United Kingdom as Esso. I have been unable to verify this claim but chose to include it here as it further exemplifies the myths that surround entrepreneurs (Shane 2008).

11. Waterfield's interview with 'Jenny Love' can be found in volume 4, number 3 of the adult magazine *Experience*.

12. This location eventually became home to the Scala cinema, which pushed the boundaries of what was deemed acceptable to be screened at British cinemas. See Giles (2018).

13. *R v. Waterfield* (1975).

14. According to the Crown Prosecution Service, 'Severance may be ordered where the admissibility of the evidence is not the same against each defendant or where the case would otherwise be too long and complicated'. See: https://www.cps.gov.uk/legal-guidance/drafting-indictment.

15. *R v. Waterfield* (1975).

16. Like many of the other pornography entrepreneurs discussed in this book, Lindsay had a propensity for fabrication and untruth. Kerekes (2000) uses a series of magazines Lindsay self-produced sometime in the mid 1970s to construct his autobiography. Each of these magazines contain the same self-eulogy of his career up until the first obscenity trial. Such sources are useful but must be treated with suspicion and corroborated wherever possible. But as Portelli (2010: 2) notes, 'rather than being a weakness, this is however, their strength: errors, inventions, and myths lead us through and beyond facts to their meaning', telling us more about how pornographers chose to present themselves.

17. The National Archives, UK, Director of Public Prosecutions, DPP 2/5884, Lindsay, John Jesner and Pritchard, Gwynn: possible offences under the Obscene Publications Act 1959 on 8 February 1975 in London W11, 1975.

18. The date of *Miss Bohrloch's* production is contentious. Sheridan (1999) identifies 1970, but this may have been based on an incorrect assumption that the film was shown at the Wet Dreams Festival in Amsterdam, 1970. It is very difficult to identify exact dates of production, due to the undocumented, clandestine nature of film making in the alternative economy. That said, Bartkowski's label Tabu de Luxe used lavish packaging that differed greatly to that used at the time, particularly when hardcore pornography was not legalized in Germany until 1975 (Heineman 2011). All of Bartkowski's distributed films had a seemingly consecutive catalogue number. Given that Tabu de Luxe does not appear in the catalogue until number 71 and is preceded by a film titled *Watergate* – catalogue number 64 – it seems unlikely that *Miss Bohrloch* was made earlier than this title. The Watergate scandal took place in 1972, with the hearings occurring in 1973, suggesting that *Miss Bohrloch* was made in 1972 or, more likely, 1973. Lindsay had built a reputation as a professional filmmaker at that point in his career, making this dating more plausible.

19. Studio Film Laboratories was one of Britain's longest running film laboratories, established in 1922. 'Phillip Black' an interviewee formerly involved in London's film industry,

believes that Lindsay's films were also processed by Colour Film Services laboratory in Marylebone, London.

20. As mentioned in Chapter 2, issue 6 of *Adult Fantasy Magazine* (1985) published extracts from what seems to be Mary Millington's biography. From page 31 onwards, she speaks of working for John Lindsay and recounts how they made a film together in the Netherlands. She suggests that European locations, such as Denmark, Sweden, Netherlands and Germany, were used by roller makers as they allowed them to easily have the films processed once they were made.

21. Glamour photographer and filmmaker George Harrison Marks also worked for Bartkowski around the same time as Lindsay, selling hard versions of his glamour films to the German entrepreneur. A Director of Public Prosecutions document found in a file relating to Lindsay describes a police investigation that took place on Harrison Marks following a raid on his studio in 1973. They discovered fourteen 'unprocessed 16mm colour films'. Harrison Marks told the officers that 'they were shot for the German market'. These were unprocessed as he was due to travel to Germany with the films, where they would be developed, edited and sold. The Obscene Publications Squad sought legal advice on whether Harrison Marks could be prosecuted. They were advised that it would not be possible for an English jury to determine whether the publication of an article in Britain could deprave or corrupt a foreign audience. Harrison Marks was released without charge. See: The National Archives, UK, Director of Public Prosecutions, DPP 2/5884, Lindsay, John Jesner and Pritchard, Gwynn: possible offences under the Obscene Publications Act 1959 on 8 February 1975 in London W11, 1975.

22. Derek Ford, who received 'extensive training in radio, television and "straight" cinema', is notable in the history of British hardcore filmmaking as he made hardcore export versions of his films *Diversions* (aka *Sex Express*, Derek Ford 1975) and *The Sexplorer* (Derek Ford 1975) for the international market (McGillivray 2017: 65–68).

23. The American version of *The Pornbrokers* was recut to include American-produced hardcore sex scenes.

24. Lindsay also had his own modelling agency named Ragdolls, but it is not clear when it was founded.

25. The argument for the public viewing the films was that it informed debate on censorship and the boundaries of obscenity.

26. *Convent of Sin* is reported as being filmed in North Wales. A man had visited his son-in-law's neighbouring cottage and found that an altar had been built: 'I went in to check that everything was all right. I found a green curtain had been hung, covering the window and the fireplace. There were candlesticks and it sort of looked like an altar' (*Birmingham Post*, 18 October 1974).

27. According to Simon Sheridan (1999: 149), Karl Ordinez was 'a mysterious "German backer" (sometimes he was Swedish too), but Mr. Ordinez was ever the elusive faceless film producer, and there is some doubt as to whether he actually existed'. Given Lindsay's regular reference

to making films for foreign producer, it seems likely that Ordinez was a pseudonym for Lindsay, and Karl Ordinez Films Limited was a formal company registered with Companies House in 1978, eventually removed from their register in June 1985 (https://www.thegazette.co.uk/London/issue/50176/page/8795/data.pdf). However, one interviewee indicated that Ordinez was a real person, but used a pseudonym. If this is so, Walter Bartkowski is a plausible candidate.

28. Performers were again found guilty of their involvement in rollers, similar to the Watford Trial, although they did plead guilty. *The Guardian* (21 November 1974) reported that a spokesman for the Defence of Literature and the Arts Society asked that the co-conspirators who pleaded guilty on the advice of their council be granted a royal pardon as Lindsay had been found not guilty. It is not clear whether this request was granted.

29. The National Archives, UK, Director of Public Prosecutions, DPP 2/5884, Lindsay, John Jesner and Pritchard, Gwynn: possible offences under the Obscene Publications Act 1959 on 8 February 1975 in London W11, 1975.

30. See Long and Sheridan (2008: 148–49) for Stanley Long's recollection of discovering the BBC crew filming Lindsay at work in his flat.

31. Ari Van Der Heul was a significant transnational player from the early 1970s onwards, being the second biggest wholesale distributor of pornography in the Netherlands next to Charlie Geerts. Based in Rotterdam, conveniently located to a port, he ran the company Hygron, which distributed films for Walter Bartkowski's Tabu, Lolita and Diamant labels, as well as Lasse Braun's films. He was involved in the European arm of the American pornography company CalVista and played a key role in distributing pornography to Australia in the late 1980s, loaning AUD 6 million to brothers, Eric and Kenneth Hill, to setup CalVista Australia (*The Age from Melbourne*, 11 February 1995). Van Der Heul became a person of interest for the Obscene Publications Squad in the early 1980s as he exported hardcore pornography to Britain; Tate (1990: 75) alleges that this included child pornography. He appeared in an episode of the late-night television show *Central Weekend* (20 June 1986), where, in a recorded segment, he spoke in silhouette about being hounded by the British police. It is likely that Van Der Heul was one of many transnational operators who financed Lindsay's films.

32. Watts was a retired barrister and wrote many letters to the press, recommending prosecuting obscene or potentially morally corrupting articles (see *The Times,* 30 January 1976).

33. *Strip Poker* features 'Big' John English and is a typical roller, depicting group sex with two females and a male. The film is further evidence of English's reputation as a reliable male performer, being regularly hired by a range of producers.

34. *R* v. *Hatiatt* (1976) concerned the book *Inside Linda Lovelace*, a ghost-written autobiography of the American pornography performer Linda Lovelace. The book was found not guilty of obscenity and, as Robertson (1979: 141) observes, generated 'enormous publicity' for the title, increasing its sales.

35. Curiously, the Criminal Law Act 1977 now made the possession of 8mm film libraries for personal screenings a possible criminal offence, although the Law Commission advised that domestic viewing should not be prosecuted (Robertson 1979: 268).

36. As with *R v. Lindsay* (1974), I could find no legal documents relating to Lindsay's later trials, again having to rely on newspaper reportage and the National Campaign for the Reformation of the Obscene Publications Act archive, which attempted to support and draw attention to the injustice of Lindsay's legal battles.

37. This was defined as 'photographs and films whose production appears to the court to have involved the exploitation for sexual purposes of any person where either (a) that person appears from the evidence as a whole to have been at the relevant time under the age of sixteen, or (b) the material gives reason to believe that actual physical harm was inflicted on that person' (Williams 2015: 213).

38. Lindsay likely imported these video tapes from America, possibly via his associate Ari Van Der Heul, who was affiliated with the US company CalVista.

39. 'Geoff Gold' is likely a reporting error, the actual name being Godfrey Gold. NCROPA letters identify his involvement in running of Lindsay's Taboo Cinema chain.

40. Freeman, Honey and Stephens all claimed to have had a BDSM titled *Sex Slave* planted by the police. Freeman made a film titled *Sex Slave* in the early 1980s, but the film Honey and Stephens describe differed in that it depicted physical harm to genitals and breasts. Both Honey and Stephens denied any knowledge of owning it, but *Sex Slave* featured in their prosecutions. Lindsay Honey, interview, 12 September 2017; Terry Stephens, interview, 7 November 2017.

41. Manchester (1986: 240–55) reproduces Westminster Council's sex establishment licence application form. The form states that the council refunded returned £4000 to unsuccessful applicants, keeping £1000.

42. Westminster Council soon responded by dropping the requirement from 10 per cent to 5 per cent, but this did little to deter pseudo sex shops.

43. See Simpson (1983: 111–38) for more on the BBFC's introduction of new classifications.

## Conclusion

1. From the data given, it is interesting to note that the use of the Obscene Publications Act 1959 significantly reduced from 2001 onwards, following the re-evaluation of the R18, and fell even further after the introduction of the CJAIA.

2. https://www.cps.gov.uk/legal-guidance/obscene-publications.

## Epilogue

1. Gerd Wasmund, interview, 9 November 2020.

2. A mysterious producer by the name of John Fortune made several films in the late 1970s for Walter Bartkowski. Some of these were hardcore versions of softcore films released by pornography entrepreneur Russell Gay, who began as a glamour producer in the late 1950s – early 1960s, before moving into softcore magazine publishing.

3.  Lasse Braun's films that make up *Sex Maniacs* appear to be: *English Schoolgirl* (1977), *Tit Friction* (1977), *Locked Out* (1977), *Jealousy* (1977), *Blondie's Lessons in Statistics* (1977), *Uncle Roger* (1977), *Country Life* (1977), *Nazi Games* (1977), *Call Girls* (1977) and *Satin Party* (1977).
4.  See Hebditch and Anning (1988: 215–16) for a summary of Wasmund's experience of working in the United States and the problems making *Las Vegas Maniacs* (Gerd Wasmund 1985).
5.  See blogger Gav Crimson's website for further details on this film: https://tinyurl.com/7eaudpp4.
6.  Early American adverts for hardcore videos show that the films were made available in Europe's PAL and SECAM formats, as well as the American video format NTSC. This shows that video entrepreneurs were well aware of the transnational demand for hardcore pornography.
7.  Freeman claimed that he chose the name Freeman to indicate that he was now a 'free man'. This could have also been to distance himself from his criminal past.
8.  Freeman was not the only pornographer to receive support from the Department of Trade, an issue of *Late Night Video* mentions Freeman's success alongside Martin Denning of the company Red Tape.
9.  This was established in an appeal relating to the video screening of hardcore pornography at basement premises in Soho. See Attorney General's Reference (No. 5 of 1980) [1980] 3 All ER 816.
10. Lindsay Honey, an employee of Freeman's, corroborated this claim, telling me: 'Videx was making a ton of money as far as I can remember. There would be a couple of Royal Mail sacks every day with a mixture of cash and cheques. Lot of cash as you can imagine. Probably about 3 to 4 hundred quid a day coming in'. Lindsay Honey, interview, 10 October 2017.
11. Tuppy Owens, interview, 19 April 2015.
12. Gonzo is a term used to describe 'successful wave of first-person and more "realistic" pornographic products that sprung seemingly out of nowhere at the end of the 1980s' (Biasin and Zecca 2016: 332).
13. See *R* v. *Holloway* (1982) for further details.

# Bibliography

Abbott, S. A. (2010), 'Motivations for pursuing a career in pornography', in R. Weitzer (ed.), *Sex for Sale: Prostitution, Pornography and the Sex Industry*, New York: Routledge, pp. 47–66.

Albury, K. (2018), 'Heterosexual casual sex: From free love to Tinder', in C. Smith, F. Atwood, and B. McNair (eds), *The Routledge Companion to Media, Sex and Sexuality*, Abingdon: Routledge, pp. 81–90.

Alilunas, P. (2014), 'The necessary future of adult media industry studies', *Creative Industries Journal*, 7:1, pp. 62–66.

Alilunas, P. (2016), *Smutty Little Movies: The creation and regulation of adult video*, California: University of California Press.

Anon. (1972), *Pornography: The Longford Report*, London: Coronet.

Arnberg, K. (2010), *Motsättningarnas marknad: Den pornografiska pressens kommersiella genombrott och regleringen av pornografi i Sverige 1950–1980*, Sekel bokförlag.

Arnberg, K. (2012), 'Under the counter, under the radar? The business and regulation of the pornographic press in Sweden 1950–1971', *Enterprise and Society*, 13:2, pp. 350–77.

Arnberg, K. (2017), 'Before the Scandinavian "porn wave": The business and regulations of magazines considered obscene in Sweden, 1910–1950', *Porn Studies*, 4:1, pp. 4–22.

Arnberg, K. and Marklund, C. (2016), 'Illegally Blonde: "Swedish Sin" and pornography in American and Swedish imaginations, 1950–1971', in M. Larsson and E. Björklund (eds), *Swedish cinema and the sexual revolution: Critical essays*, Jefferson: McFarland, pp. 185–200.

Arnberg, K. and Marklund, C. (2016), 'Illegally imaginations, 1950–1971', in M. Larsson and E. Björklund (eds), *Swedish cinema and the sexual revolution: Critical essays*, Jefferson: McFarland, pp. 185–200.

Bakehorn, J. (2010), 'Women-made pornography', in R. Weitzer (ed.), *Sex for sale: Prostitution, pornography, and the sex industry*, New York: Routledge, pp. 91–111.

Barker, M. (1984), *The Video Nasties*, London: Pluto Press.

Barnett, V. L. (2018), '"The most profitable film ever made": *Deep Throat* (1972), organized crime, and the $600 million gross', *Porn Studies*, 5:2, pp. 131–51.

Basu, G. (2013), 'The role of transnational smuggling operations in illicit supply chains', *Journal of Transportation Security*, 6:4, pp. 315–28.

Baumol, W. J. (1990), 'Entrepreneurship: Productive, unproductive, and destructive', *The Journal of Political Economy*, 98:5, pp. 893–921.

Becker, H. S. (1966), *Outsiders: Studies in the Sociology of Deviance*, New York: Free Press.

Bentley, C. (2013), *Tonight At 8*, Scotts Valley: Createspace Independent Pub.

Beresford, S. (2014), 'Obscene performative pornography: R v *Peacock* (2012) and the legal construction of same-sex and gendered identities in the United Kingdom', *Porn Studies*, 1:4, pp. 378–90.

Berg, H. (2014), 'Labouring porn studies', *Porn Studies*, 1:1–2, pp. 75–79.

Biasin, E. and Zecca, F. (2016), 'Introduction: Inside Gonzo porn', *Porn Studies*, 3:4, pp. 332–36.

Bichler, G., Bush, S. and Malm, A. (2013), 'Bad actors and faulty props: Unlocking legal and illicit art trade', *Global Crime*, 14:4, pp. 359–85.

Bomback, R. H. (1958), *Processing Amateur Movies*, London: Fountain Press.

Bosworth, M. (2001), 'The past as a foreign country? Some methodological implications of doing historical criminology', *British Journal of Criminology*, 41:3, pp. 431–42, https://academic.oup.com/bjc/article-abstract/41/3/431/436836.

Bowring, J., Leavey, C., Ross-Houle, K., Carline, A. and Gunby, C. (2018), 'The UK Adult Film Performer Project: A case for being pro-performer voice', *Porn Studies*, 5:4, pp. 457–60.

Brewster, F., Fenton, H. and Morris, M. (2005), *Shock! Horror*, Guildford: FAB Press.

Brown, G. (2000), 'Divorce reform', *Law & Justice*, 145, p. 57.

Buckley, P. J. and Casson, M. (2001), 'The moral basis of global capitalism: Beyond the eclectic theory', *International Journal of the Economics of Business*, 8:2, pp. 303–27.

Button, J. (2019), *A Dictionary of Green Ideas*, London: Routledge.

Cannatelli, B. L., Smith, B. R. and Sydow, A. (2019), 'Entrepreneurship in the controversial economy: Toward a research agenda', *Journal of Business Ethics*, 155:3, pp. 837–51.

Carlin, G. (2007), 'Rupert Bare: Art, obscenity and the *Oz* trial', in M. Collins (ed.), *The Permissive Society and Its Enemies*, London: Rivers Oram Press, pp. 132–44.

Carter, O. (2018a), *Making European Cult Cinema: Fan Enterprise in an Alternative Economy*, Amsterdam: Amsterdam University Press.

Carter, O. (2018b), 'Original climax films: Historicizing the British hardcore pornography film business', *Porn Studies*, 5:4, pp. 411–25.

Carter, O. (2021), 'The Watford Blue Movie Trial: Regulating rollers in 1970s Britain', *Porn Studies*, 9:1, pp. 82–100, https://doi.org/10.1080/23268743.2021.1947881.

Carter, O. (2022), 'Satisfaction guaranteed: Your choice and the transnational distribution of hardcore pornography between the Netherlands and Britain', *Enterprise & Society*, 23:3, pp. 1–27, https://doi.org/10.1017/eso.2022.13.

Chibnall, S. (1998), *Making Mischief: The Cult Films of Pete Walker*, Surrey: FAB Press.

Chibnall, S. (2003), *Get Carter*, London: I.B. Tauris.

Church, D. (2016), *Disposable Passions: Vintage pornography and the material legacies of adult cinema*, London: Bloomsbury.

Church, D. and Schaefer, E. (2018), 'In focus: Why adult film history matters', *Journal of Cinema and Media Studies*, 58:1, pp. 141–46.

Cleveland, D. and Pritchard, B. (2015), *How films were made and shown*, Essex: *Lavenham Press Ltd*.

Cocks, H. (2016), 'Conspiracy to corrupt public morals and the "unlawful" status of homosexuality in Britain after 1967', *Social History*, 41:3, pp. 267–84.

Collins, A. (2004), 'Sexual dissidence, enterprise and assimilation: Bedfellows in urban regeneration', *Urban Studies*, 41:9, pp. 1789–806.

Collins, M. (2007), 'Introduction: The Permissive Society and its Enemies', in M. Collins (ed.), *The Permissive Society and its Enemies*, London: Rivers Oram Press, pp. 1–40.

Coopersmith, J. (1998), 'Pornography, technology and progress', *Icon*, 4, pp. 94–125, https://www.jstor.org/stable/23785961.

Cox, B., Shirley, J. and Short, M. (1977), *The Fall of Scotland Yard*, Middlesex: Penguin.

Dahl, E. and Næsby, B. (1970), *Sex 69*, San Diego: Greenleaf.

Daly, A. (2018), *Playland*, London: Mirror Books.

Dean, T., Ruszczycky, S. and Squires, D. D. E. (2014), *Porn Archives*, London: Duke University Press.

Deslandes, P. R. (2015), 'The cultural politics of gay pornography in 1970s Britain', in B. Lewis (ed.), *British Queer History*, Manchester: Manchester University Press, pp. 267–96.

Di Lauro, A. and Rabkin, G. (1976), *Dirty Movies: An Illustrated History of the Stag Film, 1915–1970*, New York: Random House *Value*.

Dodd, S. D. and Anderson, A. R. (2001), 'Understanding the enterprise culture paradigm: Paradox and policy', *The International Journal of Entrepreneurship and Innovation*, 2:1, pp. 13–26.

Douglas, J. (1969), *The Age of Perversion*, London: Canova Press.

Doyle, G. (2013), *Understanding Media Economics*, London: SAGE.

Drucker, P. (2015), *Innovation and Entrepreneurship*, London: Routledge.

Dunning, J. H. and Lundan, S. M. (2008), *Multinational Enterprises and the Global Economy*, 2nd ed., Chichester: Edward Elgar Publishing.

Elert, N. and Henrekson, M. (2016), 'Evasive entrepreneurship', *Small Business Economics*, 47:1, pp. 95–113.

Farge, A. (2013), *The Allure of the Archives*, Connecticut: Yale University Press.

Farmer, R. (2017), 'The Profumo affair in popular culture: The Keeler Affair (1963) and the commercial exploitation of a public scandal', *Contemporary British History*, 31:3, pp. 452–70.

Ferris, P. (1993), *Sex and the British*, London: Michael Joseph.

Fisher, T. (1993), 'Permissiveness and the politics of morality', *Contemporary Record*, 7:1, pp. 149–65.

Flexner, S. B. (1982), *Listening to America*, New York: Simon and Schuster.

Flint, D. (1999), *Babylon Blue: An Illustrated History of Adult Cinema*, London: Creation Books.

Franzosi, R. (1987), 'The press as a source of socio-historical data: Issues in the methodology of data collection from newspapers', *Historical Methods: A Journal of Quantitative and Interdisciplinary History*, 20:1, pp. 5–16.

Freeman, M. J. (2011), I Pornographer, Amazon Kindle.

Freeman, M. J. (2012a), *Rich Man (I Pornographer Book 5)*, Amazon Kindle.

Freeman, M. J. (2012b), *Poor Man (I Pornographer Book 6)*, Amazon Kindle.

Freeman, M. J. (2013a), *Making Movies (I Pornographer Book 3)*, Amazon Kindle.

Freeman, M. J. (2013b), *The Trailblazer (I Pornographer Book 4)*, Amazon Kindle.

Freibert, F. (2021), 'Distribution, bars, and arcade stars: Joe Anthony's entrepreneurial expansion in Houston's gay media industries', *Synoptique*, 9:2, pp. 33–54.

Frewin, A. (2000), *London Blues*, Harpenden: No Exit Press.

Gertzman, J. A. (1999), *Bookleggers and Smuthounds: The Trade in Erotica, 1920–1940*, Philadelphia: University of Pennsylvania Press.

Gibson-Graham, J. K. (2006), *A Postcapitalist Politics,* Minnesota: University of Minnesota Press.

Giles, Jane. (2018), *Scala Cinema 1978–1993*, Guildford: FAB Press.

Gillespie, A. A. and Ost, S. (2016), 'The "higher" age of consent and the concept of sexual exploitation', in I. Reed, M. Bohlander, N. Wake and E. Smith (eds), *Consent: Domestic and Comparative Perspectives*, London: Routledge, pp. 161–76.

Godley, A. and Casson, M. (2012), 'History of entrepreneurship: Britain, 1900–2000', in D. S. Landes, J. A. Mokyr and W. J. Baumol, (eds), *The Invention of Enterprise*, Princeton, New Jersey: Princeton University Press, pp. 243–72.

Gold, D. (2012), *Solid Gold: My Autobiography: The Ultimate Rags to Riches Tale*, Amazon Kindle.

Gold, R. (1997), *Good as Gold: The Rags to Riches Story of the Gold Brothers*, London: Robson Books.

Goldstein, M. (2005), *Naked Jungle*, London: Silverback Press.

Gorfinkel, E. (2017), *Lewd Looks*, Minnesota: University of Minnesota Press.

Gorfinkel, E. (2019), 'Editor's introduction: Sex and the materiality of adult media', *Feminist Media Histories*, 5:2, pp. 1–18.

Gottschalk, P. (2009), *Entrepreneurship and Organised Crime: Entrepreneurs in Illegal Business*, London: Edward Elgar Publishing.

Gray, C. (2002), *Enterprise and Culture*, London: Routledge.

Gustafsson, T. (2016), 'The open secret: Illegal screenings of pornographic films for public audiences in Sweden, 1921–1943', in E. Bjorklund and M. Larsson (eds), *Swedish Cinema and the Sexual Revolution: Critical Essays*, North Carolina: McFarland and Co, pp. 101–15.

Hagedoorn, J. (1996), 'Innovation and entrepreneurship: Schumpeter revisited', *Industrial and Corporate Change*, 5:3, pp. 883–96.

Hale, F. (2003), '"Time" for sex in Sweden: Enhancing the myth of the "Swedish Sin" during the 1950s', *Scandinavian Studies*, 75:3, pp. 351–74.

Hall, S. (1980), 'Reformism and the legislation of consent', in Anon. (ed.), *Permissiveness and Control: The Fate of the Sixties Legislation*, London: Palgrave Macmillan, pp. 1–43.

Hammersley, M. and Atkinson, P. (2007), *Ethnography: Principles in Practice*, London: Routledge.

Hammond, P. (1976), *French Undressing*, London: Futura Publications.

Hebditch, D. and Anning, N. (1988), *Porn Gold: Inside the Pornography Business*, London: Faber and Faber.

Heffernan, K. (2015), 'Seen as a business: Adult film's historical framework and foundations', in L. Comella and S. Tarrant (eds), *New Views on Pornography: Sexuality, Politics, and the Law*, California: Praeger, pp. 37–56.

Heffernan, K. (2016), 'Sex entertainment for the whole family to mature pictures: I Jomfruens Tegn and transnational erotic cinema', in A. Fisher and J. Walker (eds), *Grindhouse: Cultural Exchange on 42nd Street, and Beyond*, London: Bloomsbury, pp. 129–44.

Heineman, E. (2011), *Before Porn Was Legal: The Erotic Empire of Beate Uhse*, Illinois: University of Chicago Press.

Henry, S. (1978), *The Hidden Economy*, London: Martin Robertson and Company.

Hill, N. (1937), *Think and Grow Rich*, Forgotten Books.

Hobbs, D. (1988), *Doing the Business*, Oxford: Oxford University Press.

Hobbs, D. (1995), *Bad Business*, Oxford: Oxford University Press.

Hubbard, P. (2012), *Cities and Sexualities*, Oxon: Routledge.

Humphries, S. (1991), *A Secret World of Sex: Forbidden Fruit: The British Experience 1900–1950*, London: Sidgwick & Jackson.

Hunt, L. (1998), *British Low Culture: From Safari Suits to Sexploitation*, London: Routledge.

Hunter, I. Q. (2013), *British Trash Cinema*, London: Palgrave MacMillan.

Hunter, I. Q. (2014), 'Naughty realism: The Britishness of British hardcore', *Journal of British Cinema and Television*, 11:2&3, pp. 152–71.

Hutchinson, T. (2013), 'Doctrinal research: Researching the jury', in D. Watkins and M. Burton (eds), *Research Methods in Law*, London: Routledge, pp. 8–39.

Jarossi, R. (2018), *The Hunt for the 60s Ripper*, London: Mirror Books.

Jefferson, T. (1993), 'Cultural responses of the Teds', in S. Hall, and T. Jefferson (eds), *Resistance through Rituals Youth Subcultures in Post-war Britain*, London: Routledge, pp. 67–70.

Johnson, D. K. (2019), *Buying Gay: How Physique Entrepreneurs Sparked a Movement*, New York: Columbia University Press.

Jones, M. (2007) 'Down the Rabbit Hole: Permissiveness and Paedophilia in the 1960s', in M. Collins (ed.), *The Permissive Society and its Enemies: Sixties British Culture*, London: Rivers Oram Press, pp. 112–31.

Jones, S. and Mowlabocus, S. (2009), 'Hard times and rough rides: The legal and ethical impossibilities of researching "shock" pornographies', *Sexualities*, 12:5, pp. 613–28.

Joyce, S. (2011), *Knock Down Ginger*, Amazon Kindle.

Kane, B. (2019), 'Ecclesiastical court records for social and cultural history', in R. Sandberg, N. Doe, B. Kane and C. Roberts (eds), *Research Handbook on Interdisciplinary Approaches to Law and Religion*, Cheltenham: Edward Elgar, pp. 37–53.

Kelland, G. (1986), *Crime in London*, London: Random House.

Kendrick, W. M. (1987), *The Secret Museum: Pornography in Modern Culture*, London: Viking Penguin.

Kennedy, E. L. and Davis, M. D. (2013), *Boots of Leather, Slippers of Gold*, London: Routledge.

Kerekes, D. (2000), '*Jolly Hockey Sticks!*', in J. Stevenson (ed.), *Fleshpot: Cinema's Sexual Myth Makers and Taboo Breakers*, Manchester: Headpress, pp. 191–96.

Kerekes, D. and Slater, D. (2000), *See No Evil: Banned Films and Video Controversy*, Manchester: Headpress.

Killick, M. (1994), *The Sultan of Sleaze: The Story of David Sullivan's Sex and Media Empire*, London: Penguin.

Kirby, D. (2018), *Scotland Yard's Gangbuster*, Barnsley: Pen and Sword True Crime.

Kirzner, I. M. (1973), *Competition and Entrepreneurship*, Chicago: University of Chicago Press.

Knight, A. and Alpert, H. (1967), 'The history of sex in cinema: Part Seventeen – The Stag Film', *Playboy*, November, pp. 154–58, 170–89.

Koch, G. (1990), 'On pornographic cinema: The body's shadow realm', *Jump Cut*, 35, pp. 17–29.

Kuhn, A. (2002), *Everyday Magic: Cinema and Cultural Memory*, London: I.B. Tauris.

Kutchinsky, B. and Snare, A. (1999), *Law, Pornography and Crime: The Danish Experience*, Oslo: Pax Forlag.

Kyrou, A. (1964), 'D'un Certain Cinema Clandestin', *Positif: Revue de Cinéma*, June/July/August, pp. 205–23.

Larsson, M. (2015), 'A national/transnational genre: Pornography in transition' in T. Gustafsson and P. Kääpä (eds), *Nordic Genre Film: Small Nation Film Cultures in the Global Market-Place*, Edinburgh: Edinburgh University Press, pp. 217–29.

Larsson, M. (2016), *The Swedish Porn Scene: Exhibition Contexts, 8mm Pornography and the Sex Film*, Bristol: Intellect.

Larsson, M. (2018), 'Oh Paris! The journeys of Lasse Braun's 8mm pornography', *Journal of Cinema and Media Studies*, 58:1, pp. 158–63.

Lauret, J. C. (1970), *The Danish Sex Fairs*, London: *Jasmine Press*.

Leathard, A. (1980), *Fight for Family Planning*, London: Springer.

Lee, E., Sheldon, S. and Macvarish, J. (2018), 'The 1967 Abortion Act fifty years on: Abortion, medical authority and the law revisited', *Social Science & Medicine*, 21:2, pp. 26–32.

Leeson, P. T. and Coyne, C. J. (2004). 'The plight of underdeveloped countries; institutions and the direction of entrepreneurial activity with evidence from Romania', *Mercatus Center at George Mason University*, https://www.mercatus.org/system/files/The_Plight_of_Underdeveloped_Countries_Institutions_and_the_Direction_of_Entrepreneurial_Activity_with_Evidence_from_Romania_Working_Paper.pdf.

Linnane, F. (2016), *London's Underworld*, London: Pavilion Books.

Lobato, R. and Thomas, J. (2015), *The Informal Media Economy*, London: Polity.

Long, J. (2012), *Anti-Porn*, London: Zed Books Ltd.

Long, S. and Sheridan, S. (2008), *X-Rated: Adventures of an Exploitation Filmmaker*, London: Reynolds and Hearn.

Madsen, S. A. (2013), *Historien Om Ugens Rapport*, Copenhagen: Lindhardt og Ringhof.

Maina, G. and Zecca, F. (2021), 'Turn on the red light: Notes on the birth of Italian pornography', *Porn Studies*, 9:1, pp. 118–42, https://doi.org/10.1080/23268743.2021.1961604.

Malpass, P. (1999), 'Continuity and change in philanthropic housing organisations: The Octavia Hill Housing Trust and the Guinness Trust', *The London Journal*, 24:1, pp. 38–57.

Manchester, C. (1982), 'Indecent Displays (Control) Act 1981', *Statute Law Review*, 3:1, pp. 31–39.

Manchester, C. (1986), *Sex Shops and the Law*, Hampshire: Gower.

Marcus, S. (2017), *The Other Victorians*, Oxon: Routledge.

Mark, R. (1979), *In the Office of Constable*, Glasgow: Fontana.

Marwick, A. (1988), 'The 1960s: Was there a "cultural revolution"?', *Contemporary Record*, 2:3, pp. 18–20.

Marwick, A. (2007), 'The international context', in M. Collins (ed.), *The Permissive Society and its Enemies*, London: Rivers Oram Press, pp. 169–84.

McCarthy, D. M. P. (2011), *An Economic History of Organized Crime: A National and Transnational Approach*, Oxon: Routledge.

McClister, C. G. (1994), 'Prohibition of obscene imports in the United Kingdom – A violation of Article 36 of the Treaty Establishing the European Community', *Penn State International Law Review*, 13:2, pp. 329–46.

McConville, M. and Chui, W. H. (eds) (2007), *Research Methods for Law*, Edinburgh: Edinburgh University Press.

McGillivray, D. (2017), *Doing Rude Things*, London: Wolfbait.

McGlynn, C. and Ward, I. (2009), 'Pornography, pragmatism, and proscription', *Journal of Law and Society*, 36:3, pp. 327–51.

McKee, G. (1978), *Film Collecting*, London: *The Tantivy Press*.

McKee, A., Byron, P., Litsou, K. and Ingham, R. (2020), 'An interdisciplinary definition of pornography: Results from a Global Delphi Panel', *Archives of Sexual Behavior*, 49:3, pp. 1085–91.

McKenna, M. (2020), *Nasty Business: The Marketing and Distribution of the Video Nasties*, Edinburgh: Edinburgh University Press.

McRobbie, A. (1989), 'Second-hand dresses and the role of the ragmarket', in A. McRobbie (ed.), *Zoot Suits and Second-Hand Dresses*, London: Springer, pp. 23–49.

Mort, F. (2010), *Capital Affairs: London and the Making of the Permissive Society*, London: Yale University Press.

Müller, T. (2015), 'Moral entrepreneurship revisited: Police officers monitoring cannabis retailers in Rotterdam, the Netherlands', *Contributions from European Symbolic*

*Interactionists: Reflections on Methods*, 9 March, pp. 139–57, http://dx.doi.org/ 10.1108/ S0163-239620150000044007.

Nead, L. (1997), 'Mapping the self: Gender, space, and modernity in mid-Victorian London', *Environment and Planning A*, 29:4, pp. 659–72.

North, D. C. (1990), *Institutions, Institutional Change and Economic Performance*, Cambridge: Cambridge University Press.

North, D. C. (2005), *Understanding the Process of Economic Change*, Princeton: Princeton University Press.

North, P. (2007), *Money and Liberation*, Minneapolis: University of Minnesota Press.

O'Toole, L. (1999), *Pornocopia*, London: Serpents Tail.

Paasonen, S. (2010), 'Labors of love: Netporn, Web 2.0 and the meanings of amateurism', *New Media and Society*, 12:8, pp. 1297–312.

Paasonen, S. (2017) 'Smutty Swedes: Sex films, pornography and good sex', in D. Kerr and D. Peberdy (eds), *Tainted Love: Screening Sexual Perversion*, London: I.B. Tauris, pp. 120–36.

Pearson, J. (2015), *The Profession of Violence: The Rise and Fall of the Kray Twins*, London: William Collins.

Perkins, M. (2012), 'Pornography, policing and censorship', in P. Johnson and D. Dalton (eds), *Policing Sex*, London: Routledge, pp. 85–98.

Petley, J. (2011), *Film and Video Censorship in Contemporary Britain*, Edinburgh: Edinburgh University Press.

Petley, J. (2019), 'Loosening the gag: The Crown Prosecution Service's revised legal guidance on the Obscene Publications Act 1959', *Porn Studies*, 6:2, pp. 238–44.

Pezzutto, S. (2019), 'From porn performer to porntrepreneur: Online entrepreneurship, social media branding, and selfhood in contemporary trans pornography', *About Gender*, 8:16, pp. 30–60.

Portelli, A. (2010), *The Death of Luigi Trastulli and Other Stories: Form and Meaning in Oral History*, Albany: SUNY Press.

Porter, M. E. (1998), 'Clusters and the new economics of competition', *Harvard Business Review, November–December*, pp. 77–90.

Pullen, B. (2008), 'Photography and censorship: The photographs and ideals of Jean Straker', *Photography and Culture*, 1:2, pp. 227–38.

Reekie, D. (2007), *Subversion: The Definitive History of Underground Cinema*, London: Wallflower.

Roberts, M. J. D. (1985), 'Morals, art, and the law: The passing of the Obscene Publications Act, 1857', *Victorian Studies*, 28:4, pp. 609–29.

Robertson, G. (1979), *Obscenity*, London: Weidenfeld and Nicolson.

Roodhouse, M. (2013), *Black Market Britain*, Oxford: Oxford University Press.

Rose-Ackerman, S. (1996), 'The Political Economy of Corruption: Causes and Consequences', *World Bank*, Washington, DC., © World Bank, License: CC BY 3.0 IGO, https:// openknowledge.worldbank.org/handle/10986/11629.

Samers, M. (2005), 'The myopia of "diverse economies", or a critique of the "informal economy"', *Antipode*, 37:5, pp. 875–86, https://onlinelibrary.wiley.com/doi/abs/10.1111/j.0066-4812.2005.00537.x.

Sandbrook, D. (2011), *State of Emergency: The Way We Were in Britain 1970–1974*, London: Penguin.

Sanders-McDonagh, E., Peyrefitte, M. and Ryalls, M. (2016), 'Sanitising the city: Exploring hegemonic gentrification in London's Soho', *Sociological Research Online*, 21:3, pp. 128–33.

Saunders, R. (2020), *Bodies of Work: The Labour of Sex in the Digital Age*, London: Palgrave Macmillan.

Schaefer, E. (2002), 'Gauging a revolution: 16mm film and the rise of the pornographic feature', *Cinema Journal*, 41:3, pp. 3–26.

Schaefer, E. (2005), 'Dirty little secrets: Scholars, archivists and dirty movies', *The Moving Image*, 5:2, pp. 79–105, https://muse.jhu.edu/article/190409/summary.

Schaefer, E. (2007), 'Plain brown wrapper', in J. Lewis and E. Smoodin (eds), *Looking Past the Screen: Case Studies in American Film History and Method*, Durham: Duke University Press, pp. 201–26.

Schaefer, E. (2012), 'The problem with sexploitation movies', *Iluminace*, 3, pp. 148–52.

Schaefer, E. (2014), '"I'll take Sweden": The shifting discourse of the "sexy nation" in sexploitation films', in E. Schaefer (ed.), *Sex Scene: Media and the Sexual Revolution*, Durham: Duke University Press, pp. 207–34.

Schlosser, E. (2004), *Reefer Madness*, New York: Mariner Books.

Schumpeter, J. (1939), *Business Cycles*, New York: McGraw-Hill.

Schumpeter, J. (2017), *Theory of Economic Development*, Oxon: Routledge.

Shane, S. A. (2008), *The Illusions of Entrepreneurship*, London: Yale University Press.

Shelby, H. C. (1970), *Stag Movie Review*, California: Viceroy Press.

Sheridan, S. (1999) *Come Play with Me*, Guildford: FAB Press.

Sheridan, S. (2005) *Keeping the British End Up: Four Decades of Saucy Cinema*, Richmond: Reynolds & Hearn.

Short, M. (1990), *Inside the Brotherhood*, London: Harper Collins.

Simpson, A. W. B. (1983), *Pornography and Politics*, Exeter: Pergamon Press.

Slade, J. W. (1984), 'Violence in the hardcore pornographic film: A historical survey', *Journal of Communication*, 34:3, pp. 148–63.

Slade, J. W. (2000), *Pornography in America*, Santa Barbara: ABC-Clio.

Slade, J. W. (2006), 'Eroticism and technological regression: The stag film', *History and Technology*, 22:1, pp. 27–52.

Smith, C. (2005), 'A perfectly British business: Stagnation, continuities and change on the top shelf', in L. Z. Sigel (ed.), *International Exposure: Perspectives on Modern Pornography 1800–2000*, New York: Rutgers University Press, pp. 146–72.

Smith, C. (2007), *One for the Girls*, Bristol: Intellect.

Smith, C. (2018), 'Policy, politics and porn', *Sexualities*, 21:8, pp. 1351–59.

Smith, R. (2009), 'Understanding entrepreneurial behaviour in organized criminals', *Journal of Enterprising Communities: People and Places in the Global Economy*, 3:3, pp. 256–68.

Smith, R. (2020), 'The evolution of "entrepreneurial policing": A review of the literature', *Journal of Entrepreneurship and Public Policy*, 9:1, pp. 1–20.

Spicer, A. and McKenna, A. T. (2013), *The Man Who Got Carter*, London: Bloomsbury Publishing.

Stoops, J. (2018), *The Thorny Path*, Montreal: McGill-Queen's Press.

Strub, W. (2011), *Perversion for Profit: The Politics of Pornography and the Rise of the New Right*, New York: Columbia University Press.

Sullivan, R. and McKee, A. (2015), *Pornography: Structures, Agency and Performance*, London: John Wiley and Sons.

Summers, J. (1989), *Soho: A History of London's Most Colourful Neighbourhood*, London: Bloomsbury.

Sutherland, J. (1982), *Offensive Literature: Decensorship in Britain, 1960–1982*, Junction Books, London.

Sweet, M. (2006), *Shepperton Babylon*, London: Faber and Faber.

Taormino, T., Penley, C., Shimizu, C. P., Miller, M. and Hill-Meyer, T. (2013), *The Feminist Porn Book: The Politics of Producing Pleasure*, New York: The Feminist Press at CUNY.

Tate, T. (1990), *Child Pornography*, London: Trafalgar Square.

Taylor, L. S. (1970), *Decision in Denmark: The Legalizing of Pornography*, California: Academy Press.

Thompson, B. (1994), *Soft Core*, London: Weidenfeld and Nicolson.

Thompson, D. (2007), *Black and White and Blue Adult Cinema from the Victorian Age to the VCR*, Toronto: ECW Press.

Tomkinson, M. (1982), *The Pornbrokers: The Rise of the Soho Sex Barons*, London: Virgin.

Trevelyan, J. (1973), *What the Censor Saw*, London: Michael Joseph.

Tsaliki, L. (2016), *Children and the Politics of Sexuality: The Sexualization of Children Debate Revisited*, London: Palgrave Macmillan.

Turquier, B. (2016), '"Bolex artists": Bolex cameras, amateurism, and New York Avant-garde film', in G. Fossati and A. van den Oeve (eds), *Exposing the Film Apparatus: The Film Archive as a Research Laboratory*, Amsterdam: Amsterdam University Press, pp. 153–62.

Upton, J. (2016), 'Electric blues: The rise and fall of Britain's first pre-recorded videocassette distributors', *Journal of British Cinema and Television*, 13:1, pp. 19–41, https://www.euppublishing.com/doi/abs/10.3366/jbctv.2016.0294

Voss, G. (2012), '"Treating it as a normal business": Researching the pornography industry', *Sexualities*, 15:3–4, pp. 391–410, https://journals.sagepub.com/doi/abs/10.1177/1363460712439650.

Waldroup, H. (2020), 'The nude in the album: Materiality and erotic narrative', *Visual Resources*, 36:2, pp. 195–214.

Walsh, D. (2004), 'Doing ethnography', in C. Seale (ed.), *Researching Society and Culture*, London: Sage, pp. 225–37.

Watney, S. (1997), *Policing Desire: Pornography, AIDS and the Media*, Minneapolis: University of Minnesota Press.

Waugh, T. (1996), *Hard to Imagine: Gay Male Eroticism in Photography and Film from Their Beginnings to Stonewall*, New York, Chichester: Columbia University Press.

Waugh, T. (2001), 'Homosociality in the classical American stag film: Off-screen, on-screen', *Sexualities*, 4:3, pp. 275–91.

Weeks, J. (2012), *Sex, Politics and Society: The Regulation of Sexuality Since 1800*, Oxon: Routledge.

Wickstead, H. (2020), 'Soho typescripts: Handmade obscene books in post-war London bookshops', *Porn Studies*, 7:2, pp. 1–25.

Williams, B. (2015), *Obscenity and Film Censorship*, Cambridge: Cambridge University Press.

Williams, C. (2006), *The Hidden Enterprise Culture: Entrepreneurship in the Underground Economy*, Cheltenham: Edward Elgar.

Williams, J. E. H. (1960), 'The Street Offences Act, 1959', *The Modern Law Review*, 23: 2, pp. 173–79.

Williams, L. (1989), *Hard Core: Power, Pleasure, and the Frenzy of the Visible*, Berkeley: University of California Press.

Wood, F. (2017), *The Naked Truth About Harrison Marks*, London: Wolfbait.

Woozley, A. D. (1982), 'The tendency to deprave and corrupt', *Law and Philosophy*, 1:2, pp. 217–38.

# Index

8mm film 2, 4–5, 12, 28, 52–4, 57, 59–60, 62, 68, 70, 81, 114, 149, 226
*8mm Magazine* 13, 59, 60, 126
9.5mm film 53
16mm film 12, 28, 53, 55–60, 62, 63, 81, 114, 116
35mm film 53, 55, 226
*100% Lust* (1966) 28, 75–6, *75*, 81, 108, 321n22

## A

Abortion Act 1967 29–30
Academy label 162, *163*, 190–1, *190*, 206, 245–6
Action Films 118, 246
*Action Girl* (1968–72) 326n19
*Adult Fantasy Magazine* 328n20
Adult Loop Database 3, 12, 81, 239
*Afternoon Lust* (1964–67) 65
*After Sales Service* (1969) 88
age of consent 98, 99, 219
Alilunas, P. 4, 5, 9, 12, 14, 224, 226
Alpert, H. 17, 55, 218
*Alpine Lust* (1970–72) 191, *192*
alternative economy
    casual roles 325n12
    emergence of alternative economy 17–50
    entrepreneurship as framework 217, 219, 220
    entrepreneurship in alternative economy 14–15

expanding roller trade 92, 102, 113, 133, 135
making the roller market 57, 63, 68, 70, 72, 89–90
overview 17–19
pornography as 6–9
regulating the roller trade 15, 17–19, 138, 171, 172
video and 1980s laws 237
Alton, Leslie xxiii, 37, 40, 74–5, 111, 114, 126
*Amateur Cine World* (magazine) 57, 58, 59, 60–1, 63, 81
*Amateur Photographer* (magazine) 44, 72, 161
America 4, 55, 177, 218, 225
*An American Buttman in London* (1992) xxvii
Amör Films 246–7
Amsterdam xxvii, 17, 125–6, 131, 237
anal sex xxvi, 165, 168
*And the Rain Came* (1970–72) 191
Anglo Continental label 158, 161, 162, 165, *165*, 191, 247
Anning, N. 4, 59, 70, 75, 76, 106
Ann Summers 175
Anwyl-Davies, Judge Marcus 167, 169–70
Apollo Films 162, 248
*Arabian Nights* (1969) 147, 325n9
archives xxix, 11–12, 13, 222, 223, 324n1

Arnberg, K. 177, 322n28
Arriflex ST 16mm cine camera 191
*Artic Fuck* (1970–72) 191, *192*
Assman Productions 77
Aston Manor school, Birmingham 194, 196, 197
Australia 330n31
*Auto Sex* (1968) 76
Aventura 227

**B**

Bartkowski, Walter (Charlie Brown) xxii, 79–81, 89, 107, 125, 127, 139, 151, 153, 191, 206, 225, 322n28, 328n18, 329n27, 331n2
Basu, G. 153
Baumol, W. J. 8, 20
BBC (British Broadcasting Corporation) 186, 202, 204–7
    BBC Blue Movie Case 204–7
BBFC *see* British Board of Film Censors; British Board of Film Classification
BDSM (bondage, discipline and sadomasochism) 159, 210, 213, 221, 227
Becker, H. S. 8, 177, 220
Ben Dover brand 237 *see also* Honey, Lindsay
Ben's Books 227
Bentley, Chrissie 318n2, 318n3
Beresford, S. 159, 213, 234
bestiality 37, 117, 143, 168, 326n21, 327n5
Betamax 228, 232
Bichler, G. 20
*Birmingham Post* 150, 196, 197
Birmingham Trial (*R* v. *Lindsay*) 25, 195–8, *199*, 201–2, *202*, 207, 209
Blackburn, Raymond 174, 176
*Black Magic* (1963–67) 65
black market 8, 95, 216, 218, 236
blue movies 2, 54, 55, 64, 318n1
blue movie shows 64, 66–8, 73–4, 81, 89, 180

Blue Scene Films 81–9, *85*, 133, 149, 249–50, 322n29, 322n30, 322n34
Blue X label 250–1
Boffa, Tony *see* Sonenscher, Tony
Bolex H16 camera 57–8, *58*, *59*, 114, 191
Bomback, R. H. 60, 62
*Bondage* (1966–67) 108
bondage, discipline and sadomasochism (BDSM) 159, 210, 213, 221, 227
Bon Homme Press 46
bookshops
    bookshop owners 34–8
    Court Bookshop image *41*
    emergence of alternative economy 14, 17, 23, 25, 26, 31, 32–4, 39–42, 43, 46–8
    erotic drawings 96
    expanding roller trade 104
    making the roller market 80–1
    map of Soho's bookstores *49*
    regulating the roller trade 141, 155, 159
    Soho Postcards and Bibles 43, 46, 47
    the underworld 39–42
*The Bookworm* (1971–72) 154
Bosworth, M. 13
Braun, Lasse (Alberto Ferro) xix, 4, *59*, 76, 127, 156, 183, *183*, 191, 194, 225
    *Golden Butterfly* 59
    'London Series' 225
    *Sex Maniacs* 331n3
*Breakfast Service* (1990) xxvi
Brewer Street, Soho *18*, 33, 39
British Board of Film Censors (BBFC) 5, 21, 28, 53, 64, 179, 194, 209, 214, 215
British Board of Film Classification (BBFC) 22, 235, 237
British Broadcasting Corporation *see* BBC
British Film Institute 223
*British Journal of Photography* 72, 86, 88
British Library 11, 12, 118

British Newspaper Archive 12, 138, 324n1

British Videogram Association 232

brothels 31, 67

Brown, Charlie *see* Bartkowski, Walter

Brown, G. 30

Buenos Aires 54

buggery 123, 168, 169, 170, 171

*The Builders* (1970–71) 191

Bunny Films 133, 251

Buster, Dolly xxvi

*Butterfly* (1972) *229*

Byrne, Bob xix

Byrne, Gerald 33–4, 35, 39, 154


C

Caborn-Waterfield, Michael 175

CalVista 227, 330n31, 331n38

cameras 44, 57–9, 114, 191

Campaign Against Censorship 21

Canby, Vincent 325n7

Candy Films 143, *143*, 147, 251

Capstick, Brian 209

Carlin, G. 327n2

*Carnaby Kinks* (1968) *17*, 107

Carnaby Kinks label 53

Casanova Film 252

Case, Donald 'Duke' (aka Nick Valentine) xix, 158–9, *160*

CD-Film 204

censorship 7–8, 169, 179, 182, 185, 209, 232, 235–6

*Central Weekend* (TV show) 214, 330n31

chair system, of bookshops 33, 34, 36, 37, 47

*Charity Begins at Home* 196

Charlie Brown Produktion 151

Cherub label 133, 252–3, 322n34, 326n19

Chez M. Pigeon (1960–65) 57, 62, 64

Chibnall, S. 5, 53, 54, 70, 318n4

*Chick* (magazine) 111, *128*, 131, 188, 194, 222

'Chicko' (bookshop chair) 105

child pornography 21, 37, 100–1, 102, 143, 174, 208, 210, 323n10

*Chinese and Passion* (1970–72) 142

'Christine' (roller performer) 2

cinema clubs
    distributing hardcore films 176, 179–82, 185–6, 203–4, 206, 208, 211, 214–16
    *The Frost Programme* 173
    Holloways trial 234
    and Lindsay 203–4, 206, 208, 211, 214
    making the roller market 59, 63, 64, 68
    regulating pornography 22
    and Waterfield 179, 181–2, 185–6

Cinemas Act 1985 21, 216

Cinematograph Act 1909 21, 216

Cinematograph Act 1952 21, 179, 182, 216

Cinematograph (Amendment) Act 1982 21, 215, 216, 236

Citron, Gerald 40, 184

Clark, Patricia xxii, 179, 180, 182, 183, 185, 236, 237, 327n8, 327n10

class 24, 42–3, 67, 94

Cleveland, D. 57

Climax Films
    bookshop 126, 127
    catalogues *129*, 132
    and Cook 70, 71, 75, 76
    expanding roller trade 92, 105–13, 114, 127–33, 135
    and Keeler rumours 75–6
    labelography 239, 240, 253–61
    making the roller market 3
    and Phillips 14
    regulating the roller trade 141, 146, 148, 149, 153, 154
    title cards *109*

Climax in Color 154

Climax Original 107, *128*, 253–61, 323n11

*Climax Story* blog 323n9

clip joints 31, 179

clustering 47

Cocks, H. 22, 28, 30

'Colin' (producer) xix, 35, 43, 47, 71

collectors xxiii, 12

Collingbourne, Anthony
    Academy label 190, 206
    death of 170
    image *161*
    imprisonment 170, 176
    making the roller market 70
    move to Europe 212
    overview xix
    regulating the roller trade 15, 137, 158,
        161–2, 163–70, *163*
    Watford Blue Movie Trial 163–70

Collins, A. 31

Color Climax 84, 89, 106, 107, 142, 156,
    183, *183*, 184, 324n3, 326n21, 327n6

*Color Climax* magazine 148

colour film 67–8, 71–2, 127–8, 132, 158,
    328n19

common law charges 22, 24, 30, 68, 73, 166,
    171, 235

Community Levy for Alternative Projects
    (CLAP) 181

Compton Cinema Club 179, *180*

conspiracy charges 22, 24, 68, 166, 171, 205,
    208

contact magazines 118

contact printers 62–3, 116

*Continental Film Review* 13, 124, *125*

continental market labelography 303–13

contraception 29, 219

*Convent of Sin* (1972–73) 197, 200, 329n26

Cook, Ivor
    *100% Lust* 108
    *British Journal of Photography* advert
        86

Chibnall on 5, 318n4

death of 90

emergence of alternative economy 50

entrepreneurship as framework 218–19

expanding roller trade 92, 96, 106, 116,
    133

Germany links 322n26

making the roller market 14, 51–2, 63,
    70–6, 78, 79, 81, 86, 88–90

overview xx

police interview 320n2

regulating the roller trade 140, 145, 148

Soho Postcards 89

Coopersmith, J. 7

Copenhagen 17, 76, 79–80, 89, 131, 139,
    321n24

coprophilia 210

Cornell, George 324n17

Cornwall Gardens raid 73, 74, 79, 322n26

Court Bookshop 40, *41*, 42, 113, 114

Cox, B. 5, 140

Cox, Derek 127, 324n18

Coyne, C. J. 7

credits 10

Criminal Justice and Immigration Act 2008
    20, 21, 198, 221, 240, 331n1

Criminal Justice and Immigration Act 2018 22

Criminal Justice and Public Order Act 1994
    21

Criminal Law Act 1977 208, 230, 330n35

Crimson, Gav 332n5

Crispie, Stuart xxii, 106, 140

Crown Prosecution Service (CPS) 221,
    328n14

Culver, Officer 47, 105, 145, 147

Customs and Excise Act 1952 184, 186

Customs Consolidation Act 1857 183

Customs Consolidation Act 1876 21, 23, 213

customs laws 21, 23, 59, 183–4, 186, 212–13,
    216, 234, 237

**D**

Dahl, E. 142

*Daily Mail* (newspaper) 126, 194, 196

*Daily Mirror* (newspaper) 55, 104, 167, 185, 188, 197, 201

Daly, Anthony 326n22

Danish Blu Films 147, 261, 325n9

Darby, John
    Academy label 190, 206
    distributing hardcore films 176, 196–8
    garage image *137*
    and Lindsay 176, 186–91, 194
    mail-order catalogue 206
    move to Europe 212
    overview xxii
    regulating the roller trade 15, 136–7, 150, 155–8, *157*, 162, 166, 168
    seized materials 192

'Dave' (distributor) xxi, 42, 159, 176, 208, 210, 227

Davey, Ronald 'The Dustman' xxii, 35, 43–7, 111, 124, 146

Davis, M. D. 12

Dean, T. 11

*Deep Throat* (1972) 173, 178–9, 185

*Degenerate's Orgy* (1968) 118–20, *119*, *121*, 122, 123

Delilah Deluxe 133, *134*, 263

Denmark
    Blue Scene Films 81, 88, 89
    and Cook 71, 76, 78, 79–81
    'Danish blue' 190, 325n7
    emergence of alternative economy 17, 22, 31, 38
    expanding roller trade 107, 125, 127–8, 131–3
    film processing 59
    legalization of pornography 47, 89, 127, 139, 148, 184, 218, 325n7
    making the roller market 14, 71, 76, 78–81, 88–90
    red-light districts 17
    regulating pornography 22
    regulating the roller trade 139, 141–2, 145, 146, 148–50, 153, 155, 156
    sex fairs 324n19
    transnational trade 148–50
    Universal Films 141–2, 145, 146, 148

Denning, Lord 55, 171

Denning, Martin 332n8

'Derek' (producer) xix, 63, 68–9, 99, 147

De Wallen, Amsterdam 17

*Dial a Guy* (1981–82) 232, 234, 235

digital pornography 9, 132, 221

Di Lauro, A. 12, 55, 76, 84, 238, 239, 319n7

Director of Public Prosecutions 13, 15, 22, 93, 102, 123, 137, 166, 168, 171, 184, 195, 204, 239

'The Dirty Squad' 34 *see also* Obscene Publications Squad

disorderly house charge 68, 182, 208

distributing hardcore films in Britain 173–216
    Lindsay and Birmingham trial 194–202
    Lindsay and dirty work 203–6
    Lindsay and exports 186–94
    Lindsay as a wanted man 207–14
    list of distributors xxi–xxii
    moral battlefield 174–8
    overview 15, 173–4, 214–16
    *R* v. *Waterfield* (1975) 182–6
    Waterfield and members-only clubs 178–82

Divorce Reform Act 1969 29, 30

Doc Johnson 227

doctrinal research 13

*Dog Fun* (1967–68) 117

*Dog Lovers* (1971–72) 168, 169, 170

*Dog Orgy* (1967–68) 117

*La Dolce Vita* (1960–65) 64, 239

Dolly Films 133, 143, *143*, 147, 263–4, 325n9

Double X 162, *163*, 264–5

Douglas, J. 32–3

Dover, Ben *see* Honey, Lindsay

*Down Town* (n.d.) 53

Doyle, G. 56

*DPP* v. *Jordan* (1976) 25, 209

drawings 96, 97, 99

*Dream Orgy* (1970–72) 251

Drew, Linzi 230

Drucker, P. 30

Drury, Ken 154

dubbing xxvi

Du Cann, Richard 171

*Duet* (1968) 86, 87, 322n33

Dunning, J. H. 127

DVDs xxvii, xxviii


E

*Easiest Way* (1930–35) 55

educational videotapes 237

Eighteen, Kenneth 91–2, 114, 126, 127

*Electric Blue* series 234

Elert, N. 19–20

English, 'Big' John 84, 106, 225, 322n31, 322n34, 330n33

*English Joys* (1940–43). 55

enterprise cultures 3, 8, 56, 218, 229

entrepreneurial policing 220

entrepreneurship

    distributing hardcore films 176–8

    emergence of alternative economy xxix, 14, 19–20, 30–1, 35, 39, 42, 48

    entrepreneurship as framework 217–23

    entrepreneurship in alternative economy 14–15

    evasive entrepreneurship 7, 19–20, 48, 76, 176, 219

    historical studies 5

    home video 224, 237

making the roller market 56, 89, 90

moral entrepreneurs 15, 174, 176–8, 187, 236

pornography as an alternative economy 6–8

entrepreneurship in expanding roller trade 91–135

    Climax Films 105–13

    Freeman as born entrepreneur 92–100

    Freeman as pornographer at the pictures 113–18

    Freeman blackballed 118–27

    Original Climax Films A/S 127–32

    overview 91–2, 132–5

    Phillips 100–5

'Ernie' (casual supplier) 325n12

Eros Films 116, 118, 132, 265–8

erotic drawings 96, 97, 99

*Erotic Images* (1980) 230

erotic literature 28, 45, 139

*Escort Agency* (1966) 108

Esland, Geoff 204, 205

ethnohistory xxix, 10, 11, 222

Eureka Nudist Camp 234

*Euston Capture* (1972) 206

evasive entrepreneurship 7, 19–20, 48, 76, 176, 219

Excelsior Films 189, *189*, 191, 268–9

*Exchange and Mart* (magazine) 13, 124, 126, 156, 175, 230

*Experience* (magazine) 13, 180, 181

Exxon Cinema Club 179, 180, *181*, 182, 185–6, 327n10


F

*Family Fun* (1967–68) 117

Family Planning Act 1967 29, 30

*Fanny* (1967) 86

*Fanny Hill* (Cleland) 139

Fantasy label 133, 162, *163*, 269–70, 326n19

*Fantom Kiler* films xxviii

fantrepreneurs 6

Farge, A. 13

Farmer, R. 321n23

Fat Bill (Billy Hicks) 38, 101, 113, 114

female performers 10, 69, 106, 111, 117, 167–9, 197–8, 219–20

female producers 10, 220

Ferro, Alberto *see* Braun, Lasse

Festival of Light 138, 151, 174, 176, 207, 327n2

fetishes 143, 210

*Film Making* magazine *151*

film processing 59–62, 67, 69, 110, 192, 222, 223

Fisher, T. 27

*Fisherman's Luck* (1965–67) *51*, 81–4, *82*, *83*, 110, 322n29

flat-farming 39

Fleetwood Films 158, 159, *160*, 161

Flesh Films 142, *156*, 204, 239

Fletcher, Simon 11

Fletcher, Tom 35

Flexner, S. B. 318n1

Flint, D. 76

Forbes, Peter 66

Ford, Derek 329n22

*For Men Only* (1967) 320n5

Fortune, John 331n2

*Forum* magazine 13, 181, 182

France 17, 33, 35, 42, 55, 320n17

Franzosi, R. 12

Freedom of Information (FOI) 13, 221, 323n2

*Free for All* (1966–67) 131

Freeman, Mike (Michael Muldoon)
    allegations of police planting 213
    archives 323n2
    choice of name 332n7
    Climax Films 324n3
    death of 93
    drug use 231

entrepreneurship as framework 219, 220, 222

entrepreneurship in alternative economy 14–15

Eros Films 132

expanding roller trade 91–2, 100–1, 102–4, 105, 133, 135

film equipment 193

Freeman as born entrepreneur 92–100

Freeman as pornographer at the pictures 113–18

gay pornography 231–2

*Hardcore Guaranteed* documentary 11, 93

Hawley murder 91–2, 126–7

historical studies 4–5

and home video 224, 228–33, 234–6

image *93*

imprisonment 104, 127, 176, 220, 235

interviews 11

*I Pornographer* book series xxviii, 11, 93, 113, 122, 123, 126, 234, 235

on Ivor Cook 71–2

mail-order companies 123

making the roller market 57, 62, 64, 71–2, 75, 76

overview xxi

'Pornographer at the Pictures' series 116–17

on postcards 323n10

regulating the roller trade 146, 148

sexual offences 100–1, 104, 105, 114, 126

trials 234–6

the underworld 38

Videx label xxix, 229, 230

freemasonry 46, 320n20

*Free Sample* (1970–72) 87–8, 149

Frewin, Anthony 321n22
*The Frost Programme* 173–4, 182, 194, 197
*Full Treatment* (1966–67) 111, *112*

**G**
gangsters 38, 39, 91
garage labs 60, 69, 148
Gardner, William 73–4
Gatsby label 239, 270
Gay, Russell xxi, 53, 106, 227, 324n15, 331n2
*Gay Boys* 159
*Gay News* 232
gay pornography xxviii–xxix, 23, 108, 142–3, 159, 213, 221, 231–2
Geerts, Charlie 183, 227, 330n31
Geismar, Ulrich *195*
General Post Office Film Unit (GPO) 55, 320n8
General Video 227
Germany xxvi, 4, 125, 131, 151, 191, 322n26
Gestetner photocopiers 46
*giallo* (Italian film cycle) xxviii, 6
glamour films 28, 53–4, *54*, 81, 84, *125*
glamour photography 43, 161, 320n4
Global Cinelux 133, 270–1
Gold family 175, 212, 213, 327n4, 331n39
*Golden Butterfly* (1967) 59
Golden Phallus award 191, 318n3
Goldstar 212
Goldstein, Murray 53, 320n3
gonzo porn 231, 332n12
*The Good Life* (1966–67) 111
Goodman, Edward xxiv, 21
Gorfinkel, E. 162
*Gorgeous Blondes* (Soho Bible) 111, *112*
Gottschalk, P. 95
Granby, Martin xx, 71, 113, 145–8, 323n6, 325n8
Gray, C. 133

group sex 108, 117, 142, 164, 165
Gustafsson, T. 64

**H**
Hammersmith Nude Murders 100
Hammond, P. 320n17
*Hardcore Guaranteed* (2019 documentary) 11, 92, 93, 220
hardcore pornography
    defining 9
    development in Britain 218
    emergence of alternative economy 8, 14, 16, 20, 22, 26, 30–1, 48
    financial scale 48
    and Freeman 228–9
    historical studies 3–5
    home video 227–30, 237
    legalization xxvii, xxix, 15, 47, 60, 89, 224, 232, 237
    making the roller market 52, 54–5
    regulating xxix, 20, 22
    researching 9–10
    *Truth or Dare* 230 *see also* distributing hardcore films in Britain
*Hard Dollar Hustler* (1977) 232, *233*
Harrison Marks, George xx, 5, 28, 53, 81, 106, 227, 320n4, 329n21
Hawksford, John xxii, 34–5, 43
Hawley, Gerald (Gerry) 91–3, 126–7, 146, 220, 222
Hayward, Dr Lionel 198
*Health Farm* (1975–77) 206, *207*
Hebditch, D. 4, 59, 70, 75, 76, 106
Heffernan, K. 4
Henley, Richard 319n13
Henrekson, M. 19–20
Henry, S. 99
Heritage Films 53, 106
Her Majesty's Customs and Excise (HMCE) 183, 212

Hicks, Billy (Fat Bill) 38, 101, 113

*High Society* (1970–72) 191, *192*

Hill, Eric 330n31

Hill, Kenneth 330n31

Hill, Napoleon 179, 180

*HIM* magazine 232

*History of Hardcore* (2002 documentary) 203

Hobbs, D. 8, 13, 35, 39, 94, 101, 220

Hodas, Marty 158–9

Holborn Police Station 26, 37

Holloway, Ben 40, 227

Holloway, Christopher 234

Holloway family 159, 227–9, *228*, *229*, 234

Hollywood 76, 226

*Home from School* (1969) 147

Home Office Committee on Obscenity and Film Censorship 209

home video xxviii, xxix, 6–7, 15–16, 69, 224–37

*Homework* (1967–68) 116

homosexuality 28, 29, 188, 213, 234 *see also* gay pornography

Honey, Lindsay (aka Ben Dover) xx, 5, 213, 230, 231, 237, 331n40, 332n10

Hoopers Hotel brothel 31

horror films xxv, 227

*Hotel Sexi* (1960–65) 64, 239

*The Hot Girls* (1974) 194

*House of Mirrors* (1972) *136*, 163–5, *164*, 167, 168

Hulpert, Frankie 72–3, 74, 75

Humphreys, James xxii, 140, 141, 154, 184

Humphries, S. 30

Hunt, L. 5, 27, 201

Hunter, I. Q. 5, 197

Hunter, Mike (Gerd Wasmund) xx, 84, 225, 332n4

*The Hunter* (1969) 87

Hutchinson, T. 13

Hygron 330n31

**I**

Ilford's (photography shop) 64, 98, 100, 108, 129

*I'm Not Feeling Myself Tonight* (1976) 213

incest 117, 143

*Incest* (1967–68) 117

*Incestral Home* (1967) 86

indecency 21–2, 183, 185, 186, 216

Indecent Displays (Control) Act 1981 21, 214, 236

Index on Censorship 319n6

*In Drag* (1967) 108

insider accounts 4, 13

institutional frameworks 8, 19–20, 26, 177, 220

*Intensive Care* (1974) 211

International Films 157, 206, 239, 271–2

internet pornography xxvii, xxx, 221

interracial pornography 142

inter-titles 84

interviews 10, 11, 222

*Invitation Sex* (1969) 86

*I Pornographer* book series (Freeman) xxviii, 11, 93, 113, 122, 123, 126, 234, 235

Italian film xxviii, 4

Italian Tony *see* Sonenscher, Tony

**J**

Jack the Stripper case 100

James, Rupert 231

Janes, Joseph 'Joey' xxii, 32, 40, 41–2

Jeal, Billy 145

'Jenny Love' 327n11

'John' (distributor) xxi, 40

*Jolly Hockey Sticks* 196, 197, 206

Jones, M. 197

Jones, S. 198

Joyce, Sandra 91–5, 97–9, 102–5, 114, 116–17, 126–7, 220, 318n2, 323n1

    *Knock Down Ginger* 93, 104, 113, 116, 220, 323n4

*Joyride* (1969–71) 190, *190*
Julian, Charles (Charles Marandola) 155

**K**
Kamera 106
Karl Ordinez label 197, 206, 212, 272–5, 329n27
Kay's Laboratory 204, 205
Keeler, Christine 18, 28, 76–8, 77, 78, 81, 90, 108, 321n23, 321n25
Kelland, Gilbert 155, 176, 189
'Ken' (collector) xxiii, 321n25, 322n30
Kendrick, W. M. 9, 42–3
Kennedy, E. L. 12
Kennedy, Sarah 234
Kenny Lynch Record Centre 32
Kentish Town Cine (KTC) 322n30
Kerekes, D. 194, 240, 328n16
Killick, M. 175
*Kinky Schoolgirls* (1971–72) 196
*Kinky Vicar* (1970– 72) 191
Kinsey Institute for Sex Research 3, 12, 55, 81, 84, 116–17, 223, 238–9, 318n7
Kirby, D. 326n17
Kirzner, I. M. 96, 113
*Klimaks* (magazine) 106
Klinger, Michael 179
Knight, A. 17, 55, 218
Koch, G. 67
Kodak 44, 52, 59, 148
Kray twins 91, 102, 103, 126, 324n17
KTC (Kentish Town Cine) 322n30
Kuhn, A. 10
Kutchinsky, B. 131

**L**
labelography 238–313
	branded 245–94
	continental market 303–13
	overview 238–40

unbranded 240–5
unknown 294–302
unknown Lindsay titles 302–3
laboratory processing 59–62, 192
*Lady Chatterley's Lover* obscenity trial 28
*Lady Victoria's Training* (1981–82) 230
languages 64
Larsson, M. 4, 76, 189, 222
*Late Comer* (1969) 143, 251
*Late Night Video* (magazine) 13, 224, 227, 230, 332n8
*Lavabora* (1960–65) 64, 239
Leathard, A. 29
Lee, E. 29–30
Leeson, P. T. 7
Leidibird 189, 190, 275
*Lesbian Model Agency* (1980) 230
*A Lesson in French* 143
Letraset 45, 64, 191, 240, 321n15
licensing system
	distributing hardcore films 176, 208, 215
	emergence of alternative economy 8–9, 15, 19, 26, 31, 35–7, 39–42, 45–7
	entrepreneurial policing 217, 220
	expanding roller trade 93, 102, 111, 113, 114, 118, 123, 124, 133, 135
	making the roller market 56, 72–3
	regulating the roller trade 137, 162
	removal of 137, 176
	the underworld 39–42
Lindsay, John Jesner
	BBC Blue Movie Case 204–6
	and Blue Scene Films 81
	*Central Weekend* 214
	Chibnall on 5
	Customs and Excise 212
	death of 186
	distributing hardcore films 15, 176, 186–94, 195–8, 201, 203–14, 216
	entrepreneurship as framework 217

fabrication 328n16

film equipment 191

filming in Europe 60

*The Frost Programme* 173–4, 194, 197

home video 224, 225, 228, 229, 232

images 187, *195*

imprisonment 213, 214

'John Linden' alias 190

Karl Ordinez label 329n27

Lindsay and exports 186–94

Lindsay as a wanted man 207–14

London Blue Movie Centre 202

mail-order advert *199*

Millington on 321n14, 328n20

overview xx

Ragdolls modelling agency 329n24

regulating the roller trade 146, 149, 171

*R v. Lindsay* (1974) 25, 195–8, *199*, 201–2, *202*, 207, 209

tax bills 214

trials 212, 213, 330n36

Lindsay, Penny 206

Linnane, F. 39

Local Government (miscellaneous provisions) Act 1982 214, 215, 236

Lockwood, Irene 100

*Lolitas* (1969) 131

London Blue Movie Centre 202, 209

London Revolutionary Feminist Anti-Pornography Consciousness-Raising Group 208

Long, Stanley 53, 204, 320n4, 330n30

Longford, Lord (Frank Pakenham) xxiv, 15, 48, 137, 138, 150, 151–2, 173, 174, 176, 187

Longford Report 48, 152, 173, 194, 210

Long Shop 35, 36, 102, 146

Look Films 162, *163*, 275–6

loops 2, *54*

*Love for Sale* (1967–68) 111

Lovelace, Linda 330n34

*The Love Pill* (1972) 194

*The Lover's Guide* (1991) 237

*Loving Dollies* (1966–69) 131

Lowe, Stanley 102

*Lucky Girl* (1968) 84–5, 86, *86*, 87

Lundan, S. M. 127

Lynch, Kenny 32, 41


**M**

magazines xxvi, 4, 12–13, 47, 59, 63, 90, 222

*Maidservant* (1970–72) 143, *144*

mail order xxv–xxvii, 3, 15, 53, 123–5, 136–7, 145, 150, 155–8, 171, 228, 237

making the roller market 51–90

    before rollers 52–6

    Blue Scene Films 81–9

    early pioneers 63–70

    from Soho to Copenhagen 76–81

    Ivor Cook 70–6

    making rollers 56–63

    overview 51–2, 89–90

'Mal Mallister' (collector) xxiii, 64, 66, 321n23

Malmo Films 133, *134*, 147, 148, 276

Manchester 25–6

Manchester, C. 37, 42, 175, 213, 215, 331n41

*Manhunt* (1969–72) 86–7, *88*

Manifold, Laurie 140, 141, 151–3, 193

Mansfield family 123–4

Marcus, S. 319n7

'Mark' (distributor) xxi, 149–50, 325n12

Mark, Robert 155

Marklund, C. 177

Marwick, A. 27

Mason, Ronald Eric 'John' xxii, 35–9, 42, 45–6, 102–3, 105, 111, 113, 132–3, 314–17

masturbation 182, 185

*Mayfair* (magazine) xxvi

Mayfair Film Productions 193, 212

McCabe, Stuart 51, 320n1

McClister, C. G. 183

McGillivray, D. 76, 212, 213, 214

McKee, A. 6, 9

McKee, G. 52, 149

McManus, Aidan xxiii, 32

McRobbie, A. 32

Meadows, Paula 230, 231

MediaStream 12

*Mella v. Monahan* (1961) 23

*Men* (1966–67) 107, 108

Mercer, John xxix

Messina Brothers 29, 38, 39

Metropolitan Police
 A10 unit 145
 distribution of hardcore films 15, 174, 176, 194
 emergence of alternative economy 8, 19, 33–5, 38, 39
 Hammersmith Nude Murders 100
 and mail order 123
 making the roller market 72, 88
 regulating the roller trade xxix, 145, 155
 researching 10, 13

Mifsud, 'Big' Frank 39

'Mike' (Danish blogger) 322n27

Millington, Mary 191, *193*, 321n14, 328n20

Milton, Berth xix, 90, 177, 194, *195*, 327n6

mini-movie machines 158–9, *160*

*Miss Bohrloch* (1972–73) 191, *193*, 206, 318n3, 328n18

Mistral 227

Mitchell, Ian 233

Modern Books 34

Moody, Alfred William 'Bill'
 and Cook 73, 74, 79
 expanding roller trade 101, 104, 111, 113–14, 124, 133
 and Granby 325n8
 obscenity and permissiveness 36–7, 40, 46
 overview xxiii
 regulating the roller trade 145, 146

moral entrepreneurs 15, 174, 176–8, 187, 236

morality 15, 24, 27, 28, 30, 138, 174–8, 187, 216, 236

*More La More I* and *II* 322n34, 326n19

*More Suds and Sex* (1967) 86

Mort, F. 18, 27, 76

Moser, Hans 4, 17, 71

Mountain 142

Mowlabocus, Sharif xxix, 198

Muldoon, Michael *see* Freeman, Mike

Muldoon, Sandra *see* Joyce, Sandra

Müller, T. 177

*Music Masters I / II* (1965–67) 86, 243

*The Mysteries of Verbena House* 42

N

Næsby, B. 142

*Naked as Nature Intended* (1961) 28

National Archives, London 13

National Campaign for the Reform of the Obscene Publications Act (NCROPA) xxix, 12, 208, 211, 213, 330n36

National Health Service (NHS) 29

Nationwide Petition for Public Decency 174, 327n2

*Naughty!* (1972 documentary) 191, 192, 193

NCROPA *see* National Campaign for the Reform of the Obscene Publications Act

Nead, L. 31

*Negro* (1970–72) 142

Nestville Photography 99, 114, 124, *125*

Netherlands 17, 22, 125–6, 131, 141, 184, 212

New Private label 239, 276–8

*News of the World* (newspaper) xxvii, 33, 45, 91, 120, 123, 126, 170, 204, 205, 206

newspapers 12–13, 138, 222

Nielsen, Sven 59

*No Mercy for Susan* (1967–68) 131

North, D. C. 8, 9, 19, 20, 177

*Now and Then* (TV series) 320n1

Nowiki, Roman xxviii
nudism 28, 43, 234, 321n23
nudity 53, 161, 175
*Nympho Artist* (1969–72) *189*, 191

**O**

Obscene Publications Act 1857 31
Obscene Publications Act 1959
　distributing hardcore films 3, 174, 178,
　　179, 182–3, 186, 198, 201–2, 205,
　　210, 213, 216
　emergence of alternative economy 7–8,
　　14, 16, 19, 20–6, 28, 31, 33, 40
　entrepreneurship as framework 217,
　　218, 220, 221
　expanding roller trade 91, 92, 98, 101, 135
　falling use 331n1
　home video 227, 228, 230, 234, 235
　and Lindsay 193, 198, 201, 202, 205,
　　210, 213
　making the roller market 53, 68, 73, 74
　permissive turn 28, 31
　problem with obscenity 24–6
　regulating pornography 20–4
　regulating the roller trade 15, 137, 147,
　　152, 157, 159, 162, 165, 166, 169, 171
　and Waterfield 179, 182, 183, 186
Obscene Publications Act 1964 amendment
　23–4, 179
Obscene Publications Squad
　bookshop owners 31, 34–8
　and Cook 71–4
　'The Dirty Squad' 26
　distribution of hardcore films 176, 176,
　　178, 184, 188, 205, 208
　emergence of alternative economy 5, 8,
　　15, 19, 26, 31, 34–8, 41–2, 45–7
　entrepreneurial policing 220
　entrepreneurship as framework 217,
　　220, 222

expanding roller trade 93, 102, 103–5,
　111, 114, 118, 123–4, 126, 133, 135
fall of 152, 154
and Freeman 93, 102, 114, 118, 123,
　126, 230–2, 234
home video 227, 230, 231, 232, 234
licensing system 26, 35–7, 56, 93, 102
making the roller market 56, 69–74, 90
and Phillips 103–4
regulating the roller trade 15, 140–1,
　145–7, 150, 152, 154–6, 159, 162,
　171
researching 10
Soho Postcards and Bibles 45–7
the underworld 38, 41, 42
obscenity 20–6, 152, 165, 183, 185, 208–10,
　221
obscenity, permissiveness and the dirty square
　mile 17–50
　bookshop owners 34–8
　overview 17–19, 47–50
　permissive turn 26–31
　problem with obscenity 24–6
　regulating pornography 19–24
　Soho as Dirty Square Mile 31–4
　Soho Postcards and Bibles 42–7
　underworld 38–42
obscenity trials 9, 13, 22, 25, 28, 172, 187,
　210–13, 234, 327n2
Offences Against the Person Act 1861 29
*Office Party* (1970–72) 252
Old Compton Street, Soho 35, 42, 227, 234
Oliver, Matthew xxiv, 48, 152, 154, 155
online harms 9, 221
Open University 204
Operation Innocents 100
Orchid Film 191, 197, 278
Ordinez, Karl 329n27 *see also* Karl Ordinez
　label
orgies 73

Original Climax Films 139, 140, 324n3
Original Climax Films A/S 127–32, *128*, 139, 153, 324n2, 324n20
Oslo Club, Southampton 185
O'Toole, L. 23
Owens, Tuppy 230–1
*Oz* (magazine) 327n2

**P**

Paasonen, S. 132, 191
packaging design 206, 223, 328n18
Paillard Bolex H16 camera 57–9, *58*
Pakenham, Frank *see* Longford, Lord
Pannell, Jayson 327n8
Paramount Publications *151*
*The Part-Time Job* (1962–63) 84, 110
Pearl Films 278–9
Pearson, J. 126
*Peeping Tom* (n.d.) 68
*Penthouse* (magazine) 186–7, 188, 189, 191
*The People* (newspaper) 34, 64, 73, 106, 138–9, 140, 147, 151
*People and Work* (TV programme) 204
performers 10–12, 117–18, 120, 122–3, 171, 198, 219–20
periodicals 12–13
permissiveness 3, 26–31, 67, 138, 208, 210
permissive society 14, 19, 27, 48
*Personal Advertiser* (magazine) 13, 118, 122
*The Personal Touch* (n.d.) 76
Peter Street, Soho *18*, *18*
Petley, J. 210, 215, 235
Peyrefitte, M. 17
'Phillip Black' (collector) xxiii, *55*, 322n30, 328n19
Phillips, Evan 'Big Jeff'
    Chibnall on *5*
    Climax Films 105–7, 108, 111, 113, 191
    death of 176

entrepreneurship in alternative economy 14–15
expanding roller trade 92, 100–8, 111, 113, 114, 126–9, 131–3, 135
image *103*
imprisonment 176
labelography 240
making the roller market 59, 64, 71
Original Climax Films A/S 127–9, 131
overview xx
regulating the roller trade 139–41, 148–9, 151–3, 155–6
Phoenix International 191, 279
photography 3, 9, 23, 43–5, 57, 74, 96, 98
Pickard, Dr Christine 201
*Pick Up* (1970–72) 246
pimps 29, 38, 39
piracy xxv, xxvi, 81, 237
*Playboy* (magazine) xxvi, 188
Playboy Classic 280
Playboy Films 133, 280–1
Playland arcade 326n22
police
    academic studies 5
    bookshop owners 35–6, 38–9
    corruption 13, 33–5, 38–9, 47–9, 90, 216
    distribution of hardcore films 15, 174, 176, 194, 211, 216
    doctrinal research 13
    emergence of alternative economy 8–9, 19, 25–6, 33–9, 41, 47–9
    entrepreneurial policing 220
    expanding roller trade 93, 94, 102, 114, 124, 135
    Hammersmith Nude Murders 100
    Lindsay on 211
    list of police characters xxiii
    and mail order 123
    making the roller market 68, 72–3, 88, 90

police statements 222

regulating the roller trade xxix, 145, 155

researching 10, 13

Soho 33–5

the underworld 38–9, 41

popular music 28

*The Pornbrokers* (1973) 194, *195*, 197, 329n23

PornHub xxviii, 9

*The Porn King, the Stripper and the Bent Coppers* (1998 documentary) 324n18

porno chic 218

'Pornographer at the Pictures' series 116–17, *117*

pornography

as an alternative economy 6–9

archives 11–12

costs of making 42–3, 58–9

decriminalization 31, 207

defining 9–10

distributing hardcore films in Britain 15, 173–216

emergence of alternative economy 14, 16, 17–50

entrepreneurship as framework 15, 217–23

entrepreneurship in expanding roller trade 14–15, 91–135

financial scale 48, 158

historical studies 3–5

home video 224–37

investigating the illicit 9–14

labelography 238–313

legalization xxvii, xxix, 15, 47, 60, 89, 174, 177, 184, 187, 201, 218, 221, 224, 232, 237

legalization in Denmark 47, 89, 127, 139, 148, 184, 218, 325n7

list of rollers seized from John Mason 314–17

making the roller market 14, 51–90

regulating xxix, 19–24, 187, 220–1

regulating the roller trade 15, 136–72

pornography entrepreneurship 20, 31, 218–19

*Pornography in Denmark* (1970 documentary) 131, 325n7

pornography studies 218, 220

Portelli, A. 328n16

Porter, M. E. 47

possession 22–4

postcards 43, 76, 98–9, 145, 320n17 *see also* Soho Postcards

*Postif* filmography 238

*Post Mercury Gazette* 100

Post Office Act 1953 21, 171, 205

*Primitive London* (1965) 320n1

printers 62–3, 114–16, 193

Pritchard, Brian xxiii, 57, 59, 60, 62, 67, 81, 110–11, 116

Pritchard, Gwynn 204, 205

*Private* (magazine) 175, 177, 194

*Private Eye* (magazine) 38, 39

Private Films label xxviii, 90, 133, *134*, 281–2

processing film *see* film processing

producers xix–xxi, 45

Profumo Affair 18, 28, 70, 76, 90, 321n22, 321n23

prohibition 177

prostitution 28–9

Protection of Children Act 1978 21, 22–3, 208, 235, 323n3

public good defence 25, 152, 166, 171, 185, 198, 201, 209, 216, 319n6

Public Order Act 1984 21

Pussy Film 282

*Pussy Galore* (1966–67) 75, 107, *108*

Q

Queen of Hearts 282

**R**

R18 (Restricted 18) certificate xxv, 5, 11, 22, 215, 221, 235, 237, 331n1

Rabkin, G. 12, 55, 76, 84, 238, 239, 319n7

'Rådhusantikvariatet' bookstore 80, 107

Radio Nord 188

Ragdolls modelling agency 225, 329n24

rag markets 31–2

raids 36, 45, 73, 118, 124, 141, 146, 147, 159, 194, 210–11, 325n12, 326n17

Rally Against Permissiveness 138

Rambooks 42

*Randy* (1965–66) 28, 76, 77, 81

Rape Action Group 208

Raymond, Paul 53

*Razzle* (magazine) xxvi

*Rear Admiral* (1969) 322n29

Reclaim the Night 208

red-light districts 17–18

Reekie, D. 60

*Regina* v. *Murray and Others* (1965) 67

regulating the roller trade 136–72

    House of Mirrors 158–63

    Longford and fall of Obscene Publications Squad 151–5

    mail-order business 155–8

    overview 136–7, 170–2

    time of crisis 138–41

    transnational trade 148–51

    Universal Films 141–8

    Watford Blue Movie Trial 163–70

religion 197, 198, 236

*The Rent Man* (1963–65) 220, 318n2

Rice Davies, Mandy 321n23

*Ring Up for Love* (1966–67) 107, 108–10, *108*, 111

Rippledale label 227, *228*, 229

'Rob' (police officer) xxiii, 39

Robertson, G. 22, 23, 24, 25, 48, 152, 163, 166, 182, 183, 330n34

Robinson, Alan 'Big Bill' 319n13

Rodox 324n3

Rodox Color Teknik laboratory 148

rollers

    archives 3, 12, 223

    before rollers 52–6

    Blue Scene Films 81–9

    Climax Films 105–13

    and Cook 70–6

    costs of making 42–3, 58–9

    definition 2, 52

    early pioneers 63–70

    emergence of alternative economy xxix, 6, 28, 47

    entrepreneurship as framework 15, 217–23

    entrepreneurship in expanding roller trade 91–135

    Freeman as born entrepreneur 92–100

    Freeman blackballed 118–27

    from Soho to Copenhagen 76–81

    labelography 238–313

    list of rollers seized from John Mason 314–17

    making rollers 56–63

    making the roller market 51–90

    name derivation 55

    Original Climax Films 127–32

    and Phillips 100–5

    regulating the roller trade 15, 136–72

    researching 10–13

    time of crisis 138–41

    transnational trade 148–51

    Universal Films 141–8

'RonnieX' (collector) xxiii, 55–6

Roodhouse, M. 7, 95

Rose-Ackerman, S. 36

Rosen, Monty 102

Rotterdam 184

Royal Film Productions 282–3

rule enforcers 8, 177–8, 209, 216, 219

Rumbelows 232

*R v. Hatiatt* (1976) 207, 330n34

*R v. Hicklin* (1868) 24, 152

*R v. Lindsay* (1974) 25, 195–8, *199*, 201–2, *202*, 207, 209

*R v. Stanley* (1965) 21

*R v. Waterfield* (1975) 21, 181, 197

*R v. Whyte* (1972) 25


**S**

Samuels, Bernard 179

Sanders-McDonagh, E. 17

satellite television xxix–xxx, 237

Savile, Jimmy 152

Scala cinema 328n12

Scandinavia 79, 107, 149, 155–7, 176, 326n14

Schaefer, E. 3, 4, 11, 53, 55, 146

schoolgirl theme 117, 194–5, 197–8, 240, 323n10

*School-Girl träumt von King-Kong* (1977–79) 225, *226*

Schumpeter, J. 7, 8, 20, 56

Scotland Yard 38, 55, 72, 100, 194, 196

Screentime Ltd 212

*Seduction Susan* (magazine) 84, 86, 89, 322n35

*Sex 69* trade exhibition, Copenhagen 131, 139, 142, 189

sex cinemas 214, 215

sex comedies 194

sex fairs 131, 324n19

*Sex Maniacs* (1977) 225

*The Sexorcist* (magazine) *187*

sexploitation films 138, 194

*Sexposed* (2018 documentary) 10

sex shops xxv, 17–18, 22, 176, 208, 214, 215, 237

*Sex Slave* (1981–82) 234, *235*, 331n40

sex toys 227

sexual culture 14, 27–31, 138

sexual economy 17, 19, 31

sexual education 198

*Sexual Freedom in Denmark* (1970 documentary) 325n7

Sexual Offences Act 1956 98, 101, 123, 168, 171

Sexual Offences Act 1967 29, 30, 189

Sexual Offences Act 2003 323n3

sexual revolution 3, 28

sex workers 18, 28–9, 31, 39, 40, 66–7, 100

Shakespeare (photographer) 147

Shaw, Robert 71

*Shaw v. DPP* (1962) 22

Shelby, H. C. 218

Sheridan, Simon 318n3, 320n4, 322n31, 328n18, 329n27

Short, M. 320n20

*Sight and Sound* 216

Silver, Bernie xxii, 29, 38–40, 42

Sim, Dr Myre 198

Simpson, A. W. B. 179, 208, 331n43

*Sin Dreamer* (1977) 225

SJD Properties Limited 36

Slade, J. W. 4, 9, 55, 110, 120, 132, 218, 238, 240

Sloman, Chuck 211

small-gauge film 14, 59, 63, 226

*A Small Hotel* (1968-72) 326n19

Smart, Elizabeth 318n2

Smith, C. 5, 7, 20, 21, 175, 216

smuggling 56, 59, 133, 140, 153, 184

Snare, A. 131

softcore pornography xxvi, 4, 9, 28, 48, 53, 194, 215, 227, 327n3

Soho
  bookshops xxviii, xxix, 96, 98, 102, 104
  bookshops map 49
  as 'dirty square mile' 17, 31–4
  distributing hardcore films 214, 215
  emergence of alternative economy 8, 14, 17–19, 26, 29, 31–4, 38–42, 47–50
  historical studies 4–5
  home video 227, 234
  making the roller market 53, 55, 76
  name derivation 32
  regulating the roller trade 141
  researching 10
  the underworld 38–42
Soho Bibles 3, 37, 45–6, 46, 47, 111, 112, 117, 223
'Soho George' (historian) xxiii, 100
Soho: People Live Here Too (TV news feature) 210–11
Soho Postcards 3, 43, 44, 47, 51, 71, 72, 88–9, 96–9, 97, 103, 111, 123, 145, 223
Soho Society 207
Soho Striptease (1960) 53
Soho Typescripts 3, 45 see also Soho Bibles
'Soho Walk-ups' 18
soliciting 28–9
Sonenscher, Tony (Tony Boffa, Italian Tony) xxii, 31–2, 38, 40, 41–2, 41, 43, 49, 113
soundtracks 148, 183, 191
Spar Sex Corporation 154
Der Spiegel 153
'spivs' 95, 218
The Stage 229, 230
stag films 2, 17, 55, 66, 76, 110, 120, 132, 188, 218
Steinle Films 133, 189, 190, 190, 283
Stephens, Dr Anton 201
Stephens, Terry xxi, 213
'Steve' (distributor) xxi, 24, 174–5, 176

Stoops, J. 5, 56, 106, 323n10
Straker, Jean 23, 319n4
Streamone Ltd 212
Street Offences Act 1959 29, 31
Streisand, Barbra 76
strip clubs 31, 39, 53, 182
Strip Poker (1970–72) 173, 205–6, 330n33
striptease 28, 53
Strub, W. 177, 236
Studio Film Laboratories 192, 328n19
Studio Hire 161
studs 84
Sturman, Reuben 159, 227, 234
Suds and Sex (The Handyman) 322n32
Sullivan, David 175–6, 180, 208, 214, 327n5, 327n6
Sullivan, R. 6
Sunday People (newspaper) 90, 106, 114, 127, 141, 152–5, 159, 175, 181, 182, 193, 202
Super 8 films 2, 28, 53, 148–9, 183, 225, 226, 232
Sutherland, J. 218
Svensk Films 133, 143, 143, 147, 283–4, 325n9
Swap Orgy (1968) 118, 119, 120, 122, 123
Sweden 4, 12, 64, 81, 86, 88, 89, 125, 146, 190, 222

T
tabloid newspapers 12, 69, 120, 152, 222, 235
Taboo (label) 206, 207, 210–11, 228, 284
Taboo & Phoenix Productions 157, 191, 284–6
Taboo Cinema Club 203, 204, 212, 213
Taboo of Sweden/Taboo Films of Sweden 157, 191, 286–7
Tabu de Luxe 191, 206, 328n18
Tarantula label 287

Taylor, L. S. 4

Taylor, 'Skinny' Ken xix, 63, 69–70, 90, 161–2, 326n19

Teddy Boys 94

Teenage Productions 191, 197, 288–9

*The Teen Scene* (1966–67) 111

television xxix–xxx, 12

*Temptation* (1972–73) 197

Tenser, Tony 179

Thatcher, Margaret 187, 214, 219, 229, 235

Theander, Jens xx, 80–1, *80*, 89, 106, 131, 324n20

Theander, Peter xx, 80–1, *80*, 106, 322n27, 324n12, 324n20

Theander Brothers 84, 89, 106, 107, 131, 148, 225, 325n11, 327n6

Thompson, B. 5, 207, 208, 210, 215

Thompson, D. 4, 70, 76

Thompson, Peter 174

Thorpe, Leonard xx, 63, 64, 67–8, 71, 133

*Thrilling Drilling* (1974) 211

*Timber* (1970–72) 161

*Tit Friction* (1977) 225

title cards 108, *109*, 117

Todd Tanks 60, *61*

Tomkinson, Martin xxiv, 4, 26, 30, 33, 35, 37–9, 43, 45, 47, 98

*Tonight at 8* (1966–67) 1–3, *1*, 108

Topsy Films 142

transnational trade 9, 76, 90, 127, 131, 133, 148–51, 194, 216

trans performers 108

transvestite pornography 143

*Traveller's Rest* (1972) 64, 164–5, *165*, 168

*Triangle* (1966–67) 131

*Truth or Dare* (1981) 224, 230

Tsaliki, L. 138

tube sites xxviii, 9

Tudor Price, David 209

*Turkish Delight* (1967–68) 65, 86, 87, 89

Turquier, B. 57

*Twist Contest* (n.d.) 54

*Two's Enough* (1967–68) 131

typescripts 9, 45, *57 see also* Soho Bibles

*Tyrollean Love* (1970–72) 191, *192*

U

Uhler printers 62, 114, *115*, 116, 193

Uhse, Beate 4, 181–2

*UKPressOnline* 12

underage performers 102, 106, 114, 323n10

underworld 38–42, 126

United Productions 289

United States 4, 55, 177, 218, 225

Universal Films 141–8, *143*, 157, 289–92

*Up Against the Law* (magazine) 181, 184, 185

Upton, J. 5

*Up, Up and Away* (1968) *91*, 129–31, *130*

urolagnia 210

V

V2000 format 228

Valentine, Nick (aka Donald 'Duke' Case) xix, 158–9, *160*

van Batenburg, Willem xxi, 59

Van Der Heul, Ari xxii, 205, 206, 330n31, 331n38

VCR *see* video cassette recorder

Venus Films 106, 118, 292–3, 324n15

Venus Tempel Sex Museum, Amsterdam 131

Vesterbro, Copenhagen 17

VHS (Video Home System) xxvi–xxvii, xxviii–xxix, 12, 69, 226–8, 232

Victorian morality 24, 27, 210

video cassette recorder (VCR) xxvi, xxvii, 52, 224, 226

Video Collection Exchange 227, *228*

video nasties 69, 233, 235

Video Recordings Act 1984 16, 21, 216, 235–6, 319n1

videotapes 23, 211, 226–30, *232*, 233–7, 332n6

*Video World* (magazine) xxvi, xxvii, 13, 224, 227, 230

Videx label xxix, 229, 230, *231*, *232*, 233, 234, 235, 332n10

*The Videx Video Show* (1982) 234–5

Viking Films 239, 293–4

Vinn, George 111

*Vintage Erotica* website 12, 322n35

Virgo, Wallace 'Wally' xxiii, 37, 140, 141

Voss, G. 6

*Vue* (magazine) 59, 222

**W**

Waldroup, H. 223

Walker, Pete xxi, 53, 106

Walker's Court, Soho 18, *18*, 32, 36, 40, *41*, 47

Walton 52, 53, *54*

Warren, Norman J. xxi, 54

Wasmund, Gerd (Mike Hunter) xx, 84, 225, 332n4

Waterfield, David xxii, 15, 21–2, 173–4, 176, 178–82, *178*, 185, 197, 213, 216, 217, 236–7, 327n8, 327n10

Watergate scandal 328n18

watersports xxvi, 143

Watford Blue Movie Trial 2, 15, 69–70, 137, 155, 163–70, 190, 192–4, 197

Watney, S. 231

Watts, Hugh 205, 330n32

Waugh, T. 12, 44, 55, 66, 188

Webb, David xxiii, xxix, 208, 211

Webb, Duncan 34, 39

Weeks, J. 27, 28, 138, 236

*We Had to Do It* (1969–71) 190, *190*

Wells, Dave xix, 71, 90

Westminster Council 19, 215, 331n41, 331n42

Wet Dreams film festival 131, 318n3, 328n18

*What a Gay Day?* (1981–82) 232, 234, 235

*What the Butler Saw and Did* (1965–67) 86

Whitehouse, Mary xxiv, 138, 176, 187, 208, 235, 236, 327n2

Wickstead, Bert 91, 126

*The Wife Swappers* (1969) 194

Wilhelmus, Joop xx, 194, *195*, 197, 205

Williams, Bernard 209

Williams, Frances 61, 63

Williams, L. 9, 11, 66

Williams Committee 209–10

Wolfenden Report (1957) 22, 28–9, 30

women

    performers 10, 69, 106, 111, 117, 167–9, 197–8, 219–20

    producers 10, 220

Wood, F. 320n4

Woozley, A. D. 24

*Wrens at Play* (1967–68) 117

**X**

xHamster xxviii, 9

**Y**

Yaffe, Maurice 198

Young, Brian 40

Your Choice xxvii, 186, 236, 237, 326n15, 327n8

**Z**

Zodiac Films 191, 294

Lightning Source UK Ltd.
Milton Keynes UK
UKHW051441100123
415114UK00001B/1